SOCIAL WORK PRACTICE

SOCIAL WORK PRACTICE:

MODEL AND METHOD

ALLEN PINCUS • ANNE MINAHAN

University of Wisconsin, Madison

F. E. Peacock Publishers, Inc.
Itasca, Illinois

Peacock Series in Social Work

The Assessment of Social Research: Guidelines for the Use of Research in Social Work and Social Science, 2nd ed.
By Tony Tripodi, Phillip Fellin, and Henry J. Meyer

Differential Social Program Evaluation
By Tony Tripodi, Phillip Fellin, and Irwin Epstein

Ethical Decisions for Social Work Practice
By Frank Loewenberg and Ralph Dolgoff

The Emergence of Social Welfare and Social Work, 2nd ed.
By Neil Gilbert and Harry Specht

Family Counseling and Therapy
By Arthur M. Horne and Merle M. Ohlsen

Family Treatment in Social Work Practice
Ed. by Oliver Harris and Curtis Janzen

Fostering Participation and Innovation: A Handbook for Human Service Professionals
By Jack Rothman, Joseph G. Teresa and John L. Erlich

Group Skills in Social Work: A Four-Dimentional Approach
By Sue Henry

Introduction to Social Welfare Policy: Power, Scarcity and Common Human Needs
By Joseph Heffernan

Rural Human Services: A Book of Readings
Ed. by H. Wayne Johnson

Skills in Helping Individuals and Groups
By Lawrence Shulman

Skills of Supervision and Staff Management
By Lawrence Shulman

The Social Services: An Introduction
By H. Wayne Johnson

Social Work Research and Evaluation
By Richard M. Grinnell, Jr.

Strategies of Community Organization: A Book of Readings, 3rd ed.
Ed. by Fred M. Cox, John L. Erlich, Jack Rothman and John E. Tropman

Tactics and Techniques of Community Practice
Ed. by Fred M. Cox, John L. Erlich, Jack Rothman and John E. Tropman

Women's Issues and Social Work Practice
Ed. by Elaine Norman and Arlene Mancuso

Copyright © 1973
F.E. Peacock Publishers, Inc.
All rights reserved
Printed in the U.S.A.

Library of Congress
Catalog Card No. 73-82647
ISBN 0-87581-132-9
Fourteenth printing, 1982

DEDICATED TO

THE MEMORY OF

OUR COLLEAGUE

VIRGINIA FRANKS

Contents

Preface

This book has grown out of our experiences over a five-year period in developing and teaching a basic course in social work practice for first-year graduate students in social work. A basic assumption in developing the course was that regardless of the many forms social work practice can take, there is a common core of concepts, skills, tasks, and activities which are essential to the practice of social work and represent a base from which the practitioner can build. Our goal was to interrelate these elements in a framework or model which would identify a frame of reference for analyzing and dealing with situations of concern to social work. Such a framework should reflect and readily make apparent the essential unity and cohesiveness of the profession and provide the basis for a professional identity for those who practice social work.

Building the Model for Practice

We both had been students and teachers in traditional social work method courses: casework, group work, and community organization. We became aware of the similarities in the knowledge, skills, and values underlying these methods and began to examine them in search of general principles and a model of practice that would fit all three.

However, we found it difficult to break away from the thinking implied in each of the traditional models—that social workers specialize in working with one size of system—individual, small group, or community. We knew that caseworkers work with groups, group workers with individuals, and community workers with individuals and groups, as well as that all social workers work with organizations and segments of communities. Thus we abandoned our search for a common core of social work practice through a study of the traditional social work methods and began anew. Our criticisms of traditional social work theory suggested the following criteria for developing a model for social work practice:

First, a model should avoid conceptualizing social work practice in such dichotomous terms as person/environment, clinical practice/social action, and microsystems/macrosystems. We believe the strength of the profession lies in recognizing and working with the connections between these elements.

Second, a model should account for the fact that the worker has tasks to perform and relationships to maintain with a variety of people in any planned change effort. Work with people other than the client should be seen as deliberate and purposeful activity. A model should focus on the relationship of these people to the planned change effort and on skills in working with them as well as the client.

Third, the worker will often have to work with and through many different sizes and types of systems (one-to-one relationships, families, community groups) in helping a client. The methods of practice suggested by the model should not be tied to any one size system. The appropriate size and type of system or systems to work through should be determined by the nature of the task at hand.

Fourth, while the model should not be based on any one substantive theoretical orientation, such as learning theory, ego psychology, communication theory, or conflict resolution, it should allow for the selective incorporation of such theoretical orientations in working with specific situations. The social work model for practice, however, should be clearly differentiated from any substantive theoretical orientations being utilized. In many practice models the two become so intertwined that the theoretical orientation appears to dictate the purpose of the social worker's practice. A social work frame of reference, derived from a clear notion of the function and purpose of the profession, can avoid this problem by serving as the primary guide in analyzing and dealing with social situations.

Fifth, while the model should be applicable to analyzing social work in the wide variety of situations and settings in which it is practiced, it should account for the skills, tasks, and activities of the social worker at a very specific level, rather than an abstract one.

In addition to the above criteria, our model building was guided by our view of social work practice as a goal-oriented planned change process. Thus, in developing our model, we began by examining the tasks of the social worker in action as he works to change elements in a social situation in order to achieve a specified goal or outcome. Our model grew by bits and pieces as we isolated and identified basic elements in practice that were reflected in these tasks. We borrowed concepts from the existing literature which we found useful in understanding and interrelating these elements.

We want to make it clear that our model for practice does not propose a supramethod of practice that incorporates various specific methods or combines casework, group work, and community work. Rather it represents a reformulation of the base of social work practice which gives social work a clear place among the human service professions. Our model is not intended to provide a base for a generalist practitioner, as opposed to the specialist. It can set the foundation for either one, depending on how the practitioner builds on it and incorporates his special knowledge and interests regarding particular social problems, client groups, resource systems, theoretical orientations, and social science knowledge.

Finally, we should note that we tried to develop a "middle-range" model. It is designed to be specific enough to be useful in teaching concepts and techniques the student can apply in the field and use to analyze his activities and role as a change agent, but general enough to be applicable to a wide variety of settings and situations and provide the student with an adequate overview of social work practice. As mentioned above, the model does not rest on any one substantive theoretical orientation but does utilize a general systems approach in organizing the elements of the model.

Whom the Book is Intended For

The book was written for students taking a beginning course in social work practice at the undergraduate or graduate level. However, it has been our experience that seasoned practitioners will find our framework useful in helping them integrate their various activities as a social worker and provide them with a fresh perspective on their role. Because we have placed social work in the general context of planned change, students and practitioners in other human service professions and allied fields may also find many aspects of the book useful.

Organization of the Book

The book is divided into three parts. Part I provides an orientation to social work practice and the role of the practitioner. Its five chapters build a framework for understanding and analyzing social work practice. The reader who is interested in what social work practice is about, rather than in the how-to-do-it aspects, will find this part of the book especially helpful.

The second part of the book focuses on eight practice skill areas essential for carrying out any planned change effort in social work. Here the reader will find discussion both on ways of understanding the skills and how to utilize them in practice. The order in which these skill areas are presented is not meant to imply any special sequence in which they are utilized in practice. As our discussion of the process in social work in Chapter 5 will make clear, the practitioner draws on all their skill areas throughout the planned change process.

Part III offers three previously published case studies which nicely illustrate the kind of social work practice we have discussed. Since we refer to them throughout the book we would suggest that the reader start with the case examples before reading the rest of the book. Especially for the reader without any social work experience, the case examples should make it easier to relate to our discussions in Parts I and II.

Acknowledgments

We are indebted to many people who helped us in our thinking and encouraged us to develop and write this book. Martin Loeb, Director of the School of Social Work at the University of Wisconsin, Madison, created a conducive climate at the school for our collaborative work and supported us every step of the way. Our faculty colleagues in field and classroom teaching offered many insights and ideas and much criticism and gave generously of their time in helping us develop our model. Students in our classes over the past five years who have been exposed to turbulence and change on the campus, in society, and in the social work profession offered us both strong criticism and enthusiasm and strove to keep us close to reality. We owe special thanks to Alfred Kadushin, Claire Kentzler, Russell Leedy, and Betty Pincus, who commented on first drafts of our early chapters, although we accept sole responsibility for their content.

Beckie Romnes was invaluable to us throughout our work by typing our manuscripts and taking care of a myriad of details with cheerfulness, calmness, and great dispatch. Isabelle Minahan, Betty, Michael, and Ellie Pincus also deserve to take a bow for their emotional support. Finally, we are grateful to the people at Peacock Publishers—Ted Peacock, Tom LaMarre, Joyce Usher, and Gloria Reardon—for their faith in our undertaking and their able assistance.

ALLEN PINCUS
ANNE MINAHAN

PART I

A FRAMEWORK FOR SOCIAL WORK PRACTICE

CHAPTER 1

THE NATURE OF
SOCIAL WORK
PRACTICE

It is logical to expect a book on social work practice to begin with a definition specifying its purpose and the reason for its existence. Such a definition will not be clear, however, unless we first discuss the particular social situations that are of concern to social work. The purpose of social work as stated here is designed to provide workers with a perspective or frame of reference for viewing social situations. The discussion of the nature of social work practice in this chapter also considers the functions, tasks, and activities social workers perform to achieve their purpose and the relationships between art and science in the practice of social work.

SOCIAL SITUATIONS AND RESOURCE SYSTEMS

The focus of social work practice is on the interactions between people and systems in the social environment. People are dependent on systems for help in obtaining the material, emotional, or spiritual resources and the services and opportunities they need to realize their aspirations and to help them cope with their life tasks.

The concept of life tasks was elaborated by Harriet Bartlett, who describes it as follows:

As used in social work, the task concept is a way of describing the demands made upon people by various life situations. These have to do with daily living, such as growing up in the family, learning in school, entering the world of work, marrying and rearing a family, and also with the common traumatic situations of life such as bereavement, separation, illness, or financial difficulties. These tasks call for responses in the form of attitude or action from the people involved in the situation. They are common problems that confront many (or all) people. The responses may differ but most people must deal with the problems in some way or other.[1]

In early American society the family was the major system to provide people with the resources[2] they need to help them cope with their life tasks. As society has become industrialized, urbanized, and bureaucratized, the family has given up many of its former functions. People have become increasingly dependent for help from extrafamilial resource systems such as places of work, schools, and units of government. At the same time, these systems have become increasingly complex and difficult to negotiate.

People today can find help from three kinds of resource systems: informal or natural, formal or membership, and societal. *Informal or natural resource systems* consist of family, friends, neighbors, coworkers, bartenders, and other helpers. The aid given by such informal relationships includes emotional support and affection, advice and information, and concrete services or resources such as baby-sitting or loan of money. Such systems also can assist in gaining access to and using formal and societal resource systems by providing help in locating appropriate resources or filling out application forms and using influence to cut red tape.

Formal resource systems are membership organizations or formal associations which promote the interests of their members. These systems may supply resources directly to members or help them negotiate with different societal systems. For example, labor unions may provide recreational and social activities for their members as well as help them to deal with employers. The negotiations of a membership orga-

---

[1] Harriet M. Bartlett, *The Common Base of Social Work Practice* (New York: National Association of Social Workers, 1970), p. 96.

[2] We will use the single term "resource" to include the concepts of resources, services, and opportunities.

nization with societal systems may benefit not only its members, but also other people who need help from such systems. For example, an organization of parents of mentally retarded children may influence a school board to expand school services for retarded children, which will benefit not only families in the organization but all families of retarded children in a community.

There is a host of membership organizations in American society; some are long-term organizations, others are short-term, ad hoc groups. They may be connected directly to a specific societal resource system or related to several systems. Examples include parent-teacher associations, professional associations such as the National Association of Social Workers or the American Medical Association, cooperatives, Better Business Bureaus, welfare rights groups, tenant's unions, and neighborhood associations.

Through public activities and voluntary citizen action, society has established a great variety of *societal resource systems*. People become linked to several of these systems. Some, such as hospitals, adoption agencies, vocational training programs, and legal services are designed to meet short-term or special needs. People become linked to other societal resource systems such as schools, day-care centers, place of employment, and social security programs by virtue of their age or some on-going social role (work role, student role) they perform. In their roles as citizens and members of a community, people are linked to numerous other governmental agencies and services such as public libraries, police agencies, recreation departments, and housing authorities.

Despite the help potentially available from the network of informal, formal, and societal systems, there are situations in which people are unable to obtain the resources, services, or opportunities they need to cope with their life tasks and realize their aspirations. Existing systems may prove to be inadequate for a number of reasons.

Inadequacies of Informal Resource Systems

There are several reasons why informal systems may not provide the help people need.[3] First, a person may lack an informal helping system. A young couple may be new to a community and not have any relatives nearby; an elderly widow may have survived all her friends and family.

Second, a person might be reluctant to turn to friends, relatives, or

---

[3] For a discussion of the inadequacies of informal resources as reported by clients, see John E. Mayer and Noel Timms, *The Client Speaks: Working Class Impressions of Casework* (New York: Atherton Press, 1970).

neighbors for help. A young mother whose child is having difficulty in school may fear loss of face; an elderly woman may not want her adult children to perceive her as a burden.

Third, even if a person does turn to an informal helping system, it may be unable to meet his needs. People often receive conflicting, ineffective, or unacceptable advice when they turn to confidants among their friends and relatives. The natural informal system also may lack the resources necessary to help. If a mother has to spend some time in a hospital, her friends might not be able to look after her children while she is gone or attend to her needs while she recuperates at home. Although the informal helping system may be adequate for meeting small everyday needs, its resources may be overtaxed in extraordinary or crisis situations such as a death in the family or the loss of a job.

Inadequacies of Formal Resource Systems

There are many factors that prevent people from receiving the help they need from the network of formal groups or organizations which provide resources to their members and help them negotiate with societal systems. First, such groups may not exist. There may be no neighborhood association to help community residents in seeking better protection from the police department or more adequate staffing of playgrounds from the recreation department.

Second, people may be reluctant to join a membership organization. They may fail to see how the organization can help them, disagree with some of its goals and activities, believe they will not be welcome or acceptable to the other members, or think they lack the skills to participate.

Third, people may be unaware of the existence of a formal resource system. Parents who have just discovered that a child is mentally retarded may not know that an association of parents of retarded children exists in their community.

Fourth, an existing organization may not have the necessary resources and influence to provide services to its members or to negotiate on their behalf with a societal resource system. A tenant's union may be unable to get the housing authority to enforce certain housing codes, or a PTA group may be unable to resolve conflict between parents and the school resulting from some new policy adopted by the school. A neighborhood association might not have enough members or financial support to provide needed recreation services.

Inadequacies of Societal Resource Systems

People often encounter difficulties in obtaining help from societal resource systems at the local community level. First, needed resources may not exist, or may not exist in sufficient quantity, to provide adequate services for all who need them. A neighborhood center may lack personnel and money to reach out into the neighborhood to work with teen-age runaways. A community may not have comprehensive mental health services or a sufficient number of day-care centers.

Second, a needed resource or service may exist but not be geographically, psychologically, or culturally available to those who need it. A Mexican-American migrant family settling in a new community may be hesitant to ask assistance from a downtown Anglo agency. A depressed individual may be afraid to seek counseling at a mental health agency because he is afraid of being called mentally ill. An existing service may have eligibility restrictions which effectively screen out minority groups, poor people, or those with specific disabilities.

Third, a needed resource may exist but people may not know about it or how to use it, especially if obtaining help requires dealing with complicated bureaucracies. Francis Purcell and Harry Specht, in their case study "The House on Sixth Street," which is given in Part III, describe the problems of a woman who came to a neighborhood service center in New York City to complain that there had been no gas, electricity, heat, or hot water in her apartment house for more than four weeks. The difficulties of the tenants in the building were intricately connected with other elements of the social system related to the housing problem. For example, dealing with problems of water supply alone, required contact with six different city departments.

Fourth, even if people are using one or more societal resource systems, the very operation of these systems can create new problems or aggravate existing ones. For example, a public welfare system could encourage dependency by following a policy of reducing welfare payments by the full amount that a recipient earns from a part-time job. Further, sometimes the role requirements of being a client of a resource system present problems. Zelda Foster's case study, "How Social Work Can Influence Hospital Management of Fatal Illness," included in Part III, describes a hospital ward for patients suffering from a fatal blood disease in which the ward culture operated to "protect" patients from learning the nature of their illness. By denying patients the right to participate in the planning for their families, the hospital was adding to the stress and burden of both patients and families.

Fifth, when people are linked to more than one resource system, the systems may work at cross-purposes, trapping the individual in a web of conflicting demands and contradictory messages. For example, Lynn Hoffman and Lorence Long, in the case study "A Systems Dilemma," in Part III, describe the problems of a black family in a large city. Mr. Johnson, the husband, had worked for 11 years as a chef. His wife was working in a home for brain-damaged children and between them they made enough money to keep a 15-year-old daughter in a private school and a 19-year-old daughter in college. Their combined income was above the limit for the low-income housing apartment where they had lived for 17 years, and they were threatened with eviction. Mr. Johnson, who was subject to dizzy spells, was drinking heavily and having dizzy spells more frequently.

In regard to their problems, this one family received communications from the Housing Authority, three doctors, legal services, Mr. Johnson's union, two employers, the Veteran's Administration, a loan company, and Workmen's Compensation. Hoffman and Long illustrate how the elaborate interplay of the host of resource systems in the situation contributed to the breakdown of the father, "a breakdown which might otherwise seem to be the result of some disorganizing process within the person himself."

Other Inadequacies of Resource Systems

In general, informal, formal, and societal resource systems may not provide the resources, services, and opportunities people need because: (1) a needed resource system may not exist or may not provide appropriate help to people who need it, (2) people may not know a resource system exists or may be hesitant to turn to it for help, (3) the policies of the resource system may create new problems for people, or (4) several resource systems may be working at cross-purposes.

In addition to these inadequacies any one of the systems may not be functioning properly because of internal problems that hamper its effectiveness. A family, a membership organization, or a societal system may be hampered by internal conflict between its members, inadequate procedures for making decisions and solving problems, or faulty internal communications. Thus the internal functioning of the systems established to help people meet their life tasks and realize their values and aspirations may be the cause of problems for people within the systems. It may also keep the systems from aiding people who come to them for help.

types of interaction: among people within a resource system (informal, formal, or societal), between people and resource systems, and between resource systems. Consider a social worker in a community mental health center who is asked to help a low-income family with young children who are having difficulty in school. The social worker's assessment of the situation would include the problems within the family, the problems the children are having in the school, and the problems the school is having in teaching these and other low-income children. The goals of the social worker, to help the family and the school improve the ways they deal with each other, may call for intervention on several levels: (1) influence the school to change its transactions with this low-income family and other low-income children and families; (2) help the individual family members improve the social interactions within the family to enable each family member to achieve his maximum growth; (3) help the family to change its interactions with the school; and (4) help the family and other community institutions to improve the ways they deal with each other.

If the social worker ignored the possibility of changing the way the school was dealing with the family and focused only on the family, the family would continue to have problems with the school which could create continual anxieties and discord. On the other hand, if he concentrated only on changing the way the school deals with the family, the personal problems of the family might continue to aggravate its relationship with the school. A study of social work approaches to the resolution of *problems of malperformance* in the public schools by Robert Vinter and Rosemary Sarri concluded that both the personal characteristics of students and conditions within the school contributed to malperformance and that the social worker must deal with both:

If he addresses himself primarily to attributes of the pupil (or his family situation) which seem to be contributing to malperformance, the effectiveness of his helping efforts will be greatly reduced. It seems important, therefore, that the social worker retain dual perspectives, and attempt to resolve problem *situations* or *processes:* both pupils and school conditions should be targets of his interventive activity. He must find ways of serving specific individuals while simultaneously dealing with the sources of pupil difficulties within the school.[4]

The case studies in Part III also illustrate how problems can be viewed as being rooted in the interactions within and among various

[4] Robert D. Vinter and Rosemary Sarri, "Malperformance in the Public School: A Group Work Approach," *Social Work* 10 (January 1965):13.

Further, individuals unable to cope with their life tasks may find themselves overwhelmed by physical, emotional, economic, or social conditions. Such people may be unable to achieve satisfying relationships within a natural system or to take advantage of existing formal and societal systems.

THE PURPOSE OF SOCIAL WORK

The definition of social work practice to be used in this book focuses on the linkages and interactions between people and resource systems and the problems to be faced in the functioning of both individuals and systems. The definition is:

Social work is concerned with the interactions between people and their social environment which affect the ability of people to accomplish their life tasks, alleviate distress, and realize their aspirations and values. The purpose of social work therefore is to (1) enhance the problem-solving and coping capacities of people, (2) link people with systems that provide them with resources, services, and opportunities, (3) promote the effective and humane operation of these systems, and (4) contribute to the development and improvement of social policy.

A SOCIAL WORK FRAME OF REFERENCE

Each helping profession needs its own perspective or frame of reference for viewing the situations it is concerned with. Such a framework should reflect the purpose of the profession and provide it with a unique handle for dealing with those situations. Three characteristics of the social work frame of reference reflect the types of social situations to which social work practice is addressed.

Performing Life Tasks

In viewing a social situation, our first concern is with the life tasks confronting people and the resources and conditions which could facilitate their coping with these tasks, help them realize their values and aspirations, and alleviate their distress.

For example, consider an unmarried 25-year-old man who is being discharged from a mental hospital. The social work frame of reference would focus on such questions as: What tasks does he face in making the transition from the restricted environment of the hospital to the community? What problems will the stigmatizing label of former mental patient present for him? What kind of life does he want for himself? Does he have a family or other informal system he can be integrated with? What tasks do informal helpers face in helping him adjust to the community and how ready and able are they to provide this help? What kind of assistance in problem solving will he need? Does he need housing, a job, help in planning for leisure time? What formal and societal resource systems exist in the community to help him with any of these tasks?

As another example, consider a family in which one of the children is mentally retarded. The concern of social work here is not with the mental retardation per se but with the tasks that having a mentally retarded child present to the family and their ability to cope with these tasks. Do the parents have the knowledge and time to deal with any special problems the child might present? Are there resources in the community such as special day-care centers and schools? Are the parents aware of and able to use such resources? Is there an organized group of parents of mentally retarded children which could provide the parents with information and advice, help link them to needed resources as the child grows up, provide an outlet for sharing problems and concerns, and act as an advocate for their interests?

The three case studies in Part III further illustrate the distress people experience in coping with tasks and trying to realize their aspirations in the face of difficult obstacles. The tenants in the tenement house on Sixth Street (Purcell and Specht), in trying to improve their housing conditions, needed help in forming a membership organization as well as information, advice, encouragement and other assistance to deal with the extremely complicated bureaucratic system of city agencies. The patients in the hospital ward (Foster) were frustrated in their efforts to maintain a responsible family role by the subculture of the ward. They needed the help of the worker with the tasks of communicating the nature of their distress to the doctors, and they needed the support of the worker in confronting the ward culture. The network of resource systems the black family (Hoffman and Long) was caught up in was frustrating the father's efforts to maintain his work and family roles and achieve his aspirations for his children's education. The family needed the assistance of the worker in dealing with the societal systems that were intruding upon them as well as the worker's information and his use of confrontations to force them to alter their roles and tasks within the family resource system.

Thus the first dimension of the social work frame of reference directs

attention to the tasks people are confronted with in social si and the resources and conditions necessary for facilitating t formance of these tasks.

Interacting with Resource Systems

A second characteristic of the social work perspective on soci tions is its focus on people *in interaction with* their network of r systems. This means that we do not view problems as an attri people; rather, we see people's problems as an attribute of thei situation. The question is not *who has* the problem, but how ments in the situation (including the characteristics of the pe volved) are interacting to frustrate people in coping with the

For example, suppose the residents of an inner-city neighb are not making use of a newly established health clinic in the a the residents the problem because they are reluctant to use th or is the clinic the problem because it is not reaching the resid viewing the situation, the social worker would focus on the pr communication and interaction between the two systems (cli neighborhood) in an effort to improve the linkage between t the residents don't know about the clinic, the means of adver may not be adequate. Perhaps posters should be placed in b grocery stores. If the residents know about the clinic but feel fortable about going there, it might help if some of the sta indigenous to the neighborhood. There may need to be some p for child care at the clinic so parents can talk with the doctors being distracted. The residents may have had previous bad exp with public clinics or may be angry at not being consulted w clinic was being established.

As another example, in exploring the problems experienced parents of a mentally retarded child the worker will look at th actions of the family as a resource system for its members. T of each parent must be examined in the context of the roles c family members. How does the presence of a mentally retarde affect the interaction of the other family members? Do the agree on how the mentally retarded child should be handled? I ways do they help or support one another? How do other c react to the attention that the parents pay to the mentally r sibling? Does the father see his role in relation to the retarde differently than his role in relation to the other children?

Most situations confronting a social worker involve looking

social systems that are related to a social situation. In the Foster study, the problem—the role expectations for the patient—is rooted in a single system—the ward system, which tied together the patients, their families, and the hospital. In the other two studies, problems such as poor housing and family equilibrium are embedded in a great number of different systems.

This second aspect of the social work frame of reference, then, moves beyond a dichotomous view of people and the resource systems in their social environment, or even people within their systems in the social environment, to a focus on the nature of the linkages and interactions between people and their resource systems.

Relating to Public Issues

The third aspect of the social work frame of reference directs the practitioner's attention to the relationship between the private troubles of people in a social situation and the public issues which bear on them. C. Wright Mills discusses the differences between personal troubles and public issues:

Troubles occur within the character of the individual and within the range of his immediate relations with others; they have to do with his self and with those limited areas of social life of which he is directly and personally aware. Accordingly, the statement and the resolution of troubles properly lie within the individual as a biographical entity and within the scope of his immediate milieu—the social setting that is directly open to his personal experience and to some extent his willful activity. A trouble is a private matter: values cherished by an individual are felt by him to be threatened.

Issues have to do with matters that transcend these local environments of the individual and the range of his inner life. They have to do with the organization of many such milieu into institutions of an historical society as a whole, with the ways in which various milieu overlap and interpenetrate to form the larger structure of social and historical life. An issue is a public matter: some value cherished by publics is felt to be threatened.[5]

Many personal troubles cannot be dealt with by an individual or family because problems of personal milieu are linked to public issues. Reciprocally, problems of public issues cannot be handled without

---

[5] C. Wright Mills, *The Sociological Imagination* (New York: Oxford University Press, 1959), p. 8.

examination of their impact on personal troubles. As William Schwartz puts it:

> . . . the polarization of private troubles and public issues cuts off each from the reinforcing power of the other. There can be no 'choice'— or even a division of labor—between serving individual needs and dealing with social problems, if we understand that a private trouble is simply a specific example of a public issue, and a public issue is made up of many private troubles.[6]

Thus Schwartz sees the social agency as not just a means of providing services and resources but as an arena for the conversion of private troubles into public issues. Indeed, social workers might agree with Mills that the task of liberally educated men is to translate personal troubles into issues, and issues into their meaning for individuals.[7]

To illustrate the relationship between personal troubles and public issues, consider the problems of health needs of elderly people. An aged person who needs but cannot find adequate nursing home care has a private trouble. However, the shortage of good quality nursing care and the existence of substandard nursing homes is a public issue. If social workers concentrate on helping individual aged people find scarce nursing home care, they are only dealing with private troubles. They cannot alleviate many of these private troubles, however, without also working on the public issue—the expansion of quality nursing home care. And, in order to substantiate the need for nursing home expansion and improvement, social workers must cite the need for such care by many individuals and describe the private troubles related to the public issue.

To summarize, the social work frame of reference leads the practitioner to focus on three related aspects of social situations: (1) the life tasks people are confronted with and the resources and conditions which would facilitate their coping with these tasks; (2) the interactions between people and their resource systems, as well as the interactions within and among resource systems; and (3) the relationship between the private troubles of people and public issues which bear on them.[8]

---

[6] William Schwartz, "Private Troubles and Public Issues: One Social Work Job or Two?" *The Social Welfare Forum, 1969* (New York: Columbia University Press, 1969), p. 38.

[7] C. Wright Mills, *The Power Elite* (New York: Oxford University Press, 1957), p. 319.

[8] The social work frame of reference will be elaborated in Chapter 6, Assessing Problems.

FUNCTIONS OF SOCIAL WORK PRACTICE

In defining what the social worker does to achieve the purposes of social work, the major focus is not on problems of people or problems of resource systems, but on the interactions between people and resource systems and between resource systems. The social worker will perform some functions with people who need help from resource systems and others with people within various resource systems.

Seven major functions of social workers in carrying out the purposes of the profession can be differentiated. The intervention activities and tasks performed by social workers are designed to accomplish one or more of the following functions:

1. Help people enhance and more effectively utilize their own problem-solving and coping capacities.
2. Establish initial linkages between people and resource systems.
3. Facilitate interaction and modify and build new relationships between people and societal resource systems.
4. Facilitate interaction and modify and build relationships between people within resource systems.
5. Contribute to the development and modification of social policy.
6. Dispense material resources.
7. Serve as agents of social control.

In practice, a given activity might be performed to achieve several of these functions at the same time. Further, because of the interactional (or transactional[9]) nature of the linkages that exist within, between, and among people and their resource systems, a specific activity or task of the worker that creates a change in the nature of one linkage may set off reciprocal changes in several of the other linkages and thus accomplish other functions.[10]

Enhancing People's Problem-Solving Capacities

Because people may not be able to cope with their life tasks and may experience distress because of physical, emotional, economic, or social

[9] For a discussion on the utility of using systems theory for viewing persons in situations transactionally see Carol Meyer, *Social Work Practice: A Response to the Urban Crisis* (New York: Free Press, 1970), pp. 124–37.

[10] See the Hoffman and Long case study in Part III for an illustration of the worker's conscious use of interventions aimed at achieving several functions (help the family members enhance and more effectively utilize thir own problem-solving capacities, establish initial linkages between family and resource systems, facilitate interaction and modify relations between the family and societal resource systems, and facilitate interaction and modify relationships within the family).

problems, it is a function of the social worker to *help people enhance and more effectively utilize their own problem-solving and coping capacities.* These problems may prevent an individual, who could be connected to several systems (family, place of work, school), from functioning satisfactorily within them. Individuals may also be so over-whelmed and confused by the life tasks facing them that they may need help in establishing realistic goals and aspirations for themselves and in deciding what they can do to achieve them.

The social worker may even use himself as a resource in performing several kinds of activities to help people to establish goals and formulate plans to reach their goals. The social worker ordinarily is employed within a social agency to deliver social services; he thus is representing a societal system when he uses himself as a resource. The social worker who is a private practitioner is representing the profession of social work, which also is a societal resource.

WORKER TASKS AND ACTIVITIES. First, the social worker identifies and contacts people who need help in coping with their life tasks. Some people with problems will contact a social worker directly. A lonely young mother who is a single parent and is overwhelmed with problems of raising her children may go to a social worker in an agency for help. A teacher unable to cope with disruptive children in her classroom may ask a social worker in the school for assistance. Often, however, people with problems will not seek out a social worker. Carol Meyer discusses the importance of social workers being located where people are when they are performing their life tasks and may be faced with problems in coping with crisis situations. Thus she suggests they should serve in employment offices, hospitals, schools, and day-care centers.[11] Social workers in these settings can reach out to contact people and offer help.[12] They may aggressively seek potential applicants who might become clients.

Second, the social worker can provide understanding and support and encouragement for people who are in a crisis. In this role he could help an individual who has lost his job and is anxious about the future, a woman who has lost her husband and is overwhelmed by feelings of grief and inadequacy in planning for her future, or a frightened child who has been admitted to a hospital.

Third, the social worker can provide an opportunity for people to talk about their difficulties. Describing his situations and airing his

---

[11] Meyer, *Social Work Practice.*
[12] Chapter 8, Making Initial Contacts, and Chapter 9, Negotiating Contracts, discuss methods of reaching out to people.

feelings may help an individual to organize his thinking, see his situation in new ways, and make a plan to cope with it. A teacher overwhelmed by problems of teaching Mexican-American children who are new to the school, speak little English, and are creating a disruption in the classroom may talk over his difficulties and decide to learn Spanish and study Mexican-American culture. A teen-ager who has dropped out of high school and is having trouble obtaining jobs may air his discouragement and decide to return to school. A tenant having difficulties getting adequate light and heat from his landlord may vent his frustrations and decide to join a tenant's union.

Fourth, the social worker can help people examine alternative ways of solving problems and provide information to help them make decisions. An unwed pregnant teen-ager may need help in understanding her options with regard to having an abortion, having and keeping the baby, or giving up the baby, and the tasks and consequences presented by each option. In such a case the worker will have to help the girl think through her situation and establish her own objectives before she is ready to consider what resources she might need. In the Purcell and Specht case study in Part III, the worker helped the tenants think through their problems and provided information which helped them decide what actions they should take and what resources they should use to try to improve their housing situation.

Fifth, the social worker can confront people with the reality of their situation by giving them information which upsets their equilibrium and motivates them to make changes. He can use confrontation with people who are apathetic and believe change is impossible or who blame their problems on someone else. A mother who is neglecting her children could be told by a social worker that the court could take the children away.

Finally, the social worker can teach skills to help individuals realize their aspirations and accomplish their life tasks. Rural people who have moved to a large city may need help in acquiring knowledge and skills needed to cope with urban life. People who have problems in social interactions with others can learn new communication skills from a worker.

Through the performance of such tasks and activities, the social worker can enable individuals to solve their own problems and to use the resources they already are linked to more effectively. Thus people will not always require long-term assistance from social workers in becoming linked to new resource systems or in utilizing their own resources. As a result of the worker's initial contacts, however, they often decide they want to use other resources and may require the worker's help in obtaining them. They may also need the worker's further help in negotiating with the systems to which they are connected. In these instances, the worker will perform some of the other functions discussed below.

Establishing Linkages to Resource Systems

It has been noted that people who need resources may not be linked to informal, formal, or societal systems because they may not know of their existence or how to use them, because they may be reluctant to use the systems or believe they will not meet their needs, or because a needed resource system does not exist. Several kinds of activities are engaged in by social workers to *establish initial linkages between people and resource systems.*

WORKER TASKS AND ACTIVITIES. First, the social worker helps identify and locate people who are in need of certain resources or entitled to certain benefits but who are not aware of their eligibility to receive them. The worker could organize a program employing elderly people to reach isolated elderly people who may not be aware of such community services as "meals on wheels" or homemaker services or their eligibility for Medicare. He could make arrangements with others who are likely to come into contact with people in need, such as visiting nurses or delivery boys, to act as referral agents. He could help a membership organization reach out to and recruit new members who need the assistance of the organization and who in turn would help strengthen it.

Second, the social worker provides people with information on what resources are available, what they are entitled to, and what procedures to follow to obtain the resource. A neighborhood association might need information on possible sources of funds or businesses which may donate equipment. An unemployed person being discharged from a mental hospital may need information on job possibilities or employment services as well as leads to social clubs he might join to help him meet other people.

Third, the social worker can assist people in overcoming practical problems that prevent them from getting or using a needed resource. A worker might arrange for baby-sitting so that a mother can attend a vocational training program or for a member of a senior citizen's club to accompany a prospective member to a meeting, both to offer support and to help him find his way.

Fourth, the social worker makes referrals and assists people in getting a needed resource. He could make a phone call to help pave the way, accompany a person to an agency to help cut red tape, help him in filling out forms, or provide other such assistance. A social worker might help a community group write up an application for funds for some new program or put the group in touch with experts who can provide such help. He could refer a person who has problems with an absentee landlord to a local neighborhood group working on landlord-tenant problems. The worker will often follow up to make sure the needed service or resource is being provided.

Fifth, the social worker acts as an advocate on behalf of people who are experiencing difficulty in obtaining a resource or negotiating a system. In the Purcell and Specht case study, the tenants needed the worker to advocate for their interests in dealing with the reluctant landlord and municipal agencies. A neighborhood organization may need the help of the social worker in asking the board of directors of a community center to give it space for an office, or a welfare rights group might use a worker to help it convince a county board to change some policy. A patient being discharged from a mental hospital might need the social worker to persuade his former employer to give him his old job back.

Sixth, the social worker by providing information and advocacy, can stimulate an existing societal resource system to examine policies that prevent it from serving some population groups and help the system make itself more accessible. This could involve such things as working to locate offices of the system near where people live, helping to simplify application forms and procedures, arranging to have receptionists who speak the same language or are of the same culture as the people who use the system, providing for evening and weekend hours, and devising better means of publicizing the resources available.

Finally, the social worker enables people to act as resources for one another by forming new systems to link them together. For pregnant teen-agers reluctant to seek advice or comfort from friends and relatives, the worker might form a group in which they can share mutual concerns, offer each other support, and share ways of coping with their situation. Workers have organized telephone reassurance programs in which isolated elderly people in the community call one another every day to check if everything is all right and to summon help if needed. The worker thus creates a new informal helping system, linking together those in the community who did not have such a system naturally. Social workers also are instrumental in organizing membership organizations such as neighborhood or special-interest groups so people can work together on common problems. Some systems which social workers help build are temporary or ad hoc groups which cease to function when their short-term purpose is realized. Other systems, such as a neighborhood council may be more permanent.

Facilitating Interaction with Resource Systems

After initial linkages have been formed between people and societal resource systems, problems may occur which prevent societal systems from being responsive to their consumers and keep people from receiving the help they need.[13] Indeed, the nature of the interactions between people and resource systems may aggravate rather than reduce problems, or may create new problems. Thus it is the function of the social worker to *facilitate interaction and modify and build new relationships between people and societal resource systems.*

The operation of some societal systems actually dehumanizes the people they were established to serve. Procedures in a mental hospital may force patients into a daily regimen that denies them basic human dignity, personal privacy, and opportunities to make decisions for themselves, thus decreasing their feelings of self-worth and reducing their motivation to change.

Some societal systems are unresponsive to those who come to them from natural or membership systems because members of the societal system and the consumers disagree as to the nature of the problems and what should be done about them.[14] Unless consumers have a voice in determining the nature of the response of societal systems, they may not receive the resources, services, or opportunities they want.

Within large societal resource systems such as hospitals or schools, people may not be receiving all the appropriate services the systems can provide. A patient in a hospital may not know that members of a social service department will help him make plans for his family while he is hospitalized.

If consumers are receiving services from several subparts of a societal system, or from many societal systems, they may find that these systems are working at cross-purposes. The Hoffman and Long case study in Part III illustrates how individuals and families are linked to many

---

[13] For the purpose of this discussion we are not considering people who are consumers of societal systems and who may become part of them for short or long periods as full permanent members of the systems, because they are viewed not as providing the resource, but as receiving (or consuming) it.

[14] See discussion in Chapter 9, Negotiating Contracts, on reasons for disagreement between workers and others.

societal resource systems which may give contradictory messages and place contradictory demands on consumers of the service, as was noted above.

Many of the social worker's activities are designed to make his own societal system more responsive to its consumers and to change the ways other societal systems interact with consumers.

WORKER TASKS AND ACTIVITIES. First, the social worker can ensure that information is provided to a societal resource system to illustrate problems that its operating procedures are causing for its consumers. The worker himself may provide the information, or he can encourage staff to examine existing information. The Foster case study in Part III, discussed above, illustrates how a social worker helped confront the staff on a hospital ward with information on how the existing practice of not telling patients the nature of their illness exaggerated the fears and increased the stress of the patients and their families. The worker used the information to help the ward staff make changes in the way they related to the patients and families.

Instead of providing existing information himself, the worker can stimulate staff of a societal system to do a self-study of their interactions with consumers. He could convince a mental health agency to collect information on the number of people who do not return after a first interview, the service objectives that were established by workers and consumers, and the extent to which these objectives were reached. The results of this self-study could motivate the agency to change its methods of offering service.

Second, the worker can serve as a consultant to a societal system and suggest different methods of operation. A worker in a hospital or school could help physicians and teachers to develop procedures to identify people who need special services, such as outpatient facilities or special tutors.

Third, the worker can consult with informal systems to assist them in obtaining new or expanded services from societal systems. A worker could help a family with a child who is having difficulties in school by explaining school policies, describing different services the school offers, helping the family decide what additional or changed services they want from the school, and supporting them in their decision to talk to school administrators.

The worker also can consult with and teach skills to people to help them deal with the conflicting demands and requirements of the many systems they are linked to. The worker in the Hoffman and Long case study helped the family to assess the demands made by different systems and helped them decide how they should respond. A worker could also assist a membership organization such as a PTA to deal with conflicting requests made to it by different parts of a societal system—the school board, principal, or special education teachers.

Fourth, the worker can bring people in one societal system together or link people from many societal systems to enable them to arrive at a coordinated plan and approach for a family or an individual. Within a large societal system such as a school or children's institution, the worker may coordinate the work of different parts of the system and help different staff members, such as teachers, special tutors, guidance counselors, remedial reading staff, and other special staff, to arrive at a unified plan and approach with a particular consumer of the service.

Fifth, the worker can serve as a consumer advocate with societal systems. He can make an agreement with a natural or membership system to act as an advocate on its behalf. The worker could advocate on behalf of an aged person who is receiving public assistance for additional special-purpose funds or with a judge for release of a juvenile from a detention home. A school social worker could help persuade the principal to accept a PTA recommendation for changes in the way parent-teacher conferences are conducted.

In addition to advocating on behalf of specific consumers, the worker can advocate for the inclusion of consumers in the decision making of societal systems to make the system more responsive to them. He can encourage societal systems to involve consumers in evaluating with staff the services they have received and to include consumers on advisory boards and agency boards of directors.

Sixth, the worker can organize consumers into a new membership organization to advocate on their own behalf or help an existing organization to do so. A worker could organize a council of residents of a nursing home, not only to plan activities for themselves but also to advocate for changes in the home operation, or he could organize residents in a low-income neighborhood to advocate for changes in the host of societal resource systems they are connected to. The worker can also increase the effectiveness of existing membership groups in advocating with a societal resource system by providing assistance such as plans for a membership campaign and advice on strategy and tactics.

Finally, the worker can mediate and resolve disputes and conflicts between natural informal systems, membership organizations, and societal systems. He could mediate a dispute between an organization of low-income people and a neighborhood association of property owners on the appropriate enforcement of housing codes and the need for new housing regulations for an inner-city neighborhood. He could assist members of these groups in reaching agreement on specific desired changes in housing regulations and help them form an ad hoc coalition to influence the city council and housing inspectors. If parents believe the teen-age programs offered by a neighborhood center exert a bad influence on their children, a worker could mediate the dispute between family members and the center. A hospital which operates a drug rescue unit may need the help of a social worker in reducing conflicts over appropriate police involvement with young people who abuse drugs.

Facilitating Interaction within Resource Systems

The activities of the social worker discussed in the previous section focused on efforts to change interactions *between* people and resource systems. Here we will consider activities of the worker aimed at changing the interactions of people *within* an informal, formal, or societal resource system in order to enable the system to meet the needs of its members[15] and, in the case of societal resource systems, to improve their ability to provide resources for their consumers. Thus the social worker's function is to *facilitate interaction and modify and build relationships between people within resource systems.*

The worker may be seeking to help family members change the way they relate to each other, to help them provide emotional support and affection for one another, to help members of a neighborhood association deal with problems of internal dissension, or to help staff members of a hospital redefine their working relationships. In all these situations, the worker's activities are directed toward helping individual members of the system carry out their roles within the system, as well as improving the operation of the system as a whole. For example, the worker in the Hoffman and Long study sought to help the husband assume and carry out different roles within the family but also focused on changing the way all the members related to one another. Roles in any system are reciprocal, and if one member changes a role (a father tries to assume more authority within the family), other members are going to react to this new role (a mother may fight the father's attempt).

---

[15] In this discussion, "members" refer to all people in informal and membership systems and to employees in societal resource systems. Problems between consumers of societal resource systems, be they residents in institutions or people with limited contacts, and staff of societal resource systems were discussed in the last section.

In working to change transactions between people in a resource system, the worker operates on the assumption that if he helps the system provide satisfaction for its members, the system will be better able to achieve its goals. If the morale of employees of a societal resource system is improved, the services they offer to consumers will be affected. Types of problems that may hamper the functioning of a system include apathy, conflict between members, poor communication, and inadequate procedures for making decisions and solving problems. Further, the distribution of power and authority in the system and conflicting values among members may prevent some members from achieving satisfaction in their roles.[16]

Problems of internal functioning of a system may have been in existence for a long time, or a sudden crisis or change in membership or in positions in a system may create problems. For example, a death in a family, the birth of a retarded child, the election of a new president of a welfare rights group, or a shift in executives in a social agency may create new problems of internal functioning for the system or exacerbate existing ones.

The worker may be a member of the system he is trying to help or outside it (a family, a special-interest group, another societal system). He may be a member of a societal resource system (a staff member of a hospital or social agency). Further, the worker in his own societal system may or may not have formal administrative responsibility, but he is responsible for trying to change faulty functioning of his system that prevents it from serving in the best interests of its consumers.

WORKER TASKS AND ACTIVITIES. First, the social worker transmits information from one part of a system to another. Ronald Lippitt, Jeanne Watson, and Bruce Westley illustrate how the worker, serving as a friendly, neutral intermediary between people in a system, may correct misconceptions and reduce hostility and conflict between subparts and thus help correct distortions in communication or the way people listen to one another.[17] Thus the worker could improve understanding and communications between parents and children, between members of a formal organization, between administrators and workers, or between different staff units in a formal organization.

Second, instead of serving as a neutral intermediary, the worker can take sides and advocate for the interests of one part of a system which

---

[16] For a discussion of problems of internal relationships with different size systems see Ronald Lippitt, Jeanne Watson, and Bruce Westley, *The Dynamics of Planned Change* (New York: Harcourt, Brace and World, Inc., 1958), pp. 21–48.

[17] Lippitt, Watson, and Westley, *Dynamics of Planned Change*, p. 47.

lacks power, is not included in decision making, or is not receiving satisfaction from its role within the system. The worker could advocate on behalf of child-care workers in a children's institution and confront the rest of the staff with the harm that is done to the children because child-care staff do not participate with professional staff in making plans for the children.

Third, the social worker can help organize subparts of a system and help them advocate and work for changes in their own behalf. He could encourage members of a tenant's union to work together and to attempt to change the operating rules of the union, which vest much of the authority in the president, or to elect a new president.

Fourth, the worker can serve as a consultant to members of a system, pointing out problems of internal functioning and suggesting changes in operating procedures and role assignments. If members of the system are apathetic and believe that change is impossible to achieve, the worker may need to provide them with hope that change is possible, point out examples of other systems that have changed, and enumerate the benefits that will accrue to members if changes are made. A worker could show leaders of a neighborhood organization who have difficulties in mobilizing members how other organizations have succeeded in mounting successful action programs by involving members in decision making, thereby gaining their commitment and interest in working for change.

Fifth, the worker can teach skills to members of the system which will enable them to perform their present roles more satisfactorily or assume new roles within the system. He could help a newly elected president of a membership organization plan an agenda for a meeting and develop methods to improve group discussion. The worker could model, and thus teach, problem-solving procedures to a family by asking each member to present his ideas about family problems and how they should be solved and then asking all the members to discuss the alternative suggestions that have been made.

Sixth, the worker can try to introduce new members into the system or encourage present members to drop out in order to improve the system's functioning. A worker could help recruit members of a formal organization who are well regarded by the rest of the members and who have skills that will help in reducing conflicts between members, or he could encourage parents to allow a 19-year-old son, whose life style conflicts with theirs, to leave home.

Finally, the worker can involve members of the system in self-diagnosis of problems in their interactions by encouraging discussion of their difficulties or establishing feedback mechanisms with the system itself. The worker could videotape a family's interactions or a staff meeting of an organization, play it back, and help members examine their own problems in interactions.

Influencing Social Policy

The responsibilities of social workers to become involved with public issues that have an impact on the private troubles of people and to influence people within societal systems to make them more responsive to present and potential consumers have been pointed out above. A related function of social workers is to work for changes in social policies that affect people in many informal, formal, and societal resource systems. Thus social workers *contribute to the development and modification of social policy* made by legislative bodies, elected heads of government, public administrative agencies (Department of Health, Education and Welfare), voluntary funding institutions (United Fund), and people in positions of authority in societal resource systems.

In efforts to make changes in social policy, social workers are faced with constraints that limit and otherwise affect the specific objectives they may establish and their ability to achieve their objectives.[18] It is useful here to distinguish between basic fundamental changes in social policy and middle-range levels of policy change.

Fundamental change in social policy involves changes in the basic structure of societal institutions, such as changes of national priority in the allocation and distribution of the resources of a society. Examples of such change would be replacing current public assistance programs with some form of guaranteed annual income, or the diversion of funds from the space program to programs to improve elementary school education in the inner cities.

Social workers, who continually deal with problems of people, are painfully aware of needed changes in basic social policy at the national level. The problem of poverty requires a more equitable distribution of money; the answer to unemployment lies in the creation or availability of jobs. Problems of inadequate medical care require new forms of health-care delivery systems, and those of inadequate housing in urban slums require a greater proportion of resources to be allocated

---

[18] For a discussion of the dilemmas faced by members of the social work profession who work to influence public issues see Meyer, *Social Work Practice*, pp. 2–34; Harry Specht, "The Deprofessionalization of Social Work," *Social Work* 17 (March 1972):3–15.

to the rehabilitation of housing and building of new housing. While social workers can and should work toward bringing about some of these changes, they must recognize the severe limitations they face in trying to do so.

One limitation is the fact that fundamental social change is brought about in the political area through political processes. The force that a profession can bring to bear on a problem is technical know-how and expertise. Battles in the political area, however, depend on political power, which in this society means mobilization of a powerful constituency. Such activity is more suited to social reform movements and political parties than to a profession.

A second is that issues of basic social policy changes are too important to be left solely in the hands of any profession. Our democratic traditions dictate that special-interest groups and experts should not have the only right or the decisive right to determine public policy in their areas of technical competence. Society would resist efforts of the medical profession to dictate health policy, of the legal profession to dictate legal policy, or of the social work profession to dictate social service policy. Indeed, the value base of social work within the framework of democratic decision making restrains social workers who are tempted to impose their own views of social change on the people affected.

A third limitation is that social work is dependent on society for its sanction and support. It has been repeatedly demonstrated that society will not support any activity which has an objective of bringing about fundamental changes in the very fabric of social institutions.[19]

Awareness of these limitations should not be used as an excuse for ignoring fundamental policy issues; indeed social workers may support fundamental changes in basic social policy. Rather, this awareness should caution social workers against promising more than it is possible to deliver. Neither should they accept the blame for the continuance of social problems that have their roots in faulty social institutions.

Because of these limitations, social workers in the public issue arena ordinarily operate in what Jack Rothman and Carol Meyer call the middle level or range of social change.[20] Social workers, often in cooperation with others, work for many social policy objectives. They call attention to unmet needs and gaps in present resources (lack of home-care services to the aged) and the dysfunctional aspects of existing

---

[19] For a discussion of this point see Peter Marris and Martin Rein, *Dilemmas of Social Reform* (New York: Atherton Press, 1967).

[20] Jack Rothman, "An Analysis of Goals and Roles in Community Organization Practice," *Social Work* 9 (April 1964): 24–31; Meyer, *Social Work Practice*, p. 24.

social policy and legislation (deducting the full amount of earnings of a public assistance grant may discourage recipients from working). Social workers help design and promote the establishment of new services, coordinate and integrate existing societal resource systems (establishing a coordinated approach of many public and voluntary services to drug abusers and their families), and work to influence and sometimes help shape social policy and legislation designed to alter the social conditions and restraints under which people live (removal of practices that discriminate against minorities or classes of people).

Social workers may work through their professional association, the National Association of Social Workers, to contribute to the development and modification of social policy. Many social work activities also influence social policy.[21]

WORKER TASKS AND ACTIVITIES. First, the social worker collects and analyzes information on problems and conditions which point to the need for a change in social policy. While data collection is implicit in the tasks and activities of social workers in carrying out other functions, it is fundamentally important in social policy development.[22] No matter where a social worker is employed, he has intimate contact with data on social problems, social conditions, and the deficiencies of existing societal resource systems.

The social worker can analyze and summarize information existing in his own agency files, such as the number of aged and physically handicapped people who had to go to nursing homes because of the lack of adequate home care services. He can establish procedures to collect information, such as conducting a survey of the housing available to low-income people or produce data through the monitoring of a demonstration project that indicates objectives achieved and consumer reaction.

Second, the social worker can encourage his agency or other societal resource systems or formal organizations such as civic groups to take public positions on issues. He could help them mount an educational

---

[21] For a discussion of activities of social workers aimed at influencing social policy, see Irwin Epstein, "Social Workers and Social Action: Attitudes toward Social Action Strategies," *Social Work* 13 (April, 1968): 101–8; Patrick V. Riley, "Family Advocacy: Case to Cause and Back to Case," *Child Welfare* 50 (July 1971): 374–83; Harry Specht, "Casework Practice and Social Policy Formulation," *Social Work* 13 (January, 1968): 42–52; Robert Sunley, "Family Advocacy: From Case to Cause," *Social Casework* 51 (June 1970): pp. 347–57; Alan D. Wade, "The Social Worker in the Political Process," *The Social Welfare Forum, 1966* (New York: Columbia University Press, 1966), pp. 52–67.

[22] The importance of the role of the social worker as data collector to influence the political process is highlighted in Wade, "Social Worker in the Political Process."

campaign through the mass media, printed material, and public meetings.

Third, the social worker can form new systems to work for changes in social policy. He can form special study committees, task forces, or membership organizations to study problems and conditions and needs of people and make recommendations for legal changes, for the creation of new services or the elimination of old ones, or for better coordination of existing resources. A worker could form or serve on a citizen's committee to study the problems of people in a specific neighborhood, the adequacy of day-care services for a community, or the need for changes in state legislation on drugs.

Coalitions of existing organizations to work together to influence social policy can also be established by the social worker. He could help form a coalition of welfare rights groups, civic organizations, churches, and members of societal institutions to work for a change in existing public assistance laws and regulations.

The worker can also be instrumental in forming a group of people from several existing societal systems to help them coordinate their services. He could help representatives of all community services for mentally retarded children devise a coordinated plan to provide a continuum of services to the children and their parents. One agency may be designated as a fixed point of referral to ensure that families and children make their way through the appropriate services.

Fourth, the social worker can provide information to the makers of social policy and advocate for changes. He could testify at a legislative hearing, or talk personally to a legislator, mayor, city council member, or administrator responsible for devising procedures for implementing social policy, such as licensing regulations for day-care centers. The worker could write letters to policy makers and provide documentation from his data collection or from a study committee.

Fifth, the social worker can encourage others to advocate directly with policy makers for changes. He can provide them with information and serve as a consultant on tactics. The worker could assist the chairman of a citizen's committee that has studied day-care needs to prepare a presentation for a city council or a United Fund. A worker in a neighborhood center could encourage a prominent citizen member of his board of directors to testify at a city council meeting about the impact of a new zoning ordinance on residents of the neighborhood. The worker could consult with a welfare rights group on strategy to use to influence a state board which makes policy decisions on financial grants for special needs of families.

Sixth, the social worker can help design services and programs and draft legislation and proposals to change existing laws and policies and establish needed services. He could design new programs and proposals to offer social services in a rural area or help draft state legislation to change drug laws or to authorize additional state social services.

Finally, social workers, in cooperation with others, can test existing laws and administrative policies by taking specific cases to court or through an appeal procedure. The social worker can not only test the legality of the application of a policy in one individual case but change policy in future cases. Further, the testing of existing laws may lead to a future change in the law itself. For example, social workers have successfully challenged and changed the policy of welfare departments to make midnight inspections of the homes of women receiving Aid to Families with Dependent Children to determine if a man was in the house and supporting the family.

All of the functions discussed above are designed to accomplish the purposes of the social work profession. Thus they are aimed at enhancing the coping ability of people, linking people and needed resource systems, promoting the effective operation of informal, formal and societal resource systems, and contributing to the development of social policy. In addition to these functions, social work historically has performed two other vital societal functions: dispensing material resources and serving as agents of social control. Society has sanctioned the performance of these functions by the social work profession, in cooperation with other professions and occupations. Social workers have accepted these functions and developed competence in performing them.

Social workers who perform these essential societal functions bring to their performance their particular perspective and skills in improving the interactions between people and their social systems. Indeed, some knowledge and skills of social work have been developed by practitioners who have performed these functions. However, we believe the performance of these functions *alone* is not, and should not be, the central core or focus of the social work profession.

Dispensing Material Resources

A historic function of social workers is to *dispense material resources—* money, food, adoptive and foster homes, homemaker services, and other resources that are crucial for people's survival. Some of these resources (financial assistance) are granted to public agencies by legislative action. Public and voluntary agencies are sanctioned and licensed by law to develop and dispense other resources (foster and adoptive homes, day-care services). Other resources are developed on the initiative of social agencies (homemaker services, foster homes for discharged mental hospital patients). Thus ordinarily when social workers dispense material resources, they are operating as agents not only of a social agency but also of society. They are bound by legislative and agency mandates, regulations, and standards. In addition, social workers themselves have developed professional standards of practice in this area, such as in the fields of foster care and adoption.

Social workers who dispense resources also perform the other functions and tasks and activities discussed above. A social worker could help family members receiving financial assistance to enhance their own problem-solving capacities and to utilize resources of membership organizations and societal resource systems. Social workers locate people who need material resources, work to make their own and other societal systems responsive to people receiving financial assistance, and advocate for changes in the provision of income to poor people.

In addition to the above tasks and activities, there are also some specific tasks which social workers perform in dispensing material resources.

WORKER TASKS AND ACTIVITIES. First, the social worker determines the need and appropriateness of resources for people and determines if they are eligible for a resource. He could determine if a child needs a foster home or if his needs could be better met in his own home, a group home, or an institution. Social workers determine if people are eligible for financial assistance.

Second, the social worker forms new informal resource systems for people. Social workers who place children for adoption or discharged mental hospital patients in foster homes are actually creating an informal system for them.

Third, the social worker locates resources. When people themselves are potential resources (a potential foster family), social workers determine if they can provide the resource effectively. The worker could develop foster-home-finding programs and then screen prospective parents to determine if they can provide a good home for children with special needs or for an elderly person.

Fourth, the social worker provides knowledge and skills to people who are acting as resources. He could initiate training programs for homemakers and consult with them on special problems they encounter.

Fifth, the social worker prepares people for the use of a resource and helps them use it effectively. He may need to give a great deal of information and support to children or aged people both before and after they enter foster homes. He could provide help in budgeting to a person receiving financial assistance.

Finally, the social worker monitors and supervises the use of the resource. He could visit aged people in their foster homes to determine if their needs are being met effectively, if the situation could be improved, or if the aged person should move to another foster home or other facility.

Serving as Agents of Social Control

Some societal systems have been granted the authority to *serve as agents of social control* for people whose behavior deviates from societal laws and norms and to protect people who may be harmed by the behavior of others. Societal systems exercise their authority to confine people whose behavior has been labeled deviant in prisons, mental hospitals, and other institutions. They also supervise people in the community who have committed deviant acts, remove children and other dependent people (severely mentally retarded or physically handicapped people) from situations where they may be harmed, and establish and enforce standards for care of dependent people.

Social workers who serve as agents of social control receive their sanction and authority through their employment in societal resource systems. In addition to carrying out their social control function, these social workers also perform the other functions and tasks and activities already discussed. For example, a social worker who is supervising a man on probation will help him enhance his own problem-solving capacity, acquaint him with needed resources in the community, work to make societal systems responsive to him and his family, help him and members of his family provide support to each other, and may work for a change in laws and policies which establish regulations and conditions for people on probation. However, the worker also performs specific tasks and activities related to his social control function.

WORKER TASKS AND ACTIVITIES. First, the social worker supervises people who have been labeled deviant by society. He monitors their behavior to determine if they are conforming to laws and rules established by legislation, by court order, or by administrative policy. Social workers supervise people who are on probation or parole or are placed under informal supervision by a court to see that they comply with the conditions established for their behavior. Workers also may play a supervisory, monitoring role with people in an institution.

Second, the social worker investigates complaints of abuse and neglect. A worker in child or adult protective services collects information to determine if a dependent person is being neglected or abused and may recommend to the court that he be removed from the custody or care of parents, guardians, or other caretakers.

Third, the social worker licenses resource facilities to ensure that adequate care is provided for people who need the resources. The licensing function extends to foster homes, day-care centers, children's institutions, nursing homes, and other informal and societal resource systems.

The seven functions performed by social workers in carrying out their purposes in specific tasks and activities as we have outlined them are not independent from one another. It should also be noted that others have categorized social work functions and tasks differently. Some have preferred to describe social work functions according to major roles enacted by workers: advocate, educator, facilitator, and organizer of systems. We believe that such a classification confuses the functions social workers perform with the methods they use to carry out their functions. Indeed, if we examine the first five major functions we have outlined, which focus on changing and improving the interactions between people and their social systems, we discover that to perform each function the social worker plays the roles of advocate, educator, facilitator, and organizer of systems. Thus our classification makes it clear that the social worker cannot choose between major role stances to achieve all his functions, but must select, for a particular situation and change effort, the appropriate role and activity that will help him achieve his goals. In the selection of his activities, the social worker is guided by the science and art of practice.

ART AND SCIENCE IN SOCIAL WORK PRACTICE

In the course of this book we will be referring to social work practice as a *planned change* effort. The term "planned change" was deliberately chosen because of its connotations. The word "plan" conveys the idea of a purposeful and well-thought-out scheme, method, or design for the attainment of some objective or goal. The word "change" implies movement, a difference in or alteration of a situation or condition from one point in time to another. We view social work as a conscious, deliberate, and purposeful planned change effort.

By placing social work in such a context we are not denying the artistic and intuitive components of practice. We view art and science as allies, rather than adversaries. Unfortunately they are often not seen this way.

Young people today talk about the value of honesty in communications; of trusting, open relationships; of love and understanding between people. Students may be wary of theories and concepts which attempt to explain and predict human behavior and give guidelines for engineering change. They may fear that if they try to apply theories and act consciously to achieve a goal, they will destroy their ability to relate to others with spontaneity, love, and intuition.

We believe that while love is essential, love is often not enough. In order to help others change, we need to combine our creativity, spontaneous feelings, individuality, concern, and love for others with a body of knowledge about human behavior, the social environment, and processes of change; with proficiency in using techniques or procedures; and with a method of problem solving that utilizes our knowledge and techniques and provides a systematic guide for *our change efforts.*

Let us consider again the example of a worker in a mental health clinic who is asked to help a low-income family with young children having difficulty in school. The social worker will begin by making contact with the family and the school to explore the problems they are having with each other. He brings to these encounters his knowledge about: growth and development of all children, particularly low-income children; interactions within a family; particular problems of low-income families; functioning of organizations, particularly school systems; ways that families and schools ordinarily deal with each other; resistances to change that exist in all systems (individuals, families, organizations, and communities); and ways that families and organizations can be influenced to change. He also brings his knowledge of this particular community, the school system, the family's neighborhood, and the life style and problems of low-income people in this neighborhood and town.

In his contact with the family and the school, he uses interviewing and observational techniques to gain information. He has learned how to ask questions, pick up cues from what is said and not said, and observe behavior and the surrounding home and school environment. He begins to make sense and order out of the information he collects by matching it to his body of knowledge and theory and forming hypotheses about what is causing and maintaining the problems and what can be done to resolve them. His problem-solving method guides him as he takes his next steps to form a working agreement with the family and the school, establishes goals, and works to achieve them. As he moves along in the planned change process, he will test what is happening against his knowledge and apply a variety of interventive techniques.

The worker may have had experience with many similar families and schools which will help him in his work, but there will be unique aspects of this problem which will require his creativity and intuition in combining his knowledge and techniques and in using his problem-solving method. Joseph Eaton notes that knowability in the practice of social work is never absolute:

Areas of ignorance and error always exist no matter how much research and experience are applied to the solution of a human problem. In certain respects every man is (1) like all other men, (2) like some other men, (3) like no other man. (1) and (2) make it possible to apply science to practice; (3) represents the limiting condition. Social workers know that "every case is different," but this fact does not preclude the application of experiences derived from similar cases. Knowledge, while no key to certainty, contributes to a more modest goal, namely, to increase the frequency of socially appropriate decisions at the expense of the number of inappropriate or erroneous ones.[23]

Thus, while social workers acquire knowledge and skills which guide them in understanding a problem and selecting the appropriate interventive measures, they must use creativity and intuition in applying them because knowledge is never complete and each situation has unique aspects. Ernest Greenwood has described this as the interpretive process:

The interpretive process, the development of a formulation which will account for a series of facts, is essentially a free-wheeling, speculative one. It is an inferential process whereby the inquiring mind churns the available information over and over, employing all the logical devices and bringing to bear upon it any and all kinds of relevant knowledge. The process allows for a considerable play of the imagination, and the final formulation bears the personal imprint of its formulator.[24]

A social worker brings to his practice his own personality, values, life style, and feelings about other people along with his knowledge and skills. If he denies his own feelings, he may come across as a mechanistic technician and will have difficulty in engaging other people in problem-solving efforts. If he foregoes the selective use of knowledge

---

[23] Joseph Eaton, "Science, 'Art', and Uncertainty in Social Work," *Social Work* 3 (July 1958): 3–4.

[24] Ernest Greenwood, "The Practice of Science and the Science of Practice," in Warren Bennis, Kenneth Benne, and Robert Chin (eds.), *The Planning of Change* (New York: Holt, Rinehart, & Winston, Inc., 1961), p. 77.

and skills, he will operate at the same level as a concerned layman. Instead of assuming an antagonism between knowledge and art in practice, it should be recognized that one enhances the other. Helen Harris · Perlman notes their interdependence in her belief that "the artist's creativity is freed when he has grasped firmly the essential structure and forms of his particular activity. Only when he has incorporated these into his practice are his energies fully released to feed his senses, perceptions, responses, imaginations."[25]

William Schwartz has some reassuring words for those who may question their ability to creatively combine intuition, style, and personality with skills and knowledge to become an effective social worker:

There is, after all, no sphere of knowledge, no personal strength, and no field of competence which is irrelevant to the responsibilities of the human relations worker. And yet we know that the tasks of helping are not performed best by paragons but by those who want to help, know what they are trying to do, and have sufficient mastery of themselves and of social realities to offer their strengths in the struggles of others. Thus, the central problem for the helping agent does not lie in his nearness to perfection but in the extent to which he can mobilize the powers he does possess in the service of others. In order to find the common ground, he must use certain specific knowledge about human beings; in order to contribute data, to reveal his own stake in society, to define the rules, and to challenge the obstacles in the learner's path, he must be free to share what he has of sensitivity, science, and personal maturity. Where the worker proceeds from a clear sense of focus and function, his own strengths are tools that he uses in the specific tasks that he is called upon to face. As such, his powers are not pitifully inadequate replicas of a formidable ideal but full-blown strengths which he is free to own and to share.[26]

Although science and art will merge in the style of a particular social worker, he needs to know when he is operating from the basis of knowledge and when from creativity and intuition. A worker acting on the latter basis can examine the results, decide if he needs to try alternate approaches, and add to his own knowledge base. The next chapter elaborates on this idea in its discussion of the reliance on values and knowledge as a guide to practice.

---

[25] Helen Harris Perlman, *Social Casework—A Problem Solving Process* (Chicago: The University of Chicago Press, 1957), p. 6.

[26] William Schwartz, "The Social Worker in the Group," *Social Welfare Forum, 1961, National Conference on Social Welfare* (New York: Columbia University Press, 1961), p. 170.

CHAPTER 2

VALUE DIMENSIONS

AND DILEMMAS OF

THE CHANGE AGENT

ROLE

Placing social work in the context of planned change forces consideration of the issue of values and ethics. By whose *standards* do we determine that change is necessary? How are the *goals* of the change process
determined? What are the legitimate *means* for effecting change? How
do we *evaluate* the outcomes obtained? All such questions address
themselves, at least in part, to the values of the practitioner and his
profession.

It is impossible to structure an effective change effort in which an
implicit or explicit imposition of values is totally absent. If social
workers lay claim to some expertise in effecting change, they must
assume some responsibility for the nature and consequences of such
change. While this responsibility can be pointed out easily, it is a difficult one to discharge. This chapter is designed to help with this task.

The reader looking for a list of ethical do's and don'ts will be disappointed. The purpose of this chapter is to help make the practitioner aware of the value dimensions which permeate his practice and

the ethical dilemmas within which he must operate. Some observations will also be offered on coping with the ethical ambiguities built into the social worker's role. The intention is not to "dispose of" the value question in this chapter, however; the issues identified here will be referred to throughout the book.

VALUES AND KNOWLEDGE

In the discussion of values it is useful to distinguish between knowledge and values and to define the role each plays in guiding social work practice.

Values are beliefs, preferences, or assumptions about what is desirable or good for man. An example is the belief that society has an obligation to help each individual realize his fullest potential. They are not assertions about how the world is and what we know about it, but how it *should* be. As such, value statements cannot be subjected to scientific investigation; they must be accepted on faith. Thus we can speak of a value as being right or wrong only in relation to the particular belief system or ethical code being used as a standard.

What we will refer to as knowledge statements, on the other hand, are observations about the world and man which have been verified or are capable of verification. An example is that black people have a shorter life expectancy than white people in the United States. When we speak of a knowledge statement as being right or wrong, we are referring to the extent to which the assertion has been confirmed through objective empirical investigation.[1]

Values of Social Work Practice

A statement of the values held by the profession of social work can be found in The Working Definition of Social Work Practice developed by the National Association of Social Workers. The following six values are listed as basic to the practice of social work:

1. The individual is the primary concern of this society.
2. There is interdependence between individuals in this society.

---

[1] Concepts (and analytical frameworks and models built from them) comprise another category of knowledge. These are abstractions from our empirical knowledge base and represent ways to view, think about, and organize knowledge. Concepts cannot be referred to as right or wrong. Rather, we speak of them in terms of how useful they are in serving their purpose. "Social roles" and "coping mechanisms" are examples of concepts which have been useful in social work.

3. They have social responsibility for one another.
4. There are human needs common to each person, yet each person is essentially unique and different from others.
5. An essential attribute of a democratic society is the realization of the full potential of each individual and the assumption of his social responsibility through active participation in society.
6. Society has a responsibility to provide ways in which obstacles to this self-realization (i.e., disequilibrium between the individual and his environment) can be overcome or prevented.[2]

As William Gordon noted in his critique of the working definition, some of these propositions (Nos. 2 and 4, for example) are not really values but verifiable observations (i.e., knowledge statements). When values are focused on as ultimate assumptions about man and what is desirable for him, it becomes obvious that relatively few basic or primary values exist. From these primary values, many other so-called values can be logically deduced.[3] The *primary* values of social work might be stated as follows:

1. Society has an obligation to ensure that people have access to the resources, services, and opportunities they need to meet various life tasks, alleviate distress, and realize their aspirations and values.
2. In providing societal resources, the dignity and individuality of people should be respected.

Many values discussed in the social work literature can be seen as flowing from this basic value stance. For example, value No. 6 from the working definition is directly deducible from the primary values stated above and the generally known fact that societal conditions often determine the extent to which individuals have the opportunities to realize their potential. Other values, like those that call for the worker to respect the client, maximize the client's self-determination, maintain a nonjudgmental attitude, observe the confidentiality of the client's communications, and be honest in dealing with the client, can similarly be seen as having their roots in the primary social work values.

Such values not only stem from the primary values of the profession, however. They also contribute to the achievement of goals based on these same primary values and may therefore be considered *instrumental* values. They dictate ways in which the worker should interact with others in carrying out his professional activities so as to actualize the primary values. When viewed from a pragmatic rather than an ethical

[2] National Association of Social Workers, "Working Definition of Social Work Practice," *Social Work*, 3 (April 1958): 5–9.
[3] William E. Gordon, "A Critique of the Working Definition," *Social Work*, 7 (October 1962), pp. 3–13.

perspective, the consequences of acting upon a given instrumental value can be studied in order to determine to what extent and under what conditions it does in fact serve the attainment of goals consistent with the basic values of the profession. The pragmatic reason for maximizing client participation and self-determination is that it can lead to greater commitment to the planned change process. Likewise, respect for the client's individuality and a nonjudgmental attitude can reduce defensiveness, while honesty can increase the client's trust in the worker. Commitment, openness, and trust are ingredients which facilitate an effective client-worker relationship. Ideally, the instrumental values of the profession will conform to both ethical and pragmatic demands.

Guides to Practice

The way in which values and knowledge serve as guides to practice can be best understood by examining how they relate to the purpose and functions of social work practice. As Gordon points out, the purpose of social work, in the sense of what is to be accomplished, is the achievement of the desirable outcomes stated in the profession's basic values. This general purpose is translated by the worker into more explicit proximal goals, according to the particular nature of the given problem or situation with which he is working, for example helping Mr. Smith build up his confidence for a job interview or teaching Mrs. Jones how to reinforce better study habits in her child. Proximal goals, therefore, are essentially the concrete ends toward which the day-to-day practice of social work is directed.[4]

Though knowledge and values serve different functions, technical and ethical issues are often complexly interrelated in practice, and separating them is a difficult task. A problem that is stated in terms of posited relations between means and ends (i.e., the relative effectiveness of various plans in achieving a given end) is primarily technical and basically relies on knowledge. But semantics tends to add to the confusion. Technical issues are often couched in the language of ethical predicates or value judgments such as "right" and "wrong" or "should" and "shouldn't." An example is specification of the *right* way to provide feedback to a client. At the same time, ethical issues can be stated in technical terms. Whether a worker committed to racial integration can be effective consulting with a segregationist organization is an example.

---

[4] Ibid.

Our concern in distinguishing between values and knowledge, and the role each plays in guiding practice, reflects more than semantic interest. There are several important implications for practice in this differentiation.

First, acceptance of unconfirmed (but confirmable) knowledge statements as values inhibits the development of a valid knowledge base for social work practice. For example, Martin Wollins points out that even though recent research has demonstrated that group care may be adequate for many children in need of foster care, some American social workers have difficulty accepting the idea.[5] This is because the belief that the family environment is best for raising foster children is regarded as a value rather than a knowledge statement, and it fits in with other beliefs of American social workers.

The social worker must often act on the basis of incomplete knowledge; he cannot withhold action until all the knowledge he is using is confirmed. But he must remember that if he treats the unconfirmed knowledge as values, his beliefs become more ingrained. This makes it increasingly difficult to give them up or alter them when new data become available.

Second, as Gordon states, the separation of knowledge and values would help social workers avoid tacitly incorporating as value assumptions certain cultural norms whose effectiveness in providing the greatest satisfaction for individuals or groups should be regarded as problematic rather then confirmed. He notes that "The implicit equating of financial success with self-realization, or the intact family with the attendant right to unrestricted and unlimited reproduction, could then be viewed as testable, even questionable means to valued ends, not values in themselves."[6] In the same vein, Orville Gursslin, Raymond Hunt, and Jack Roach have pointed to the tacit equating of mental health and middle-class values.[7] In fact, most theories of behavior incorporate value-laden conceptions of the "healthy" person.

Still another reason for distinguishing between knowledge and values relates to our earlier discussion of the separate function that each serves in guiding practice. If a value is used as a guide when knowledge is called for, the resulting action is apt to be ineffective. If knowledge is

---

[5] Martin Wollins, "Group Care: Friend or Foe?" *Social Work*, 14 (January 1969): 35–53.

[6] Gordon, "Critique of the Working Definition," p. 9.

[7] Orville R. Gursslin, Raymond G. Hunt, and Jack L. Roach, "Social Class and the Mental Health Movement," in Frank Riessman, Jerome Cohen, and Arthur Pearl (eds.), *Mental Health of the Poor* (New York: Free Press, 1964), pp. 57–67.

called upon when a value is needed, the resulting action may be unpurposeful or even harmful.[8] For example, for a long time social workers were cautioned not to offer direct advice to clients, since this would violate the client's self-determination and impose the worker's solutions on the client. It has been found, however, that advice giving can be a useful tool in helping a client. The appropriateness of its use is a technical issue which must take into consideration such factors as the client's dependency on the worker and the goals of the client and the worker. The worker who does not offer advice when it is appropriate to do so will be ineffective because he is using an ethical solution to a technical problem.

To take another example, a community worker who is working to organize a rent strike among residents in a building might decide not to inform them of all the risks involved, reasoning that with majority support the tenants can win gains from the landlord. But if people develop fears because of the risks, the landlord can break the solidarity of the strike, tenants may become more despondent than before, and chances for improving their situation might worsen. The worker's decision not to reveal all the risks might seem to be based on technical considerations, but he is dealing with an ethical issue. If he believes in honesty and holds that the people affected by decisions should make them, because they are the only ones in a position to evaluate the risks accurately, the issue of informing the tenants of the risks involved will be guided by ethical considerations.

Finally, the distinction between knowledge and values can keep the worker aware of his own values. This awareness is an important first step in coping with the value dilemmas that are inherent in the change agent role.

ETHICAL AMBIGUITIES OF THE CHANGE AGENT ROLE

For the practitioner who considers self-determination or the enhancement of man's freedom as a fundamental value, any manipulation of the behavior of others constitutes a violation of their essential humanity. Herbert Kelman argues that the very fact of using manipulation raises ethical problems regardless of the form that this manipulation takes and regardless of the nature of the ends toward which the ma-

---

[8] William E. Gordon, "Knowledge and Value: Their Distinction and Relationship in Clarifying Social Work Practice," *Social Work*, 10 (July 1965): 32–39.

nipulation is directed.[9] An example of such an issue is the use of punishment to control behavior versus the use of positive rewards to condition behavior.

Were it possible to effect behavior change without manipulation or imposition of values, the social worker would not have to be so concerned about the value question. But since it is impossible to structure a change effort which is totally free of manipulation or imposition of values, he is confronted with a value dilemma that is built into the social worker's role.

To begin with, the reliance on planned change itself ultimately rests on a number of value assumptions: man should not passively accept his conditions but actively intervene to change them; man should make rational use of valid knowledge; man should be future oriented and plan ahead, and so forth. Though the social worker can point to empirical demonstrations of the effects of his planned change efforts to support his faith in the process, he must nonetheless accept the sobering fact that he cannot say with certainty that the world will be better off because of his efforts. Neither can he state with conviction that a given situation might not be worsened rather than improved by his intervention.

Social workers often work with others who do not share their faith in a rational approach to problem solving. They may hold a more fatalistic outlook on life. They may believe that we cannot and should not try to change things but accept them as they are. Indeed some may place great value on suffering and discomfort in the belief that they will be rewarded in an afterlife. In working with these persons social workers often use terms such as "client apathy and resistance," "helping people develop an awareness of their problems and the need for change," or "helping people develop the capacity to deal effectively with their own problems." To some extent these may be euphemisms for instilling in clients the worker's own values and his belief in planned change.

In addition to a belief in planned change itself, most change agents subscribe to a set of values governing their working relationships. These are the instrumental values discussed above, such as openness, honesty, and collaboration. The change agent may find himself in the position of helping others who either do not share these same values

---

[9] Herbert C. Kelman, "Manipulation of Human Behavior: An Ethical Dilemma for the Social Scientist," *Journal of Social Issues*, XXI, No. 2 (1965) pp. 31-46.

or do not hold them to the same degree. In fact, the worker might diagnose the problems of the client, be it an individual, a family, or an organization, as stemming from the fact that the client is operating on values in conflict with the worker's own instrumental values. For example, the leader of a community organization may be running the organization in a very autocratic manner and neglecting to consult the members on important matters or to share enough information with them. As a result the membership may become very apathetic and fail to develop a high commitment to the organization.

Not only will the practitioner often hold different instrumental values from the client and act upon his own values (impose them) in his relationships with the client, but his very effectiveness depends on his doing so. Chris Argyris argues that the client begins to test the validity of the worker's approach by seeing if the worker himself acts upon the values he is advocating the client system to adopt.[10] For example, if the worker is not open and honest in his relationship with the organizational leader in the example cited above, the leader might question why he should adopt such an approach in working with his organization.

When the worker is faced with resistance and wants to be accepted by the client system, he may be tempted to adopt some of the client's instrumental values. But in such cases the worker is likely to be "accepted" only in the sense of becoming a part of the client system. He might not be accepted as a consultant with a set of different values which the client system ought to explore seriously. Indeed, a client might well lose confidence in a consultant he feels he can manipulate to accept his values. An individual who, in the face of stress, takes on the values and norms of the client culture will probably not be respected in that culture.

Another factor contributing to the ethical ambiguities of practice is that despite any attempts by the worker to maintain a morally neutral stance, the client can still regard the practitioner as a moral agent. There are, in fact, a number of studies which show that psychotherapists can and do influence client values. David Rosenthal found that patients who improved in psychotherapy tended to revise certain of their moral values in the direction of their therapists' values.[11] Others have shown that practitioners can condition the verbal responses of a

---

[10] Chris Argyris, "Explorations in Consulting-Client Relationships," in Bennis, Benne, and Chin, *Planning of Change* (1969), pp. 434–57.
[11] David Rosenthal, "Changes in Some Moral Values Following Psychotherapy," *Journal of Consulting Psychology*, 19 (November 1955): 431–36.

client without being aware of doing so. This is not surprising, since it is difficult to see how any practitioner interacting in a reciprocal relationship can refrain from responding to his own values.

Discussions in the social work literature of the "limits" of client self-determination[12] point to another set of factors which puts the social worker in a position of interjecting his own values into the planned change process. Though the worker may ideally see his mission as helping people do what they want, this ideal becomes difficult to apply absolutely in practice. For one thing, the client himself may not be sure about what he wants and indeed may be seeking help in making a decision. The unwed pregnant teen-ager may be ambivalent about keeping her baby, or the president of a neighborhood organization may be unsure about the advisability of merging his organization with another group in the area. In helping people explore their problems, it is likely that the worker will personally favor one decision or alternative over another. This makes it difficult for the worker not to influence the client's choice by the emphasis he places on different alternatives, the way he presents them, or the information he provides.

Further complicating the issue is the fact that people do change their minds. A client who is very angry and upset with her husband may approach the worker stating that she wants a divorce. Does the worker accept this initial statement as the final wish of the client and help her plan for the divorce? Practice experience dictates that further exploration of the problem may reveal that she really may have more positive feelings and need for her husband, and her desire for a divorce was a temporary expression of her anger over a particular problem. To accept the client's initial expression at face value and act upon it would be doing an injustice to the client. If the client persists in her desire for a divorce, this would, of course, be a different situation. The problem is at what point to accept the client's statement as an accurate expression of her self-determination.

Another illustration of the same problem is a social worker who is seeking to organize a neighborhood association. He knocks on several doors and is met with apathy and disinterest. Does he accept this initial reaction as a final decision that these people do not want to form an organization, or does he try again, perhaps in a different way, to reach them? The seasoned practitioner comes to expect to be greeted with

---

[12] See Saul Bernstein, "Self-Determination: King or Citizen in the Realm of Values?," *Social Work*, 5 (January 1960): 3–8; Alan Keith-Lucas, "A Critique of the Principle of Client Self-Determination," *Social Work*, 8 (July 1963): 66–71; David Soyer, "The Right to Fail," *Social Work*, 8 (July 1963): 72–78.

apathy and disinterest in a neighborhood where people feel powerless. He may not be doing his job if he gives up too easily. The issue is at what point he accepts the fact that the people have self-determined that they do not want a neighborhood organization. These are complex questions because they encompass technical issues and the skill of the practitioner in reading people's behavior, as well as the ethical issue of respecting clients' self-determination.

Another set of limits often referred to in the literature comes under the heading of "reality." Whether this be physical, legal, financial or other forms of reality, it places restrictions on what any client is able to do. Another type of reality is recognition of the fact that the exercise of one person's freedom may prevent others from exercising theirs. Each person must accept some limits on his own freedom to make it a viable concept for all. As Saul Bernstein notes, exercise of self-determination that disregards reality is full of fantasy and can be unhealthy and self-defeating. But he also raises the point that "reality" should not always be accepted as fixed and unchangeable.[13] Further, the question can be raised about the client's right to set unrealistic goals. David Soyer, in discussing the client's right to failure, is concerned that in the name of reality social workers may be too conservative and set their sights for helping clients too low. He also believes that the client must learn for himself what the limits of reality are.[14]

Even this brief discussion of the concept of the client's self-determination can point to the underlying ethical problem. Social work regards self-determination as a client "right," but the worker is called upon to decide whether to "grant" this right to the client, and if so, to what extent. It is a contradiction for the worker to be put in this position. If the worker is able to deny the client's right of self-determination, then it really doesn't, in fact, exist. This is another expression of the value dilemma inherent in the social work role.

COPING WITH THE VALUE DILEMMAS

In calling attention to some of the ethical problems that must be faced in the planned change process, we are suggesting neither that the social worker should avoid influencing behavior under any circumstances, nor that he should be unconcerned about the manipulation inherent in all influence attempts simply because it is inevitable. As Kelman

---

[13] Bernstein, "Self-Determination."
[14] Soyer, "The Right to Fail."

remarks, there are important differences in kind and degree of manipulation, and there are ways of mitigating the manipulative effects of various influence attempts, even if these effects cannot be entirely eliminated.[15]

How can the change agent meet his responsibility for mitigating the manipulative effects of the planned change process? Kelman suggests that the first step in coping with the value question is the recognition of its existence, but such a self-awareness is difficult to attain. Ethical questions are ambiguous and make us feel uncomfortable—we like to avoid them. It is also easy to pay lip service to a lofty set of values from a textbook and feel we are meeting our responsibilities in this manner. But abstract values such as client self-determination not only are difficult to use as guides in everyday practice but can be harmful if they lull us into a false sense of complacency. Kelman cautions the practitioner against becoming so intoxicated with the "goodness" of what he is doing for and to the client that he fails to recognize the ambiguity of the control he exercises.

Self-awareness in and of itself, however, is not enough unless it is put to use in the service of the client. One way the worker can do this is to "label" his values for the client and allow the client to "talk back" in a sort of mutual influence situation. Kelman puts it this way:

. . . from the point of view of reducing the manipulativeness of the situation, it would be important to encourage mutuality at least to the extent of acknowledging that what the therapist introduces into the situation is not entirely based on objective reality, but on an alternative set of values, which are open to question. There may be particular therapeutic relationships in which a therapist finds it difficult to acknowledge the values that he brings to them, because his own motivations have become too deeply involved. There may also be institutional settings in which the therapist is required to present the institutional values as the "right" ones, in contrast to the patient's own "wrong" values. These are danger signals, and the therapist may well consider refraining from entering a therapeutic relationship or working in an institutional setting in which he is not free to acknowledge the contribution of his own values.[16]

This "labeling" of values is important for all practitioners, not just psychotherapists. Many behaviors and social conditions become defined as problems because they threaten existing community values and norms relating to such areas as drug use, delinquency, and abortion.

[15] Kelman, "Manipulation of Human Behavior."
[16] Ibid., p. 42.

As members and often representatives of the community, social workers must differentiate between their personal views of the value issues and the professional task of helping clients. Harry Specht believes:

> The question for the professional is whether his objective is to enable people to make choices or to assert *his* choice and cast his lot with those who have arrived at *the* solution. Social work operates in a framework of democratic decision-making, and if one decides that the framework is no longer viable, then there is no profession of social work to practice.[17]

In addition to recognizing and limiting the manipulative aspects of the situation, Kelman suggests that it is important to build into the change process itself procedures that will provide protection and resistance against behavior manipulation. The situation should be structured in such a way that the client will be encouraged to explore his own values and to relate alternative actions to his own value system. At the same time, the social worker must keep to a minimum the direct and indirect constraints he exercises.

> The crucial point is that the client's own values should be at the center of attention when change is under consideration and should be readily available as criteria against which any induced behavior can be measured. To the extent to which this is true, the patient or the group will be in a better position to resist manipulation in the service of alien values. Often, however, this will require much more than non-interference on the part of the practitioner. It may require active efforts on his part to encourage the client to bring his values to the fore and measure the induced changes against them.[18]

Finally, Kelman believes that it is important to go beyond providing clients with protection against manipulation that would encroach on their freedom of choice. He urges that the actual *enhancement* of *freedom of choice* should, ideally, be one of the positive goals of any influence attempt. The worker's professional skills should be used to provide the client with experiences that enhance his ability to choose, and thus to maximize his own values.

Though Kelman offers some useful guidelines on coping with the ethical dilemma inherent in the social work role, no dilemma yields to a simple or final solution. Armed with self-awareness of values and

[17] Harry Specht, "Disruptive Tactics," in Ralph Kramer and Harry Specht (eds.), *Readings in Community Organization Practice* (Englewood Cliffs, N.J.: Prentice-Hall, Inc., 1969), p. 384.

[18] Kelman, "Manipulation of Human Behavior," p. 43.

the knowledge and skills of his profession, the worker is faced with the constant task of maintaining a balance between flexibility and integrity. Flexibility is an essential trait because there must be a mutual accommodation between the expectations of the worker and client in the establishment of an effective relationship. The worker's integrity, however, establishes the boundaries of his flexibility. As Kenneth Benne notes, the limits of the worker's adaptability to the demands of his clients are set by a system of values that determines how he will function in a worker-client relationship.[19]

Flexibility was an issue in the discussion above of the limits of client self-determination, where the question of how persistent the worker should be in trying to organize a neighborhood association was raised. If the worker gives up at the first expression of apathy, disinterest, or hostility because he doesn't want to impinge on the self-determination of the clients, it might be suspected that he is offering a rationalization to cover up his insecurity at this task. If, on the other hand, the residents have seriously considered the idea and repeatedly maintain their belief that it is not in their best self-interest to form such an organization, then the continued persistence of the worker might impinge upon their freedom.

In an unpublished speech entitled "Finding and Making Leaders," Nicholas Von Hoffman urged the community organizer to drop off as much of his personal ideological baggage as he can outside the site of his organization efforts. The organizer must respect the morals and values of the community in which he is working. Some workers may consider their freedom and integrity compromised if they have to pay attention to their dress, resist speaking out on certain political issues, and otherwise watch their life style so they do not offend the public morals of the community. But Von Hoffman would regard such workers as inflexible and immature: "The best organizers have single-track minds. They care only for building the organization. When they alienate a potential member, they do so out of organizational need, not out of the egotism of irrelevant personal values. The best organizers stifle their tastes, their opinions, their private obsessions."

Of course even a flexible worker will run into situations where he can and should stand firm on his ethical principles. For example, he may try to discourage a newly forming tenant's union from trying to keep blacks out of their building and refuse to help them if they estab-

---

[19] Kenneth D. Benne, "Some Ethical Problems in Group and Organizational Consultation," in Bennis, Benne, and Chin, *Planning of Change* (1969), pp. 595–604.

lish such a policy. When a worker is at a deadlock with a client system over an ethical issue, it is sometimes possible to shift the problem to a different basis or define it in such a way that other nonconflicting values can be brought to bear on the situation.

For example, consider the following situation. A worker has helped a group of white persons to establish a small community center in their neighborhood. A black civil rights group has applied to use a meeting room in the center. The board of the center, holding a racist attitude, turns them down, and the black group threatens to demonstrate. The board asks the worker to talk to the blacks and help keep them out of the center. The worker cannot honor this request if he is bound to the ethic of fighting racial discrimination. He can argue the ethical issue with the board, but such an approach may end in a deadlock. As an alternative, he can help the board redefine the situation from an ethical issue to a pragmatic one concerned with conflict and neighborhood disruption. Appealing to the board's value of "avoiding trouble and keeping things peaceful," he can show them how allowing the black group to use the center will help reduce conflict and tension, while denying them use of the center will promote these conditions. The issue then has been shifted from whether racial discrimination is right or wrong to what is the best way to keep peace in the neighborhood.

We should also point out that it is not always necessary for the worker to achieve a consensus in values among the people he is working with before he can take positive action. For example, a worker may be able to get a group of local businessmen to set up a program to establish and find summer jobs for youth in the community. Some may favor the program because it keeps the kids off the street and out of trouble. Others may feel that the community has a responsibility to create opportunities for youth to participate in meaningful and responsible roles, or that these jobs will help build character and teach the value of money. Still others may feel no special responsibility to youth but go along with the project because of the public relations aspect of maintaining a good public image. If the worker tries to arrive at a consensus on the basic values underlying this program, it may never get off the ground.

Similarly, the staff at a mental hospital might agree to try a new treatment program, but for a variety of reasons. The administrator might go along because it has the potential of reducing the cost of patient care. The nursing staff may agree to it because it would make their jobs more interesting and give them more autonomy. Other staff may see its main value in enhancing the patients' decision-making ability. If the worker planned to first arrive at a consensus with the staff on a set of values regarding patient care and treatment and then to set up a program to maximize these values, he might never arrive at the second step.

A resurgence of interest in and commitment to client advocacy in the social work profession has led to the issue of flexibility versus integrity being brought up in terms of moral relativism or situational ethics. Can or should a worker who maintains a moral stance incorporating such values as collaboration and honesty in his working relationships with clients alter his stance when advocating on behalf of a client against some adversary? Within certain limits set by the worker's value framework and factors of efficiency and expediency, George Brager argues that the worker should and indeed must be willing to engage in social manipulation or political behavior when it is in the best interests of the client.

The justification for the violation of any cherished value must be its inherent conflict with some other value of equal or greater import. It follows, then, that manipulation should generally be eschewed except when it is clearly in the best interests of the disadvantaged client. The magnitude of the need, the powerlessness of the client, and the rules of the game as played by his adversaries dictate the conclusion that manipulation is sometimes justified.[20]

Brager also considers the values inherent in the substantive goal or principle at issue:

Risks to life and limb, basic needs, and social justice are areas that justify political intervention. Manipulation by or on behalf of victims of discrimination in a case of clear social injustice would thus be appropriate, e.g., in response to the jailing of civil rights workers. Similarly, one could condone a lie to entice a potential suicide off a ledge, although one would be highly critical of such behavior in other instances.[21]

But Brager cautions that the potential costs and risks of political strategies must always be assessed against their potential gains, so that the worker's morality is supported by expediency.

The issues that Brager raises with regard to moral relativism have import beyond the area of client advocacy. Similar issues have been raised about the ethics of certain behavior modification techniques in

---

[20] George A. Brager, "Advocacy and Political Behavior," *Social Work*, 13 (April 1968): 11.
[21] Ibid., p. 13.

treatment. For example, the use of certain procedures such as punishment might be justified with a severely retarded or psychotic patient
who has not responded to any other treatment approach, but not in
other cases. The reasoning is that it would be more inhuman to leave
the patient in his present state if there is a possibility for improvement
through the use of techniques involving punishment.

To cope with the ethical ambiguities of the change agent role, the
social worker must maintain a balance between flexibility and integrity. Self-awareness, technical expertise, and a tolerance for ambiguity
will help in this task. But the worker also needs to set some "bedrock"
values that establish the outer boundaries of his flexibility. These bedrock values should assure that the worker never loses sight of the mission of his profession—to serve in the best interests of the client. They
can also help contain the anxiety which may arise as he experiences
the inherent value dilemmas in the change agent role.

CHAPTER 3

FOUR BASIC

SYSTEMS IN

SOCIAL WORK

PRACTICE

Social workers work with many different kinds of people in their planned change efforts. Consider the following examples, all of which will be considered as the discussion of the four basic systems in social work practice is developed.

A probation officer works with probationers, their families, schools, employers, courts, lawyers, his own agency, and other community agencies.

A social worker in a nursing home works with the residents, the director and other institutional staff people, families, family doctors, social security and welfare department personnel, hospitals, churches, volunteer groups, and other community resources.

A neighborhood-center worker works with families, people of different ages and with different interests (teen-agers, young children, the aged, welfare mothers, local businessmen), landlords, city building inspectors, public health departments, employment services, and a host of other community people and institutions.

A worker in a community mental health clinic works with individual families and other groups, schools, treatment institutions, and other community organizations and groups.

Each social worker must decide what his purposes and relationships should be in working with all the various people he encounters. He needs to be clear about who will benefit from his change efforts, who has given him sanction to work for change, who will need to be changed or influenced, and whom he will need to work with in order to achieve different goals in his change efforts. The activities of the social worker can be viewed in relation to four types of systems: change agent, client, target, and action.

THE CHANGE AGENT SYSTEM

The term "change agent" originated with Ronald Lippitt, Jeanne Watson, and Bruce Westley, who use it to describe the variety of helpers with different specialties who work with different size systems.[1] In most change efforts there is one primary change agent who carries major responsibility. Two change agents may share this responsibility, as when cotherapists work with a family. A change agent could work with several other helpers in an action team that assists in the change efforts, while retaining the primary responsibility of change agent working with the team. A probation officer who works with school personnel, a welfare worker, employment office personnel, and so forth can be charged with the responsibility of coordinating all of their activities.

A social worker can be viewed as a change agent and the public, voluntary, or profit-making agency, organization, or community institution that employs him as a *change agent system.* When a social worker is a private practitioner, he alone composes the change agent system unless he contracts on a regular basis to work with other change agents such as clinical psychologists, doctors, and lawyers in a profit-making organization.

In our view, a change agent is a helper who is specifically employed for the purpose of creating planned change. This differs from the view of Roland Warren, who defines a change agent as "any person or group, professional or nonprofessional, inside or outside a social system, which is attempting to bring about change in that system."[2] We

[1] Ronald Lippitt, Jeanne Watson, and Bruce Westley, *The Dynamics of Planned Change* (New York: Harcourt, Brace, & World, Inc., 1958), p. 12.

[2] Roland L. Warren, *Truth, Love and Social Change and Other Essays on Community Change* (Chicago: Rand McNally & Co., 1971), p. 285.

differ from Warren because we believe the "paid" change agent is influenced in his change efforts by the system that employs him and pays his salary.[3] Thus he operates differently from an individual attempting to bring about change as a private citizen.

The impact and influence of the change agent system on the change agent will vary depending on whether the agent's intent is to change his own system from within, like a social worker employed by a nursing home who attempts to change procedures within the home, or to change a system of which he is *not* a part, like a worker with a mental health agency who is asked for help by a woman who has an alcoholic husband, or a neighborhood-center worker who is trying to change policies of a local school.

Similarly, the change agent operates with different sanctions, constraints, and opportunities when he is working from the inside to change his own change agent system than the ones he is subject to when he is working to change a system from the outside. When the social worker is *outside* of the system he is helping to change, he is not personally entangled on an ongoing basis with all the people in the system and can maintain objectivity by standing somewhat apart as a representative of his own agency–change agent system (and indirectly the community) and his profession. When the change agent views people in his own agency as targets of change and tries to change his system from *inside*, he will not be able to stand apart from his own system and must recognize that his ongoing relationships with other people in his system and his own aspirations for job security, promotion, and status will affect his change efforts. Furthermore, his own organization may not view his change efforts as legitimate work activity. On the other hand, change agents working from the inside to change their own systems have advantages over outside change agents in their special access to people within the system (other staff members, agency directors, members of boards of directors, and clients) who may provide information and become allies in efforts to change internal policies and procedures.

Organizations occasionally employ change agents whose major func-

---

[3] Many social work writers have described the impact of a social worker's own organization on his change efforts. See Andrew Billingsley, "Bureaucratic and Professional Orientation Patterns in Social Casework," *Social Service Review*, 38 (December 1964): 400–407; George A. Brager, "Institutional Change: Perimeters of the Possible," *Social Work*, 12 (January 1967): 59–69; Irwin Epstein, "Social Workers and Social Action: Attitudes toward Social Action Strategies," *Social Work*, 13 (April 1968): 101–8, and "Professional Role Orientations and Conflict Strategies," *Social Work*, 15 (October 1970): 87–92; Warren, *Truth, Love and Social Change*.

tion is to help the organization change to remain relevant, increase creativity and productivity, or adapt to changing circumstances.[4] Under these conditions, the change agent still is working from a position within his own system, even though he is sanctioned to work for organizational change, and his relationships to other people within the system and his personal aspirations will affect his work.

THE CLIENT SYSTEM

The term "client system" also is derived from Lippitt, Watson, and Westley, who use it to signify the specific system that is being helped.[5] This idea that the client is any expected beneficiary of the services of a change agent has been used for a long time by many social workers. We take a somewhat different view and consider the client system as the individual, family, group, organization, or community that, in addition to being the expected beneficiary of service, is a system that asks for help and *engages the services* of a social worker as a change agent.[6] And we add a third dimension to our view of a client system— the idea that people become clients only when a working agreement or contract has been established between them and a change agent. The contract clarifies the purpose or goal of the change effort and the methods that will be used in the change activity.[7] This working agreement or contract may be with the entire client system or some subpart of it (one member of a family, the board of directors of an organization, one organization in the community). The social worker can also attempt to enlarge the client system by involving other members of a larger system. For example, the worker in the mental health clinic may start only with the wife of an alcoholic husband as a client and then attempt to include the husband and children in the client system. Or the social worker may reduce the client system by limiting his contractual agreements. The neighborhood-center worker, for example, may agree to work with an entire neighborhood organization to help it solve some internal organizational friction. He may later decide he

---

[4] Warren G. Bennis, Kenneth D. Benne, and Robert Chin expand on this role of a change agent in *The Planning of Change* (New York: Holt, Rinehart & Winston, Inc., 1961), pp. 16–17.

[5] Lippitt, Watson, and Westley, *Dynamics of Planned Change*, p. 12.

[6] This view is shared by George A. Brager in "Advocacy and Political Behavior," *Social Work*, 13 (April 1968): 5–15, and to some extent by Bennis, Benne, and Chin, *Planning of Change* (1961), which on p. 17 refers to "the party who asks for help and desires some change in performance" as the client system.

[7] Chapter 9 is devoted to negotiation of contracts.

cannot form a working agreement with the whole organization and limit his contract to a few members who are attempting to make drastic changes in the organization.

Thus, in summary, we believe a change agent may regard as clients only those who have sanctioned (or asked for) his services, are expected to be beneficiaries of the change efforts, and have entered into a working agreement or contract with the change agent. The term "client" is used with the same connotations as in other professions.

There are certain implications to our definition of client systems. For one thing, we must examine the source of the social worker's sanctions to engage in change efforts. Two types of sanctions are available here. The first is the sanction which gives him the right or opportunity to make his services available to the public and certifies his competence. This sanction comes from his profession and, in some areas, from state statutes. The second type of sanction gives him the right to engage in specific activities on behalf of a specific client. This sanction comes from the client himself when he voluntarily contracts for the services of the practitioner. For example, a social worker may be sanctioned to do family counseling in a given community, but he cannot work with the Jones family, residents of that community, without that family's permission.

Initially a probation officer or a neighborhood-center worker who wants to form an organization in his neighborhood will not have voluntary contracts and sanctions from the probationer or neighborhood residents. They are *potential* clients, not actual clients. The workers' sanctions to engage in specific activities with them come from the agencies employing the workers (the change agent systems) and thus indirectly from the community that supports the agencies. The community, then, in a sense is the client and expects to benefit from the workers' activities. In some circumstances, such as those of a worker in a nursing home who wants to change the staff procedures in the home and does not have its sanction to do so, the social worker must fall back on his sanction from his profession.

We believe that, when possible, a change agent should attempt to obtain sanction and a working agreement or contract from the expected beneficiaries of his change efforts.[8] Both the value and knowledge com-

---

[8] Sanction and contracts cannot be obtained, obviously, when the expected beneficiary is unable to give sanction or make a contract due to age or physical or mental condition, or when it would not be good "strategy" or timing to involve the beneficiary.

ponents of social work practice discussed in the last chapter support this belief.

Ethically, we believe people have the right to self-determination and participation in decisions that affect them. Warren suggests that most social workers:

> . . . not only are constrained by agency controls; they are constrained by their own attitude toward the client. They identify with him as a person who needs help, which it is to be hoped will be generously given. They do not identify with him as a citizen demanding his legal rights or as a person demanding social justice. They identify rather with the agency, with the system.[9]

Our view of a change agent forming a contract with a client system respects the rights of clients as citizens.

Pragmatically, we think change agents can best gather information from and about the expected beneficiaries of their services if the beneficiaries participate in the process as collaborative partners. Furthermore, we think people will more readily follow through on a change effort and, if necessary, make changes themselves if they have sanctioned the change efforts and been involved in establishing the goals for change and the methods to achieve them.

Thus, in the examples cited above, when the change agent has sanction only from his profession or agency and community, and the people he wants to help are *potential* clients and not *actual* clients, one of his important tasks will be to try to influence these people to become actual clients. Thus his sanction will be shifted directly to those with whom he seeks to work. This is not always easy or possible to accomplish. When it cannot be achieved, the change agent should be aware that he cannot establish truly collaborative relationships and must devise alternate strategies.[10]

THE TARGET SYSTEM

We call the people the change agent needs to change or influence in order to accomplish his goals the "target system." The term "target" has been used frequently in recent social work literature.[11] Although

---

[9] Warren, *Truth, Love and Social Change*, p. 51.

[10] Relationships and the strategies flowing from them are discussed in Chapter 4.

[11] Mary E. Burns and Paul H. Glasser, "Similarities and Differences in Casework and Group Work Practices," *Social Service Review*, 34 (December 1963): 416–28; Ralph M. Kramer and Harry Specht, *Readings in Community Organization Practice* (Englewood Cliffs, N.J.: Prentice-Hall, Inc., 1969); Harry Specht, "Disrup-

some regret the connotations of the term, we have not found an adequate substitute.

An important diagnostic task of the social worker, usually in collaboration with the client system, is to establish the goals for change and then determine the specific people—the targets—that will have to be changed if the goals are to be reached. To illustrate, the neighborhood worker may be asked by members of a group to help them achieve the goal of improving their housing conditions. The change agent agrees, and together they identify several targets: landlords, city housing inspectors, members of the city sanitation department, and others. Some of these targets may agree readily to make changes; others may be recalcitrant and resist or fight the change efforts. There are two important considerations in such a situation. First, the client system is not always the system that needs to be changed (in other words, it is not always the target) in order to reach the change goals.[12] And, second, it cannot be assumed that the target system always will be resistant to the change efforts; it may agree readily, be indifferent, or fight change.

The social worker may work with or on behalf of the client system. Under some circumstances, he can intervene through direct interaction with the target system. For example, the mental health agency worker may work directly with the wife (client system) and her alcoholic husband (target system) and in face-to-face encounters attempt to influence the husband to admit he has a drinking problem, to ask for help, and to become a client and participate in rehabilitative activities. If the social worker has little or no direct interaction with the target system, he can bring other influences to bear on the target system. For example, the neighborhood worker and community group seeking better housing conditions could ask their alderman to influence a city sanitation department inspector (target system) to enforce sanitary regulations in the neighborhood. They could try to influence a newspaper reporter to write a story about housing conditions in the neighborhood which identifies prominent citizens who are absentee landlords (target system) of the deteriorating property in an attempt to force them to improve it.

Sometimes the client system and the target system are the same, as

---

tive Tactics," in Kramer and Specht, *Readings in Community Organization Practice;* Roland Warren, "Types of Purposive Social Change at the Community Level," Brandeis University Papers in Social Welfare, No. 11 (Waltham, Mass., 1965); Brager, "Advocacy and Political Behavior."

[12] Burns and Glasser, "Similarities and Differences," were among the first to point out this distinction, as were Purcell and Specht in their case study in Part III.

when a change agent accepts an individual client for help in solving a personal problem. In other cases, the client system may be considered the target system in working toward some goals, but in respect to other goals, the target and client systems may differ and be apart. In the example cited above, a neighborhood group and a worker have identified target systems—inspector of the city sanitation department and landlords—outside the client system and asked the alderman and newspaperman to try to influence the targets. Members of the group also may want to talk directly with city officials but be afraid to present their problems in this way and lack confidence in their ability to gain access to these people and to present an effective case. The worker may need to give them encouragement and help them plan and rehearse what they will say. In this activity the worker views the members of the group as another target system, and his goal is not only to help them with their housing problems but also to enhance their feelings of self-worth and give them confidence which will help them deal with other problems and situations. Another example would be a worker in a community mental health center who may be working with a mother to change her ways of handling her children (client system also the target system) while he is serving as her advocate in getting the welfare department to increase her assistance grant (client system different from the target system).

Client and target systems often partially overlap. For example, after the wife (client system) of the alcoholic husband (target system) has come to the mental health worker to ask for help for her husband, the worker may discover that her behavior is contributing to her husband's drinking problem. In addition to working with the husband, the worker may attempt to influence the wife to modify her behavior, in which case she becomes a target.

In other cases, the target and client systems are completely separate. For a neighborhood worker trying to open up jobs in the community for former migrant workers, the employers are the target system and the former migrant workers the client system.

When the social worker seeks to change the policy makers in his own agency in order to provide better service for the community and his clients, the change agent system itself may become a target system.

In any one change effort, the change agent will identify several goals over a period of time. Different people may be considered targets for different goals at different times. For example the neighborhood worker may view former migrants who have moved into the neighborhood as people he would like to work with and assist, thus he considers them as potential clients. Because his first goal is to make them actual clients, they can be considered targets in relation to that goal. If, after the worker contacts the migrants they decide to work with him and become clients, they no longer are targets in relation to the worker's first goal, which has been accomplished. Together the former migrants and worker agree on a goal of securing employment, and employers are identified as targets for that goal. The migrants also may identify goals for themselves such as learning English or becoming acquainted with their new community. In respect to these goals, the migrants are targets.

Thus the change agent may deal with several targets to reach several goals.[13] The relationships he maintains with these different target systems, the types of influences he brings to bear upon them, and the tasks he performs will be dictated to varying degrees by a number of factors: his goals; the separateness or overlapping of the client, target, and change agent systems; the perceptions the target systems have of his change efforts; and their reactions to these efforts.

THE ACTION SYSTEM

As indicated by the examples illustrating interactions between the change agent, client, and target systems, the change agent does not work in isolation in his change efforts; he works with other people. We use the term "action system" to describe those with whom the social worker deals in his efforts to accomplish the tasks and achieve the goals of the change effort. An action system can be used to obtain sanctions and a working agreement or contract, identify and study a problem, establish goals for change, or influence the major targets of change.[14]

In any one problem situation the change agent may work with several different action systems to accomplish different tasks and achieve different goals. The purpose of a particular action system could be to influence people who are *potential* clients, and at present only targets, to become *actual* clients. For example, if the nursing home worker had been sanctioned and asked by the home's director to influence the staff to change their attitudes and behavior toward the residents, at that

---

[13] The analysis of target systems has been presented from the change agent's point of view. From another perspective the change agent himself may be viewed as a target by people he wants to influence. Client, target, and action systems may attempt to influence the change agent to change his view of the cause of a problem and the methods to be used in solving it.

[14] Roland Warren first used the term "action system" to describe new systems created to perform community action tasks, in *The Community in America* (Chicago: Rand McNally & Co., 1963). We have broadened this definition.

point the worker could consider the director as the client system and the rest of the staff as targets. However, the change agent may believe he will have more success in working with the staff if they ask for his help. In this case he would consider the staff as potential clients and might form an action system with the director in an attempt to influence the staff to ask for his help and become his clients.

An action system could also be formed to study and collect information about a problem. The neighborhood worker may help form a group to study housing conditions in the neighborhood and identify targets that need to be changed. Another action system could be formed to perform the intake function of an agency. For example, couples who have applied to adopt a child may have their first face-to-face contact with the agency in a group meeting at which expectations and procedures of the agency and state laws are explained and couples have an opportunity to raise questions and voice concerns.

It may be necessary to form one or more action systems to influence the target to change. The neighborhood worker seeking to improve housing conditions would enlist the support of the alderman, a newspaper reporter, and others in efforts to influence the city sanitation department inspector and absentee landlords. In addition the worker can help members of the action system of neighborhood residents meet with landlords and city officials directly.

Depending on the situation, an action system could be:

1. A new system put together by the worker with the expectation that the members of the system will be in direct interaction with each other. For example, the nursing home social worker could form a group of residents to plan activities and programs or to give advice to the staff on operating the home.

2. An existing system already in operation. Examples are the family with an alcoholic husband, or a teen-age gang operating in the area of a neighborhood center.

3. Several people who may not at any one time be engaged in direct interaction with one another but whom the worker will coordinate and work with to change a target on behalf of a client. For example, the probation officer may coordinate the activities of an employment office worker, employers, a welfare worker, a teacher at a vocational school, and others in his work on behalf of the probationer.

Thus change agents may work with a number of different types of action systems at different steps in their change efforts. In some cases, however, they may work with the same action system throughout. If a husband and wife with no children ask the social worker for help in solving their marriage problems, he could deal only with the two of them throughout the change effort. In this case they are the client system, and the target system and, along with the worker, the action system. In other cases, the action system does not include the client system or the major target (the alderman and newspaper reporter in the neighborhood housing example), or the client and action systems may be the same and the target system may lie outside them (the nursing home director and the social worker, with the staff as targets).

CLASSIFICATION BY SYSTEM

In any change effort, the change agent can clarify his purpose and relationships with the people with whom he will be working by classifying them as members of one or more types of systems. We have named them above as:

1. *Change agent system:* The change agent and the people who are part of his agency or employing organization.
2. *Client system:* People who sanction or ask for the change agent's services, who are the expected beneficiaries of service, and who have a working agreement or contract with the change agent.
3. *Target system:* People who need to be changed to accomplish the goals of the change agent.
4. *Action system:* The change agent and the people he works with and through to accomplish his goals and influence the target system.

It should be emphasized that change agents are working to change *people*, not vague abstractions such as "the community," "the organization," or "the system." When we say that communities or organizations or families or groups are client or target or change agent systems, we are referring to the people who make up these systems. If the goal of the change agent is to change the structure of a system—the web of patterned relationships between people—he does this by influencing people in the system to change the ways they interact with one another.

It should be also emphasized that the change agent does not become a permanent, integral, interacting part of the client, target, or action systems. He is, however, an integral part of his change agent system. He forms an action system or works with an existing one, works with the client system, and seeks to influence the target system, but he does not become a part of these systems on the same basis as the other members.[15]

IMPLICATIONS OF SYSTEMS FOR PRACTICE

All the information we have presented about different types of systems is not just so much jargon. It can make a real difference to the social work practitioner. There are a number of implications for social work practice in viewing the activity of the social worker in relation to the four types of systems. Nine of these are noted below.

First, the social worker is provided with a framework he can apply to the many types of situations and the many people related to a change effort. He can analyze change efforts in social work, described in Chapter 1 as aimed at improving the social interactions between people and their environment. Among the purposes and functions of social work specified were enhancing the problem-solving and coping capacities of people; facilitating interaction between and within informal, formal, and societal resource systems; making resource systems more responsive to people; and contributing to the development and modification of social policy. The framework lends flexibility to the social worker's efforts to analyze and determine his goals and relationships with people in all the systems involved.

Second, the framework can help the social worker identify the tasks that must be accomplished in a change effort. It can be used in diverse efforts, whatever the primary target—an emotionally disturbed individual who needs help with personal problems, a family in conflict, absentee landlords of slum properties, or a social agency unresponsive to the needs of its consumers. It helps the social worker to identify common tasks that must be performed in all change efforts, such as to form a contract with a potential client system or to establish an action system.

The framework can help the worker approaching any change effort gain perspective on where he is, where he wants to go, what tasks he needs to perform and in what order or time sequence he should perform them. An early task may be to obtain sanction and a working agreement or contract from the expected beneficiary of the change efforts, as has been noted.

---

[15] The hazards of the change agent becoming a part of the client system and adopting the client's values were discussed in Chapter 2. The nature of relationships formed by change agents with different systems is discussed in Chapter 4.

After the change agent has identified a target, his next tasks are to determine and form the action system that will be most effective in reaching it. Because situations change or are clarified as change efforts unfold, additional *potential* client, target, and action systems will become evident. The change agent who uses the systems framework knows he has the tasks of moving from the potential to actual stage in gaining additional clients, specifying new targets, and forming new action systems. As new systems are identified and developed over time, he must consider the impact of the new systems on those he has identified and with whom he is still working.

When the worker is clear about the tasks that are common to all change efforts, he can concentrate on the unique features of each change situation and the particular skills and techniques it requires.

Third, the systems framework shows the social worker he cannot assume that the people who ask for his help are the major targets of intervention. As the examples above indicated, to help a client the worker often has to "help" a system apart from the client to change. In past social work practice, as Purcell and Specht point out in their case study in Part III: "too often . . . the client system presenting the problem becomes the major target for intervention."

Fourth, the framework makes clear that no assumption can be made that any size or type of action system is the most appropriate to deal with the problem presented by the client system. Only after the purpose and goal of the change efforts have been established can a worker determine if a one-to-one relationship, a face-to-face group, or another type of action system is most appropriate.

Many observers have pointed out that the breakdown of social work practice into three methods—casework, group work, and community organization—has led social workers to automatically select a specialized method for solving problems that confront them, instead of allowing the problem to dictate the required method.[16] Abraham Kaplan's "law of the instrument" is explained as "give a small boy a hammer,

---

[16] In particular, see Harriet M. Barlett, *The Common Base of Social Work Practice* (New York: National Association of Social Workers, 1970); Herbert Bisno, "A Theoretical Framework for Teaching Social Work Methods and Skills, with Particular Reference to Undergraduate Social Welfare Education," *Journal of Education for Social Work*, 5 (Fall 1969): 5–17; Carol Meyer, *Social Work Practice: A Response to the Urban Crisis* (New York: Free Press, 1970); Alice Overton, "The Issue of Integration of Casework and Group Work," *Social Work Education Reporter*, 16 (June 1968): 25 ff.; William Schwartz, "The Social Worker in the Group," *Social Welfare Forum, 1961*, National Conference on Social Welfare (New York: Columbia University Press, 1961), pp. 146–71. Also see Purcell and Specht in Part III.

and he will find that everything he encounters needs hammering."[17]

Fifth, the social worker is forced to recognize that he has social work tasks to perform and must establish relationships not only with clients but with people who are not clients. As Yvonne Fraley points out:

> The concentration of the profession on the development of knowledge and skills in client relationships has tended to relegate to obscurity social work relationships with persons who are neither clients nor clientele. Yet these relationships have always been important in direct service. They are increasingly important . . . we need to develop a model which will facilitate the identification, analysis, and comparison of all professional relationships in which social workers engage.[18]

The framework also helps the social worker recognize that he can transfer the knowledge and skills he has gained in working with one type of system to working with another. For example, many of the principles and skills used in interviewing to gather information or influence another person can be applied to interviewing for other purposes—a client who has asked for help with a personal problem, a community leader, or a school teacher having difficulty with a child and his family. Some of the same principles of group formation apply in forming an action system for group counseling and a community action system. Some of the knowledge and skills that apply to working with a one-to-one action system also apply to working with a group.

The change agent working with different sizes and types of systems can be alerted not only to similarities in the skills and knowledge required but also to differences in situations requiring the use of specialized theories of influence (learning theory, ego psychology, community development) and knowledge about particular problems (mental retardation, the aging).

Sixth, the importance of viewing organizations as systems involved in social change is made obvious. In the three-method view of social work practice (casework, group work, and community organization), the organizational system is often ignored in moving from the group to the community and usually is discussed only in the context of administration. However, the organization is often a target of the worker's intervention in dealing with a problem, and he must know how to operate

---

[17] Abraham Kaplan, *The Conduct of Inquiry: Methodology for Behavioral Science* (San Francisco: Chandler Publishing Co., 1964), p. 28.

[18] Yvonne L. Fraley, "A Role Model for Practice," *Social Service Review*, 43 (June 1969): 146–48.

in relation to this system just as he does in relation to the individual, the group, or the community.

Seventh, the deliberate focus on the agency (change agent system) as a potential target of change not only emphasizes that social workers may need to change their own agencies in order to help clients but also demonstrates the need for understanding the process of changing agencies from within as well as from without.

Eighth, the emphasis on the action system as the system the worker works with and through to influence the target points out the necessity for the change agent to keep the action system operating smoothly. The worker will need to continually diagnose the way the action system is operating. If this system is not operating in a way conducive to achieving the desired change, the worker will need to determine the cause of the dysfunction and then alter its composition, size, or operating procedures.

To illustrate the importance of the operation of the action system, consider the personal rivalries and feuds that can develop in a community task force and keep the group from accomplishing its tasks. Or consider a child in an institution for emotionally disturbed children who is the target of an action system composed of administrators, child-care workers, social workers, teachers, custodians, and cooks. If this action system is not coordinating its efforts in a unified plan to change the child, he may receive conflicting messages. Indeed, he may end up manipulating each member of the action system to cater to what he wants, thus negating the change goals.

Ninth, social work practitioners, students, and writers are currently debating the appropriate use of collaborative, bargaining, and conflictual relationships between social workers and other systems. The workers' use of manipulation, advocacy, and a partisan stance on behalf of clients, as opposed to acting as a communication builder, teacher, enabler, and guide are also topics of debate.[19]

The appropriateness of the use of different relationships, roles, and strategies by the change agent can be clarified by examining the particular pattern of overlapping and separate types of systems the worker must deal with in a given problem. By establishing contracts or working agreements with client systems, social workers usually maintain collaborative relationships with them. Thus, if the client system is the same as or partially overlaps with the target and action systems, the worker

---

[19] See Specht, "Disruptive Tactics"; Warren, "Types of Purposive Social Change"; and Brager, "Advocacy and Political Behavior."

may choose collaborative strategies and act out such roles as enabler and teacher. However, when the target system is *outside* (is not the same as) the client action systems, the worker has a choice of relationships and roles. His selection will depend on the readiness of the target to change and the amount and kind of influence available to both the target and change agent systems. The social worker may choose whether he will play the role of communication builder or adversary, or whether he will form collaborative or conflictual relationships.

A social worker working with a client in a face-to-face action system will be guided by the traditional social work values of self-determination and honesty. However, when the target system lies outside his client and action systems, the worker may select manipulation and other tactics that reflect other values, if he believes these tactics will influence the target system to change and thereby help the client system.[20]

---

[20] Brager, "Advocacy and Political Behavior," makes a similar point in his discussion of the appropriate use of manipulative behavior in social work practice, as pointed out in Chapter 2.

CHAPTER 4

WORKER

RELATIONSHIPS

The worker's position and purpose influence the type of relationships he forms with the various systems he encounters in his change efforts. These relationships are the medium through which he carries out his activities. This chapter will (1) describe common elements of all social work relationships, (2) identify different types of relationships, (3) discuss the factors that influence the worker in his formation of relationships, and (4) point out the impact of worker style on relationships.

COMMON ELEMENTS OF PROFESSIONAL RELATIONSHIPS

Although social workers form different types of relationships with different systems, there are common elements in all professional relationships which make them different from personal relationships. Three major characteristics of social work relationships can be identified.

First, social workers form relationships for a professional purpose. In everyday life, a satisfying personal relationship may be an end in itself. The social worker forms a professional relationship for a purpose related to his planned change work.

Second, in professional relationships the worker devotes himself to the interests of his clients and the needs and aspirations of other people, rather than his own interests.

Third, the worker forms relationships based on objectivity and self-awareness which allow him to step outside of his own personal troubles and emotional needs and to be sensitive to the needs of others.

Of course, social workers do experience personal satisfactions and frustrations in their professional activities, but ordinarily they concentrate on problems external to themselves and their own worries and concerns. The social worker involved with job-related problems in his own agency that affect him personally is an exception—he is personally entangled with the people in the system and his personal and professional relationships may coincide.

There are several reasons why the three professional characteristics named above are essential in social work relationships. Social workers receive sanction from specific client systems and from the community that establishes and pays for social work service. These sanctioning sources expect the social worker to use his knowledge and skills to provide impartial, objective service in the best interests of the client. He is expected to be motivated by ideals of service to others rather than personal profit and gain.

The social work professional organization, the National Association of Social Workers, establishes professional norms to regulate and guide social work practice and requires its members to subscribe to a code of ethics, which states in part:

As a member of the National Association of Social Workers I commit myself to conduct my professional relationships in accord with the code and subscribe to the following statements:

I regard as my primary obligation the welfare of the individual or group served, which includes action for improving social conditions.

I will not discriminate because of race, color, religion, age, sex, or national ancestry, and in my job capacity will work to prevent and eliminate such discrimination in rendering service, in work assignments, and in employment practices.

I give precedence to my professional responsibility over my personal interests.

I hold myself responsible for the quality and extent of the service I perform.

I respect the privacy of the people I serve.

I use in a responsible manner information gained in professional relationships.

I treat with respect the findings, views, and actions of colleagues, and use appropriate channels to express judgment on these matters.

I practice social work within the recognized knowledge and competence of the profession.

I recognize my professional responsibility to add my ideas and findings to the body of social work knowledge and practice.

I accept responsibility to help protect the community against unethical practice by any individuals or organizations engaged in social welfare activities.

I stand ready to give appropriate professional service in public emergencies.

I distinguish clearly, in public, between my statements and actions as an individual and as a representative of an organization.

I support the principle that professional practice requires professional education.

I accept responsibility for working toward the creation and maintenance of conditions within agencies which enable social workers to conduct themselves in keeping with this code.

I contribute my knowledge, skills, and support to programs of human welfare.

Sanctions from the community and the social work profession call for social workers to devote themselves to the interests of their clients and other people. However, if the social worker does not maintain relationships based on objectivity and self-awareness, his own emotional reactions to other people will have an impact on his ability to achieve his purposes. The worker may have "gut" reactions that cause him to feel anger, hostility, or affection toward others. Indeed Ernest Beier believes the worker's own reactions can be a valuable source of data. If a person evokes strong feelings in the worker, he might be expected to provoke these same feelings in others. Thus the worker can form hypotheses about that person's usual behavior and the responses he usually receives. However, if the worker is to be helpful, he cannot afford to be caught up with his own feelings or to respond from them.[1]

The social worker can also use his own reactions and emotions as data in assessing attitudes and behavior of individuals and groups in organizations and the community. Here, too, however, he cannot allow himself to respond from his own feelings, or he may lose his ability to act in a purposeful manner on behalf of his client.

A further consideration is the fact that social workers work with people who may be hesitant to discuss personal problems.[2] John Mayer

[1] Ernest Beier, *The Silent Language of Psychotherapy* (Chicago: Aldine Publishing Co., 1966).

[2] See discussion in Chapter 1 on why informal resource systems may not provide the help people need.

and Noel Timms conducted a study of clients of English social agencies to determine (1) why some people did not turn to informal systems—family, friends, and neighbors—for help with personal problems, (2) what people who did turn to informal systems for help thought about the assistance they received, (3) why people were reluctant to turn to societal institutions for help, and (4) what benefits they believed they received from societal systems. They found that many people were reluctant to turn to families and friends for help because of embarrassment or fear—fear of loss of face, fear that they would have to disclose more than they wanted to, or fear that the other person might not keep the information confidential and might be untrustworthy in his use of it. People also were reluctant to burden others with their problems and were not sure they would receive the help they needed. Some of those who had turned to their family and friends for help reported that they received conflicting, ineffective, or unacceptable advice and, in some cases, the people they turned to had withdrawn and refused to help them. On the other hand, Mayer and Timms found that although the clients they interviewed had been reluctant to turn to a social agency, when they did they believed they were helped. They perceived the worker as someone they could talk to, who was interested in them, whom they could trust, and who lessened their feelings of shame in having to seek help.[3]

This study of English agency clients indicates the utility of relationships that are objective and focus on the needs of the client, not those of the helper. Although Mayer and Timms's study deals with relationships with individuals, the same principle of limiting the relationship to the purpose of the intervention can be applied in working with any size system.

Social workers working to change the ways members of a family interact or to help a family and community agencies establish mutually satisfactory linkages must try not to impose their own religious, political, or other personal beliefs on the people whose behavior they are attempting to change. As was pointed out in Chapter 2, the worker needs self-awareness to know when he is imposing his values and beliefs on the client. He must decide when he can maintain flexibility on ethical issues and when to stand firm on his bedrock beliefs, label them to the client, and interject them consciously into the change effort.

If the social worker does not focus on the major purpose of the

---

[3] John E. Mayer and Noel Timms, *The Client Speaks: Working Class Impressions of Casework* (New York: Atherton Press, 1970).

intervention and the needs of his client system and instead pushes his own *personal* beliefs, he may alienate and offend those he is attempting to influence because of an issue which is not relevant to his major goals. Nicholas von Hoffman spelled out this point in an unpublished speech to college students interested in organizing in slum neighborhoods:

You are building a power group, a mass organization to serve a partic-ular consistency, one that has certain paramount issues to be met. The demands are remote from "peace" or from any number of other perhaps laudable but irrelevant interests. In other words, don't act like cultists. If you are a vegetarian, keep it to yourself, hide it, because there are a certain number of butchers in your community and you want them in the organization too.

Although all social workers form relationships to achieve purposes related to the needs of client systems, there are significant differences in social work relationships established to achieve different purposes with different systems.

TYPES OF RELATIONSHIPS

A relationship can be thought of as an affective bond between the worker and other systems operating within a major posture or atmos-phere of collaboration, bargaining, or conflict. The characteristics of these three types of relationships and the factors that lead to their development can be differentiated analytically. While in practice every relationship contains elements of all three, at any point in time, a worker may be relating to another system in a manner which essentially is collaborative, bargaining, or conflictual.

Collaboration

Social workers normally have collaborative relationships with clients; indeed, the essence of forming a working agreement or contract with a client is for the social worker and the client to agree on the goals for the change process and the methods to achieve these goals. Collabora-tive relationships with clients are facilitated by social work values that stress self-determination and democratic decision making. People will more readily follow through on a change effort and, if necessary, take risks and make changes themselves, if they have sanctioned the change efforts, have helped establish the goals for change, and have developed trust and confidence in the worker, as we have noted.

Collaborative relationships with clients who have problems of interpersonal social functioning have been described by many writers in
terms of the change agent's creation of an accepting atmosphere by the
way he relates to clients. This atmosphere promotes feelings of trust,
genuineness, and honesty between clients and workers.[4] Some writers
on organization and community change also stress the utility of collaborative relationships in working for change.[5] However, recent studies
of community action programs by Roland Warren and Harry Specht[6]
indicate that true collaborative relationships are possible only when
there is agreement on the goals of the planned change effort and the
methods for achieving the goals between the worker and his target system—those people the change agent needs to change or influence in
order to accomplish his goals. Thus a change agent working with a
community action system may use collaborative strategies to change a
target (school system, social welfare agency, police department, county
welfare board) only when the goals of the worker and his action and
target systems are congruent. This same principle would apply when a
worker is trying to influence an individual or group (prison inmate,
youth gang) which does not want to become a client and collaborate
with the worker.

Interestingly, even if the worker believes his goals and the goals of
his target are the same, if the target system *perceives* the goals as being
different, it may resist collaborative relationships. Both Carl Rogers
and Harry Specht stress the importance of the target's *perception* of
the worker's goals and methods. Rogers summarizes research which
demonstrates that the client's perception of the attitudes and procedures of the worker are crucial growth-promoting or growth-inhibiting
characteristics of a helping relationship.[7] Specht, in discussing the kind

---

[4] See Felix B. Biesteck, *The Casework Relationship* (Chicago: Loyola University
Press, 1957); Florence Hollis, *Casework—A Psychosocial Therapy* (New York:
Random House, Inc., 1972); Helen Northern, *Social Work with Groups* (New
York: Columbia University Press, 1969); Carl R. Rogers, *Freedom to Learn*
(Columbus, Ohio: Charles E. Merrill Publishing Co., 1969), and *On Becoming a
Person* (Boston: Houghton Mifflin Co., 1961).

[5] Chris Argyris, "Explorations in Consulting-Client Relationships," in Warren
Bennis, Kenneth Benne, and Robert Chin (eds.), *The Planning of Change*, 2d ed.
(New York: Holt, Rinehart & Winston, Inc., 1969), pp. 434–57; Murray Ross,
Community Organization: Theory and Principles (New York: Harper & Row,
Publishers, 1955).

[6] Roland Warren, "Types of Purposive Social Change at the Community Level,"
Brandeis University Papers in Social Welfare, No. 11 (Waltham, Mass., 1965);
Harry Specht, "Disruptive Tactics," in *Social Work*, Vol. 14, No. 2 (April 1969),
5–15.

[7] Rogers, *On Becoming a Person.*

of response the target system will make to the issues raised by the change agent and the action system, points out that:

> The response to an issue, whether rational or not, tells us how the issue is *perceived* by different parties to a change; perception determines response. Whatever the reality, perceptions which the different parties to a change project have of what the change will mean for them is crucial in determining their response.[8]

In discussing change at the community level, Specht also points out that collaboration is a viable strategy when the "other" (the target) perceives the goal of the change agent as a rearrangement of community resources with which the target is in essential agreement because it perceives the reorganization of services as not placing great demands upon it or causing it to lose a great deal of money, power, status, or prestige—in fact, it may believe it will gain.[9] Thus, collaboration seems to be possible when the target believes it is in his self-interest to collaborate or, at the minimum, he will not lose through collaboration. We believe this principle can be applied to social change efforts with other size systems. It can be hypothesized that collaborative relationships with any size target system are feasible when the target sees the goal of change as desirable and in its self-interest and believes that the demands placed upon it will not require major changes in its existing power and status relationships.

Collaborative relationships based on trust and mutual agreement on means and ends are feasible in many different situations, including the following:

1. A worker at a mental health clinic and a family agree to work together on the problems the family is having with the neighborhood school and other community institutions.
2. A school social worker agrees to help a teacher work with a child who is disrupting a classroom.
3. A social worker at a child-welfare agency meets with a group of pregnant unmarried women to help them think through alternative courses of action.
4. A worker with a community health-planning agency helps agencies coordinate their services to the mentally retarded.
5. A worker at a family service agency forms a task force of workers within his own agency to discuss developing an agency program to work with families concerned with teen-age drug abuse.

---

[8] Harry Specht, "Disruptive Tactics," p. 6.
[9] Specht, "Disruptive Tactics."

Thus the worker may form a collaborative relationship when the system he is interacting with will assume a complementary one. If the worker is perceived to be interested in the same goal as another and indicates that he wishes to work cooperatively, a trusting, collaborative relationship can be built between the parties.

Bargaining

When social workers make their first contact with a pot ntial client, action, or target system, the systems, in a sense, are in a bargaining relationship—each is testing the other to determine what the other's goals are, what demands will be placed on all parties, and what the outcomes of the change efforts might be. If, after this initial testing, the conditions described above as amenable to collaborative relationships emerge, then a contract can be reached and collaborative relationships can follow.

However, if the other system perceives that the goals of the change agent may not be entirely in its own self-interest and that demands will be placed on it to develop new skills or ways of relating and working with others, the bargaining relationships may continue. As Specht puts it, bargaining is likely when "one or the other parties expects that he will end up with more or less of something—money, facilities, authority."[10]

The word "bargaining" implies that each party has something to gain as well as something to lose in the effort. George Brager and Valerie Jorrin note that often "each party would rather concede something to the other than fail to reach agreement at all."[11]

Social workers and other systems may enter into bargaining agreements for four reasons. First, the cultural norm or value placed on working together to resolve differences appears to mandate at least a show of minimal cooperation and some attempt to resolve differences. This value makes it possible for a social worker to persuade several people to work with him, even if some of them mistrust him and one another and they share different goals. For example, a neighborhood-center social worker may be able to bring together representatives of the welfare department, police, health inspectors, landlords, and neighborhood residents who have been in conflict over neighborhood issues, and a worker may be able to secure agreement from all members of a

---

[10] Ibid., p. 7.

[11] George A. Brager and Valerie Jorrin, "Bargaining: A Method in Community Change," *Social Work*, 14 (October 1969): 73.

family to work with him in joint family therapy, even if some are resistant to change efforts.

Second, a bargaining relationship may be the only way a system can acquire desired resources. Thus a patient in a mental hospital may agree to cooperate with a social worker and enter group therapy in return for special privileges. A teen-age gang may decide to tolerate a neighborhood-center worker in return for special outings and use of sports equipment. A group of agencies may agree to work together in a planning council which has the authority to allocate federal and state funds. An alderman may agree to help a neighborhood group obtain city resources in the hope of securing their votes.[12]

Third, the status or power relationships between different systems may force a bargaining situation. A truly collaborative relationship may be difficult to achieve between people of different statuses, because as Warren Bennis, Kenneth Benne, and Robert Chin suggest, collaboration often requires a distribution of power in which each party has an opportunity to influence the other.[13]

Fourth, the force of law may cause parties of unequal status into a bargaining situation. A parolee is forced into a contract with his parole officer. Unless a voluntary contract based on shared goals evolves, the two are essentially in a bargaining relationship.

Community action groups and social workers attempting to bargain with agency and institutional officials are often at a power and status disadvantage. Brager and Jorrin note that officials "are, in large part, in control of the decisions at issue, while the community groups are clamoring at the gates." Officials are better organized and command vastly superior resources, but for bargaining to occur, there must be some parity between the parties. Brager and Jorrin suggest three leverage points for increasing parity in bargaining: threats of embarrassing the officials or of causing disruption, damaging the self-image of an institution or group of officials, and using all existing legal mechanisms.[14]

In some bargaining situations, the social worker is bringing parties together to enable them to bargain, and in others the social worker himself is in a bargaining stance vis-à-vis another system. In the first

---

[12] When the social worker is bargaining with a potential client, both parties are bargaining about the conditions under which help will be given or received. When either party "loses" something in this effort, they are losing, or giving up, a condition they believe is desirable if they are to work together. Further, the social worker may be losing the opportunity to engage a client system in change efforts.

[13] Warren G. Bennis, Kenneth B. Benne, and Robert Chin, *The Planning of Change*, 2d ed. (New York: Holt, Rinehart & Winston, Inc., 1969), p. 147.

[14] Brager and Jorrin, "Bargaining," p. 74.

case, the social worker may have collaborative relationships between himself and the individual bargainers and may be viewed by all concerned as a neutral, trustworthy mediator. In the second, the social worker is not neutral and may be seen as an advocate of a point of view trying to help a client system obtain something in the bargaining process. In the latter case, the social worker can be expected to use tactics of persuasion, negotiation, and even confrontation—and, occasionally, guile—to enhance his bargaining position.

In summary, a social worker becomes involved in bargaining relationships when (1) there is a perceived difference between, on the one hand, the shared goals of the change agent and client systems and, on the other, those of the target system, (2) the target system perceives the change goals as not entirely in its self-interest, (3) the target system believes moderate demands for change will be placed on it, and (4) conditions are present which force the parties into a bargaining situation where there is at least a possibility for agreement or accommodation.

Conflict

If the bargaining relationships break down and the parties cannot reach agreement or accommodation, or if polarization occurs between the perceived differences in the goals and demands of all parties, conflictual relationships may follow. They may also be inevitable if the shared goals of the change agent and client systems appear to pose a serious threat to the self-interests of the target system and are perceived by the target as requiring major changes in its functioning. Conflict is also likely to follow if the conditions that led to the establishment of a bargaining relationship were not present at the outset of the change effort, and if there appears to be no desire to negotiate differences.

Specht believes conflictual relationships involve modes of intervention in which contest and disruption are the prevailing tactics.

Contest or disruption is rooted in the competition for power in human relations. Status relationships refer to the social arrangements (that "institutionalized system") by which promises, expectations, rights, and responsibilities are awarded, and those social arrangements always award more to some than to others; a threat to the system of relationships which give some people power over others is the basis for this kind of response whether it involves parents and children, welfare workers and clients, students and teachers, or blacks and whites. None surrender that power voluntarily. . . . When community issues are perceived by one or another party as eliminating or diminishing their power over others, the response may be predicted as dissensus, and contest and disruption the result. . . . In these kinds of change efforts, the action system and target system are distinctly separate, and the client system is closely aligned or identical with the action system.[15]

The social worker faces situations when the use of conflictual relationships is required in order to achieve the shared goals of the worker and client system. A social worker acting on behalf of the community as client may have essentially a conflictual relationship with parents accused of child abuse. One working with an action and client system of neighborhood residents may enter into conflictual relationships with landlords and city officials.

A social worker thus involved in conflictual relationships on behalf of his client system may not always operate with the expected social work values of openness, mutual trust, and honesty vis-à-vis the target system. He may use such tactics as protest demonstrations, open confrontation, threats, and court orders in his efforts to influence the target system, be it individual, group, or community organization or institution.

Critics of the social work profession have accused social workers of avoiding bargaining and conflictual relationships. Indeed, some social workers cite social work values that emphasize self-determination and honesty as the justification for avoiding relationships that are not collaborative.

Social workers who prefer collaborative relationships are often in a dilemma because they are involved in situations where collaborative strategies are not possible or are not effective in achieving the worker and client goals. And, as Brager points out: "For the social worker . . . to eschew political behavior [bargaining or conflictual relationships] or to counsel his clients or constituents to avoid it, even indirectly, is to diminish still further the ability of the disadvantaged and their professional advocates to influence community change."[16] It should be noted, however, that few social workers advocate using tactics involving violence in conflictual situations. Indeed, as was noted in Chapter 1, social workers are limited in their choice of intervention strategies by constraints that stem from the professional base of social work, from social work values, from the organization that employs the social worker, and from society.

---

[15] Specht, "Disruptive Tactics," p. 7.
[16] George A. Brager, "Advocacy and Political Behavior," *Social Work*, 13 (April 1968): 6.

Just as collaborative relationships call for complementary relationships to be held by both the worker and the other party, in conflictual situations both parties must be willing to play the proper role, or the conflict will not be maintained. In a sense, a contract is established to maintain conflictual relationships. Of course, if the target tries to adopt a collaborative relationship and asserts that his goals and those of the change agent and client systems are really the same, they may be threatened with co-option. The target may convince the social worker that there is no need for disagreement because they both share the same goal—perhaps helping welfare recipients obtain all they are legally entitled to. If, in fact, they do share the same goal, there is no need for conflict. But, if the worker acquiesces and the target does not do everything within its powers to obtain the maximum benefits available to the worker's clients because it is no longer pressured to do so, the worker has been co-opted and is no longer serving in the best interests of his clients.

FACTORS INFLUENCING RELATIONSHIPS

The purpose of the social worker and the goals, interests, and expectations of all parties concerned in a change effort are major factors influencing the type of relationships the worker will form—collaborative, bargaining, or conflictual. Table 1 summarizes the perceptions held by others in each of these possible relationships between the worker and others.

In any given change effort, the social worker may be working with many client, action, and target systems, including people within his own change agent system. He may have different relationships with different systems. This is not surprising, since the worker occupies many different positions in a system of social relationships of power and status within his own agency, with clients, and with other systems in the community. Yvonne Fraley points out that

Not only do different social workers occupy different positions in a system of social relationships, but the same social worker may occupy different positions in the system. The direct-service worker, supervisor, administrator, consultant, and researcher occupy different positions. But the same worker may be a supervisee in relation to one person and a supervisor in relation to another. With some people he will be a peer, with others he will not. . . . Most social workers will also interact on the job, in their community's social welfare system, and in a number of its

TABLE 1
FACTORS INFLUENCING SOCIAL WORKER'S RELATIONSHIPS WITH OTHERS*

Type of relationship	Other's perception of outcome	Other's perception of demands placed on him
Collaborative—trust, mutual agreement on means and ends	Desirable—in self-interest	Minor—can be met within existing capacities and resources
Bargaining—adversary relationships, with willingness to negotiate differences	Not entirely in self-interest	Moderate—requires development of new capacities and skills or modification of existing ones and reallocation of resources
Conflictual—distrust, disagreement on means and ends	Undesirable—not in self-interest	Major—requires change in basic status and power relationships and control over resources

* Some items on this chart are adapted from Harry Specht, "Disruptive Tactics," in Ralph M. Kramer and Harry Specht, Readings in Community Organization Practice (Englewood Cliffs, N.J.: Prentice-Hall, Inc., 1969), p. 375.

subsystems. Each of these positions evokes different expectations, attitudes, and behavior from him and from others in relation to him.[17]

The framework of four types of systems presented in Chapter 3 can help the worker define his position, purpose, and relationships with all the systems he encounters. Further, the worker's relationships are influenced by the particular pattern of overlapping or separate types of systems he must deal with in a given change effort. Social workers have contracts, and thus collaborative relationships, with clients and members of action systems. Thus, if the target system is the same as or partially overlaps with the client and action systems, collaborative or bargaining relationships can occur. However, when the target system is outside (is not the same as) the client and action systems, the worker may engage in collaborative, bargaining, or conflictual relationships.[18]

Any relationship may have elements of collaboration, bargaining, and conflict. If the three types of relationships are considered to be on a continuum, the worker and other systems would move back and forth

---

[17] Yvonne L. Fraley, "A Role Model for Practice," Social Service Review, 43 (June 1969): 149.
[18] Brager, "Advocacy and Political Behavior," makes a similar point in his discussion of the appropriate use of manipulative behavior in social work practice.

between collaboration and conflict, and often would be in the middle—in a bargaining relationship. The worker may be in a bargaining relationship with a potential client at the beginning of the planned change process and move toward collaboration as the contract is negotiated. Workers and other systems may move back and forth between bargaining and conflict as they seek the parity that is needed between parties in a bargaining effort, as Brager and Jorrin point out. Change agents and community groups often use conflictual relationships to achieve parity with a target.

> Community groups . . . often resort to dramatic action before bargaining can begin. This pre-negotiation phase serves to establish them as a seriously contending party by demonstrating their ability to invoke sanctions. Bargaining which eventuates from public confrontation between community groups and officials carries the implicit or explicit threat of further contest should an impasse develop. Community groups are therefore often involved in a bargaining process which follows a pattern of alternating public confrontation and private discussion.[19]

The use of conflict and bargaining to enable a change agent to achieve collaboration is also seen as necessary by Bennis, Benne, and Chin:

> Collaboration is always an achievement not a gift. It is usually attained through open and grueling confrontation of differences, through conflicts faced and resolved, through limited areas of collaboration growing into larger areas of collaboration as fuller trust develops . . . change agents who expect collaborative ways of working to occur without mutual confrontation, effort and learning have limited understanding of either collaboration or conflict.[20]

Although change agents and members of opposing factions in bargaining or conflictual relationships may recognize that there are serious conflicts between them, often they also want to establish more cooperative sets of attitudes. Richard Walton believes that two different strategies, conflictual power strategies and collaborative change strategies, place contradictory demands on a worker and force him to choose between them or to find some basis to integrate the two in some broader strategy of change. Walton suggests three ways of coping with this dilemma:

1. Sequencing or alternating the emphasis placed on collaboration and conflict.

---

[19] Brager and Jorrin, "Bargaining," p. 74.
[20] Bennis, Benne, and Chin, *Planning of Change* (1969), p. 152.

2. Having contradictory strategies implemented by different persons or groups.

3. Choosing tactics that minimize the dilemmas: selecting conflictual tactics that have the least negative impact on collaboration and choosing collaborative strategies that detract least from conflictual power strategies.[21]

When the worker shifts relationships with the same system over time, the other system will have to shift relationships accordingly and perceive the worker in a different way. At one point in time the target of the social worker may be outside and separate from his action system and he may be in a bargaining or conflictual relationship with it. Later if the worker wants to form another action system to include representatives of the target system and seeks to form collaborative relationships with it, he may be unable to do so because the target may view him with hostility and suspicion. When the other system will not shift relationships, the social worker may need to adopt Walton's second strategy and ask another social worker and agency to establish collaborative relationships with the target system and, possibly, work to bring the client and target systems together.

In summary, social workers will adopt many types of relationships in their interactions with others in a single change effort. In working with one system, the social worker's relationship may fluctuate between conflict, bargaining, and collaboration if the other system will also adapt and change its reciprocal relationship with the worker.

WORKER STYLE

In the conscious, deliberate, purposeful process of social work, a number of factors that influence the worker's selection of appropriate relationships in his change efforts have been identified. This may have implied that every social worker has at his disposal an array of different types of relationships—a bag of tricks—from which he can select the appropriate tool for his purpose and, like a versatile actor, play out many different kinds of relationships.

We do not view social workers as skilled actors or chameleon technicians whose feelings and actions are skin deep and can be turned on and off at will. In discussing the art and science of social work in Chapter 1, we pointed out that social workers need to combine their skills and knowledge with creativity, spontaneous feelings, individual-

---

[21] Richard E. Walton, "Two Strategies for Social Change and Their Dilemmas," in Fred M. Cox et al., *Strategies of Community Organization: A Book of Readings* (Itasca, Ill.: F. E. Peacock Publishers, Inc., 1970) pp. 343–349.

ity, and concern for others. Our discussion of values in Chapter 2 pointed out the necessity for the social worker to balance flexibility in his actions on the client's behalf with his own integrity and ethical beliefs. The concept of "worker style" is helpful in blending these ideas of art and science and flexibility and integrity.

By worker's style we mean the sum of his personality, values, and predisposition. A worker doesn't merely adopt different relationships but must modify and integrate them into his life style—make them his own, so to speak. Some workers are at home in a conflict situation. Others prefer operating more in a collaborative framework. Some workers are comfortable being provocative and confrontive while others are not. However, a worker who limits himself to one major relationship stance also limits his ability to help his clients when change goals require the use of a variety of worker relationships.

Social workers who do modify their styles and experiment with the use of new forms of relationships must be aware of how they are perceived by other people. Rogers, who cites research pointing to the importance of genuineness on the part of the worker, believes what the worker says must match his own feelings. The worker must appear to be dependably real.[22] Von Hoffman urges college student organizers to act like themselves and, at the same time, to be aware of others' opinions:

At the risk of sounding like mother, may I say that impressions do count. I'll mention clothes. It is one thing to wear overalls in Mississippi where many of the people actually do wear them—it is another to wear them as an occasional stunt in a big northern city, but to indulge in peculiarities of dress and speech simply makes you look like youthful faddists. . . . White middle class girls from Des Moines, to be extreme about it, did not grow up referring to males as "cats" and when they do it on the south side of Chicago they sound either patronizing or idiotic—take your pick.

Nothing is so reassuring as a person who acts like himself. If you don't know who you are, stay out of organizing until you do and are willing to accept yourself as yourself. When you do, you will find that other people will.

In summary, in order for the social worker to make conscious use of his relationships, he must be aware of his own emotions, hang-ups, and preferences and try and keep them from interfering with his work. He needs a great deal of objectivity in order to use himself as an instrument for influencing and helping others.

[22] Rogers, *On Becoming a Person.*

CHAPTER 5

PROCESS IN

SOCIAL WORK

PRACTICE

In building toward an understanding of social work practice, this chapter will discuss some factors which help define the tasks the worker must perform in a planned change effort and show how these tasks are interrelated and directed toward realization of the goals of this effort. Since many essential tasks and skills used in practice will be identified, this chapter will also serve as a bridge to Part II, which deals with eight practice skill areas.

PROCESS, PURPOSE, AND TASK

"Process" can be defined as a systematic series of actions directed toward some purpose (or designed to bring about a particular result, end, or condition). Process and purpose are thus related concepts. To understand the process in social work practice it is useful to begin with the idea of purpose—what determines the worker's purpose in a given practice situation at any point in time and how these purposes change. While the focus of social work spelled out in Chapter 1 and

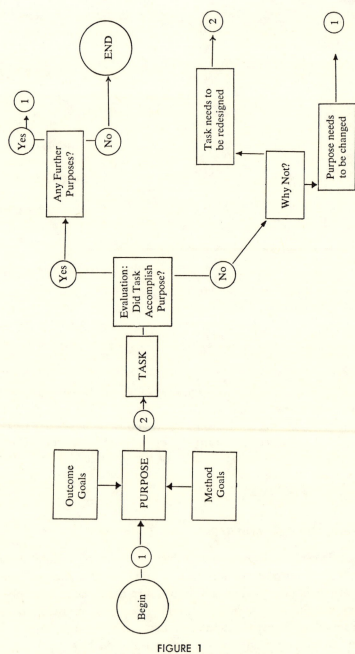

FIGURE 1
THE PROCESS IN SOCIAL WORK PRACTICE

the value stance of the profession discussed in Chapter 2 set the general purpose within which the social worker operates, the interest here is in the more specific purposes and ends toward which the social worker's day-to-day tasks are directed.

The process in social work practice, illustrated in Figure 1, calls for the worker to have a purpose for each activity, as well as for the whole planned change effort. Therefore the same process applies not only to the whole planned change effort but to each activity of the worker within the change effort.

Two major factors help define the worker's purpose: the outcome goals of all systems (client, action, target, change agent), and the method goals of the worker. The worker's purpose is achieved through the accomplishment of specific tasks, as will be discussed in the final section of this chapter.

OUTCOME GOALS OF SYSTEMS

An outcome goal is an envisioned end state, or, to paraphrase Robert Vinter, a specification of the condition in which we would like to see a situation at the end of a successful planned change effort.[1] Since by our definition the client system is the expected beneficiary of the worker's services, the client's outcome goals should be paramount in determining the worker's purpose. But the outcome goals of the client cannot be viewed in isolation; they must be understood in relation to the outcome goals of all systems involved in a planned change effort. The feasibility of attaining the client's outcome goals will to a great extent depend on the kind of cooperation the worker can get from others involved in the planned change effort. The nature of the relationships (collaborative, bargaining, or conflictual) the worker establishes will depend on the congruence of the outcome goals of all those involved. Thus the worker's purpose will be influenced by the outcome goals of the action, target, and change agent systems, as well as by those of the client system.

Client System

The worker cannot proceed very far with any clarity of purpose unless he comes to some agreement over outcome goals with the client system.

---

[1] Robert D. Vinter, *Readings in Group Work Practice* (Ann Arbor, Mich.: Campus Publishers, 1967), p. 13.

While these goals may be incorporated into a contract between the worker and client, this is not to say that once such goals are agreed upon they remain static. Goals may change as new information becomes available, different aspects of a problem come to light, the resolution of certain problems creates new ones, or the failure to obtain outcome goals suggests the setting of different ones. When these outcome goals change so will the worker's purpose. When major shifts in goals occur, it may be necessary to renegotiate the contract.[2]

The more specific the outcome goals of the client system are, the more useful they will be in helping the worker define his purpose in a given case. Outcome goals stated on as general a level as "improving social functioning" or "feeling better" are too vague to be of any use.[3] When necessary, the worker must help the client formulate concrete goals. Some examples of outcome goals are: reducing absenteeism from school (client system is a school); finding a part-time job (client system is a teen-ager); obtaining funding for a playground (client system is a neighborhood organization).

Action System

When the action system, which consists of the people the worker works with and through in a planned change effort, contains persons other than clients, their outcome goals must also be taken into consideration. Though the cooperation of action system members can be more easily secured if they support the outcome goals of the client system, they may participate in a change effort for their own individual gains as well. For example, a worker may be helping a group of migrant workers (the client system) settle permanently into a community. The action system may include diverse segments of the community such as school people, businessmen, clergy, union leaders, and police officials. Union leaders might agree to an apprenticeship program not only to help the migrants but also to make sure that they join the unions and do not undercut them by working for lower wages. Local businessmen might agree to sponsor a summer job program for teen-agers, not so much for what it will do for the youth, but for the public relations value for their businesses.

In the above cases, while the outcome goals of the client and action system may be different, they are not incompatible. However, if the

---

[2] The process of coming to agreement on goals and negotiating a contract will be discussed in Chapter 9.

[3] See Chapter 6 for a discussion of goal setting.

goals of the two systems conflict and members of the action system try to achieve their own outcome goals at the expense of those of the client system, the worker will have to exert influence on the action system members to support the client system.

Target System

The target system (the persons the change agent needs to change or influence to accomplish his goals) may be the same as or different from the client system. When the target system is outside the client system, it may be agreeable with or antagonistic to that system's goals. The kind of relationships the worker forms and the strategies he must employ will be affected by whether or not the target system sees the client's goals as being in its self-interest, placing too great demands on it, or conflicting with its own goals. Ultimately these considerations will affect the feasibility of attaining the client system's outcome goals.

Change Agent System

Each social work agency often develops its own general service focus. An agency may concentrate on some population group, such as the elderly; on some problem area, such as mental retardation; or on some geographic area, such as an inner-city neighborhood. An agency may also establish some specific outcome goals with respect to its focus, such as improving the housing conditions in a neighborhood or reducing rates of mental hospital admissions in an elderly population. These outcome goals of the agency, which often get translated into policy, will also influence the worker.

In some situations the worker may reach out and initiate contact with a potential client system such as a delinquent street gang, a mother suspected of child neglect, or tenants in a deteriorating apartment house. Initially in such cases there is no client system, except for the community, in the broader sense. In these situations the outcome goals of the agency (reducing incidence of delinquent behavior, improving housing conditions) play a large part in guiding the worker's purpose.

The worker himself may have some particular outcome goals of his own he would like to accomplish. Perhaps he is interested in developing proficiency in the use of some treatment approach and is working with a case which lends itself to that approach. Or the case may involve working with a school system, and a worker can use the opportunity to develop a referral source for the agency within the school. The worker with a broad social action goal may use a case to dramatize a problem. Of course the outcome goals of the worker should not take precedence over those of the client; that is, the worker should not meet his needs at the expense of the client.

In summary, the worker, in collaboration with the client system, will establish specific outcome goals for a planned change effort. While the goals of the client system should be paramount, they must be examined in relation to those of the other systems involved in the change effort. The outcome goals give purpose and direction to the planned change effort.

METHOD GOALS OF THE WORKER

While outcome goals refer to the condition in which we would like to see a situation at the end of a successful planned change effort, method goals refer to what must be done in order to bring about this condition. The formation of an action system, the negotiation of a contract with a client, the collection of data about a problem, the conversion of a target system into a client system, and the development of adequate decision-making procedures in a committee are examples of method goals. Thus method goals are not sought as ends in themselves but as means to further the achievement of outcome goals.

A key issue is what determines which method goal or goals the worker will pursue. This issue will be considered from the perspectives of phase models of planned change and system maintenance requirements.

Phase Models of Planned Change

There are a number of descriptive and prescriptive models which divide the activities of a social worker in any planned change effort into predetermined sequential steps or phases. Each phase is characterized by some broad method goal which must be accomplished before moving on to the next one.

For example, in examining the work of a variety of change agents such as social workers, psychiatrists, and organization consultants, Ronald Lippitt, Jeanne Watson, and Bruce Westley conclude that most change processes pass through the following seven phases:

1. Development of a need for change.
2. Establishment of a change relationship.
3. Clarification or diagnosis of the client system's problem.

4. Examination of alternative routes and goals; establishing goals and intention of action.
5. Transformation of intentions into actual change efforts.
6. Generalization and stabilization of change.
7. Achievement of a terminal relationship.[4]

Reflecting the scientific method of investigation and problem solving, most phase models, in one variation or another, account for (1) recognition and engagement with the problem (2) data collection (3) diagnosis (4) intervention, and (5) evaluation and termination. While such models are useful in helping the worker think through what needs to be done in a planned change effort, any logical linear sequencing of tasks is an oversimplification of the actual process. The worker may be operating in more than one phase at any one point, and with different types of systems. He may also repeat certain phases at various times. For example, in any one period a social worker who has a working agreement or contract with a neighborhood council to help it get better garbage collection services might be:

1. Working with the council (client and action systems) to plan its strategy.
2. Contacting neighboring community groups (potential client and action systems) to see if they want to join the effort.
3. Meeting with newspaper people (potential action system) to make them aware of the problems and solicit their support.
4. Establishing a working agreement with a lawyer (action system) who has offered legal services to the council.

If problems arise and the council or worker believe the goals or tactics need to be changed, the worker might want to renegotiate his contract with the council to make sure he can still supply the kind of help and resources it will need.

Similarly, at some point in working with a couple on their marital problems, the worker may decide that the in-laws should be brought into the action system. If the couple is resistant to the idea, the worker may have to reclarify with them his understanding of the nature of the client system's problems and secure a recommitment to the goals and methods of the change effort. If the couple agree, this would then require establishing contact with the in-laws and convincing them of the need to be involved.

---

[4] Ronald Lippitt, Jeanne Watson, and Bruce Westley, *The Dynamics of Planned Change* (New York: Harcourt, Brace & World, Inc., 1958), pp. 131–43.

As Lippitt, Watson, and Westley comment:

Most change processes probably proceed by a kind of cyclic motion, starting over and over again as one set of problems is solved and a new set is encountered; hence the different phases become mixed up and the final objective may be achieved by a process which seems rather muddled to the observer who is looking for a clear-cut developmental sequence.[5]

Another problem with essentially linear task-accomplishment models is the implication that one phase waits upon the previous one—intervention waits on diagnosis, diagnosis waits on data collection. It is difficult to break out of this pattern of thinking and recognize that all of these activities are occurring throughout the process.

GUIDE POSTS FOR THE PROCESS. Any model designed to indicate what method goals should be pursued at any one point should therefore take into consideration the cyclical nature of the worker's activity: data collection, diagnosis, and intervention can be present at all steps. It should also consider the different systems the worker relates to in any planned change effort. With these considerations in mind, three successive points can be identified which can act as guideposts for the worker in assessing where he is and what method goals he should pursue with respect to each of the four basic systems with which he is working. These points are contact, contract, and termination. The change agent will always be working toward one of these points with any given system.

Contact is the initial engagement of a worker and an actual or potential client, action, or target system. When a potential client approaches a worker for help with a particular problem, the change effort begins at this point for the worker, although the potential client may have done a lot of thinking about and planning for the initial contact. In cases where the worker "reaches out" or initiates contact with a potential client, action, or target system, careful preparation by the worker for the initial encounter is necessary in order to maximize his effectiveness in influencing them to become a part of the change effort. Indeed, a worker who is new to a community may spend weeks or months studying it and identifying a variety of potential client, action, and target systems before establishing any contact related to a specific change effort.

The working agreement or *contract* that must be established by the

---

[5] Ibid., p. 130.

worker with the client system can be referred to as the primary contract. In addition, the worker will need to come to working agreements with others related to the change effort (action, target, and change agent systems). These agreements are secondary contracts.

To some extent the evolution of the contract is a continuing process, as it may be frequently renegotiated. But at some point the worker needs to establish at least a temporary working agreement which defines the nature of his relationship with other persons, the goals and methods of the change effort, and the responsibilities of each party. The terms of a contract, as well as commitment to it, may be implicit or explicit.

After a contract is established, the worker will be moving toward the end point in the process, *termination*. The amount of time he spends reaching the goals of the change process will, of course, vary a great deal from one situation to another, depending on the complexity of the goals and the difficulties encountered along the way. For example, consider a social worker in a hospital who is helping a family cope with the crisis caused by the illness of the mother. Within a week the worker may have arranged for homemaker and after-care services, provided some needed psychological support for the family and, having helped them through the crisis, terminated his relationship with them. As chairman of a committee to improve the coordination of hospital services with other community agencies, this same worker may spend a year before reaching that goal and termination. Since members may be added to and dropped from the various systems throughout a given change process, the worker may reach the termination point with different people at different times in the overall process.

To illustrate with an example, suppose a worker at a county social services department is concerned about the apathy and lethargy of residents of a nursing home in which several welfare recipients reside. The social worker asks a friend of his, a doctor who knows the nursing home director, for advice on how to present his concerns to the director. He may also ask the doctor to sit in on the initial meeting with the director in order to help legitimate the worker's position. At this point the doctor may be considered part of the action system established to make contact with the nursing home director. After the initial contact the doctor may cease his involvement in the situation but remain a potential member of a future action system should the worker need to use his influence at some later date. After making contact, the worker's goal is to convince the director (who at this point is an actual target and potential client) that a problem does exist at the nursing home and to accept the worker's help in dealing with the inactivity and apathy of the residents. Since the worker sees himself as acting in behalf of the residents of the nursing home and they are expected to benefit from his services, they might also be considered as a potential client system.

In this same case several weeks later, the worker may have established a contract with the nursing home director (change from potential to actual client), who will use the social worker for case consultations and staff development. The worker and director have identified the staff as action system members responsible for changing the residents' behavior. But the staff can also be considered as targets, since some of their attitudes and approaches to patients need to be changed. The worker may be meeting with the staff to work out a secondary contract or working agreement with them. He may be planning ways of contacting the residents, perhaps meeting with them as a group or on an individual case-by-case basis.[6]

In the simplest case, where the target, client, and action systems are one and the same—such as when a couple comes for help with a marital problem and the social worker works with the two of them to resolve it—there is no need to keep track of the progress being made with each system. In such situations it is possible to characterize the progress of the whole change effort in terms of the point toward which the worker is moving (contact, contract, or termination). Thus when the basic systems completely overlap, a simple linear model suffices. But in most situations confronting the worker there will be some differences in the composition of the client, action, and target systems, and there will often be more than one action or target system to deal with.

To summarize, while with any one system the worker moves in the direction from contact to contract to termination, there is no simple way to characterize the sequencing of the worker's method goals with respect to the whole change effort. However, though at any one point the overall picture may appear chaotic, the three guideposts proposed here can help the worker tease out the pieces and assess his progress with any one system. They can help clarify what must be done in relation to what system in order to move the planned change effort toward the realization of the outcome goals that have been established.

The guideposts also sensitize the worker to changes over time in such factors as the nature of the contracts he is negotiating, modes of con-

---

[6] We should note that in any situation where there is more than one client system, the worker must be prepared to cope with the possibility of conflicting demands and expectations being placed on him by different client systems.

tacting people, and shifts in the size and composition of systems. They call for the worker to make use of all his skills in data collection, diagnosis and intervention in working toward all points in the planned change effort.

System Maintenance Requirements

An action system, like any social system, has two major concerns—to achieve specific outcome goals, and to maintain itself as a well-functioning unit. Social systems theory refers to this dual focus as goal achievement and system maintenance. Therefore the method goals of the worker can also be viewed from the perspective of the system needs of the various action systems he forms and works with.

It is important for the worker to keep the action systems functioning smoothly so they can serve as vehicles for the planned change effort. Each action system is an entity in itself and may develop problems which hinder its ability to perform tasks and achieve goals. Problems such as apathy, inability to make decisions, poor communication, conflict, or power struggles may arise whether the action system is a community task group, a treatment group, a family, or a one-to-one relationship. In any action system the worker must coordinate the efforts of different persons and maintain communications. The larger and more complex the action system, the more time and energy the worker will have to put into system maintenance activities. The worker must not only deal with these problems when they arise but try to form the action system in a way that will minimize their occurrence.

Chapters 10 and 11 will discuss in detail the formation and maintenance of action systems. Some of the method goals the worker focuses on are dictated by the needs of these systems, and at different points in their development action systems may pose different problems. Accordingly, the method goals related to action systems will change through time.

The issue of the relationship between method goals which stem from system maintenance needs and those which derive from phase models of planned change has been raised by Roland Warren. Writing in the context of community organization and social action, he has proposed a phase model based on changes in the structure of the action system itself rather than on a sequence of tasks to be accomplished by the change agent. His stages for analyzing the development of the action system are:

1. Initial systemic environment in which the action system emerges.

2. Inception of the action system.
3. Expansion of the action system.
4. Operation of the action system.
5. Transformation of the action system.

Warren makes it clear that the action system may focus on various tasks (such as developing an awareness of problem or goal, gathering facts, seeking possible solutions, choosing a course of action, and implementation) at different phases in its development. For example, in some situations the gathering of facts and consideration of various courses of action may take place before the expansion of the action system, while in other situations these tasks may be saved for the expanded action system. He also points out that an important consideration in studying any community action system is the manner in which task-accomplishment phases are related to stages of development of the action system.[7]

FROM PURPOSE TO TASK

After the purposes toward which the process of social work is directed have been determined, the next step is the translation of these purposes into specific tasks that must be accomplished in order to achieve them. The designing and carrying out of these tasks is the heart of practice.[8]

The worker draws on two main sources in linking purposes to tasks. The first is his general knowledge of practice skills. For example, if the worker's purpose is to gather information about a given problem, he will draw on his proficiency in designing and using data collection techniques and his knowledge of which one is most appropriate for collecting the needed data. The task designed to gather needed information may range from an interview at a client's home, to observation of family interaction in a laboratory setting, to a walk around a neighborhood.

Often a task will be designed with more than one purpose in mind. For example, consider a mother who has come to a mental health center because of the excessive acting-out behavior of her six-year-old

---

[7] Roland Warren, *The Community in America* (Chicago: Rand McNally & Co., 1963), pp. 315–20.

[8] For an elaboration of the task concept as central to social work practice, see William J. Reid, "Target Problems, Time Limits, Task Structure," *Journal of Education for Social Work*, 8 (Spring 1972): 58–68, and Elliott Studt, "Social Work Theory and Implications for the Practice of Methods," *Social Work Education Reporter*, 16 (June 1968): 22–27.

child. The mother wants the staff to help the child with his problem. After the initial interview the worker may design a data collection task which requires the mother to record the frequency of certain behaviors of the child at home. In designing this task the worker might have two purposes in mind: to collect more data about the behavior of the child and to get the mother to see that she will have to take an active part in the treatment process.

To cite another example, suppose a client is in need of a resource such as a homemaker service. The worker, using his knowledge of the resources in the community and how to get them, may engage in activities (making phone calls, filling out forms) to obtain the resource for the client. However, if one of the purposes of the worker is to help the client become more independent and take more initiative in dealing with his problems, the worker might encourage him to get the information on his own. Again, the way in which a task is designed will depend on the worker's purpose, which in turn depends on the outcome and method goals in the planned change effort.

A second source the worker draws on in linking purpose to task is his knowledge of theories of behavior and the dynamics of interactions of individuals, families, groups, organizations, and communities. For example, suppose in a given case the worker's purpose is to help alleviate the client's feelings of depression. In order to do this, he must operate on some assumptions about what causes and maintains such behavior and what can be done to change it. If the worker subscribes to a psychodynamic theory that depression is a result of anger turned inward, he might design a task which involves helping the client express his feelings of anger. Another worker, working from a learning theory perspective, may view the depressive behavior as a learned response and design a task which involves the reinforcement of nondepressive behavior. Similarly, workers may have different views on what is causing and maintaining a community problem and what should be done about it.

Since human behavior and the functioning of social systems are complex topics, any one theory cannot be expected to be adequate for all situations. Further, while some theories offer competing explanations, many are complementary, offering different perspectives on the same situation. Ideally the worker will be familiar with several approaches and pick the one most suitable for his purposes. But often the worker will come to a situation with a particular theoretical bias which may influence not only the way he designs tasks but also his purpose. Social work itself holds no unique theories of behavior and the functioning of social systems. The worker must draw on the knowledge base of the social sciences in linking purposes to tasks.[9]

The worker may design tasks which (1) he performs himself (2) the client or others involved in the change effort perform themselves, or (3) the worker performs jointly with others. Once a task is completed, the final part of the process is evaluating the extent to which it accomplished its given purpose. The importance of clarity and specificity in purpose is underscored here. If the worker's purpose is not clear, it will be difficult to tell if and when his purpose has been accomplished. If a given task has failed to accomplish a purpose, or only accomplished it in part, the worker must decide if the task is not appropriate and needs to be redesigned or if he should reexamine his purpose. If a given purpose has been achieved, the process repeats itself until all remaining purposes have been accomplished.

In the process of social work practice, which involves the defining of purpose and the translation of purpose into task, many different skills are called for. Eight essential practice skill areas can be differentiated: (1) assessing problems, (2) collecting data, (3) making initial contacts, (4) negotiating contracts, (5) forming action systems, (6) maintaining and coordinating action systems, (7) exercising influence, and (8) terminating the change effort. These are the topicis of the chapters making up Part II.

---

[9] For a discussion of criteria for selecting knowledge from the behavioral sciences, see Edwin Thomas, "Selecting Knowledge from Behavioral Science," in Edwin Thomas (ed), *Behavioral Science for Social Workers* (New York: Free Press, 1967), pp. 417–24.

PART II

PRACTICE
SKILL
AREAS

CHAPTER 6

ASSESSING

PROBLEMS

_____

Throughout the planned change process the worker continually assesses situations and makes decisions about what needs to be done and how to do it. This chapter will focus on the worker's overall approach to assessing a problem, formulating outcome and method goals, and planning intervention. The kinds of assessments the worker makes in determining how to best utilize the various practice skills to implement his planning and achieve his goals will be examined in subsequent chapters.

We are beginning the second half of this book with a consideration of problem assessment skills because it helps place the other skill areas in perspective. The problem assessment, which serves as a guide to the planned change effort, is elaborated as the worker engages in his other practice activities. It should be remembered that many of the social worker's skills are utilized simultaneously in his day-to-day activities and cannot be neatly organized into any step-by-step formulation of a planned change effort. Skill areas have been differentiated only to facilitate analysis of practice situations.

After defining the nature of a problem assessment, this chapter will center on the content of the assessment—what the worker takes into consideration in making an assessment of a problem. The final section will briefly examine some factors that influence the worker's decision making during the assessment process. The focus throughout the chapter will be on the analytical activity of the worker. Reasons for and methods of involving the client system and others in the assessment and decision-making processes will be considered in subsequent chapters, particularly Chapter 9, Negotiating Contracts.

NATURE OF THE PROBLEM ASSESSMENT

The purpose of the worker's problem assessment is to help him understand and individualize the situation he is dealing with and to identify and analyze the relevant factors in a particular situation.[1] Based on this understanding he will make decisions on which aspects of the situation he will deal with, goals for the change effort, and means of achieving these goals. The problem assessment is never an end in itself. Its purpose is not to classify, categorize, or assign diagnostic labels to a person or situation. Rather, the decisions about the future course of the planned change effort are the products of the assessment process.

When a worker makes a decision he is in effect making a choice between two or more available alternatives, be it alternative goals, tasks, or courses of action. The problem assessment should help identify these alternatives and provide a basis for selection among them. It is important for the worker to realize that whether or not he explicitly identifies the alternatives, when he takes a given course of action he is in effect making a decision to select one alternative and forego the others. Part of what characterizes a professional change agent is that he considers relevant alternatives and makes a conscious selection among them based on his understanding of the individual situation and his background of appropriate knowledge and values.

We must recognize, however, that the worker's decision-making ability is limited by the fact that a complete understanding of a situation

---

[1] The term "relevant," as used here, has several meanings. The first is in relation to the purpose and functions of social work. The social work frame of reference for viewing social situations discussed in Chapter 1 is one basis for determining if the worker is dealing with relevant variables. The second, which has to do with utility, views relevance from a pragmatic basis. Edwin Thomas suggests that for a variable to be useful it must be easily identifiable, accessible and manipulatable, potent, and able to be manipulated without excessive cost. A third meaning of relevance relates to the theoretical orientation used in analyzing a situation. For example, while early-life psychosocial developmental data may be considered relevant from a psychodynamic orientation, learning theorists would not regard it in the same way. See "Selecting Knowledge from Behavioral Science," Edwin Thomas (ed.), *Behavioral Science for Social Workers* (New York: Free Press, 1967).

often takes time to develop, and the existing knowledge base is never perfect. The social worker therefore must often act on the basis of incomplete information; he does not have the luxury of postponing decisions until he is satisfied that he has an adequate basis for making them. Many situations are urgent and require the worker's immediate intervention.[2] This means that the social worker often must make assumptions and hypotheses about what is wrong in a given situation and what should be done about it. These assumptions serve as the basis for further data collection as well as for taking action. Often the worker can test the validity of his assumptions and change and modify them only after he has evaluated an action he has taken.

A pitfall in this process is the temptation for the worker to hold on to his initial assumptions and try to make the facts fit them, rather than the other way around. Knowing when and how to alter initial assumptions is essential to the exercise of professional judgment. It is helpful for the worker to keep in mind competing hypotheses and assumptions as new information becomes available, because the problem assessment is not a static assessment but changes as the planned changed process proceeds. Though it acts as an initial guide for the planned change process, it is a blueprint that is modified and detailed as the process proceeds.[3]

CONTENT OF THE PROBLEM ASSESSMENT

Many factors enter into the worker's problem assessment. Though the format will vary from one work setting to another, any problem assessment will include the following: (1) identifying and stating the problem, (2) analyzing the dynamics of the social situation, (3) establishing goals and targets, (4) determining tasks and strategies, and (5) stabilizing the change effort. Consideration of all these factors should result in a written statement of the problem assessment.

---

[2] For an elaboration of this point, see Ernest Greenwood, "The Practice of Science and the Science of Practice," in Warren Bennis, Kenneth Benne, and Robert Chin (eds.), The Planning of Change (New York: Holt, Rinehart & Winston, Inc., 1961), pp. 73–82, and Joseph Eaton, "Science, Art, and Uncertainty in Social Work," Social Work, 3 (July 1958): 3–10.

[3] In this regard Rosemary Sarri et al., "Diagnosis in Group Work," in Robert Vinter (ed.), Readings in Group Work Practice (Ann Arbor, Mich.: Campus Publishers, 1967), pp. 37–71, discuss three kinds of assessments the worker makes at various points in the planned change process: preliminary diagnosis, working diagnosis, and terminal diagnosis.

Identification and Statement of the Problem

A first step in assessing a problem is to obtain as clear a statement as possible of the problem that is being presented to the worker or that he has chosen to address himself to. It is useful in this context to define a problem as a social situation or social condition which has been evaluated by someone as undesirable. In this view, no social situation is in itself inherently a problem. When a situation is referred to as a problem, it must be realized that an implied evaluation of it has already been made. If we accept this definition, a problem can be seen as constituting a cluster of three related parts: (1) a social condition or social situation, (2) people who are evaluating the social condition or situation as problematic, and (3) the reasons or bases for their evaluation.

For example, consider a situation where some unemployed teen-age boys who have dropped out of school have taken to hanging around a street corner. To the local storekeepers their behavior may be defined as a problem because they fear that the presence of the boys may ward off potential customers. The parents of the boys may define their behavior as a problem because they feel it reflects badly on them as parents. The police may be concerned that their behavior will lead to vandalism or other delinquent activities. A social worker at a local community center may define their behavior as a problem because they are wasting their potential and setting a bad example for other youth in the community. The boys may view their own behavior as a problem because they are bored and unable to find jobs.

Thus in arriving at a statement of a particular problem, the worker must consider the three elements that comprise any problem. He must identify the behaviors or social condition in question, the people who are evaluating it, and the reasons for their evaluation.

Getting a clear statement of a social situation is not a simple matter. Descriptions and evaluations are often interwined. Statements such as "He has a disrupting effect on the classroom," or "We are being harassed by the police" or "The agency is not responsive to our needs" are not descriptions of social situations but an evaluation or judgment that has been placed on them. The worker must go beyond such statements and determine the objective factors comprising the situation. What does the boy actually do in the classroom, how frequently and under what conditions does he do it, and in what way do the teacher and other pupils react to him? What was occurring when the police interfered, how were they summoned, what action did they take, did the police act differently in this situation than in others? What needs of people are not being met, how have they attempted to communicate their needs, and what was the specific response of the agency?

In clarifying the social situation the worker will begin by identifying those involved in or affected by the situation. This is also the first step in identifying potential members of client, action, and target systems. Next the worker will want to ascertain the reasons why they are evaluating the situation as a problem. Social situations become defined as problems for many different reasons. A frequently used one is that they violate social norms or values, in which case the behavior in question often is defined as deviant. Humanitarian and altruistic concerns may lead some to define situations such as poor housing or lack of day-care facilities for the mentally retarded as problems. People experiencing stress and discomfort will define a situation as problematic simply because of their distress. Fear of disruption in the functioning of a social system is another reason why social situations are often defined as problems.

Often there will be more than one reason for assessing a situation as a problem. Further, the same social situation may be defined as a problem in one social system or subsystem and not in another, or it may be defined differently in different systems or subsystems. In the Foster case study in Part III, the social situation that the worker was concerned about was the patient role on the ward. In this role patients were not to be told that they had a terminal illness and, further, were not to raise questions about their condition. The social worker on the ward defined this situation as problematic partly because it violated the clients' right of self-determination—if the clients didn't know about their condition they couldn't be involved in the planning for it with their families. Further, the patients were revealing anxiety and fears to the worker, and the families were experiencing stress in helping to conceal the information from the patients. From the physicians' point of view, however, the maintenance of the role expectation was not seen as a problem. They viewed it as meeting their ethical responsibility for protecting patients from undue pain.

People who have been referred to the worker by a third party may have very different evaluations of their social situations than others involved in them. Examples of such third-party referrals, which are often involuntary, are a delinquent referred by the court or a mother suspected by a neighbor of child abuse.

It has been noted that the worker should not view a problem as the property of a given person or persons, but as characteristic of their interactions. It is common for people to identify others as "the problem" (the teacher, the husband, or the welfare worker is *the* problem). With such an orientation it is easy to fall into the trap of considering the problem assessment as consisting of tagging problems on people. This is not to say that specific individuals are not identified as targets for a change effort, i.e., who has to be influenced in what way to achieve what goal. But this is not the same as assigning blame or tagging someone as *the* problem. This may be a proper function for a judge, but not for a social worker. By keeping in mind the definition of a problem discussed above (a social situation or condition which has been evaluated as undesirable), the worker can help avoid such a trap.

A starting point in building a statement of the problem is what is often referred to in social work as the *presenting problem*, the reason that brings the worker and client system together. In cases where a potential client initiates contact, the worker will start with the problem that the client identifies. Where the potential client is referred by a third party or the worker reaches out to him, the worker will start with the situation as defined by the referral agent or himself. From the presenting problem the worker branches out to identify its various dimensions: the nature and the scope of the social situation, how it is being experienced and evaluated by relevant individuals and groups, what tasks the situation poses for those involved, how the tasks are being coped with, and what resources, services, or opportunities seem to be lacking. The seriousness or urgency of the situation must also be considered. Unmet needs or conditions people are experiencing may pose a danger and require immediate attention.

In branching out from the presenting problem it is useful to keep in mind the connections between personal troubles and public issues discussed in Chapter 1. The presenting problem reflects a particular vantage point from which a situation is being evaluated. Although a presenting problem might be stated in terms of a private trouble, the social worker must be alert to the possible public issues involved in order to fully assess the situation. Consider the situation in which an elderly widow asks for the help of the social worker in finding a nursing home placement. If adequate nursing home facilities exist in the community, the problem may be simply dealt with by informing the client of the available resources, providing her with whatever assistance she needs in making the necessary arrangements, and perhaps helping her cope with her feelings about entering a nursing home. On the other hand, the worker may have difficulty in finding a nursing home placement because there is a shortage of adequate nursing home care in the community or the expense of such care is prohibitive. If the worker has encountered such difficulties in other cases, he can begin to link the presenting problem (a private trouble) to the lack of sufficient community resources (a public issue). While he has a primary responsibility for dealing with the private troubles of his client, when he is aware of the related public issue he also has a professional obligation to address himself to it. He may not have the time, inclination, or expertness to deal with the issue of adequate community nursing care facilities, but he does have the responsibility to see that relevant persons and groups are made aware of the issue and will begin to work on it. This is what William Schwartz means when he says that an agency should serve as an arena for the conversion of private troubles into public issues.[4]

The presenting problem itself might be stated in terms of a public issue. For example, out of concern for the elderly members of their congregations, a group of clergy might approach the social worker about establishing additional nursing home facilities in the community. In assessing such a situation the worker must link the public issue to his knowledge of the private troubles of people. The worker might know, for example, that if more home-care services were available, there would be less need to refer people to nursing homes because most elderly people prefer living at home as long as possible. Such home-care programs would also be financially less costly than building and maintaining new institutions. Further, once such facilities are built there is a pressure to fill all empty beds in order to operate the institution most economically and make the most efficient use of costly resources. The pressure to use the institutional space may hamper the development of home-care services, to the detriment of the elderly citizens. In this situation the worker translates the public issue into its meaning for dealing with the private troubles of individuals. In this particular example the worker might help the group of clergymen to redefine the presenting problem.

The data and insights gathered by the social worker in identifying and obtaining a statement of the problem will guide him in deciding what his next step should be. There are several options. The social worker may decide that the situation is not one that requires professional intervention. Or, considering his agency's purpose and resources to be inappropriate to the problem, he may help link the people involved with more appropriate resources or services. If the problem

4 William Schwartz, "Private Troubles and Public Issues: One Social Work Job or Two?" *The Social Welfare Forum, 1969* (New York: Columbia University Press, 1969), pp. 22–43.

seems to be one in which the social worker can be of additional help, or if he needs more information in order to make a decision, he can continue to explore the dynamics of the situation.

Analysis of the Dynamics of the Social Situation

Before identifying alternative goals, targets, tasks, and strategies for the planned change effort, the social worker must elaborate the initial statement of the problem into a more detailed analysis of the dynamics of the problematic social situation. He needs to know how the pieces of the picture identified in the statement of the problem fit together. In doing this the worker will not be directing his efforts at pinpointing any single causal factor. Rather he will aim to develop an understanding of how the various elements of the situation are operating to produce or maintain the given behaviors or social conditions.[5]

In elaborating the initial statement of the problem the worker must identify the relevant social systems in which the problematic situation is rooted, including the informal, membership, and societal resource systems discussed in Chapter 1. For example, in the Foster case study in Part III, the problem was rooted in the ward system, composed of physicians, nurses, and patients, to which the patients' families became linked. In the Hoffman and Long study, the systems related to the problem included the family, the housing authority, the health department, the college loan fund, and the place of employment, to mention a few. The systems the worker considers are those which affect or are affected by the social situation which has been defined as a problem. As the planned change effort unfolds, new systems may come into consideration and previously identified systems may be excluded.

Identifying the relevant social systems helps define the boundaries of the situation the worker is exploring and points to potential members of client, action, and target systems. For example, in the Purcell and Specht case study, the landlord was a key system in the housing problems of the tenants. When the worker formed a contract with the tenants, the landlord became one of the target systems in pursuing the client's goals of getting the building repaired and services restored.

---

[5] For other discussions of assessing a problematic situation from this same viewpoint, see Harriet M. Bartlett, *The Common Base of Social Work Practice* (New York: National Association of Social Workers, 1970), pp. 84–127; Carol Meyer, *Social Work Practice: A Response to the Urban Crisis* (New York: Free Press, 1970), pp. 106–46; and Max Siporin, "Situational Assessment and Intervention," *Social Casework*, 53 (February 1972): 91–109.

In another context it is conceivable that the landlord could have approached the worker for assistance and formed a contract around his goal of realizing a profit from his investment in the tenement. It is financially impossible for many landlords to correct all the housing code violations in their buildings, even if they wanted to. Purcell and Specht note that "If the problems of landlords were not selected as a major point of intervention, they would still have to be considered at some time since they are an integral part of the social context within which this problem exists."

As the social worker identifies the systems within which problematic social situations are rooted, he should keep in mind the factors which impede people's ability to cope with their life tasks and realize their aspirations and the reasons why informal, formal, and societal resource systems may fail to provide needed resources, services and opportunities.[6] This can give him a perspective from which to understand the dynamics of problem situations. More specific understandings will grow out of the application of various theoretical concepts and theories for explaining individual behavior, social interaction, and the functioning of social systems.[7] Current theories and concepts employed in social work are drawn from many sources, including ego psychology, learning theory, role and social systems concepts, organizational theories, theories of social conflict, transactional analysis, and various communications theories. We do not intend to even briefly summarize these theories and concepts or discuss how they are applied in practice, but we wish to point out that they are brought to bear in the assessment process.

Goals and Targets

On the basis of his understanding of the dynamics of the problem, the social worker, with the client, must establish goals for the planned change effort and decide upon targets with respect to these goals. Together they must translate the client's needs or requests into specific goals. The establishment of outcome and method goals was discussed in Chapter 5. Three facets of goal setting that are important to problem assessment will be considered here: (1) goals and subgoals, (2) feasibility, and (3) priorities.

GOALS AND SUBGOALS. In any problem situation it will usually be

---

[6] See Chapter 1.
[7] See Chapter 12 for a discussion of the knowledge base of the social worker.

necessary to consider a multiplicity of goals in relation to the client, action, target, and change agent systems. There may be a general (or global) goal, such as resolving a conflict between a housing authority and tenants or improving services to the mentally retarded. If the worker's problem assessment is to serve as a useful guide in the planned change process, these global goals must be broken down into a number of smaller, more specific subgoals. These can be viewed as either small pieces of the general goal or as a series of steps toward its accomplishment. In the process of determining tasks and strategies for the planned change effort, the elaboration of subgoals (especially method goals), as well as the analysis of feasibility, will be a continuing process.

FEASIBILITY. The planned change goals that are established should not only be specific and relevant to the client's problem, they must also be feasible. Unrealistic goals can lead to frustration, reinforce apathy, and lead to withdrawal from the planned change effort. In considering the feasibility of attaining any goal, two main factors must be examined: the resources which can be brought to bear on it, and the resistances and difficulties likely to be encountered.

In assessing resources the social worker must take into consideration his own personal and professional resources as well as those of the actual and potential members of the client, target, action, and change agent systems. Such resources might include time, money or other material resources, access to influential people in the community, special knowledge, motivation and interest, social skills, and existing formal and informal resource systems discussed in Chapter 1. Too often social workers and other human service professionals are oriented to analyzing weaknesses and pathology and overlook the strengths within the people and systems they work with. Resources must always be viewed in relation to the specific situation; what is a resource in one situation may not be one in another. For example, if the worker and action system members cannot spare the time to conduct a broad community survey, they may either have to use alternative means of determining the needs of the community or alter their goal. On the other hand, what may be required to help effect a change in an agency's policy is access to someone who has influence over members of the board of directors. If such a resource is not available to the worker, then having all the time in the world will not make this goal any more feasible.[8]

---

[8] See Chapter 12, Exercising Influence, for a discussion of influence resources and the means through which they are brought to bear on a situation.

Any planned change effort will to some extent involve changes in the attitudes, beliefs, and behavior of the people involved. Whenever such changes are not seen by people as being in their self-interest or worth the cost involved, the social worker will meet with resistance. Anticipating the amount and kind of resistance and how it might be manifested is, therefore, an important element in determining the feasibility of accomplishing a goal. A large part of Chapter 8, Making Initial Contacts, will be devoted to analysis of the sources of motivation and resistance to participation in a planned change effort.

The examination of previous efforts by the client system and others to deal with the problematic situation (or similar ones) often will be useful in pointing out both resources and resistances and difficulties.

PRIORITIES. While the determination of feasibility is primarily a technical issue, the defining of priorities is implicitly or explicitly a value problem. Priorities are not just a matter of long-term versus short-term goals, but which goals should be given preference in the face of limited resources.

It might seem, then, that in determining priorities a first step should be the identification and clarification of values and securing agreement on them by the client and action system members. But as Charles Lindblom cautions, in complex social problems this is often an impossible task. Not only is there likely to be a conflict in values between different people related to a change effort, but also a conflict among the various values held by any one individual. Consider the example offered by Lindblom of an administrator who must relocate tenants living in tenements scheduled for destruction:

One objective is to empty the buildings fairly promptly, another is to find suitable accommodation for persons displaced, another is to avoid friction with residents in other areas in which a large influx would be unwelcome, another is to deal with all concerned through persuasion if possible, and so on.

How does one state even to himself the relative importance of these partially conflicting values? A simple ranking of them is not enough; one needs ideally to know how much of one value is worth sacrificing for some of another value. The answer is that typically the administrator chooses—and must choose—directly among policies in which these values are combined in different ways. He cannot first clarify his values and then choose among policies.[9]

---

[9] Charles E. Lindblom, "The Science of 'Muddling Through,'" in Fred M. Cox et al., *Strategies of Community Organization: A Book of Readings* (Itasca, Ill.: F. E. Peacock Publishers, Inc., 1970), pp. 293–94.

Alleviating immediate distress and providing for the basic necessities such as food, housing, and medical care will always be a priority in serving clients. But once we move beyond such basic necessities, establishing priorities becomes more difficult. As another example consider a young unwed mother who wants, at the same time, to accomplish four goals: to work so she doesn't have to be dependent on her parents or public welfare, to continue her education so she can get a better paying and more satisfying job, to avoid leaving her infant at home with a baby sitter all day, and to improve her relationship with her parents, who want her to give up the child for adoption. The point that Lindblom makes is pertinent also to this kind of example. While the worker will help the client sort out her own values and aspirations so she can decide on a course of action, her decisions on ends and means must be intertwined.

For funding agencies and agencies considering the adoption of new programs, the determination of priorities can be a major task. It may be helpful for them to compare programs or services on a common set of variables, such as the number of people affected by the problem a service addresses itself to and the current share of resources devoted to the problem, in order to facilitate decision making regarding priorities.

Tasks and Strategies

All of the steps in the problem assessment discussed above will affect the decisions the worker makes regarding a course of action for a planned change effort. Identification and statement of the problem, analysis of the dynamics of the situation, and the setting of goals and targets provide help in three specific areas: (1) determining actual and potential members of client, action, and target systems with respect to method and outcome goals; (2) suggesting points of entry in dealing with the problem, and (3) indicating resources the worker will be able to utilize, resistances he is likely to encounter, and the kinds of relationships he will be able to establish.

The development of an intervention plan is the *raison d'être* of the problem assessment and the ultimate test of its adequacy. In detailing a course of action the worker must specify who is to do what in what order and at what point in time. The costs of various alternative courses of action will also have to be evaluated, as measured in terms of money, time, psychological stress, altered status, or foregone alternatives.

As noted in Chapter 1, social workers engage in various activities in carrying out the functions of the profession. Each problem situation will call for the performance of some combination of these functions. Activities and tasks to suit the needs of the specific situation being dealt with must be chosen to facilitate these functions.

Social workers' activities can be characterized under one of three approaches to intervention which encompass all the various worker functions. These approaches can be called education, facilitation, and advocacy.

The *education* approach covers a cluster of roles such as those of the teacher, expert, and consultant. The objective is to help people and systems acquire information, knowledge, and skills. Typical activities the worker might engage in are giving information and advice, providing feedback, teaching skills, role playing and modeling, and demonstrating behavior. This role cluster operates within the general stance of collaborative relationships.

A second general approach, *facilitation,* encompasses a role cluster including the enabler, supporter, mediator, and broker. Objectives are to stimulate and mediate linkages within and between systems, strengthen the integration of systems and help them overcome apathy and disorganization, and help systems mobilize internal resources as well as secure external ones. The approach also aims to help create and build new systems. The worker's activities might include eliciting information and opinions, facilitating expression of feelings, interpreting behavior, discussing alternative courses of action, clarifying situations, providing encouragement and reassurance, practicing logical reasoning, and recruiting members. Activities are usually carried out within the context of a collaborative or bargaining relationship.

The third general approach, *advocacy*, includes the roles of advocate on behalf of specific client or client groups and helper for people who want or need to advocate on their own behalf. The objective of this strategy is to help an individual or system obtain a needed resource or service or to obtain a policy change or concession from a resistant, disinterested, or unresponsive system. Typical activities include organizing demonstrations and protests, presenting forceful arguments, calling attention to situations, and documenting accusations. The advocacy approach operates within the general stance of bargaining or conflictual relationships with respect to the target system.

Stabilization of the Change Effort

A final consideration in a problem assessment is anticipation of what new problems might arise as a result of the planned change effort and what needs to be done to see that the change is maintained once it is achieved. Changing one aspect of a social situation will have consequences for other aspects, and new problems may be brought to light. This is why helping to develop the coping and problem-solving capacities of people involved in a planned change effort is always an implicit goal, if not an explicit one.

While the social worker does not have access to a crystal ball, anticipation of possible unintended consequences of the planned change effort can help keep him alert to new problems as they arise. Stabilization of the planned change effort will be discussed more fully in the last chapter, Terminating the Change Effort.

The Written Problem Assessment Statement

The final step in the process of problem assessment should be a written statement covering the aspects discussed above. A written statement has many advantages. It forces the worker to make explicit what he does and doesn't know about the situation, helps him identify the assumptions he makes, acts as a tool in negotiating and establishing contracts, serves as a yardstick in measuring progress, and facilitates communication about the situation with others.

To be useful the problem assessment statement should be highly specific and discriminatory. It should clearly differentiate and individualize the situation being dealt with. As Alfred Kadushin notes, universally valid statements that apply to the majority of clients the social worker deals with are useless because they tell him no more than he knew before he met the client.[10] Examples of such statements are: "The client needs support in dealing with stressful situations," or "There should be improved communication among groups in the community."

The statement should be focused on the specific issue and clearly written. Specific descriptions of behaviors and events should be included, and the use of evaluative labels and jargon which can be easily misinterpreted should be avoided.

FACTORS AFFECTING THE WORKER'S DECISION MAKING

Throughout the assessment process, as in the entire planned change effort, the worker is called on to exercise his judgment in making many

---

[10] Alfred Kadushin, "Diagnosis and Evaluation for (Almost) All Occasions," *Social Work*, 8 (January 1963): 12–19.

decisions.[11] We have defined a decision as a choice between two or more alternatives. As decisions with regard to assessment, goal setting, and intervention planning are made in day-to-day practice activities, they are open to many influences aside from the criteria already discussed.[12] A number of factors operate to bias the worker's decision making.

Bias can be defined as "a particular tendency or inclination, especially one which prevents unprejudiced consideration of a question."[13] In a biased decision, one alternative is more likely to be selected than the others, not because the relevant criteria suggest it, but because other factors are operating to affect the decision. While such bias can never be completely eliminated, hopefully its effects can be reduced if the worker is aware of those factors.

One major source of bias in decision making is the agency or organizational context in which the change agent is working. Organizations can influence the workers' decisions by formally or informally limiting the alternatives and information available to him or by *a priori* giving preference to certain alternatives.[14] As an example, Scott Briar, in a study of workers' decisions to place a child in a foster home or institution, found that a good predictor of the worker's decision was the particular agency in which he worked.[15] Some agencies may favor one type of placement over another or simply have more access to one than the other. A child welfare agency that has foster care, group home, and institutional programs will consider using any one of these resources, while an agency that has only a foster care program will concentrate on these placements. Similarly, the worker's judgment as to when a patient is ready for release from a mental hospital is subtly (and often not so subtly) influenced by pressure from administrators to make room for new patients. The worker must be careful not to substitute agency conceptions, policies, and practices for independent professional judgment.[16]

---

[11] The terms "judgment" and "decision making" can be used interchangeably.

[12] For discussion of decision-making models relevant to social work practice, see A. Z. Arthur, "A Decision-Making Approach to Psychological Assessment in the Clinic," *Journal of Consulting Psychology*, 30 (October 1966): 435–38; Roland Warren, "Two Models of Social Planning," in *Truth, Love and Social Change and Other Essays on Community Change* (Chicago: Rand McNally & Co., 1971, pp. 54–71; and Lindblom, "Science of 'Muddling Through.'"

[13] *American College Dictionary* (New York: Random House, 1948).

[14] For a discussion of this point see Herbert A. Simon, *Administrative Behavior* (New York: Free Press, 1957), pp. 1–20, 45–109, 123–71.

[15] Scott Briar, "Clinical Judgment in Foster Care Placement," *Child Welfare*, 42 (April 1963): 161–69.

[16] Saari *et al.*, "Diagnosis in Group Work," pp. 50–51.

A second major source of bias is the processing of data in decision making. Methods of using data can result in such disparities as the "lock-in" effect and the "anchoring" effect.[17] The lock-in effect refers to the tendency to make judgments before accumulating all available evidence, thus locking in initial impressions in the early stages of information processing. Change agents often form tentative hypotheses to guide data collection, subject to rejection or confirmation as additional information is gathered. However, like the researcher, rather than rejecting the hypothesis, the practitioner will sometimes reject the data when it does not confirm a dearly held hypothesis. Henry Miller and Tony Tripodi reported a study in which social workers listened to tape recordings of interviews with prospective adoptive parents. Both during and after the interview the social workers were asked to make judgments about the suitability of the couple as adoptive parents. The judgments made after the first half of the interview were similar to judgments made after the entire interview.[18]

The "anchoring" effect comes into play in judgments about the degree or intensity of a given variable, which are affected by the anchor point or reference point used by the change agent. This will depend on many factors, including the amount and kind of his experience with clients, his value system, and his life experiences in general. A worker in a family service agency might characterize a client as being severely depressed—and he might be in comparison to other clients seen at the agency. However, if the same client were seen at a mental hospital he might be judged as only moderately depressed. Judgments about housekeeping standards, child-care practices, organizational efficiency, and the like are similarly affected by the anchor points of the decision maker.

The process of assessment, which has been detailed in this chapter, continues throughout the planned change process. While the initial assessment serves as a blueprint, it will be modified as ideas are tested out and new data and information are gathered. The worker continually reassesses the nature of the problem, the need for supporting data, and the effectiveness of the approaches chosen to cope with it.

---

[17] For a summary of research findings pertaining to these and similar factors see Henry Miller and Tony Tripodi, "Information Accrual and Clinical Judgment," *Social Work*, 12 (July 1967): 63–69, and Tony Tripodi and Henry Miller, "The Clinical Judgment Process: A Review of the Literature," *Social Work*, 11 (July 1966): 63–69.

[18] Miller and Tripodi, "Information Accrual and Clinical Judgment," p. 64. We should caution here that increased information is no guarantee of better decisions. Miller and Tripodi also reported on a study which found that beyond an optimum point, amount of information can be inversely related to reliability.

CHAPTER 7

COLLECTING

DATA

_____

Information from and about a variety of persons and systems is needed throughout the planned change process. This chapter is designed to acquaint the practitioner with the array of available data collecting techniques and the importance of selecting those that are most appropriate for his purposes. Three general modes of data collection will be discussed: (1) questioning, (2) observation, and (3) use of existing written material.

QUESTIONING

A variety of data collecting techniques involve questioning. Verbal questioning refers to individual or group interviewing in which questions are asked verbally and verbal replies are expected. Written questioning refers to techniques in which questions are written and call for written replies, as in a questionnaire or application form. Some questioning techniques, instead of posing direct verbal or written questions, may present an individual or group with a purposefully ambiguous stimulus such as an incomplete sentence ("I wish that——") or a picture. Subjects are then asked to respond to the stimulus by completing the sentence or making up a story about the picture. Since these techniques require the individual to utilize his own perceptions and personal meanings (i.e., his frame of reference) in responding to the stimulus, they are known as indirect or projective techniques.

Direct Verbal Questioning

The regular individual or group interview is the most widely used tool for data collection and probably the single most important one. To use this tool properly requires knowledge and understanding of such topics as the interview as a communication system, verbal and nonverbal communication, motivations and barriers to communication, and roles and relationships in the interview. There are prescribed techniques for formulating and sequencing questions, preparing for and explaining the purpose of the interview, keeping it focused, making smooth transitions between topics, using probing techniques, assessing the respondent's frame of reference, and terminating the interview. Detailed information on all these aspects of interviewing are available in sources devoted to the subject.[1]

In the social work framework, the interview is seen as an action system for the purposes of data collection. There are a range of options in structuring this system. At one extreme is the nondirective interview, in which the worker follows the mood and interests of the interviewee. The worker may have in mind some areas or topics he wants to cover, but he does not formulate in advance the questions he wants to ask or the order in which he will pursue them. An alternative is to follow a preset interview schedule or questionnaire. This way of structuring the interview is necessary for collecting comparable data from a large number of persons, such as in a neighborhood survey. If the respondents are not all asked the same questions in the same way, it is difficult to analyze and summarize the resulting data. The same would hold true for an agency concerned with collecting a uniform set of demographic data on all clients for record-keeping or research purposes.

The worker also can structure an interview by establishing norms or ground rules. For example, in conducting an initial interview with a family, he might ask that each person in turn explain how he sees the family's problems. Other family members must wait their turn and must not interrupt. Further, each person might be asked to simply

---

[1] See Robert Kahn and Charles Cannell, *The Dynamics of Interviewing* (New York: John Wiley & Sons, Inc., 1957); Raymond Gordon, *Interviewing: Strategy, Techniques and Tactics* (Homewood, Ill.: Dorsey Press, 1969); and Alfred Kadushin, *The Social Work Interview* (New York: Columbia University Press, 1972).

state his point of view and not to pass judgment on what other family members have said. These rules not only allow each person a chance to talk but might also be useful in getting family members to *listen* to one another. Thus intervention as well as data collection goals would be served. Similarly, when interviewing a group such as an agency board of directors, the worker might ask each member to state his opinions before opening a general discussion. This may be an especially important technique if one or two members tend to dominate the discussion.

Attention to the physical setting of the interview is another way of structuring the situation. It may make a difference if a teen-ager is interviewed in the worker's office or on the teenager's "turf." A different atmosphere is created in the office if the worker's desk acts as a barrier between himself and the client or if both are in full view of each other.

Viewing a group or individual interview as an action system for the purposes of data collection may stimulate thinking in regard to ways of structuring the interview to overcome barriers to communication, maximize motivations, and increase the flow of unbiased information.

Direct Written Questioning

Many kinds of written questioning techniques are in use. Application forms for agency services, evaluation forms filled out by group members, self-administered attitude tests, and questionnaires filled out by an agency in reporting to a community planning group are all examples of these techniques.

The major advantages in the use of written instruments, which are self-administered, are savings in time and the greater possibility that the respondent can remain anonymous. However, these advantages must be weighed against other factors in the data collection situation, such as the demands placed on the people being questioned. For example, through the use of an application form filled out by a potential client prior to the first interview, data can be obtained on how the client sees his problems and the kind of services he wants. This can be helpful in pointing out issues which should be covered in the initial interview. However, if the client is going to be "turned off" by filling out a form and sees it as dehumanizing or evidence of a lack of personal interest in his problems, then this is not the kind of first experience he should have with the agency. Further, because self-administered questionnaires and tests often depend on the individual's literacy and ability to express himself in writing, they may prove embarrassing or frustrating for the person who lacks these skills.

Some clients, however, are able to and indeed may enjoy expressing themselves in writing. For such clients the worker can use these traits to advantage in his data collection effort. A client might be asked to keep a daily diary in which reactions to important events are summarized or a log of certain activities and their frequency, such as amount of time spent in social interaction as opposed to solitary activities.

Written questionnaires are often useful when the worker wants to assess the knowledge or attitudes of a person or group. A worker helping a group of teen-age girls with problems of sex and dating had each girl fill out a 10-question quiz on facts relating to sex and reproduction. The girls felt less embarrassed in responding to the written test than if they had to expose their knowledge (or lack of it) in front of the group. The quiz gave the worker a good idea of how much the girls did know and created a stimulus for discussion. In another group designed to promote greater communication and understanding between younger and older people, the worker began with an attitude test to measure the stereotypes held by different age groups about one another. Since people are often curious about how their answers compare to others', such a test can serve as a good way of getting the discussion underway.

Written questionnaires also provide a means of collecting data from a group without members biasing or influencing each other's answers. In a budgeting group the worker might ask each person to list criteria for allocating scarce funds to different agencies. In this way he can get some idea of the range of criteria and degree of consensus in the group without certain prominent members being able to influence the results. The worker could accomplish the same end by interviewing each group member separately, but this would take a great deal of time. Further, in an interview, workers' own biases may influence the position of the group members. A number of research studies have substantiated the superiority of nominal groups as compared to conventional brainstorming groups. In nominal groups, people work in the presence of one another, making lists or writing down ideas, but they do not interact. Interacting groups inhibit the performance of their members and generate a smaller number and variety of ideas, as well as fewer high-quality suggestions.[2]

---

[2] Andre Delbecq and Andrew Van de Ven, "A Group Process Model for Problem Identification and Program Planning," *Journal of Applied Behavioral Science*, 7 (July-August 1971): 466–92.

Written questioning techniques are also often used in interviews with families. For example, each family member is asked to write down three good traits and three traits which need changing for each member, including himself. All the lists are given to the worker. This not only avoids the possibility of one person influencing the answers of another, but family members might be willing to write things down that they are not comfortable saying to one another. In addition to getting a good picture of how family members perceive one another, the worker can feed back this data to the family in many different ways in order to open up communication and get members involved in the treatment process.

In cases where anonymity is a prime consideration, the written questionnaire may be the only feasible means of data collection. For example, if a public welfare agency is doing a survey of clients to evaluate the agency's services, clients may be reluctant to say anything negative for fear their funds or services will be cut. The self-administered questionnaire, returned by the respondent by mail, may be the only way to assure the anonymity of the respondents. However, the problem of respondent motivation is an issue in the use of mail questionnaires. Explaining how the data will be used and how the results might benefit the respondent may help increase his motivation. Keeping the questionnaire brief, making the format attractive, and enclosing a stamped self-addressed envelope also should increase the number of returns.[3]

Self-administered questionnaires designed to study the dynamics of small groups through the perceptions and feelings of the group members are known as sociometric measures. These elicit group members' perceptions on such dimensions as power (members are asked to rank each other from most to least influential) and affect (members are asked whom they like most in the group, whom they would prefer to work with again). The worker's theoretical orientation will influence what aspects of the group he will study. Sociometric devices have been used extensively in small-group research by social psychologists and can be very useful for the social worker.

For example, a group of social work students in a field unit who were having problems communicating with one another were asked to perform two tasks. First they were asked to rank other group members

---

[3] For details on questionnaire construction and community surveys, see Claire Selltiz et al., *Research Methods in Social Relations* (New York: Holt, Rinehart & Winston, Inc., 1959); Roland Warren, *Studying Your Community* (New York: Free Press, 1965); and Pauline Young, *Scientific Social Surveys and Research* (Englewood Cliffs, N.J.: Prentice-Hall, Inc., 1966).

in terms of whom they felt most comfortable criticizing and from whom they felt most comfortable accepting criticism. Second, they were asked to list the criteria they used in ranking the members the way they did. Since the members of this group had been hesitant about sharing their feelings with one another, this method of data collection was appropriate because it allowed for anonymity. The group found the task interesting, and it stimulated discussion.

Knowing how to feed back such data requires a good deal of skill on the part of the leader. Whether people who are ranked low feel they are being attacked or getting useful, constructive criticism depends on how the feedback is handled by the worker. The worker should be aware of the kinds of feelings and anxieties his data collection will stir up and be prepared to deal with them. By explaining in advance why the data are needed and how they will be used, the worker gives group members a chance to raise questions that are troubling them. Such an explanation may also help to increase respondents' willingness to participate and give accurate and complete answers.

In an ongoing group, post-meeting evaluation forms are sometimes useful in giving the worker and the group a picture of how meetings are going and what might be done to improve them. The use of the same set of questions on such forms for a number of meetings facilitates comparison and measurement of change.

In summary, written questioning techniques can be timesaving, maintain the respondent's anonymity, and help prevent respondents from influencing each other's responses. The worker must be sure, however, that the respondent has the ability and motivation to complete the task. Because it is difficult to deal with issues in any depth in written questioning and respondents' intepretation of the questions may vary, it is preferable to use such techniques in combination with a direct interview when possible. Written questioning techniques also may have the beneficial side effect of getting people interested and involved in a change effort.

Projective Verbal Questioning

Projective techniques are those that allow the respondent to impose or project his own frame of reference (personal meanings and perceptions) in responding to some stimulus, such as a picture. Therefore these techniques are especially useful in assessing an individual's attitudes and self-image. The administration and standardized scoring of projective tests is the concern of the clinical psychologist. The social worker uses projective techniques to supplement the interview, as a way of stimulating an individual to talk about things he may have difficulty expressing otherwise and obtaining leads to followup in the interview. The worker is not concerned with labeling or classifying the respondent on the basis of an interpretation of projective data.

Claire Selltiz, and her co-authors caution that the individual is not always willing or able to supply information on his own behavior, beliefs, or feelings.

People may be unwilling to discuss controversial topics or to reveal intimate information about themselves. They may be reluctant to express their true attitudes if they believe that such attitudes are generally disapproved. Or they may be unable to give the desired information, either because they cannot easily put their feelings into words or they are unaware of their feelings about the matter in question.[4]

Therefore techniques that rely on the individual's personal reactions may not always be effective.

On the simplest level the worker can make use of projective type questions to start an interview and elicit material he can follow up. If an agency director were asked how he would spend a hypothetical million dollars added to his budget, his answer would give some idea of the importance he places on different programs and services. Paul Watzlawick describes a family interview in which the mother and father were asked to discuss the meaning of the proverb "A rolling stone gathers no moss." This ambiguous proverb will be interpreted differently if "moss" is seen as something desirable (roots, friends, stability) and "rolling" is considered bad, or if "rolling" is thought to be good (prevents stagnation) and "moss" bad.[5]

Role playing is a useful projective device for data collection. In a training school for delinquent teen-age girls, the worker set up a role play of a court hearing at which a girl is sentenced to the institution. The roles of the judge, the girl, the parents, and the probation officer were all played by girls, and the role play gave a good idea of how they saw the figures they were playing. Like other projective devices, role playing often leads to a good discussion. It can be much more productive than a regular interview with the worker, especially with teen-age girls, who enjoy dramatics and see role playing as a kind of game. Similarly a worker might ask a client having difficulty finding a job to

---

[4] Selltiz et al., Research Methods in Social Relations, p. 280.
[5] Paul Watzlawick, "A Structured Family Interview," Family Process, 5 (September 1966): 256-71.

role play a job interview. This would give the worker some idea of how the client acts and how he presents himself at the interview. In working with families, it is sometimes useful to have family members switch roles in order to see how they view the roles of the other family members. In addition to data collection, role playing is useful for other purposes. It provides opportunities for rehearsing behaviors, practicing skills, and seeing things from another's point of view.

Pictures are another projective technique that can serve as a stimulus to start people talking. One resourceful worker was confronted with a depressed elderly patient in a hospital who was reluctant to talk to him. He took a Polaroid picture of the patient, showed it to her, and asked her to tell him about the person in the picture, what she was thinking about, and how she was feeling. This technique got the patient talking about her problems even though she would not initially respond when asked direct questions in an interview.

In working with a couple who were having marital problems, the worker utilized a set of pictures showing a husband and wife at home. One of the pictures showed the husband with his coat on at the door, which could be interpreted as his coming home or going out. Another showed the couple together on a couch, smiling and apparently happy. The husband and wife, individually, were asked to arrange the pictures to tell some kind of story. The wife started the story with the picture of the husband coming home, a fight taking place, and ended with the two together happily on the couch. The husband's story was just the opposite, beginning with them on the couch and ending with him leaving. In discussing this, the wife said that she had made up a story as she would ideally like to see it, while the husband's story was more realistic. This led into a discussion of their perceptions of their situation, which they had had difficulty talking about in previous interviews.

In working with very young children, where regular interviewing is not appropriate, various play activities are often used as projective devices. Little children playing with a doll house will often give clues as to how they see the family situation. Children's drawings can also be very revealing.

Written Projective Techniques

Written projective techniques share the same advantages and disadvantages as direct written questioning. Like other projective techniques, they are especially useful in assessing attitudes, perceptions, and self-images. One commonly used technique is called the sentence-completion test. Unfinished sentences related to the subject the worker is interested in are constructed, and the respondent is asked to complete them. One worker gave a sentence-completion test to a group of mental hospital patients to assess their attitudes toward the hospital and about being discharged. Sample questions were: "The aides in the ward are _____." "When I leave the hospital I _____."

Another technique calls for the respondent to describe himself in 10 or 20 brief statements. This is a useful technique for revealing an individual's self-image. People may describe themselves in physical terms (tall, fat, beautiful), affective terms (happy, sad), role or reference group terms (student, Catholic, middle class), and behavioral terms (aggressive, shy).

Written projective techniques can be assigned to the client in between meetings with the worker, thus giving him something to prepare for the next session. Projective techniques can be useful in conjunction with other data collection techniques, especially direct interviewing. Indeed, the worker should avoid relying solely on any one data collection technique.

OBSERVATIONAL TECHNIQUES

Observation is a pervasive activity and a basic means of gathering information in daily life. There are important differences between casual observations and the use of observation as a tool in data collection. Observation can be considered a technique to the extent that it is used toward some specific purpose. Procedures for observation should be planned in advance and subject to controls for bias.

Though observation is a component of almost all data collection techniques, unless deliberate use is made of the observer's powers of observation, much of what occurs will be lost or missed. Consider the example of a social worker conducting an interview with a mother at her home, during which one of the children barges in to ask something and, later, the mother stops to settle a fight between two of them. The worker might ignore these interruptions and use the breaks to gather his thoughts and perhaps jot down some notes. A more astute interviewer would observe how the mother handles the interruptions and how the child responds to the mother, thereby gaining some further information about the family. He will, however, need to take into consideration the effect that his presence might have had on the situation. Similarly, in conducting a family interview the worker may become so involved in the content of what is said that he might overlook many of the dynamics of the interactional processes in the family— who sides with whom, how disagreements are dealt with, and how family members react to one another's contributions.

In using observation techniques, the social worker can observe a natural, or real-life, situation or one he has purposefully contrived or structured. The worker might observe family members at dinner time in their home or performing an assigned task in his office.

The worker must also decide how formalized his observational procedures will be. He might observe a committee meeting to get some general impressions of the nature of the interaction in the group and the kinds of roles different group members play. In this case his observations would be guided by his general knowledge of group dynamics and his data would consist of his impressions, though he might jot down some notes while observing to aid his memory. In other cases the worker might be interested in gathering data on more specific aspects of the committee, such as which members support another's position on what issues, who contributes what kind of information, and to whom most of the questions are directed. To record this kind of detailed information, the worker will likely use some sort of prepared schedule with predetermined categories for entering and classifying his observations.[6]

Finally there is the issue of the relationship of the worker to the persons he is observing. When the worker is a member or leader of a group he is observing, he is functioning as a participant observer; when he is not interacting in the system he is studying, he is a nonparticipant observer. The people being observed may be aware of the nonparticipant observer's activity, such as when he is observing a family in interaction on some task assigned to them, or his purpose might be concealed, such as when he is taking notes on the actions of members of a legislative committee at a hearing.

The worker's choice of observational techniques will affect the quality and accuracy of the information he gathers. The type of information he seeks will determine whether he should observe a natural or structured situation, use impressionistic or formalized procedures, and act as a participant or nonparticipant observer.

An example of the way these factors operate in an observational situation is Sallie Churchill's description of a series of small group

---

[6] For details see Edgar Borgatta and Betty Crowther, *A Workbook for the Study of Social Interaction Processes* (Chicago: Rand McNally & Co., 1965).

meetings to collect diagnostic data on children at a mental health center:

In the first meeting the worker uses crafts, games and activities which are potentially highly interesting, provide opportunities for both individual and group activity and offer safe ways for constructive isolation. In the second session the worker increases the demand for peer interaction and the need for social skills, such as participation in group games or sharing of equipment. The degree of change and the pressure exerted by the program will be based upon an evaluation of individuals in the first meeting. . . . In the third meeting the social behavior of the members is tested in the community outside the safety of the meeting room by a trip to the store, to the museum or to the ball park. . . . After the third session the group worker reviews his impression of each child with the rest of the diagnostic team. Together team members determine what the group worker needs to investigate further. The final session is planned so that the observations needed for each child can be made. During all four sessions the group discusses the purpose of the group, how the group is related to the total clinic procedure, how the members feel about coming to the clinic, how they view their own problems and what help they themselves want.[7]

The worker in this case is a participant observer, since he has responsibility for conducting the group. While he does not use a prepared schedule to record his observations, he keeps in mind an outline of aspects of the child's behaviors as a guide in observations and writes a report after each meeting. The areas covered in the worker's report are described by Churchill as follows:

Primarily, his report is an evaluation of the pattern of behavior of a child in three areas: (1) relationship to other children, (2) relationship to an adult in the presence of other children, and (3) the child's knowledge and use of social skills, for example, physical and developmental tasks and expected peer roles. These patterns of behavior are reviewed in several contexts: (1) initial approach to the group situation, (2) ability to change over a period of four sessions, (3) stresses which precipitate regression, (4) behavior which provokes unhappy or unpleasant reactions from others, and (5) the child's reaction to group pressure. It is as important to observe the impact of a child's behavior on other children as to observe the child's behavior. . . .

The specific evaluation is made in terms of such patterns as inter-

[7] Sallie Churchill, "Social Group Work: A Diagnostic Tool in Child Guidance," *American Journal of Orthopsychiatry*, 35 (April 1965): 584-85. Copyright, the American Orthopsychiatric Association, Inc. Reproduced by permission.

action, reaction, provocation, modification and intensification. For example, in regard to the child's relationship to other children at the initial group meeting: (1) Can he show that he wants a relationship? (2) Can he accept friendly overtures? (3) Does he provoke feelings of protectiveness? (4) Under what situations can he relate and to whom? (5) Can he maintain relationships when tension is high? . . . In his knowledge of and use of social skills in the context of stress: (1) Can he accept appropriate roles in basic games? (2) Does he quit a game if another child gets a favorite role? (3) Will he disrupt activity when he doesn't want to play? (4) Are his social handicaps caused by lack of knowledge which can be remedied? (5) Do confused moral attitudes cause emotional rejection of activities?[8]

Because the worker in the example is an active participant in the group, his observations can easily become distorted. He is not as free as the outside observer to control and balance his observations. For example, he may be observing one child but become distracted when he has to intervene to break up a fight. Further, the effect that the worker himself has on the group members is difficult for him to evaluate and requires a great deal of self-awareness. Another consequence of his being a participant observer is that he must wait until after the meeting to record his observations. Here the worker's selective memory can distort the picture.[9]

In a similar vein, structured family interviews in which families are given tasks contrived by the worker to elicit certain kinds of interaction, or interaction around certain issues, have been described by Watzlawick and by Salvador Minuchin and Braulio Montalvo.[10] The family may be divided into various subgroupings (such as parents alone, children alone, or only male members) for purposes of observation. The following illustration from Minuchin and Montalvo shows how observation can aid in the exploration of intricate family dynamics

Tasks for the sibling group can be introduced in order to yield prognostic clues as to the degree to which a child is prevented by his family from access to a positive basis for self-esteem. For instance, in the G. family, a mother and father related derogatorily toward their children: the five boys—ranging from 7 to 14 years of age—were asked to try to

[8] Ibid., pp. 585–86.

[9] See Charlotte Wilke, "A Study of Distortion in Recorded Interviews," Social Work, 8 (July 1963): 31–36.

[10] Watzlawick, "Structured Family Interview"; Salvador Minuchin and Braulio Montalvo, An Approach for Diagnosis of the Low Socio-Economic Family, Psychiatric Research Report 20, American Psychiatric Association, February 1966 pp. 163–74.

find something positive ("good," "nice,") to say about each other. The clinician and the parents went behind a one-way mirror to watch carefully for relationships and labels used toward the child most consistently portrayed by the parents only as an "idiot, a dull kid." It became clear that the siblings were rather warmly and respectfully related to this child, and were providing buffers and antidotes to the parents' labels. They adhered to positive expectations ("You are the one who knows how to get around"), repairing to a large extent the damage created by the negative stereotypes of the parents. The child, in fact, behaved quite effectively and coherently during the presence of his siblings, providing an opportunity to train the parents' attention into an area of experience which they had come to regard as inaccessible.[11]

In this example the worker purposefully remains a nonparticipant observer to avoid becoming engrossed in the interactional processes of the family. The parents are also assigned the role of nonparticipant observers to help them gain some perspective on the siblings' interaction and see the family in a new light.

The social worker who wants to structure his method of recording observed data through the use of some kind of schedule or form must be a nonparticipant observer because of the demands of the recording process. Structured observations are important in collecting evidence to demonstrate the effects of an intervention effort. For example, consider a program designed to help low-income people become more effective members on agency boards and advisory committees. In order for the worker to know if his program is successful, he would have to translate "effective participation" into specific observable behaviors. One component of effectiveness might be related to the amount and kind of interaction in the meetings. Here the worker might create categories for recording the number and kinds of communications initiated by the person (raising questions, stating opinions) and the number and kinds of communications directed to the person (questions, seeking advice, seeking information). Another component of effectiveness might relate to the person's level of comfort at the meeting. The worker might look for and record incidents of discomfort as indicated by such behaviors as stuttering and fidgeting. If the worker recorded the frequency of these various behaviors by observing the person at a role play or actual meeting prior to the start of the program, and then again after completing the program, he would have a good basis for evaluating his program.

---

[11] Minuchin and Montalvo, *Diagnosis of the Low Socio-Economic Family*, pp. 170-71.

While most of the social worker's observation will be directed at people and social interaction, it can also be turned to inanimate objects. Oscar Lewis provides a good example of this kind of data collection in discussing what can be learned about slum families from their household furnishings:

Actually, the study of the material possessions of the poor may give us another important dimension for the definition of poverty. It can tell us about their buying and spending habits, their definition of luxury items, the relationship between income and material wealth, the proportion of goods bought in stores, markets, street stands, or from hawkers; the extent of trade or exchange of goods within slum settlements or neighborhoods, and the social consequences and concomitants thereof; the distances which they go to make purchases; the periods of economic crisis within the family as revealed by the history of pawned objects, the range and variation in the distribution of "wealth" among families who seem desperately poor; and finally, the values of the people as reflected in the relative amount of their income spent on various types of objects—for example, religious items versus modern appliances. In this connection I designed an inventory form which calls for the following information on each item found in a household: number or quantity of each article; description and condition; length of time in possession; cost; method of purchase (installment plan or cash); item new or used at time of purchase, where purchased, who purchased the item; if a gift, when given, by whom, for what occasion, new or used, and approximate value; if homemade, who made the item, when made and value; cost of replacing the item and approximate present value; whether the item had been pawned and/or redeemed; other comments.[12]

The physical plant is a rich source of data in such institutions as a home for the aged. If all the residents' rooms look exactly the same and do not reflect anything of the individual personality of the person living in them (through pictures, bedspreads, a chair brought from home), there is a good chance that the institution also represses expression of individuality in other areas. Are the newspapers and magazines in the day room up to date or are they several days or weeks old? Are there clocks and calendars in view? Some elderly people rely on such cues to help them maintain their orientation to time. Are chairs in the day rooms lined up in a row against the walls or arranged in conversational groupings? Such observations can give clues as to how concerned the institution is with the welfare of the residents.

In studying organizations, it is possible to observe obvious "status

---

[12] Oscar Lewis, *La Vida* (New York: Random House, 1965), pp. xxii, xxiii.

symbols" attesting to the place of various individuals in the organization's hierarcy. These may include the size of the office and desk and whether or not there are carpeting, wood paneling, or draperies. Even the nearness of reserved parking spaces to the entrance can reflect the status hierarchy in the organization. Similarly, the furnishings and decor of many public institutions indicate the value the community places on the functions they perform. For example, compare the waiting rooms of the public welfare office, the community mental health center, and the general hospital.

In the community, a great deal can be learned by taking a walk through a neighborhood. The ethnic composition, for example, may be apparent from the kind of food stores, pictures being shown in the movie theatre, and newspapers sold at the newsstands. The history of a community is also revealed in many ways. A synagogue which has been converted to a church can indicate changing ethnic populations, or a number of mailboxes on a large home can indicate that single-family homes have been converted to rooming houses.

While it is generally recognized that observational techniques can be powerful data collection tools, the social worker must be aware of their particular advantages and disadvantages in order to exploit their potential. One of the advantages of observational techniques is that they are largely independent of a person's ability to report on his own behavior. There are many instances when the worker may not want, or be able, to rely on people's own reports of their behavior or the behavior of others. The individuals may be too involved in a situation to give an objective report, or they may have some stake in distorting the picture. Further, they may lack the vocabulary, sensitivity, or insight to describe a situation adequately.

Another advantage of observational techniques is that they are not always dependent on people's willingness to cooperate. They place little demand on the system under study and can be used with minimum disruption on the behavior being studied. In fact, sometimes these techniques can be employed without the knowledge of those under study and without calling attention to what is being studied. For example, much can be learned about the informal staff organization in an institution by observing who takes coffee breaks with whom and who eats lunch together. The interaction and relationships observed between different occupational groups at a staff meeting often tell much about the institution. Is there a free-and-easy give and take or a more formal atmosphere? Whose ideas and comments are sought on which issues? Who makes what decisions? Are disagreements openly expressed, and if so, how do they get resolved?

Of course there are limitations to the use of observational techniques. Some behaviors or events may not be accessible to the worker, and in other cases he will be limited in the duration of his observations. Past behaviors, of course, are not possible to study through observation. Further, the worker may need permission (or want it, for ethical reasons) to gain access to observe certain groups or situations.

Value issues emerge in data collection considerations, as they do in all aspects of social work practice. In many cases it will be impossible to collect data from people without their sanction or permission—the worker cannot conduct an interview with a slum landlord who refuses to see him, or he will not be able to observe a family in interaction around a task if they refuse to participate. But there are instances when the worker can study a person or system without their being aware of his activity. For example, when he collects data about staff subgrouping through observing staff at coffee breaks and lunch hours, the staff members may be aware of his presence, but they may not be aware of his purpose. As noted in Chapters 2 and 3, the ethical stance of the social worker may depend on whether the target system is the same as or different from the client system.

USE OF EXISTING WRITTEN MATERIAL

Existing written material refers to available materials not gathered specifically for use by the social worker for his current data collection purposes. These materials may include case records, minutes of committee meetings, organizational charts, census data, newspaper stories, and police reports.

If existing material is readily available, it can be a very efficient means of data collection. It places little or no demands on the system under study and, in fact, can be carried out without the knowledge of those being studied. For example, a worker helping a tenant's union can obtain such information as the ownership and value of certain apartment houses from mortgage and tax records kept by the city. To use such information, which is a matter of public record, requires only that the worker be aware of its existence, know the procedure for gaining access to it, and know how to interpret it.

There are, of course, many limitations to the use of existing materials. Since they usually were not gathered for the purposes the worker has in mind, they may be incomplete or in a form that is not useful.

When using such materials as minutes or case records, there is the additional problem of the accuracy and validity of the data they contain. The worker must consider the possible biases and selective perceptions and evaluations of the persons who wrote the minutes or records. In fact, the worker using such sources may learn more about the person who has written the material than the subject about which the material was written.

The larger and more formal the system about which information is sought, the more likely it is that written records and materials will be kept about its operation. Existing data on given individuals or families will usually be limited to agency records, if they have had previous contacts with social agencies, or perhaps newspaper stories.

Formal groups such as committees and boards usually keep materials such as minutes and reports. A systematic analysis of this kind of material will yield more pertinent data than could be gathered through a casual inspection. A worker could go through a set of committee meeting minutes and note for each meeting such data as who attended, what topics were discussed, and who voted with whom on what issues. This could help him piece together a picture of the vested interests of committee members, subgroupings, and other characteristics of the group. For example, a worker interested in the decision-making process of the board of a community action commission, especially decisions regarding project funding, analyzed minutes of the board meetings. Considered were the items brought up at the meeting (administrative issues, policy issues, funding requests), whether they came from committees or were introduced for the first time at the board meeting, and the disposition of the item (settled at the meeting, sent to committee, tabled). By this process the worker was able to identify a key committee whose funding recommendations were always favorably acted upon by the board.

When the worker is studying a formal organization, he usually can draw on many kinds of existing material. Some are produced purposefully for public consumption, such as brochures and annual reports, and the worker will bear this in mind in interpreting the material. Such material may be more useful for understanding the image the organization wants to convey than for obtaining a true picture of it. Other material produced for internal use, such as organizational charts, procedural manuals, job descriptions, and directives, may be more helpful in studying the organization. The internal communication structure might also be studied through such "products" of communication as memos and requisition forms.

The usefulness of existing written material will depend on the imagination and resourcefulness of the worker. The availability of certain data may suggest to a worker areas that could be fruitfully studied. For example, one worker made use of the standardized statistical records kept on all state mental hospital patients, which contained such data as county of residence, diagnosis on admission, severity of illness, and length of hospitalization. Different patterns of hospital usage were found for those living near the hospital, as compared to those living further away. Since the state hospital in effect served as a local treatment facility for those living nearby, useful information for planning purposes was obtained on the projected use of proposed decentralized treatment centers.

The use of existing written material can be an efficient means of data collection, one which should be exploited by the worker. It can often serve as a useful starting point in his data collection process.

PLANNING A DATA COLLECTION STRATEGY

While a wide array of data collection techniques is available to a social worker, in any given situation he may not have much choice as to which techniques to use. When possible, planned use of appropriate techniques should yield the maximum amount of valid data.

There are a number of considerations in planning a data collection strategy. First, the use of more than one mode of data collection should be considered whenever possible. Certain techniques are best for certain kinds of data, but each technique has its own advantages and disadvantages. The disadvantages of any single technique can be minimized only if it is used in combination with other techniques. This point may seem very obvious, but it is frequently neglected in practice. While the direct interview is the most widely used and probably the single most important tool for data collection, overemphasis on this technique has often obscured other modes of data collection which could be used in place of the interview or to supplement and complement it.[13]

Second, in any data collection effort it is important to distinguish between the system (or person) about which information is sought and the system from which the needed data is to be collected. Some-

---

[13] Eugene Webb *et al., Unobtrusive Measures: Nonreactive Research in the Social Sciences* (Chicago: Rand McNally & Co., 1966) discuss the overdependence on interviews and questionnaires in social science research and suggest some novel unobtrusive methods of data collection.

times the two may be the same, as for example when the worker is observing a committee meeting in order to learn how the committee operates. Sometimes the two will be different, as when he is interviewing a policeman to get some information about a neighborhood. An individual can be interviewed in order to collect data about himself, another individual, a family, an organization, or a community. For example, the worker can interview John's teacher in order to get information about John and how he is behaving in class, the teacher herself and how she deals with classroom problems, or the school and its policies. Often the worker will have more than one purpose in mind. It should be recognized, however, that the validity of using the teacher as a source of data may be different when he is collecting data about the teacher herself, John, or the school.

Thus the worker must always evaluate the source of his data. In the example above, if the teacher felt she would be blamed by the principal for not being able to handle John's problems, she might play them down in the interview with the worker. On the other hand, if she were anxious to get John out of her class, she might play up his problems in the hope he would be transferred to a special class. When the worker questions the teacher about programs or policies at the school, the same caution must be exercised. A teacher who might be able to give an objective report on John's classroom behavior might give a distorted picture of how a certain policy is working at the school if she has some personal stake in the outcome.

A third consideration in planning a data collection strategy is sampling. If the worker is interested in the attitudes of teachers in a school toward a new social work program, he would not assume that one teacher's opinion reflected the opinion of the majority of teachers at the school. Even if he couldn't question all the teachers, he would want a larger sample than one. Often the worker will have access to only a small sample. When he is interested in generalizing from a limited sample to a whole population (from a few neighborhood residents to a whole neighborhood, or from a few organization members to the whole membership), he must consider how representative or typical the views or behavior of this sample is of the population from which it was drawn and in what ways it might be biased. For example, a worker calls a meeting of the tenants of a housing project to discuss what housing problems they face and what can be done about them. Suppose 30 people (5 percent of the adult tenants) show up. Are they a biased sample of all the tenants—the more dissatisfied ones? Would other tenants agree with their views of what should be done? These are the kinds of questions which confront the worker.

The issue of sampling comes up even when the worker is concerned with a single individual or family. For example, a worker may be interested in observing and recording the behavior of a child in a classroom in order to establish a baseline of attentive behavior (not being distracted from tasks). Since the worker cannot be present in the class all day, five days a week, he is only able to *sample* the child's behavior and, therefore, must take care that the sample he observes is not a biased one. The child may behave well in the early morning but as the day wears on become less attentive and more disruptive. If the worker observed him only in the early morning or only in the late afternoon, he would get a distorted view of the child's daily behavior. Ideally he would want to spread out his observations to include both different times of the day and different days of the week.

The worker interviewing a client or observing someone's behavior is constantly faced with this kind of sampling problem. Are the behaviors he observes and the things he hears typical of the person or persons? Is it being affected by the setting or the very presence of the worker?

The practitioner is often confronted with urgent problems or time limitations which require him to intervene in a situation even though his data collection may be incomplete or based on an inadequate sample. As Ernest Greenwood puts it, in contrast to the researcher whose main function is to explain and describe the social world rather than to change it, the practitioner "cannot afford the luxury of withholding action because of the insufficiency of validated knowledge."[14] However, this does not excuse the practitioner of the need to be aware of the limitations placed on his data by the sampling procedures he employs.

A fourth issue the worker must consider in planning a data collection strategy is the extent to which he will structure the system under study and/or the method of recording the data. The worker can structure the system under study in a variety of ways, ranging from simply setting up chairs in a circle in preparation for a group interview to the rather elaborate family interviews described by Watzlawick in which the family is given different tasks and observed in different subgroupings.[15]

---

[14] Ernest Greenwood, "The Practice of Science and the Science of Practice," in Warren Bennis, Kenneth Benne, and Robert Chin (eds.), *The Planning of Change* (New York: Holt, Rinehart & Winston, Inc., 1961), pp. 73-82.

[15] Watzlawick, "Structured Family Interview."

The advantage in structuring the system under study is that it is possible to obtain a greater amount of relevant data in a shorter period of time than would otherwise be possible. In just a few sessions the children in the diagnostic groups described by Churchill are confronted with a variety of situations which expose them to different demands and opportunities and require the use of different social and physical skills. It might take many days of studying the child at play in his own neighborhood to observe the same reactions and coping mechanisms.[16] Watzlawick has noted that those who have used his structured family interview report that in one hour they can identify typical patterns of family interaction which usually require 5 to 10 hours of conventional interviewing. In structuring the data collection situation, the worker creates situations instead of waiting for them to occur spontaneously. In effect, the sample of behaviors the worker can study in a given time period is increased.

To structure the system under study requires that the worker have a good understanding of the kinds of things he wants to look for and the kinds of situations or tasks that are likely to produce that kind of data. Preplanning can make the worker more sensitive to what is occurring in the system under study.

Depending on the purposes of the worker, structuring the system under study is not always desirable, however. For example, if the worker is interested in the classroom behavior of the child, it would probably be best to observe the child in his class rather than to create a simulated experience. However, the worker's access to this kind of daily life experience of the system under study may be limited.

Regardless of the extent to which the system under study is structured, there is also the issue of how structured the method of recording data should be. This can range from subjective impressions of the worker to systematic recording of what is heard, observed, or read. The schedule used by Lewis in observing the furnishings of a household and the schedule of items used in abstracting data from committee meeting minutes are some examples of systematic recording of data we have discussed above.

The main advantages to systematic recording are that it helps keep the worker focused on what he is looking for and can provide some objective evidence on what he has found. A lot of data can be missed if he is not looking for it. On the other hand, a particular data collection instrument can act as a blinder, keeping him focused on too nar-

---

16 Churchill, "Social Group Work."

row a field. Much depends on the purpose of the worker. A predetermined system for recording presupposes he has an adequate frame of reference for looking at the data. A new worker may want to observe a staff meeting or a committee meeting with no particular set of variables in mind, but rather to get a "feel" for the group and how it operates. Later he may want to focus on some particular aspect of the group's interaction. But suppose a worker is evaluating the effectiveness of a treatment program to increase the attentive behavior of a child in a classroom by observing his behavior before and after treatment. There would be more confidence in an evaluation based on comparisons of the frequency of attentive behavior acts as recorded on an observational form than one based on the worker's subjective impression of the differences in the child's behavior.

A fifth consideration in planning a data collection strategy is the nature of the demands it places on the system under study. Some techniques, such as the use of existing written material, require little or no participation from the system under study, while others, such as a survey of day-care needs in a community or a structured family interview, make great demands in terms of time and involvement. In selecting a data collection technique the worker should anticipate the effects it might have on those being studied. Of course, much will depend on whether the system under study views the demands as legitimate and reasonable and on the kind of relationship (collaborative, bargaining, or conflictual) which exists between the worker and those from whom he is gathering data. An absentee landlord will not be likely to volunteer information about the properties he owns in an interview with the head of a tenant's union. This data will have to be secured through other sources, such as mortgage and tax records.

Of concern also is the effect the data collection techniques used by the worker will have on his current and future relationships with the systems under study. Thus the worker who studied the decision-making structure of the community action commission board through use of meeting minutes wanted to avoid interviewing the board members at this point so as not to raise any suspicions or antagonize anyone. He wanted to leave the door open for future collaborative relationships.

The worker may intentionally or unintentionally exert influence on the system under study. Sometimes this influence is meant only to serve data collection goals. For example, in an interview conducted for the purpose of gathering information, the interviewer may plan his introduction and the way questions are formulated in a way designed to increase the interviewee's motivation to participate and lower his defensiveness. In this case, the influence exerted by the interviewer is directed toward increasing the flow of valid information during the interview. He may have no intention of changing the interviewee's behavior or attitudes in any way. Similarly, Churchill, in working with the diagnostic groups discussed above, had no interest in the group per se, or even in changing the behavior of the children while they are in these groups. But she did exert influence on them through her planful structuring of the group sessions, in order to get a better picture of each child.[17]

Some data collection strategies are designed with a dual purpose—not only to collect data but also to accomplish some change goals. The worker may help organize a neighborhood survey to collect data on problems in the community, but he may also be using the survey as a means to stimulate an awareness of existing problems, provide a new neighborhood group with a task which can give it a feeling of accomplishment, and help the group members learn some organizational skills and develop broader contacts in the community. Or a worker may involve a mother in keeping record of certain behaviors of her child, not only to collect data with which he can evaluate the intervention plan, but also to encourage the mother to assume more responsibility for dealing with the child's problems. The structured family interview described above may force family members to examine the family dynamics and begin to listen to each other's views. Similarly, in a role play used by the worker to collect data, the participants may begin to see certain problems from a new perspective. The mere fact of participating in an interview may help the respondent think through a problem he has been having difficulties with. Thus the worker's data collection activities should be viewed in the context of the goals in the entire planned change process.

A final consideration in planning a data collection strategy is the fact that the worker's biases and theoretical orientations can color his data collection efforts. The worker's data is the raw material for his problem assessment. However, because of the selectivity which must go into data collection (there is no way to collect all possible information about a given person or situation), it is all too easy for the worker

---

[17] Regardless of his intentions, the influence exerted by the worker in the course of collecting data may have beneficial or harmful side effects. For example, a lonely elderly widow interviewed in a survey of housing needs in the community may feel much better after the interview because it gave her a chance to visit with someone. For another aging respondent the interview might have the opposite effect, leaving her depressed because it made her more aware of the poor housing conditions in which she is living.

to collect data to support preconceived assessments and decisions. For example, once a person receives a label such as "psychotic" or "slow learner," his subsequent behaviors are often interpreted to confirm these labels. Similar behaviors displayed by persons not suspected of being "psychotic" or "slow learners" might well go unnoticed or give no cause for concern. There is a story of a newspaper reporter who got himself admitted as a patient in a mental hospital in order to write a story about the hospital. After finishing his story he revealed his true identity to the staff and asked to be released. His behavior was taken by the staff as further evidence of his mental illness, and the more he protested, the more sure the staff members were that they were right. After much trouble, his editor finally got him released. Or take the classic example of the psychoanalytic patient who comes late for his therapy session. The therapist can take this behavior as evidence of the patient's resistance to treatment. If the patient tries to explain his lateness, this is taken as further evidence of resistance. In other words, once the worker has set his framework, any data collected can support his assumptions. This is the basis for the so-called self-fulfilling prophecy.

The same holds true for the community worker. A worker who starts out to demonstrate that certain conditions exist in a community or that people hold certain attitudes can easily manipulate a community study or other data collection device to substantiate his initial assumptions. A worker seeking to generate conflict will probably be able to come up with data to highlight the polarity of opposing positions, while the worker seeking to restore communication and effect a consolidation will find data to highlight areas of agreement and consensus.[18]

Thus the social worker faces a dilemma in the data collection process. On the one hand, he must be selective in how he collects his data and approach the process with some orientation and assumptions to guide his effort. On the other hand, his orientation and assumptions can operate to bias and distort the data collection process to such an extent that all objectivity is lost. The worker must keep flexible enough to disregard his assumptions when they are not substantiated by the data, instead of building rigid frameworks which effectively filter out any data not supporting his original assumptions.

---

[18] Even the data collection of the researcher, who is supposed to typify dispassionate, objective inquiry in pursuit of knowledge, is often subjected to bias of values and personal interest. See Alvin W. Gouldner, "Anti-Minotaur: The Myth of a Value-Free Sociology," in Warren Bennis, Kenneth Benne, and Robert Chin, *The Planning of Change,* 2d ed. (New York: Holt, Rinehart & Winston, Inc., 1969), pp. 604–18.

CHAPTER 8

Contact is the initial engagement or coming together of a worker and a potential or actual client, action, or target system. This first encounter may occur when the system seeks out the worker on its own or through a referral by a third party. Often the worker himself will make the initial contact.

Throughout any change process, the social worker will ordinarily make initial contacts with several people. As a change effort unfolds, contact will have to be established with potential members of an action system, additional potential clients, and target systems. Since making contact is a method goal of the worker, those who are viewed as potential members of action, client, or target systems in relation to the *outcome* goals of the worker are also actual members of a target system in relation to this particular *method* goal.

This chapter will be concerned with how the worker initiates contact with other systems. After discussing reasons why the worker may have to initiate contact, the chapter will examine the motivating and resistance forces that influence people's decisions about becoming involved in a change effort. Determining what part of a system to contact and methods of initiating contact will be the topics of the final sections.

REASONS FOR INITIATING CONTACT

The social interactional view of social work practice emphasizes the importance of intervening in the many systems connected to a social problem. Although one system may seek help from a social worker (a mother with a child who is having problems with school) in order to help the client system, the worker probably will have to reach out to make contact with other systems (the school). Further, when one part of a system (one marriage partner, one member of an organization) seeks help, the worker must reach out to make contact with other system members. Thus, in helping a client system, the worker will have to initiate contact with several people and involve them in the change effort. Indeed, the major functions of social work are aimed at enhancing interactions of people between and within systems to provide them with resources, services, and opportunities.

While there is little debate among social workers about the necessity for initiating contacts with potential action and target system members, there are differences of opinion in the profession about reaching out to offer services to potential client systems.

Reasons for Not Reaching Out to Potential Clients

Some workers and agencies believe they should concentrate their change efforts with people who ask for help. Although they often have been criticized for doing this,[1] there are several reasons why they might resist reaching out to people who do not seek help.

Some social workers and other change agents believe they cannot help an individual or family that is not ready to engage in an introspective change effort or is not faced with a crisis that forces it to be

---

[1] For example, Richard Cloward and Irwin Epstein charge that private agencies used to discriminate between the morally worthy and the unworthy poor, but they now discriminate between the psychologically accessible, motivated poor and the unaccessible, nonmotivated poor. They suggest that agencies have substituted a middle-class mental hygiene view for the former middle-class morality view. See Richard A. Cloward and Irwin Epstein, "Private Social Welfare's Disengagement from the Poor: The Case of Family Adjustment Agencies," in Mayer Zald (ed.), *Social Welfare Institutions* (New York: John Wiley & Sons, Inc., 1965), pp. 623-44.

motivated to seek help. This thinking may stem from the theoretical orientation of change agents who hold that individuals develop problems because they have anxieties and tensions stemming from early-life experiences which are magnified in their present social interactions. Workers with this orientation may believe that individuals will benefit from a relationship with a worker which will help them develop insight into their problems; thus they may prefer verbal clients who are motivated to enter into an introspective change effort because they expect to find the problem rooted in themselves. Similarly, these agents believe they can best help an organization or a community to change when key people within these systems recognize that problems exist and express an interest in working to solve them. As a practical matter, the need for change agents to be paid salaries may force them to concentrate on organizations and groups that recognize a need for change and are willing to pay for it.

Further, the middle-class taxpayers or donors who pay for social work services may question the necessity of spending money to reach out to people who do not ask for help. Peter Marris and Martin Rein suggest that since social service agencies are in competition for middle-class financial support through taxes and contributions, they prefer to avoid public controversy while engaging in prestigeful activities and providing services for a motivated middle-class clientele.[2] Bredemeier goes further, to argue that since agencies need to prove to the public their effectiveness and efficiency, they are under pressure to undertake "easy" problems. Reaching out to severely socially handicapped people may be too costly to agencies in terms of time, effort, and ingenuity.[3] The tendency of agencies to avoid controversy that jeopardizes their financial support also inhibits some social workers from reaching out in attempts to change community organizations and institutions, to work for new legislation, or to improve neighborhood conditions.

Finally, it has been suggested that reaching out and offering service to people robs them of their dignity and self-respect and denies them their right of self-determination.[4] Irving Piliavin believes that "however benign its intent, the intrusion of social workers into the private

[2] Peter Marris and Martin Rein, *Dilemmas of Social Reform* (New York: Atherton Press, 1967).

[3] Harry C. Bredemeier, "The Socially Handicapped and the Agencies," in Frank Riessman, Jerome Cohen, and Arthur Pearl (eds.), *Mental Health of the Poor* (New York: Free Press, 1964), p. 108.

[4] For discussion of the value dilemmas inherent in the principle of self-determination, see Chapter 2.

lives of clients without their request is an infringement of the client's constitutional rights."[5] Henry Miller maintains that social workers often impose unsolicited advice on others who believe they are not free to reject the advice—for example, a public assistance recipient who fears his grant will be withdrawn, a parolee who fears he may be sent back to prison, or a patient in a mental institution.[6]

In summary, some social workers believe they should concentrate their services on people who ask for help rather than reaching out to those who do not actively seek it. They believe they can be of most assistance to people who are motivated to seek help on their own and that offering services to people who do not ask for it may deny them their rights of self-determination. Further, they do not wish to jeopardize their middle-class financial support. Social workers and agencies with these points of view appear to be motivated by commitment to their view of social work practice, a desire to rely on preferred theoretical orientations and known expertise, concern for the needs and rights of other people, and fear of losing community support.

Reasons for Reaching Out to Potential Clients

Despite the reasons cited above that oppose the social work practice of reaching out to offer help to potential client systems, there are also justifications for it. Some social workers reach out to contact people and offer help because they believe the major problems of people, especially the poor, are caused by conditions in their social environment. They believe they must contact these people and initiate efforts to change societal systems. When people are helped to change their institutions, their problem-solving and coping capacities can be enhanced. For example, some social workers believe, along with some social scientists, that the poor have problems because they are without power to control their lives and have no hopes of improving their condition. These workers believe the poor can achieve a different self-image, gain hope, and change their lives by working together on common problems.[7] Because they do not expect low-income people to be motivated

---

[5] Irving Piliavin, "Restructuring the Provision of Social Services," *Social Work*, 13 (January 1968): 37.

[6] Henry Miller, "Value Dilemmas in Social Casework," *Social Work*, 13 (January 1968): 27–33.

[7] For discussion on this point of view, see Warren C. Haggstrom, "The Power of the Poor," and Rudolph Wittenberg, "Personality Adjustment through Social Action," in Riessman, Cohen, and Pearl, *Mental Health of the Poor*, pp. 205–23 and 378–92.

to seek help except in urgent situations, they reach out to contact them and urge them to join membership groups and organizations (welfare rights groups, tenants' unions, neighborhood organizations) to work for improvements in their lives.

The social worker's concern with helping people realize their aspirations and values also leads him to reach out to individuals, families, organizations, and communities that have problems but may not know or believe they can be helped or know where they can obtain help; indeed, they may not want help.

Walter Haas, in a report on a New York City Youth Board project to seek out and help low-income problem families, discusses how a reaching-out approach may, in fact, enhance an individual's right of self-determination, as well as helping him cope with severe problems. Haas notes that people who are desperately in need of help may not know of the existence of a helping agency or may be unable to ask for help; thus they do not have a fair opportunity to decide if they want it. He believes that social workers, by reaching out to these people, can protect their right of self-determination by giving them a real opportunity to make a decision based on firsthand knowledge of the service and the willingness of the worker to work with them.[8]

Rachel Levine argues that the poor have never really had any options to choose services they consider useful, and their rejection of service is not a choice but a repudiation of services they consider irrelevant to their problems.[9]

Low-income people are not the only ones who may need help in obtaining service. A study of 426 depressed white patients from hospitals in 10 communities found that almost two thirds of the depressed patients had required some form of external support or assistance in seeking care.[10]

Social workers also may reach out to people in membership organizations and community groups and societal systems to help them realize their aspirations. Examples are a social worker offering to serve as a consultant to a welfare rights group, a school social worker reaching out to teachers to help them recognize and deal with disruptive children, or a social worker organizing a council of people from different

[8] Walter Haas, "Reaching Out—A Dynamic Concept in Casework," *Social Work*, 4 (July 1959): 41–45.

[9] Rachel A. Levine, "Consumer Participation in Planning and Evaluation of Mental Health Services," *Social Work*, 15 (April 1970): 41.

[10] Julian C. Hall, Kathleen Smith, and Anna K. Bradley, "Delivering Mental Health Services to the Urban Poor," *Social Work*, 15 (April 1970): 35–39.

agencies working with the mentally retarded or helping to form a neighborhood organization.

A commitment to help people fulfill their aspirations and values also leads social workers to reach out with preventive programs. These may range from case-finding efforts at early detection and treatment of handicapped people to alerting the community to conditions that create problems for people.

Another major reason for reaching out to people may be a joint community and professional concern for control of deviant or undesirable behavior that threatens the well-being of individuals or the well-being of the entire community. This social control function of social work was discussed in Chapter 1. Some social agencies are mandated by law to reach out to protect specific people, such as state agencies that perform licensing functions for nursing homes, children's institutions, day-care centers and other services. Such agencies as neighborhood centers, community mental health services, and hospital community programs have asked for and received sanction and support from public or voluntary funding sources to reach out to people whose behavior may be damaging to themselves and others.

To summarize, some social workers and their agencies reach out to offer services to potential client systems because they believe their services can help reduce the powerlessness of the disadvantaged. Further, they believe that people can more meaningfully exercise their self-determination and realize their aspirations if they are made aware of resource systems and provided the opportunity to utilize them. Finally, an obligation to protect the well-being of individuals and the welfare of the community can lead social workers to initiate contact with potential clients.

A key issue between the position of social workers who do and do not believe in reaching out to potential clients is where they draw the line between offering and imposing (requiring the acceptance of) their services. This is a value dilemma which was discussed in Chapter 2. Differences in varying views of social work practice, theoretical orientations, and sanctions received from the community that supports the social workers and their agencies seems to lead to differences in how the value dilemmas are resolved in the mind of the social worker.

MOTIVATIONS AND RESISTANCES TO CHANGE

When the social worker is initiating contact with potential client, action, or target systems, all parties may be ambivalent about beginning a change effort. In their analysis of social change efforts, Ronald Lippitt, Jeanne Watson, and Bruce Westley found that forces were operating in each system at the beginning of change efforts that both motivated people to change and caused them to resist it.[11] In fact, as Ruth Smalley points out, any beginning, any new undertaking in life, causes simultaneous feelings of hope and of fear.[12]

Thus, in order to engage people in change efforts, the social worker will need to analyze their perception of the *benefits* they believe will accrue to them from the change effort and what they believe the change effort will *cost* them. The worker can use his analysis of the target systems' perceptions of costs and benefits to plan a strategy for contact that will stimulate positive motivations and reduce or minimize resistance forces.[13]

Forces Encouraging Resistance

Several forces that may lead individuals, groups, organizations, and communities to resist change efforts have been identified. These are (1) reluctance to accept help, (2) fear of loss of position or resources, (3) belief that change is impossible, (4) reluctance to devote time, (5) practical barriers to participation, and (6) uncertainty.

RELUCTANCE TO ACCEPT HELP. People may be reluctant to admit they need help from an outsider or may believe receiving help is a sign of weakness. It is not difficult to imagine the fears of an individual, family, or small local organization with a problem that is about to become involved with a social worker and thinks it will be the target of change. These potential clients may be afraid of identifying themselves as inadequate and may fear rejection by others because of their inadequacies.[14]

---

[11] Ronald Lippitt, Jeanne Watson, and Bruce Westley, *The Dynamics of Planned Change* (New York: Harcourt, Brace & World, 1958), p. 72.

[12] Ruth Smalley, *Theory for Social Work Practice* (New York: Columbia University Press, 1967), p. 142.

[13] For discussion of motivating and resistance forces, see Irving N. Berlin, "Resistance to Change in Mental Health Professionals," *American Journal of Orthopsychiatry*, 39 (January 1969): 109–15; Robert Morris and Robert Binstock, *Feasible Planning for Social Change* (New York: Columbia University Press, 1966); Goodwin Watson, "Resistance to Change," in Warren G. Bennis, Kenneth D. Benne, and Robert Chin (eds.), *The Planning of Change*, 2d ed. (New York: Holt, Rinehart & Winston, Inc., 1969), pp. 488–97; and Lippitt, Watson, and Westley, *Dynamics of Planned Change*, pp. 72–89 and 179–82.

[14] See David Landy, "Problems of the Person Seeking Help in Our Culture," in *Social Welfare Forum, 1960* (New York: Columbia University Press, 1960), pp. 127–44, for a discussion of attitudes of potential agency clients.

Aaron Rosenblatt suggests that middle-class people who have accepted the American cultural norm of independence will have difficulty accepting the status of client.[15] A person who needs financial assistance is exposed to this middle-class norm through the attitudes of neighbors and shopkeepers; the staffs of hospitals, schools, and other societal systems; and the mass media. Thus the attitudes of low-income people toward receiving help from a social worker or social agency can be expected to range from feelings of humiliation and embarrassment at having to ask for help, to anger and hostility directed at a society that has victimized them and at the workers and agencies that are a part of this society.

Members of groups and organizations that need consultation and assistance from an outside change agent also may believe that acceptance of help will indicate weakness and reflect on their own competence and status. Irving Berlin points out that professional workers themselves often resist considering new methods of work that might threaten their personal satisfaction, which is dependent upon their self-concepts of expertise and effectiveness.[16] Workers may be hesitant to try different theoretical orientations, such as transactional analysis or crisis intervention, because they are reluctant to admit a need for consultation and help in using them.

FEAR OF LOSS OF POSITION OR RESOURCES. A major resistance force that is related to reluctance to admit weakness is the fear that a change effort will disrupt current positions and roles within a system, causing more loss than gain in prestige, power, or money. This factor was discussed in Chapter 4's consideration of collaborative, bargaining, and conflictual relationships. People in organizations will resist change efforts they perceive as threatening their financial resources, their claim to an area of expertise, or their jurisdiction over a specialized territory or service.[17]

Further, dominant factions in social agencies can be expected to resist change efforts that threaten their internal structure of authority and other bureaucratic procedures.[18] These agencies are social entities

---

[15] Aaron Rosenblatt, "The Application of Role Concepts to the Intake Process," *Social Casework*, 43 (January 1962): 8–14.

[16] Berlin, "Resistance to Change," p. 110.

[17] See Bredemeier, "Socially Handicapped and the Agencies," pp. 88–109; Marris and Rein, *Dilemmas of Social Reform*, p. 45; and Berlin, "Resistance to Change," pp. 109–15.

[18] For discussion, see Robert E. Vinter, "The Social Structure of Service," in Edwin J. Thomas (ed.), *Behavioral Science for Social Workers* (New York: Free Press, 1967), pp. 193–206; and Harold L. Wilensky and Charles N. Lebeaux, *Industrial Society and Social Welfare* (New York: Russell Sage Foundation, 1958), chap. 10.

in which role behavior for all components (staff, board, consumers, members) is prescribed, patterns of internal and external communication are stabilized, and lines of authority are established. Any change efforts that appear to threaten the existing equilibrium of an agency will be resisted by those in the organization who are satisfied and comfortable with the status quo.

Social workers and other change agents also may resist change efforts that require them to be in conflict with their own agency policy. The vast majority of social workers is employed by agencies, and in many respects these professionals do not function as individual entrepreneurs or free agents. It has been pointed out that social workers often are caught between the requirements of their agencies and the service commitments of the profession of social work.[19] Fear of disrupting agency patterns and possibly losing status, promotions, and even the job itself may cause social workers to resist involvement in change efforts that set them against their own agency policies. Andrew Billingsley found that social workers in a family counseling agency who had to choose between conflicting expectations were influenced by agency policies, professional standards, client needs, and the demands of the community, *in that order*.[20]

Members of families and small groups also may exhibit resistance to change because of fear of change in satisfying roles and positions within a system. Thus family members who are content with their present positions in relation to other members may resist change efforts that threaten to alter the existing patterns of family decision making and communication, and the leaders of a youth group may fear an erosion of their position if a social worker becomes attached to the group.

A proposed change that would require a person to give up attitudes, beliefs, and behavior patterns that he has held and used for a long time can be expected to be resisted because admission that the change is needed would imply that he has been wrong for years. Thus a professional worker, a member of a family, the executive of an agency, or a board of directors may resist any proposed change they believe reflects adversely on their past actions and statements.

BELIEF THAT CHANGE IS IMPOSSIBLE. A third factor causing people to

---

[19] See Andrew Billingsley, "Bureaucratic and Professional Orientation Patterns in Social Casework," *Social Service Review*, 38 (December 1964), pp. 400–407; George A. Brager, "Institutional Change: Perimeters of the Possible," *Social Work*, 12 (January 1967): 59–69; Mayer N. Zald, "Organizations as Polities: An Analysis of Community Organization Agencies," in Fred M. Cox et al., *Strategies of Community Organization: A Book of Readings* (Itasca, Ill.: F. E. Peacock Publishers, Inc., 1970), pp. 91–100; and Vinter, "Social Structure of Service."
[20] Billingsley, "Bureaucratic and Professional Orientation."

resist change is fear that they will not be able to follow through on the change effort because they lack the ability to perform as the effort requires and believe that change is impossible. An unemployed man who is urged to enroll in a training program to acquire specialized job skills may fear he will fail. A neighborhood group may believe it lacks the ability to acquire the expertise in housing and zoning ordinances and federal, state, and local housing development programs that is required to achieve changes in a deteriorating neighborhood. A shy, withdrawn teen-ager may believe he will be an outcast in a teen club.

A belief that change is impossible may create apathy and hopelessness. People who think their problems are caused by conditions in society and the attitudes and practices of societal institutions may assume they can't "fight city hall" or "change the system."

The resistance of people to change because of feelings of hopelessness may be intensified if, when they previously sought help from "helping" people, they met with failures. Individuals and families with problems might first have tried to solve their problems themselves and then turned to neighbors and friends, doctors, lawyers, employers, labor union counselors—even bartenders—before they arrive at a social agency. As the case study by Hoffman and Long in Part III illustrates, one family in its attempts to find help might deal with many social workers. In a discussion of the need for multiservice neighborhood centers, Michael March describes graphically what can happen to a family that attempts to find its way through a maze of specialized service organizations in the community.[21]

Groups or organizations that have been engaged in change efforts that have failed may also be resistant to further suggestions for change. The apathy toward change that exists in some neighborhoods and among some problem populations may have been magnified by unsuccessful previous attempts by change agents to organize them and seek problem solutions. Citizens who have served on community committees or public commissions whose recommendations were ignored may decline to join another such action system.

RELUCTANCE TO DEVOTE TIME. People will resist change if they perceive that they do not have the time to become involved in a change effort or do not wish to take the time to become involved. Even though a system may agree with or be neutral toward an outcome goal of the worker, it may not give it a high priority in relation to the time devoted to other interests.

---

[21] Michael March, "The Neighborhood Center Concept," *Public Welfare*, April 1968, pp. 97–111.

PRACTICAL BARRIERS TO PARTICIPATION. Allied with lack of time to become involved are practical barriers to participation such as lack of money or physical impairment. An employed father may not be able to afford to take time off from work to meet with a school social worker, attend a neighborhood meeting, or pay a fee for family counseling. A young mother may not have money for baby-sitters or carfare to attend a parent's meeting. An aged or physically handicapped person may not be able to leave his house or his room in a nursing home.

UNCERTAINTY. A resistance force which in a sense may embody all of the others named above is uncertainty about what the change effort will entail and hesitance about embarking on an unknown undertaking. This uncertainty may accompany all of the other forces making for resistance: reluctance to accept help; fear that a change effort will disrupt current satisfying positions and roles and cause part of a system or a whole system to lose resources; belief that change is impossible to achieve; hesitancy or inability to give time to the change effort; and the existence of realistic barriers to participation. All or some of these resistance forces may operate in any potential client, target, or action system.

Motivating Forces

Several forces may motivate individuals, groups, organizations, and communities to become involved in change efforts. These are (1) willingness to accept help, (2) desire to gain position or resources, (3) belief that change is possible, (4) relief from discomfort, (5) response to constraints, and (6) altruism. Some of these forces motivating people to change are the reverse of those causing resistance to change.

WILLINGNESS TO ACCEPT HELP. Instead of thinking that asking for help is a sign of weakness, some systems may believe it is a sign of strength to obtain outside assistance to improve their functioning. These systems are willing to accept help. Organizations may ask for consultation to improve internal communications and productivity. Groups may ask for advice on problem solving. At one time youth gangs in New York City considered it a sign of status to have a youth worker make contact with them. In some areas it may become the fashion or the norm to join sensitivity groups and enter into psychotherapy or group marital counseling.

DESIRE TO GAIN POSITION OR RESOURCES. Secondly, people may be motivated to embark on change efforts because they believe they will gain something (position, power, money, increased clientele, expertise) through the change effort or, at the minimum, protect their own interests. Many community organizations and institutions commit them-selves to poverty or health-planning programs because they think they can acquire new facilities and financial resources and protect their present programs in these areas. People in organizations, communities, families, and groups may welcome change efforts they believe will enhance their current status and power positions. A potential member of a community action system may agree to participate because he believes membership will enhance his prestige in the community and enable him to meet influential people.

In their review of change efforts, Lippitt, Watson, and Westley found many cases where systems were motivated to ask for or accept offered help because of the possibility of improvements in their every-day functioning.[22] An organization may ask for a consultant to advise it on ways to improve its services to clients. A family may attend family-life education programs. A social worker may cooperate in a research project or enroll in an institute to study new theories of family counseling or urban planning.

BELIEF THAT CHANGE IS POSSIBLE. People may be willing to embark on a change effort if they believe the change goals can be achieved. People who have had successful experiences with change efforts or know others who have done so may be motivated to embark on new efforts, if they agree with the change goals, because they have at least a beginning trust in change agents. Systems that have not been involved in change efforts that affected them directly may engage in change efforts with a social worker they have met in other situations. A person with a problem may ask for help from a neighborhood-center worker he has met at neighborhood meetings and activities. Organizations and community groups will more readily embark on change efforts with a social worker with a community-planning agency who has established good professional relationships with individuals, groups, and organiza-tions and is trusted and perceived as being a helpful person.

In addition to the motivating forces that are comparable to some of the resistance forces discussed in the previous section, there are other potent motivating forces.

RELIEF FROM DISCOMFORT. One of these motivating forces is hope for relief from discomfort, pain, or dissatisfaction with the current situation. The strength of this force will vary according to the urgency of the need for help. Situations that a potential client system would define as urgent could include: a financially destitute family in which the adults cannot find full employment, an unmarried woman 12 weeks

---

[22] Lippitt, Watson, and Westley, *Dynamics of Planned Change*, p. 160.

pregnant who is seeking an abortion, a city council aroused over an outbreak of violence and strife between police and citizens in a particular neighborhood, or an aged person who has suffered a stroke and can no longer live independently. In these cases, the situation of the potential client system may be so desperate it demands immediate help.

In other situations, the problems may have existed for a long time, and the request for help may have resulted from one or two precipitating incidents—the straw that broke the camel's back. For example, for parents aware that their young son has difficulty controlling sudden outbursts of temper, a call from an irate neighbor complaining that their son has beaten his child might firm up a decision to seek help. A hospital administrator may realize that many patients and their families have social and emotional problems stemming from the patients' illnesses, but he may delay consulting a health planning agency for aid in establishing hospital social work services until a particularly difficult situation comes to his attention.

RESPONSE TO CONSTRAINTS. Another motivation for agreeing to enter into a change effort is a response to the existence of real or imagined constraints that appear to force participation. Parents accused of child abuse may agree to cooperate with a social worker for fear of losing custody of their children. A voluntary agency director may agree to a change of policy strongly recommended by a United Fund because he fears losing financial support. A politician may agree to demands from an organized group of his constituents for fear of losing their support.

ALTRUISM. Finally, people may be motivated to accept involvement in a change effort they perceive will benefit others out of a spirit of altruism or concern for the needs of others. Their motive may be a desire to be a good citizen and to make a contribution to their community.

In summary, forces motivating people to change include: willingness to accept help from a change agent; a desire to gain position, power, money, or other resources; belief that change is possible to achieve; hope for relief from present discomfort, pain, or dissatisfaction; responses to constraints that force participation, and a spirit of altruism.

WHAT PART OF THE SYSTEM TO CONTACT

When a worker is reaching out, his method goal is to make contact with the system and engage it in change efforts. Thus, for this goal, the worker considers the system he is contacting the target system.

His first task is to decide what part or parts of the system to contact to begin the change effort. He may be reaching out to a multiple-person system (family, neighborhood group, another community agency or institution) or trying to make contact with other systems connected to an ongoing change effort. If the worker is proposing a change that will have an impact on the functioning of the entire system, he can expect to find resistance and motivating forces operating within the many subparts of the system. He will want to make his contacts with those parts that can exert influence within the entire system to reduce resistance and enhance motivations for change.

Lippitt, Watson, and Westley discuss the importance of selecting for a first contact people who can serve as a leverage point with other parts of the system. The leverage point, which must be accessible to the influence of the change agent, must also be linked to other parts of the target system and able to influence these other parts.[23] Robert Morris and Robert Binstock have advanced the concept of dominant factions in organizations, which may be a board of directors, an executive, the staff, the clientele, or the membership.[24] A worker who wants to make contact with an organization in a major change effort that will affect the whole organization will need to locate a leverage person who is part of the dominant faction or can influence that faction. However, the worker contacting a member of an organization to perform a function that is part of the agency's established operating procedures and will not require a change in organization policy, need not necessarily select such a person for contact.

The concept of a leverage person also is helpful when the social worker is considering forming an action system composed of representatives of various community organizations. The worker may ask each organization to select or elect a representative, or he may select someone he thinks will be a good leverage person from the organization, one who will bring the organization's thinking to the action system, take the thinking of the action system back to the organization, and, perhaps, influence his organization to change.

If the task of the proposed action system is considered by an organization to be crucial to the organization's interest, it probably will select a good representative leverage person. Experience with low-income and minority groups and special-interest organizations (senior citizens, welfare rights, migrant organizations) often indicates these "low status" organizations should select their own representatives to an action system whose purpose is of high priority to them. Representa-

---

[23] Lippitt, Watson, and Westley, *Dynamics of Planned Change*, pp. 100–4.
[24] Morris and Binstock, *Feasible Planning for Social Change*, pp. 102–4.

tives so chosen will feel they have the strength of their organizations behind them. Not only will they represent their organizations' interests, but they will be able to influence their own organization when this is appropriate. If representatives are selected by someone outside their own organizations, they may not be representative of their groups and may be co-opted by other members of the action system. However, whether the organization the worker wants representation from has high or low status, if the purpose of the proposed action system is not of high priority to the organization, it is likely to send a representative who has little status in it.

A leverage person also can be important when a social worker is contacting potential client systems such as a family; in some cultural groups it may be more appropriate to make the first contact with the husband, in others, with the wife. Making contact with the influentials in peer groups of children and teen-agers can facilitate change in the functioning of the groups. In studying strategies developed by social workers reaching out to tenants of slum hotels in New York City, it was found that some of these workers try to locate, contact, and involve dominant individuals. Others try to identify and contact subgroups and interest them in working on a special activity which could attract the participation of other residents.[25]

The social worker may need to approach several different factions in an existing group, institution, or organization and use a multiple-entry strategy, as suggested by Lippitt, Watson, and Westley.[26] It may be important that a proposal for change is not associated exclusively with any one part of a system, especially if all subparts have to agree to, and cooperate with, the proposed change and there is no dominant faction that can gain ready acceptance for it. Thus the change agent may need to identify leverage people in several different factions for his first contacts.

METHODS OF INITIATING CONTACT

After the social worker has decided on the most effective person to contact, he can choose an approach from a variety of methods.[27] He

[25] Joan Shapiro, "Group Work With Urban Rejects in A Slum Hotel," in *Social Work Practice, 1967* (New York: Columbia University Press, 1967), pp. 148–64.
[26] Lippitt, Watson, and Westley, *Dynamics of Planned Change*, pp. 82 and 117.
[27] Eugene Litwak and Henry Meyer, in "A Balance Theory of Coordination between Bureaucratic Organizations and Community Primary Groups," *Administrative Science Quarterly*, 11 (June 1966): 31–58, identify eight approaches a formal

will be aided in this choice by assessing the specific motivations and resistances of his target system toward his change effort and utilizing a change effort that will help reduce the resistance and enhance the motivations.

Social workers themselves may directly approach a potential client system—they can stop in to see a nursing home patient, knock on the door of a family known to have many problems, or ask for an appointment with the president of a newly formed neighborhood group. In regard to their outcome goals, they can approach a target system by contacting a city housing inspector, the chairman of a county or city public welfare commission, or the director of a social agency. They can also approach a potential member of an action system, through talking to a school principal, a prominent businessman, the chairman of a welfare rights group, or another social worker.

This method, in which the social worker himself makes contact, is appropriate under certain circumstances. It will be effective if the target system believes it is a sign of strength to obtain outside assistance or that it will gain something from the change effort. It will also work if the target system has had successful experiences with this social worker or other change agents or is dissatisfied with its current situation. It can even be effective if the system feels forced to participate or is motivated to cooperate with the social worker out of a desire to exhibit good citizenship.

However, if none of these motivating forces is operating, it may be more practicable for the social worker to ask someone who has influence with the system to be contacted and can help reduce its resistances to make the first contact. He could ask someone with higher status than either himself or the target system or someone who has had a previous positive experience with the target system to do this.

For example, a neighborhood-center worker who wants to approach a teen-age group of boys may ask the proprietor of the boys' favorite neighborhood hangout, who is accepted by them, to introduce him to the members. An agency executive may ask the president of his board of directors, an influential citizen, to approach a city official regarding chairmanship of an agency committee. His help can also be sought in

---

organization might use to achieve contact with families and neighborhood groups. These approaches, which are similar to the methods outlined here and are identified by Litwak and Meyer as "linking mechanisms," are: detached worker, opinion leader, settlement house, voluntary association, common messenger, mass media, formal authority, and delegated function.

interceding with a city department whose operations are imposing hardships on agency clients. A social worker may ask a schoolteacher or a public health nurse to tell children and their families how the social worker can be helpful to them. The report of a project to reach out to families found that one of the most satisfactory approaches was an introduction by a previous worker, provided the family had positive feelings about this worker.[28] It has also been suggested that a doctor's referral of a patient to a hospital social worker may help them achieve a satisfactory working relationship.[29]

Social workers might find it helpful to make a joint contact effort with staff members from other professions who have more status than they do. An example is a program of a mental development center designed to identify and contact mentally retarded children and their parents. If the physician in a hospital pediatric clinic determines that a child might be retarded, the child and his parents are referred to a screening team, composed of a pediatrician, social worker, psychologist, and research assistant.[30]

The approaches described above—asking someone with high status or someone whom the target system has learned to trust to make the first contact—may reduce its resistance. These influentials may be able to assure the target system that the social worker can be helpful, that change is possible, and that the change agent system has the ability to follow through on the change effort. They can persuade the target system that the seeking of help is a sign of strength, not weakness, and that a particular situation can be improved. An approach by someone of higher status than the target system can imply a sense of obligation to do what he suggests, for fear of displeasing the other system.

Another method of making initial contact is through people who themselves are current or recent members of the target population. Agencies have hired former drug addicts, alcoholics, ex-convicts, and poor people to reach out and make the first contact with people like themselves. These indigenous workers serve as a bridge between people with problems and social agencies. Hiring people with problems to help others with similar problems also provides jobs for low-income people and those who have difficulties obtaining them. Such workers

---

[28] Alice Overton and Katherine Tinker, *Casework Notebook* (St. Paul, Minn.: Greater St. Paul United Fund Council, Inc., 1957), p. 34.

[29] Rosenblatt, "Application of Role Concepts," p. 13.

[30] Pearl S. Whitman and Sonya Oppenheimer, "Locating and Treating the Mentally Retarded," *Social Work*, 11 (April 1966): 44–51.

are helped to improve themselves by helping others.[31] A review of the research on the effectiveness of neighborhood centers in low-income areas indicated that poor people employed by the centers changed more than other people served by the centers and that many of the employed poor gained confidence.[32]

Social workers also use indigenous people as volunteers to contact and encourage people to join action systems such as neighborhood organizations,[33] senior citizen groups, or associations of parents of retarded children. Social workers may ask former clients or other agency staff to contact potential clients. For example, in recruitment programs for adoption homes for minority children, child welfare agencies may ask parents who have adopted minority children to contact potential adoptive parents. Agency foster parents often help recruit new foster parents.

The assumptions behind these approaches are that people have influence with those who are similar to themselves because they have first-hand knowledge of the other's problems. They can communicate in the same language about shared experiences and thus can build rapport and feelings of trust.[34] People may be able to motivate others like themselves because they can give concrete examples of how they were helped, can stir up feelings of dissatisfaction with the present situation, and can reduce feelings of helplessness and anxiety about the

---

[31] Frank Riessman, "The Helper Therapy Principle," *Social Work*, 10 (April 1965): 27–32; Rita Volkman and Donald Cressey, "Differential Association and the Rehabilitation of Drug Addicts," in Riessman, Cohen, and Pearl, *Mental Health of the Poor*, pp. 600–619.

[32] Edward J. O'Donnell and Marilyn M. Sullivan, "Service Delivery and Social Action through the Neighborhood Center—A Review of Research," *Welfare in Review*, 7 (November–December 1969): 1–11.

[33] For detailed discussion of organizing efforts in neighborhoods, see Warren C. Haggstrom, "Can the Poor Transform the World?" in Ralph Kramer and Harry Specht (eds.), *Readings in Community Organization Practice* (Englewood Cliffs, N.J.: Prentice-Hall, Inc., 1969), pp. 301–14; Robert Perlman and David Jones, *Neighborhood Service Centers* (Washington, D.C.: Department of Health, Education, and Welfare, 1967), pp. 54–62; Herbert A. Thelen, *Dynamics of Groups at Work* (Chicago: University of Chicago Press, 1954), pp. 3–30.

[34] A review of research studies indicates that the hiring of neighborhood people with whom residents can identify easily makes neighborhood centers more acceptable (O'Donnell and Sullivan, "Service Delivery and Social Action," p. 4). Also see George A. Brager, "The Indigenous Non Professional Worker: A New Approach to the Social Work Technician," *Social Work*, 10 (April 1965):33–35; David A. Hardcastle, "The Indigenous Non Professional in the Social Service Bureaucracy: A Critical Examination," *Social Work*, 16 (April 1971): 56–63; Arthur Pearl and Frank Riessman, *New Careers for the Poor* (New York: Free Press, 1965); and Perlman and Jones, *Neighborhood Service Centers*, pp. 54–62.

feasibility of making changes. However, research summarized by Alfred Kadushin indicates that although agency supervisors believe paraprofessionals can establish rapport with potential clients, other problems may arise because of overidentification, pity, or annoyance with the potential client.[35]

In all the reaching-out approaches in which social workers ask other people to make the first contact, the workers themselves must contact these people and be able to persuade them to in turn contact those whom they want to involve in the change effort. In another type of approach, agencies seek to create a social climate in which people are encouraged to feel comfortable about seeking help. Eugene Litwak and Henry Meyer call this the "settlement house" approach, in which a change-inducing milieu is provided through physical facilities, geographical proximity, and the availability of staff.[36]

Examples of this approach are provided by the development in recent years of teen-age drop-in centers, storefront services for drug addicts and other problem populations, and neighborhood service centers. These programs attempt to maintain a casual informal atmosphere in keeping with the life styles of the potential clients. They are located in areas in which the target population lives, where they can serve as concrete symbols that change from a painful and apparently hopeless situation is possible and help is close at hand. This approach usually is combined with the strategy of using members of the target population as staff members or volunteers.

It has been suggested that social workers can, in effect, reach out to people by locating themselves where people are when they need help and may be facing a crisis in coping with their life tasks.[37] Social workers located in social security offices, unemployment offices, jails and public housing offices could offer services directly to people who already are in contact with a societal resource system. This is being done by social workers in schools, day-care centers, and hospitals. Further, social workers attempt to establish cooperative relationships with societal and membership resource systems that people are likely to turn to for help. Thus, social workers interpret their functions to doc-

---

[35] Alfred Kadushin, "The Racial Factor in the Interview," *Social Work*, 17 (May 1972): 95.

[36] Litwak and Meyer, "Balance Theory of Coordination," p. 40. Also see Lippitt, Watson, and Westley, *Dynamics of Planned Change*, p. 155.

[37] Carol Meyer, *Social Work Practice: A Response to the Urban Crisis* (New York: Free Press, 1970); George Hoshino and Shirley Weber, "Outposting in the Public Welfare Services," *Public Welfare*, 31 (Winter 1973): 8–14.

tors, teachers, ministers, lawyers, public health nurses, police, personnel managers, union counselors, and others to encourage them to refer people in need of social work service.

Another method used by social workers to contact people is the use of publicity or public relations, utilizing mass media, letters, brochures, and other written and oral means of communication. These methods may be aimed at an entire target population, as with newspaper articles about new treatment facilities for alcoholics and their families or a speech at a neighborhood organization meeting describing the services of a neighborhood center. They may also be aimed at specific individuals, as with individualized letters to people in a housing project inviting them to an organization meeting of a tenant's union, letters to legislators asking for support, or pleas to a selected mailing list for financial support.

The use of the mass media alone can generate many agency contacts. Articles and photographs in a Canadian newspaper dealing with hard-to-place children available for adoption resulted in at least 133 adoptions.[38] This approach, however, works only if the target population already is highly motivated toward a change effort and is willing to seek help on its own. For this reason social workers often combine the use of a public relations approach with a personal contact from a social worker or someone who can influence the target population. For example, a mother in a Head Start program may receive a written notice of a parents' meeting and also be contacted personally by another mother, who may work as an aide and who will reinforce the invitation and arrange for a baby-sitter and transportation. The president of an agency board might follow up on fund-raising letters with a personal visit to prospective givers.

When a direct personal contact is not feasible, agencies often try to utilize the personal-influence strategy by having high-status influential people publicly sanction the agency program. Sports celebrities may appear on television to encourage teen-agers to turn off drugs or use local youth centers, or a welfare rights newsletter may use testimonials from individual members describing how the organization has helped them.

After reviewing the effectiveness of different methods used by organizations to contact primary groups, Litwak and Meyer suggested that when an organization is communicating with a resistant primary

---

[38] Irving A. Fellner, "Recruiting Adoptive Applicants," *Social Work*, 13 (January 1968): 92–100.

group, close personal contact is required. They also point out, however, that organizations can reach greater numbers of people by the use of mass media.[39]

We can conclude that if a social worker and his agency wish to make contact with people who are resistant to change efforts, personal contact by a social worker or a person with influence with a target group may be required. However, if the social worker believes a target population is motivated towards his change effort, the use of publicity may be not only appropriate but sufficient. A worker who is not able to identify specific members of his target population may need to rely on the creation of a social climate that will encourage clients to seek help. Most often, social workers use a variation or combination of methods to contact people in order to reach a target group.

---

[39] Litwak and Meyer, "Balance Theory of Coordination," pp. 42–45. For discussion of linking mechanisms between professionals and community organizations, see Eugene Litwak, "An Approach to Linkage in 'Grass Roots' Community Organization," in Fred Cox et al., *Strategies of Community Organization: A Book of Readings* (Itasca, Ill.: F. E. Peacock Publishers, Inc. 1970), pp. 126–138.

CHAPTER 9

NEGOTIATING

CONTRACTS

Once the social worker and another system make contact, his major method goal is to influence people in the other system to become involved in the change effort. His first step in accomplishing this goal is to negotiate a contract with them.

When social workers and other systems begin to work together, all parties bring to the encounter some initial expectations about how they and the others should or will act, and what should or will happen. As people begin to interact with one another, their initial expectations may be modified. Patterns or norms of behavior become established. Understandings develop between the parties about the rules of the game and what they have decided to do (or not to do) together. These understandings result in formal or informal working agreements.

We will refer to these working agreements as *contracts*.[1] We use the term to call attention to the existence of such working agreements between parties in a change effort, whether or not the social worker and the other systems explicitly recognize them. The term also empha-

---

[1] We are indebted to our colleague, Sheldon Rose, for stimulating our thinking about contracts. See Diane F. Kravetz and Sheldon D. Rose, *Contracts in Groups: A Workbook* (Dubuque, Iowa: Kendall-Hunt Publishing Co., 1973).

sizes the contractual nature of the relationships, in which both parties have obligations to fulfill. Thus a contract is not something that the worker imposes on another system. Rather it is the deliberate and conscious articulation and shaping of the informal working agreements that are inherent in all relationships into a form that will facilitate the planned change process.

The process of developing a contract or working agreement will be referred to as *contract negotiation*. The term "negotiation" does not imply that both parties must start out with disagreements, but that each must be open to the other's ideas. Negotiation of a contract means that what will happen between another system and the social worker will be determined by joint agreement.

Social workers use contract negotiation as a major tool in their first contacts with other systems. The initial contacts between a social worker and another system are crucial in establishing a foundation for their future work together. It is in these contacts that the other system is induced to become engaged in the change effort. Several studies indicate that people are likely to continue in the change process when there is agreement between the worker and an individual, family, or group on core problems to be worked on, specific goals, and methods to reach these goals.[2] A genuine transactional agreement involves the other system in the planning of the change effort.

Our belief that people should be considered as clients only when a contract has been established between them and the social worker was set forth in Chapter 3. This contract between worker and client system is the *primary contract*. Workers also form *secondary contracts* with other systems related to the change effort—the action, target, and change agent systems.

The contract between the worker and another system may be negotiated in one meeting, or the negotiation may last for several sessions. A potential client system and a worker may make an initial commitment to explore the terms of the contract together for a few meetings before they decide if they want to work together. Once a contract is negotiated, it does not remain static but can be formally or informally renegotiated several times in a change effort.

---

[2] See Dorwin Cartwright and Alvin Zander, *Group Dynamics*, 3rd ed. (New York: Harper and Row, 1968), p. 228; George Levinger, "Continuance in Casework and Other Helping Relationships: A Review of Current Research," *Social Work*, 5 (July 1960): 40–51; and Jona M. Rosenfeld, "Strangeness between Helper and Client: A Possible Explanation of Non-Use of Available Professional Help," *Social Service Review*, 38 (March 1964): 17–25.

This chapter will first describe and illustrate the nature and content of the contractual agreements between the worker and the different systems with which he works. Then it will investigate techniques employed by workers in the process of contract negotiation and suggest some strategies for dealing with resistance.

NATURE OF CONTRACTS

The basic factors to be agreed upon in contracts between social workers and other systems are:
1. Major goals of the parties.
2. Tasks to be performed by each party to achieve the goals.
3. Operating procedures for the change process.

An essential element of each of these factors is a clear delineation of the responsibility of each party for meeting the terms of the contract. The terms of contracts between social workers and change agent, client, action, and target systems are illustrated below.

With Change Agent Systems

A social worker enters into a contract with a change agent system when he accepts a position. He and his employer agree on the general goals the worker will pursue. In a mental hospital, for example, they may agree that the worker's major goals are to get patients out of the hospital and help them to function in the community so that they need not return to the institution.

The social worker and the hospital further agree on acceptable tasks the worker may perform to achieve these goals. These might include the use of techniques and methods such as behavior modification and insight therapy that derive from particular theoretical orientations. His work could include meeting with patients individually, in small groups, and in ward meetings; working with families of the patients, potential employers, and community agencies; and performing tasks in cooperation with other staff within the hospital. The responsibilities and tasks of other staff members may be outlined to help pinpoint areas that are clearly social work functions, those where other staff has jurisdiction, and those in which responsibilities are shared.

The contract between worker and agency also will include agreement on specific operating procedures, such as salary of the worker and personnel policies of the institution.

The change agent system also has a contract with the community

This contract is established by legislative directives, appropriations from public and voluntary funding sources, management decisions from authorized administrative agencies, and agreements entered into by the agency with community groups and institutions. Mayer Zald suggests that organizations have constitutions which he defines as "basic zones of activity, goals, and norms of procedures and relationships." These constitutions are linked to the constituency and resource base of the organization, but the constituency is not the clientele. Rather, according to Zald, "the term refers to the groups and individuals who control the organization and to whom the agency executive or executive core is most immediately responsible—the board of directors, key legislators, officeholders, major fund-raisers or grantors."[3] Zald maintains that the constitution of an organization is its social contract, which defines its basic purposes and modes of operation.

With Client Systems

The fundamental ingredient in the contract between a worker and a client system is agreement on the goal or goals of the change effort. Tasks and operating procedures flow from these goals. For example, a worker and a family may first agree on a goal of reducing conflicts over acceptable standards of social conduct for the children and then reach agreement on the specific tasks that the parties to the contract will perform to achieve this goal.

The worker agrees to suggest tasks that each family member can perform separately and others that the family can perform together to help them understand their areas of disagreement and agreement. He could suggest, for example, that each family member write down what he thinks are sensible rules for conduct. Family members agree to perform these tasks and report their ideas at their next meeting with the worker. Family members also assume responsibility for suggesting tasks. As the change effort unfolds, other tasks are identified. Family members and worker also agree on operating procedures, including frequency, time and place of meetings, fee for counseling service, and whether the worker will meet with all members of the family together or with family members separately.

---

[3] Mayer N. Zald, "Organizations as Polities: An Analysis of Community Organization Agencies," in Fred Cox *et al.*, *Strategies of Community Organization: A Book of Readings* (Itasca, Ill.: F. E. Peacock Publishers, Inc., 1970), p. 92.

With Action Systems

In the family example above the client and action systems are the same, and there is no need for the worker to form a separate contract with the action system. However, when the action system is separate from the client system or includes others besides the client system, the worker will form an additional action-system contract.

For example, the board of directors of a neighborhood center asks one of its workers to form an action system to study the desirability of a change in neighborhood zoning ordinances and, if appropriate, make recommendations for changes. This action system may be composed of neighborhood residents and businessmen, zoning experts, and people who have influence on zoning decisions, as specified in the worker's contract with the board of directors.[4] When a potential member of the action system is contacted, an attempt is made to secure his tentative agreement on the goals of the action system—in this case, study of neighborhood zoning ordinances and recommendations for change. Agreement also is sought on the tasks that different members will perform, such as discussing different zoning ordinances and their implications for the neighborhood, talking to neighborhood residents and city officials, reading reports from other cities, and making decisions on preferred ordinances. Tentative agreement is reached on operating procedures, such as place and frequency of meetings and the expected duration of the action system. When all the members of the action system meet together as a group, they agree on terms of the contract.

With Target Systems

When the target and client system are the same, as in our previous family example, there is no need for a separate contract with the target system. Further, when a potential target system is part of the action system (in the neighborhood example above, a member of the city zoning commission may be included in the action system), a separate contract is not formed, at least at the beginning of the change effort, with that part of the target system. However, when all or part of the target system is separate from the client and action systems, some kind of contract normally is formed between the target and the worker, perhaps in conjunction with his client or action system.

If a target system agrees with the outcome goals of the change effort,

---

[4] See Chapter 10 for a discussion of factors that influence the worker's choice of members of action systems.

a contract is formed, with agreement on method goals, tasks, and operating procedures. An employer (target) could agree to hire a mental hospital patient (client) on his release, thus producing contract agreement on goals (employ the patient), tasks to be performed by each (employer will enroll patient in a training program, patient will attend training, worker will review progress of patient with employer and patient), and operating procedures (hours of work, salary).

Often when a contract is formed with a cooperative target, such as the employer of the mental hospital patient, the target becomes part of the action system formed to achieve a major outcome goal of worker and client—in this case, to sustain a former mental hospital patient in the community. At other times the target system will agree to or sanction the goals of the change effort and will not become involved as part of the action system in a specific ongoing change effort, as when a city council approves a zoning ordinance for a neighborhood. In some instances, agreement on outcome goals may be the last term in the contract with the target; tasks and operating procedures will be prescribed first. For example, in order to achieve any zoning change, a worker and a neighborhood organization will have to perform tasks and comply with procedures mandated by the city council—file petitions, present information at public hearings, or secure the opinion of the zoning commission.

If the target is resistant to the change goals of the worker and client system an implicit contract may be established in which the parties agree to disagree on goals. In these cases the tasks (tactics) and the operating procedures that may be used by each party may be played out in bargaining or conflictual relationships. These tactics and procedures may be anticipated, if not always accepted, by each party. In a sense the parties involved are playing out complementary and reciprocal roles that will either maintain the agreed-upon areas of disagreement or move towards accommodation and a more explicit collaborative contract on goals they both can agree upon.

In summary, in any contract between the social worker and other systems, goals, tasks, and operating procedures are agreed upon. Each party ordinarily assumes responsibility for suggesting the terms, carrying out the tasks, and complying with the procedures. Criteria used by the worker in formulating his suggestions for goals, tasks, and operating procedures are presented elsewhere in this text.[5] The focus here

---

[5] In Chapter 6, Assessing Problems, which discussed the establishment of method goals, it was pointed out that goals should be designed to alleviate identified problems and should be specific and realistically attainable. Chapter 5, Process in Social Work Practice, noted that goals help define purpose and that tasks are designed

is the utility of agreement on contract terms in inducing people to become engaged in change efforts and to maintain their involvement in them.

STRATEGIES AND TECHNIQUES FOR CONTRACT NEGOTIATION

In negotiating a contract with another system, the social worker uses diverse techniques to involve other people and secure a mutually acceptable working agreement. In practice he combines many of these techniques into an overall strategy, but some are particularly helpful for specific purposes, such as (1) establishing an initial relationship with another system, (2) identifying the purpose of the contract, (3) clarifying contract terms, and (4) identifying disagreements with the other system.

Establishing an Initial Relationship

While he is negotiating a contract, the worker is usually also establishing an initial relationship with the system involved. The quality of the relationship that is formed will not only affect the negotiation process but will be the basis of a continuing working relationship between the parties. Therefore it is important for the worker to be aware of and know how to deal with the dynamics operating in initial relationships.

One of the main factors influencing initial relationships are the expectations each party brings to it. These expectations are derived from many sources.

People who are meeting a particular social worker for the first time but who have had previous experiences with other change agents will have expectations about how social workers will behave. Examples of this situation are a teacher who has worked with school social workers; a person receiving financial assistance who may have had several social workers assigned to him, or a family that has had contact with service workers from a variety of community agencies and institutions.

People who have not had previous experiences with social workers

---

to achieve specific purposes. The worker draws on his general knowledge of practice skills and his knowledge of behavior of individuals, families, groups, organizations, and communities in linking tasks to purpose. Chapter 10, Forming Action Systems, will illustrate how the worker can influence the functioning of an action system by his use of operating procedures involving length of time, place of meeting, and rules for the interaction of the worker and members of the action system.

may base their expectations on what they have heard or read about them. Some people expect social workers to be helpful and to concentrate on helping them solve problems. Others may think social workers will tell them what to do or will always be on the side of the status quo and will enforce middle-class standards. Still others think of social workers as meddlers or "bleeding hearts" who offer aid and comfort to people who are too lazy to work, break laws, or are nonconformists.

Further, people who have different personal characteristics than the worker, as in race, culture, age, or sex, may expect him to have the same attitudes as others they have encountered with the same characteristics. They may stereotype him as a Whitey, Anglo, Hippy, or male chauvinist.

The social worker is also likely to have set expectations about how other people will behave. He may have little hope that a militant black leader of a neighborhood organization will enter into any kind of bargaining or collaborative relationships with any social worker, expect a policeman to be uncooperative in working with drug problems, or believe that elderly people would be uninterested in working with a young worker.

When there are differences between the characteristics of the worker and other people, the worker may consciously adapt his methods of approach to the life style of the other. Ignacio Aguilar suggests that in making initial contacts with Mexican-American families, the social worker must recognize the importance of a leisurely opening, fluency in Spanish, and understanding the Mexican-American's attitudes toward law, the influence of religion, the role of the male, and the significance of the extended family.[6]

Although any person the social worker encounters will probably be defensive about being stereotyped, those who think the worker considers himself superior to them will be particularly sensitive. In discussing ways to ease the difficulties between a white worker and a black potential client, Alfred Kadushin notes:

Because the white worker is initially regarded as a potential enemy, he should carefully observe all the formalities that are overt indications of respect—e.g. start the interview promptly, use Mr. and Mrs. rather than the client's surname or first name, shake hands and introduce himself, listen seriously and sincerely. Rituals and forms are not empty

---

[6] Ignacio Aguilar, "Initial Contacts with Mexican-American Families," *Social Work*, 17 (May 1972): 66–70.

gestures to people who have consistently been denied the elementary symbols of civility and courtesy.[7]

In dealing with all types of people, the worker must guard against overgeneralization. He cannot hope to completely understand the experiences and life styles of people from different cultures, races, professions, or social classes. Further, membership in different ethnic, age, sexual, and occupational groupings has different meanings to individuals. Consider the varied appeals of the wide variety of minority and women's groups. Thus, in an initial contact, the social worker must be aware that his own attitudes and expectations may bias his perception of the other.

When the social worker and any other person come together for the first time, each will expect the other to act in certain ways. During the encounter, each will be collecting data on the other that will either confirm or repudiate his expectations. They may test each other out and act in a manner that will provoke the other to meet their expectations. If a young delinquent expects the social worker to be punitive, he may act in a way that provokes the social worker to react in this way. Or, if the social worker expects a policeman to be uncooperative, the worker's attitude may actually create an uncooperative attitude in the policeman.

The social worker can lay the groundwork for a working relationship and help to overcome his own and others' misconceptions by focusing on the others' descriptions and views of the problem and treating their opinions with respect. If he is open to learning from others, he is demonstrating his interest in them as unique individuals and not as just another "case" or typical example of their race, age, sex, or social class. Further, his statements and questions as he begins his contract negotiation can be evidence of his objectivity and willingness to devote himself to the needs and interests of others, rather than his own.[8]

A social worker who has been involved in a previous successful change effort with the same people may be able to reestablish the relationship readily and negotiate a new contract with them in another change effort. In fact, agencies may ask a worker to undertake a specific change effort because his past relationships with the people in-

---

[7] Alfred Kadushin, "The Racial Factor in the Interview," *Social Work*, 17 (May 1972): 91.
[8] See Chapter 4 for a discussion of the characteristics of a professional relationship.

volved—a teacher, another worker, a city councilman—will help him negotiate a new contract with them.

The social worker may also find it easy to negotiate a contract with people he has met in what Robert Sunley calls a "nonproblem" approach that enables workers and potential members of client, action, and target systems to meet on neutral grounds. In a neighborhood center, for example, workers meet the neighborhood residents in a variety of ways and become part of their daily lives.[9] Thus a person with a problem may ask for help from a worker he already knows from other neighborhood contacts. Similarly, social workers attend meetings of social work and other professional organizations and may become involved in community organizations in order to establish relationships they can use in future contract negotiations.

Identifying the Purpose of the Contract

When a worker initiates a contact with a potential client, member of an action system, or target system,[10] he has the responsibility for explaining why he is there. People often are suspicious of others who come suggesting change. As Ronald Lippitt, Jeanne Watson, and Bruce Westley suggest, altruism is suspect in our society.[11] The first query to the social worker may be: "What's in it for you?"

Thus a worker reaching out to a multiproblem family, to people in a low-income area, to a potential member of a community committee, or to another social worker must be able to state why he is there in language and terms that make sense to the other. He needs to explain who he is, what agency he represents, the purpose of the agency, and then, specifically, why he has made contact with this particular person or these people. The worker may say he is there because a client asked him to come, because he is hired by his agency to work with people who have been in trouble with community institutions, because the local neighborhood center has asked him to find out what the problems are in the neighborhood and what the people want to do about

---

[9] Robert Sunley, "New Dimensions in Reaching-Out Casework," *Social Work*, 13 (April 1968): 64–74.

[10] As was pointed out in the last chapter, another person may make the first contact with the target system (the system to be engaged in the change effort). Here we are referring to the first contact made by the social worker, whether or not the target system has been contacted by another. However, the methods described can be used by anyone making contact.

[11] Ronald Lippitt, Jeanne Watson, and Bruce Westley, *The Dynamics of Planned Change* (New York: Harcourt, Brace & World, 1958).

them, or because a community planning organization has been asked to establish a committee to study and make recommendations on a community problem. He may find that a simple, honest explanation will be most readily accepted by other people. For example, a student social worker who had failed in many attempts to interest a group of teen-age girls who were creating problems in a neighborhood finally told them she had to work with them in order to get a passing grade in a school course. The girls understood this and agreed to meet with her.

In describing methods of reaching out to families, Alice Overton and Katherine Tinker suggest that workers should tell the families what information they have about them, where they got the information, and specifically what behavior or conditions they believe should be changed. They describe the first interview with a family:

. . . one worker began by telling a mother she understood her boy was unhappy at school and asking what she could do to help. The mother made no response and several unproductive visits passed with no real exchange taking place between her and the worker. Finally, the worker got up courage enough to say why she had come: two of the children had been involved in petty stealing at school; the "unhappy" boy was so dirty that other children would not sit near him; his sister was beginning to reflect in her behavior the promiscuity she observed at home. Then the worker was surprised to see the mother relax and participate in a discussion of what she might do. Up until then, the mother was fearful, wondering what the worker had up her sleeve.[12]

Thus a vague statement of purpose by a social worker "wanting to help" may create resistance because the other system is not sure what the social worker believes is the problem.

Overton and Tinker also suggest that by offering help the social worker is implying that he is the all-wise authority and members of the family are incapable of helping themselves. This approach obviously creates resistance in people by reflecting on their own competence and status. Social workers contacting other change agents and professional workers (teachers, foster parents, child-care workers in institutions, other social workers) to enlist their cooperation in working with a client can often achieve their objective by stating their specific purpose for the contact and asking for the help of the other person. This can be more effective than beginning by offering to help, which implies that the other is not performing his job properly.

---

[12] Alice Overton and Katherine Tinker, *Casework Notebook* (St. Paul, Minn.: Greater St. Paul United Fund Council, Inc., 1957).

An involuntary client may be very suspicious when change agents who have a great deal of power over them offer to help.[13] In a first interview with a young boy who had been committed by a court to a children's institution, a social worker told the boy he wanted to help him. The boy responded by asking the worker where he was going to send him. When the worker asked him what he meant, the boy told him that he first got into trouble when his teacher told him she wanted to help him and then sent him to the principal. The principal said he wanted to help him and sent him to a juvenile court worker. The court worker said he wanted to help him and sent him to the institution. The boy concluded: "You say you want to help me; where are you going to send me?"

Seymour Halleck points out that adolescents who have come to a social worker through a court action know that the worker is functioning as an agent of the community. They are sure that when the needs of the community conflict with the adolescent's needs, the community will win out. Halleck suggests that the worker should describe his position and outline what his purpose is on first meeting with the adolescent.[14] When the worker in the previous anecdote changed his tactics, rather than offering to help he told the boy what information he had about him and said his specific purposes were to explain to him why he was in the institution, to describe the institution's rules and activities, to tell him what he needed to do to get out of the institution, and to find out what the boy wanted to do and could do within the limitations of the rules of the institution and the order of the court.

Many adolescents in trouble have been exposed to adult double-talk and expect it from a worker. Halleck notes that "The sheer surprising impact of having an adult be so direct with them often in itself produces a favorable effect that encourages them to be more open."[15] Involuntary potential clients who believe they have been given a runaround by change agents may be willing to enter into voluntary contract negotiations with a worker who describes his purpose and the realistic limits placed on the activities of both the worker and the potential client.

When the worker is reaching out, he has the responsibility to start

[13] See Cartwright and Zander, *Group Dynamics*, p. 228, for a review of research indicating that resistance is aroused when a person believes he must submit to another's power and influence.
[14] Seymour L. Halleck, "The Impact of Professional Dishonesty on Behavior of Disturbed Adolescents," *Social Work*, 8 (April 1963): 48–55.
[15] Ibid., p. 54.

by explaining why he is there and what his purpose is. When another system initiates the contact (an organization of parents of retarded children, a teacher, a family with financial and medical problems), the worker's responsibility is to assist that system to state its purpose—its reason for coming. The worker uses his interviewing skills to help the other person explain why the worker is there. In first contacts with families and other groups, even if the worker has previously met the members individually, at the first meeting he will need to review the purpose of the group and assist the members to explore its purpose together.

Studies of people who come to agencies for help with their problems indicate they expect the worker to take an active role in discussing the problem that provoked the contact. When the expectations about psychotherapy of lower socioeconomic potential clients in their first visit to a psychiatric clinic were studied, it was found that they expected the therapist to take a generally active but permissive role. Those whose expectations were not met were less likely to return for treatment than those whose therapists met their expectations.[16]

A study of college students found that they also expected a potential helper to take an active role, believing that a worker who was highly motivated to help a client would assign importance to the client's problem. He would demonstrate willingness to continue to talk about the problem, attempt to reduce tension and lessen the client's discomfort in the interview situation, and structure the interview to help the client overcome decision-making difficulties.[17]

These studies support the belief of many social workers that people will not meet them a second time unless in the initial contact they have had an opportunity to tell why they have come.[18] Further, workers with experience in crisis intervention have discovered that enabling the other person to describe his problems and organize and focus his thinking about them can be therapeutic in itself. Indeed, several studies have indicated that detailed exploration of the stress that brought the

[16] Betty Overall and H. Aronson, "Expectations of Psychotherapy in Patients of Lower Socio Economic Class," *American Journal of Orthopsychiatry*, 33 (April 1963): 421–30.

[17] Edwin J. Thomas, Norman A. Polansky, and Jacob Kounin, "The Expected Behavior of a Potentially Helpful Person," *Human Relations*, 8 (1955): 165–75.

[18] See Miriam Jolesch, "Strengthening Intake Practice through Group Discussion," *Social Casework*, 40 (November 1959): 504–10, and Helen Harris Perlman, "Intake and Some Role Considerations," *Social Casework*, 41 (April 1960): 171–77.

client to the worker can sometimes be of such value that no further contact may be needed.[19]

Clarifying Contract Terms

To help all parties decide if they can agree on contract terms and reduce uncertainty about what the change effort will entail, the social worker should clarify the range or type of goals they may pursue, the tasks each of them may need to perform, and the options available on the operating procedures they may follow. He must also indicate what he will not or cannot do because of his own values, the limitations of his knowledge and skill, a lack of resources, the constraints of agency or community policy, or the requirements of contracts he has established with other systems. This clarification can serve several purposes.

First, letting the other system know what will *not* occur in the change effort can forestall false expectations. Indeed, the worker and the other system may decide they should not work together.

Second, by including in the range of goals that may be pursued the suggestions of people in other systems as well as his own, the worker demonstrates his willingness to be influenced by the other system. He reassures the other system that he will allow it to retain autonomy and will focus on goals its members perceive as consistent with their self-interest.

Third, by clarifying the types of responsibility and tasks he will undertake and those that the other system may be called on for, the worker can help all parties determine if they can mobilize the necessary resources to accomplish their goals. As William Reid points out, the problems to be dealt with and the goals to be established must fall within the scope of the combined resources of the client and worker, or the targets cannot be influenced.[20] A realistic clarification and assessment of available resources should help the worker and the other system agree on feasible goals.

Fourth, indicating that people in the other system will have tasks to perform makes them realize they will have to make an effort if change is to occur. Indeed if they are required to perform immediate tasks, they may gain a commitment to the change effort. Studies of clients in a psychological clinic revealed that those who were required

---

[19] See Lydia Rapoport, "Crisis-Oriented Short-Term Casework," *Social Service Review*, 41 (March 1967): 31–43.

[20] William J. Reid, "Target Problems, Time Limits, Task Structure," *Journal of Education for Social Work*, 8 (Spring 1972): 58–68.

to engage in activity between initial counseling sessions had more favorable views toward their workers than those who did not.[21] Of course people who do not believe they have the time or resources to engage in change efforts may withdraw for this reason. If they are shown they can successfully perform tasks from the beginning, they can gain a sense of participation as well as an early commitment to the effort.

Fifth, by indicating that he not only will help design tasks for the other system but also will undertake tasks himself, the worker demonstrates his interest in the problem and his commitment to help.

Sixth, indicating that tasks will be designed with the agreement of the people who will be undertaking them and, if necessary, with the help of the worker may reduce resistances to change due to fear of lack of ability to carry out a change effort.

Seventh, by clarifying the options of the operating procedures of the change effort, the worker can reassure people who resist change because they believe they cannot afford the money or time to participate or are uncertain about what they will be required to do in meetings of the action system. Questions that may be clarified include the fee or other costs required, arrangements for baby-sitters and transportation, who will be in the action system, how often and where the action system will meet, and what can be expected to happen during meetings.[22]

Eighth, by clarifying what his existing contracts are with his agency, the community, and other organizations, the worker can indicate what types of activity he can sanction and engage in himself. This clarification is particularly helpful in working with people who have been or may be in conflict with the law and who may try to seduce the worker into condoning deviant practices.

ESTABLISHING LIMITS OF CONFIDENTIALITY. Clarification by the worker can also establish the limits of confidentiality for the change effort. People who resist change because of a belief that receiving help from an outsider is a sign of weakness, or who believe they may lose rather than gain from a change effort, want to know what kind of record a social worker will keep and who is going to read the records or hear about their transactions. Further, people who agree to partici-

---

[21] Arnold P. Goldstein, "Maximizing the Initial Psychotherapeutic Relationship," *American Journal of Psychotherapy*, 23 (July 1969): 430–51.

[22] Considerations that guide the worker in his suggestions for size, operating procedures, and program of the action system will be discussed in Chapters 10 and 11.

pate in action systems designed to reduce conflict between groups or organizations, to recommend new community programs, or to plan protest strategy often are fearful of being misquoted or of having their deliberations made public prematurely.

The worker should indicate, at the beginning of the change effort, what kind of records he will keep, such as records of interviews to help him remember what happened or minutes of meetings. The worker can say who will see these records and explain agency policy and existing legal requirements about release of information, which can govern what information the agency will share with other agencies and what it is required by law to release to designated individuals. Agency policy in regard to press coverage of meetings also governs the confidentiality of proceedings.

The worker meeting individually with people in a multiperson system such as a family, school, or another social agency, must also clarify what information will be reported to other members of the system. In addition to discussing his own and his agency's policies about release of information, the worker should clarify in which areas the other system has the right or responsibility to determine if the information should be released. For example, a worker reaching out to engage people who may be involved in illegal acts (possession and sale of drugs, child abuse, vandalism, theft), can indicate what types of information he is required to report and what information he will not disclose, for example to schools or prospective employers, without the permission of the other.

Although people may be reassured by the worker's open statements about release of information, many will test him out before they decide to trust his statements. It may help them develop confidence in the worker if he shows them copies of records he keeps and sends to others. Overton and Tinker, in describing their work with families, report that their experience in showing clients copies of reports written to courts and other agencies "has been very convincing. We have reason to believe that carrying families along completely with what we are doing and why we are doing it tends to dispel their fear of something going on behind their backs. Instead, it gives them the feeling and responsibility of participation."[23] Members of a new organizational or community action system also may be reassured if the worker asks them to approve minutes, letters, and reports relating to their work.

PROVIDING EXAMPLES. One of the techniques the worker may use

---

[23] Overton and Tinker, *Casework Notebook*, p. 58.

in clarifying what may happen in a change effort is to provide examples of how others have been helped. In explaining terms of the contract, the worker can use verbal description, films, tapes, and written materials to provide real or fictional examples of how other people have worked to solve problems. When working with a group, the worker also can encourage other members to give examples of how people they know have been helped. Providing examples of the tasks other people have performed to reach specific goals not only helps to clarify what might happen in a change effort but also may provide hope for those who believe change is too difficult to achieve.

For example, a worker organizing a neighborhood group, a tenant's union, or an association of parents of retarded children can provide concrete examples of the changes other organizations have accomplished and how they achieved them. A school social worker attempting to inaugurate a new program in cooperation with other school staff may report on a successful change program in another school. Family members confused about demands made on them from people in community institutions may be encouraged by a worker who gives examples of other people, similar to themselves, who have been able to negotiate agreements with these institutions.

The worker's interactions with another system in his initial contacts with it also are a concrete example of what may transpire in the projected change effort. They indicate the type of transaction that is likely to continue throughout the effort.

MAKING CONTRACT TERMS EXPLICIT. It is possible for the worker and the other system to believe the contract is clear and think they are in agreement on its terms when, in fact, they are not. Each party may think it understands the agreements while each pursues a different agenda and has different expectations about the goals, tasks, and operating procedures of a change effort. Confusion, hostility, and dropouts may occur if one party does not follow through on what the other thought was an implied term of the contract. When the different members of an action system who are all working on behalf of a client system have varying ideas about their own roles, they may provide contradictory messages to the client and prevent the achievement of the agreed-upon goal. A neighborhood organization or a community committee may bog down if members have different understandings of the responsibilities and tasks they have agreed upon.

Making the contract terms explicit helps to clarify them and thus reduces misunderstandings and frustrating interactions. Some workers use verbal contracts to make agreement on the terms explicit for each party. In a study of six family agencies, it was found that when workers made an advance, conscious effort to formulate treatment objectives and communicated these verbally to clients, a high proportion of clients accurately perceived the worker's objectives. When workers did not specify objectives for their interviews, there was a striking absence of verbal communication with clients about the purpose of specific interviews, and the majority of the clients did not perceive how the interviews fit in with the worker's long-range goals.[24]

Social workers and agencies also use formal written contracts with other systems. One family agency uses written, signed contracts because its experience has indicated the necessity of an explicit understanding of the treatment goals mutually held by client and worker.[25] Social workers who form action systems on organizational and community problems often write a formal "charge" for the action system that includes a statement of purpose and goals of the system and methods to achieve these goals. When members have modified and accepted this statement and agreed upon operating procedures, a contract has been established between the members of the action system and between the action system and the worker. The ongoing written minutes of the action system may represent further modifications of the contract.

Whether verbal or written contracts are used, a contract term is only fully accepted when each party behaviorally agrees to it.[26] Behavioral agreement is indicated when members of an action system meet at the agreed-on time and place, family members perform the tasks suggested by the worker, or a welfare rights organizer and a county welfare department bargain together over eligibility standards.

There are circumstances in which the social worker may decide that an explicit contract cannot or should not be established and consciously decides not to push for one. In fact, when conflictual relationships exist with resistant target systems, an implicit contract to disagree may be established.

The worker may lose more than he will gain by pushing for an explicit contract. For example, a change agent system may be operating in areas where its sanction from the community is not clear. If the change agent system is pushed by the social worker to obtain sanction to pursue specific goals and tasks, it may receive a negative answer and

---

[24] Julianna Schmidt, "The Use of Purpose in Casework Practice," *Social Work*, 14 (January 1969): 77–84.
[25] Richard Lessor and Anita Lutkas, "Two Techniques for the Social Work Practitioner," *Social Work*, 16 (January 1971): 67 ff.
[26] Kravetz and Rose, "Treatment Contract."

be forced to withdraw from controversial areas. For example, before the Supreme Court decision on abortions, in many states public agency workers did not have a clear sanction to provide abortion counseling or to help women obtain abortions. Many public agency directors knew their workers were aiding clients to obtain abortions but did not explicitly make a contract with their workers authorizing them to provide this service. They did not seek a contract from public authorities sanctioning abortion counseling because they did not want to risk forcing an explicit prohibition.

Neither does the worker always push for an explicit contract with each member of a group action system or ask the action system to spell out all the goals of the members in advance. In a group action system, people often have different goals they want to achieve. For example, a social worker in a mental health center who works with people who abuse the use of drugs may become convinced of the need for a coordinated community approach on drug problems. He may form a group composed of people from the police, schools, hospitals, the city council, and social agencies. Each of these people may have different goals. The police may want community support to add additional members to the narcotics squad. The hospitals may want to establish a detoxification center. The worker himself may want his agency to be designated as the community information, referral, and service center for these problems. In the worker's contract negotiation with individual members and the group as a whole, he will attempt to find a general goal they all can agree to explicitly: i.e., develop a coordinated community plan to reduce problems of drug abuse. However, he will not initially attempt to make explicit the implicit goals of each member, although the members probably will be well aware of one another's goals. In fact, after the initial contract to work together on the one goal they all agree to explicitly, the meetings of this action system may be devoted to negotiating a final agreement which will designate specifically what each community agency will do. The worker will be able to keep members of this system from dropping out because each of them has an implicit goal it believes it can achieve.[27]

As this example illustrates, the worker himself may have goals which he does not want to make explicit in an action system. He also may not want to make all his goals explicit with a client system. The worker may accept the client's view of the problem and the client's

---

[27] However, if these implicit goals interfere with the achievement of the agreed-upon goals of the entire action system, the worker may need to restructure it. Restructuring of action systems will be discussed in Chapter 11.

goals and make an explicit contract to start where the client wants to start, but he may have other goals he wants to achieve which he does not share with the client. Instead he may attempt to help others reach their goals in a way that will facilitate movement towards his own goals. For example, one of the worker's goals in working with the family described in the Hoffman and Long case study in Part III was to "move the seesaw" that had locked the wife in the up position and the husband in the down one. The worker attempted to design tasks which would help family members reach their goals and at the same time would start to loosen the seesaw.

When the worker does not make all his goals explicit, however, he must be aware that his goals may subvert rather than assist the clients in reaching their goals. He must continually assess what is happening in order to avoid what Reid refers to as "double agenda" social work. The client may pursue one agenda, which may call for obtaining a needed resource or securing help in dealing with a community institution, while the social worker doggedly pursues another. And, as Reid points out, there is little evidence to suggest that social workers can bring about significant change with people who do not want to work on problems the social workers wish to pursue.[28]

Identifying Disagreements

Disagreements between the social worker and potential client may occur because of different views of the appropriate target for the change effort. The potential client may see the major target outside of himself, as in a community institution, while the worker sees the client itself as the major target. An example is given by William Reid:

... A mother is referred to a social agency by a school because family problems are interfering with her son's scholastic performance. While perhaps admitting to some domestic difficulties, the mother does not recognize any meaningful connection between them and her son's school performance. She rather sees his difficulty as due primarily to the school's mishandling. While the caseworker sees "some reality" to the mother's complaint about the school, he also sees vast vistas of family pathology. The caseworker is apt to show little interest in the former, while pursuing the latter with vigor.[29]

---

[28] Reid, "Target Problems."
[29] William J. Reid, "Target Problems, Time Limits, Task Structure," paper presented at the annual program meeting of the Council on Social Work Education, Seattle, Washington, January 1971, p. 5, 6.

Similarly, a worker attempting to organize and form a contract with a group of residents in a tenement, public housing, or a slum neighborhood may see the residents as his major target and attempt to involve them in goals relating to self-improvement. He is likely to discover that they see their major targets as their landlords and people in community institutions and want to establish goals that will change the way people in these institutions deal with them.

Even when there is agreement between the worker and the other system on the targets of change, there may be disagreements on what changes should occur in the target and what specific change goals should be achieved. A study of 315 clients and 27 counselors revealed a real discrepancy between the goals of the clients and the counselors,[30] and research into the purposes of social workers and clients in six family agencies found that clients placed value on achieving goals relating to concrete behavioral change, while workers emphasized more abstract, psychological goals.[31] In working with a family, the worker may emphasize goals related to reducing their problems with community institutions and increasing understanding and communication between parents and children; members of the family may emphasize goals relating to specific behaviors of parents and children. Or a worker may agree with tenement residents that the landlord is the major target but have different ideas about how the landlord should change.

In working with a multiple-person system, the worker may have difficulty obtaining agreement on goals from all the system members. Hoffman and Long's case study in Part III illustrates how members of one family—mother, father, and two children—all can have different goals. Similarly, members of a neighborhood organization may have widely different goals for improvement of the neighborhood.

The worker and the other system may agree on goals and targets but be in disagreement over strategies and tasks that need to be performed to influence the targets, the responsibilities of each, and the operating procedures to be employed. Research describing work in poverty areas emphasizes that the style of the poor is doing rather than talking,

---

[30] Andrew Thompson and Robert Zimmerman, "Goals of Counseling: Whose? When?" *Journal of Counseling Psychology*, 16 (1969): 121–25.

[31] Schmidt, "Use of Purpose in Casework Practice." See Rachel A. Levine, "Consumer Participation in Planning and Evaluation of Mental Health Services," *Social Work*, 15 (April 1970): 41–46, for case examples of goal discrepancies between clients and workers.

activity and action rather than cognitive reflection.[32] Thus a worker who suggests several sessions to discuss problems with some families may find that they expect more immediate action. A worker trying to involve a prominent businessman in a community committee to study and make recommendations on problems of drug abuse may meet resistance because the businessman does not want to attend a lot of meetings and prefers to work behind the scenes. A social worker trying to establish collaborative relationships between tenants and landlords may find the tenants prefer conflict in the form of immediate protest demonstrations against the landlord.

It is possible for the worker to be in personal agreement with the suggested contract terms of the other system but nevertheless be prevented from negotiating a contract with them because of his existing contracts with another system. The worker's contract with his agency prescribes the services he may offer. It sanctions the contract terms he may negotiate with other systems and prohibits other terms.

The worker and another system may not be able to work together because he and his agency cannot provide the service or resource the other system wants. Or the worker may have difficulty establishing a collaborative contract with another system that focuses on what the other system wants because the worker's contract with his change agent system does not sanction that activity. For example, Foster's case study in Part III points out that the ward staff's contract provision that patients not be told the nature of their fatal disease prohibited the worker from involving the patients in realistic planning for themselves and their families.

Further, the worker's agency may be reluctant to allow the worker to engage in activities that will jeopardize the agency's contracts with its sources of funding or with community institutions. The worker attempting to organize residents in a self-improvement group may find that his agency is hesitant to allow him to establish goals with the residents that might put it in conflict with community institutions. Indeed the targets of the residents—people from the neighborhood school, the public housing authority, or the public health inspector's office—may be members of existing action systems formed by the agency and thus parties to collaborative contracts with the agency.

---

[32] Rachel A. Levine, "Treatment in the Home," in Frank Riessman, Jerome Cohen, and Arthur Pearl (eds.), *Mental Health of the Poor* (Glencoe, Ill.: Free Press, 1964), pp. 329–35, and Frank Riessman and Jean Goldfarb, "Role Playing and the Poor," *Group Psychotherapy*, 17 (March 1964): 36–48.

Of course, the worker himself may have established previous contracts with members of client, action, and target systems which will make it difficult for him to establish a collaborative contract with another system. As indicated in Chapter 5, the feasibility of attaining the outcome goals of the client will be determined by the outcome goals of all systems involved in a planned change effort. In the case of the mother who believes the school is mishandling her son, the worker may form a contract goal with the mother to agree to see the teacher and try to change the way he behaves with the son. The worker has a primary contract with the client system (the mother) and attempts to negotiate a secondary contract with the teacher. If the teacher believes the boy's difficulties are caused by his home conditions, he may resist establishing a contract with the social worker to experiment with different methods of dealing with the boy in school. If the worker is not able to influence the teacher to accept the client's goals, he cannot form a collaborative contract with him.

In summary, workers and others may not be able to agree on proposed contract terms because they do not agree on the identity of the targets for the change effort or how the targets should change, there are difficulties in obtaining agreement from all members of a multiple-person system, there are differences of opinion on the strategies and tasks of the change effort, or the terms in existing contracts conflict with suggested terms of a new contract.

STRATEGIES FOR DEALING WITH RESISTANCE

Unless the worker is able to change suggested contract terms or renegotiate an existing contract, he may have to deal directly with the resistances of other systems to contract terms. He can use a variety of techniques to overcome resistance, including involving other systems, acknowledging resistance, upsetting equilibrium to create a temporary crisis, providing hope, establishing short-term or trial goals, getting help from other people, and using groups for intake.

Involve Other Systems

An important technique for dealing with resistance is to involve other systems in the contract negotiation. Research studies indicate that people are likely to resist change efforts they believe are coercive or have been imposed upon them.[33] In a study of workers' resistance to changes in industry, for example, it was found that management could modify or remove resistance by effectively communicating a need for change and by involving the workers in planning for it.[34]

Involvement of the other system should help reduce resistances caused by fear and uncertainty about what will happen and what demands will be made upon the other system, as well as fears that the system will not be able to follow through on the change effort. The worker and the other system can discuss the conditions for their working together, how goals will be established, and what each system should be able to expect from the other. If the other system has an opportunity to suggest, reject, or agree to terms for the partnership, their fears about what will transpire and their anxieties about their ability to participate should be reduced. People who have been coerced into a change effort, such as parents accused of child neglect or a teenager on probation for the sale of drugs, also may respond to a worker who clearly outlines the "rules of the game"—the nonnegotiable terms of the contract—and then indicates areas where the terms of the contract can be negotiated in a joint agreement.[35]

Involvement of the other system in formulating a contract also should help reduce resistances to change in people who believe receiving help is a sign of weakness that reflects adversely on their competence and status. People who fear that assuming the role of client will mean they will lose their status as an independent, autonomous system may be reassured by a social worker who, through his actions, makes it clear that he considers them true partners in the change effort who can and should influence the goals, tasks, and working conditions of the change effort.[36] Herbert Strean suggests that unless others perceive workers as being open to their influence, they will see them as a threat to their own identity and personal dignity.[37]

The fears of other systems that they will lose something—prestige, power, or money—in the change effort are also assuaged if they are involved in contract negotiation. If the other systems perceive they can

---

[33] Cartwright and Zander, *Group Dynamics*, p. 228.
[34] Lester Coch and John R. P. French, "Overcoming Resistance to Change," in Cartwright and Zander (eds.), *Group Dynamics*, pp. 336–50.
[35] See Halleck, "Impact of Professional Dishonesty," for a discussion of the impact of worker honesty in working with adolescents.
[36] See the Foster case study in Part III for an illustration of this concept.
[37] Herbert S. Strean, "Role Theory, Role Models, and Casework: Review of the Literature and Practice Applications," *Social Work*, 12 (April 1967): 77–87.

influence the direction of the change effort, and indeed that they may be able to bargain or act so they will gain more than they will lose, their resistance should be reduced.

Thus the involvement of other systems in contract negotiation should help reduce resistances to change caused by fear of the unknown and uncertainty about what may happen, fear of not being able to follow through on the change effort, fear of losing status, and fear of losing more than will be gained in the change effort. In addition to the utilitarian value of contract negotiation and the establishment of a joint agreement between the worker and the other system in inducing people to become engaged in change efforts, the values of the social work profession dictate that, ethically, people have a right, and should have the opportunity, to decide how they want to work with a social worker.

Acknowledge Resistance

Resistance to change can create open hostility or apathy toward a social worker. Although resistance can be expected to be high in people who have not asked to be involved in change efforts and those who disagree with the purpose and goals of the worker, it also can keep people from agreement in change effort contracts they themselves have initiated. Sometimes resistances can be lowered by the open acknowledgment of their existence.

The social worker can encourage a resistant person to give vent to his anger, suspicions, and negative reactions to the proposed change. Or the worker can himself suggest reasons why the other person is resisting working with him. For example, a worker attempting to change a teacher's behavior toward a child may acknowledge that the teacher has a large class of children whom he works hard to educate and control and indicate that he knows what he is asking will require extra time and effort. A worker contacting people who have been in conflict with change agents in many community institutions may say to them that they probably distrust him because they believe they have been treated unfairly by other workers.

In bringing resistances out in the open, the worker can acknowledge that they are legitimate and demonstrate a beginning understanding of the problems and feelings of the other. However, he must not imply that the basis for the resistance is so strong it will make change impossible. Just giving a person the experience of discussing his fears and reasons for avoiding change with a responsive worker may reduce his resistances enough to lead him to make at least a tentative commitment to negotiating a contract with the worker.

Upset Equilibrium

If the acknowledgment of resistances is insufficient to motivate systems to engage in contract negotiation, the worker may find that upsetting the current equilibrium of the other systems will motivate them. The concept of "unfreezing" refers to the processes that can be used to upset a system's equilibrium, thereby creating at least a temporary crisis and discomfort and a readiness to make changes to relieve the discomfort.[38]

The social worker can unfreeze a system's equilibrium by providing it with information that its perceptions of itself, other systems, and the problem are not correct. He may be able to confront other people with information from his own observations and reports from other sources that contradicts their positions or to point out discrepancies between what people say and how they act. For example, a social worker trying to influence his own agency to offer more services to Mexican-Americans may be met with the assertion that the agency already is serving a sizable number of these people. By collecting data on the number of Mexican-Americans in the community, the number receiving agency service, the number that have dropped out from agency service, the worker can demonstrate that, in fact, the agency is serving very few of them and is not able to involve many who do come for service.

The social worker may be able to persuade people to produce additional information that will change their own perceptions. When people acknowledge problems but place the responsibility on someone else, the worker should ask them to describe the problem situation in detail and then ask if it is always caused by someone else.[39] Or a worker working with a family whose son has just returned from a correctional institution and hopefully believes "He has learned his lesson" may ask how he is

---

[38] Warren Bennis names three mechanisms a social worker can use to unfreeze a system and create motivation for change as: (1) lack of confirmation or disconfirmation, (2) induction of guilt-anxiety, and (3) creation of psychological safety by reduction of threat or removal of barriers. See "Personal Change through Interpersonal Relations," in Bennis (ed.), *Interpersonal Dynamics: Essays and Readings on Human Interaction*, rev. ed. (Homewood, Ill.: Dorsey Press, 1968), pp. 357–94.
[39] Kravetz and Rose, "Treatment Contract," p. 51.

going to get along at home or school or with his old neighborhood gang.[40]

In working with a multiple-person system, the worker may arrange for feedback from members of the system to one another. Family members or members of other groups or organizations may provide information to each other verbally, in writing, or through the worker on what they think of each other's attitudes and behavior and how they think each person should change. Or the worker may ask group members to role play the behavior of other members of the group. Audio or video tapes of group sessions may be played back to participants, and the worker can help point out or question behavior to provide the participants with information on the patterns of interactions. In working to reduce conflicts between systems, the worker may use feedback devices to help people understand how their actions are perceived by people in the other system.

To confront a resistant target and force it into a change effort, a crisis can either be provoked by the worker and an action system or the worker can take advantage of an existing crisis. In these instances, the crisis upsets the system's equilibrium and not only may persuade a system to begin a change effort but also may provide information which can be used to point the direction of the change. For example, residents of rat-infested slum housing wanting to force stepped-up municipal housing inspection may organize a protest demonstration, carrying dead rats into the mayor's office, the city council chambers, or a newspaper office or depositing them in front of the landlord's home. Workers in a large midwestern city took advantage of an existing crisis in a juvenile detention home to push for changes in the policy of holding children in isolation. When a boy in isolation set fire to his mattress and suffocated, workers were quickly able to obtain changes in the center's discipline policies.

Providing new information to a system may provoke guilt and embarrassment in people, thereby upsetting their equilibrium, creating discomfort, and influencing them to agree to embark on a change effort. Guilt and embarrassment may result when a person realizes he has not lived up to his own ideals and standards or he has disappointed or lost face with someone important to him. A person may voluntarily engage in activity which is inconsistent with his own self-image, or change agents can provoke this behavior. A group of women graduate

---

[40] See Overton and Tinker, *Casework Notebook*, pp. 67 and 68, for other examples.

students attempting to influence their department to hire women professors provoked faculty men who considered themselves civil libertarians into making antiwoman remarks. The women pointed out the inconsistency between the men's avowed views and their behavior, thus embarrassing them. The women also made it clear they were personally disappointed in this behavior by professors they admired, thus withdrawing their approval. A slum landlord who values his image as a good citizen and neighbor may be so embarrassed by pickets carrying dead rats in front of his house he will enter into bargaining relationships with his tenants.

Provide Hope

The discomfort that results when a social worker unfreezes a resistant system by confronting it with information that challenges its perceptions and creates guilt and embarrassment may influence it to enter into contract negotiations with a worker. However, discomfort alone is not enough to induce people to remain in change efforts. They also must believe the change will bring them some relief from the discomfort.

Many studies indicate that discomfort or fear of future pain coupled with hope of securing relief from pain and a desire to receive rewards are potent motivating forces for change.[41] The social worker is faced with the dual task of maintaining enough discomfort in the other system to keep it from dropping out when its equilibrium is partially restored and at the same time providing realistic hope that change can occur.

Discomfort is usually at its highest level immediately after a system's equilibrium has been upset, by the worker, other people, or events in the environment, and it decides to embark on a change effort. Thus, many social workers believe help and hope should be offered immediately at that time. In practical terms this means waiting periods in agencies should be reduced and the worker should be able to respond quickly to crisis situations.

The social worker can offer hope by reassuring the other that change is possible, by offering support and understanding for the other's feelings and anxiety, and by discussing possible outcomes of the change

---

[41] See, for example, Cartwright and Zander, *Group Dynamics*, p. 225; Levinger, "Continuance in Casework"; Lippitt, Watson, and Westley, *Dynamics of Planned Change*, p. 164.

effort that might relieve the pain. While providing hope for improvement, the social worker also needs to discuss the tasks that must be performed before relief will occur and indicate the possibility that hard work and future difficulties will occur before goals are reached. If he does not help others face the realities of the effort that may be involved and indicate his willingness to help and support them through future discomfort, they may become quickly discouraged, lose hope, and drop out.

Establish Short-Term or Trial Goals

The utility of establishing specific short-term goals, often with a time limit attached, that the change agent and other system can agree to work on immediately is well recognized.[42] For example, Alice Overton and Katherine Tinker's experiences with families indicated that the families sought relief from immediate pressures and wanted to work on issues they thought were urgent.

Saul Alinsky and others who have described efforts to organize people into protest organizations emphasize the importance of selecting as an immediate, short-term goal some tangible issue that the people believe is crucial and that the organization probably can win on quickly. In examining the establishment of protest organizations in low-income neighborhoods, it is interesting to note that the first goal established by many was the erection of a stop sign at a busy intersection that children had to cross to get to school. The usual procedure was for mothers to mobilize to form a human chain across the street. When the mass media responded with coverage, support was gained from community influentials for the erection of the stop sign.[43]

The establishment and subsequent achievement of specific short-term goals reinforces hope that future changes are possible. When time-limited goals that other people want to achieve are established, their fears of having to give up their independence, autonomy and control are lessened, not only because they have participated in the establishment of goals but because they have committed themselves

---

[42] See Saul Alinsky, *Reveille for Radicals*, (Chicago: University of Chicago Press, 1946); Ralph Garcia and Olive Irwin, "A Family Agency Deals with the Problem of Dropouts," *Social Casework*, 43 (February 1962): 71–75; Lessor and Lutkas, "Two Techniques"; Overton and Tinker, *Casework Notebook*; Rapoport, "Crisis-Oriented Short-Term Casework"; Reid, "Target Problems."

[43] See Michael Lipsky, "Protest as a Political Resource," *American Political Science Review*, 62 (December 1968): 1144–58, for a conceptual presentation of why this strategy is effective.

for a trial period only.[44] Achievement of short-term goals may also alleviate people's fears that they lack the ability to carry out a change effort. By helping other people achieve immediate, concrete goals, the social worker demonstrates his competence to help others achieve change. This may enable him to propose negotiation of a long-term contract, if this is necessary.

Get Help from Other People

The social worker can use other people to help him deal with a resistant system. As in making initial contacts, people with high status, those with similar characteristics to the target system, or those who have had previous positive experiences with the target system can be used to encourage the target system to negotiate a contract with the worker. Others may be in a position to exert influence processes, such as persuasion or inducement, which are not available to the worker.

For example, a person with political influence who is a member of an action system to devise a community program for problems of drug abuse may be able to induce a police department to enter into a contract for police cooperation. A member of a Mexican-American organization may be able to persuade others to join the organization by offering support in their first contacts when they are ambivalent about committing themselves to a contract with the group.

When the worker is negotiating a contract with a multiple-person system, system members who are more enthusiastic and motivated may persuade other members to continue. For his first contact, the worker can select system members who will serve as leverage points with other parts of the system and can encourage these people to help him convince others in the system to enter into a contract with him. Examples of leverage people are the dominant parent in a family, the leader of a teen-age gang, or an influential member of an organization.

The worker may use other people to assist him in using many of the techniques for overcoming resistance in contract negotiations. Thus he can form an action system of other people in which the contract goal is to influence someone else into contract negotiations. The worker could also use a group action system to deal with resistances of the members and influence them to form a contract with him or to assist him in forming individual contracts with group members.

---

[44] See Garcia and Irwin, "Family Agency," for an example of how trial periods and time-limited goals can be used to reduce dropouts.

Use Groups for Intake

The interactions of people in a group can be an influence encouraging members to negotiate a contract. The members themselves use many of the techniques that overcome resistance and induce people to become engaged in a change effort. The worker can establish a contract with an existing group or a new group he has formed to achieve outcome goals. He can form a group only for intake purposes for people with whom he wants to establish individual contracts for a one-to-one action system or, later, for a group action system.

When workers and agencies form groups at intake rather than scheduling one-to-one interviews, waiting periods for service are reduced and people can be involved when their equilibrium is upset and their discomfort is high. A report of experiences of group intake meetings at a family agency revealed that 96 percent of families that accepted a group intake appointment continued in individual or group meetings with the agency, as contrasted with 72 percent that were placed on a waiting list and given individual service later.[45]

Use of a group may aid the worker in bringing resistances to change out in the open. When one member of the group expresses doubts, others will add theirs. Albertina Mabley cites the example of a worker with a group of potential clients in a family counseling agency who guides the discussion to help them realize that resistance to seeking help is a problem common to all. Eventually even the most resistive, angry people will take part in the discussion in order to vent their anger.[46] Similarly, in a newly formed community action system people will have an opportunity to express their fears that change may be difficult and impossible to achieve. Once the resistances are out in the open, the group can aid its members in dealing with them.

Groups also can be used to help people who believe the target of change lies outside themselves to realize that they are part of the problem and the target. Vera Dillon describes the use of group intake for mothers with disturbed children. The mothers initially came to the group meeting to describe their children's problems and disclaimed responsibility for them. Once in the group the mothers began to discuss their own feelings and to examine their own responsibility for their children's difficulties. Dillon believes "they respond in this way because of the acceptance, understanding, and permissiveness that pre-

---

[45] Albertina Mabley, "Group Application Interviews in a Family Agency," *Social Casework*, 47 (March 1966): 158–64.

[46] Ibid., p. 161.

vail in the group intake sessions and because of the fact that they do not feel the agency is accusing them."[47]

The worker in any group can encourage group members to point out to one another how they are part of the problem and to feel comfortable themselves in admitting that this is the case. The presence of others with common problems may give support and hope for change to individuals in the group. When some individuals discuss their problems, others in the group are encouraged to discuss theirs. Further, the group discussion can help people to focus their thinking on those aspects of the problem they can begin to deal with.

The worker can also use a group to specify what he and his agency can do and to clarify suggested terms of the contract. Individuals who are hesitant to raise questions individually may be emboldened to ask them when group members bring up other questions. These questions can clarify misconceptions people have about the agency service that would not come out in individual sessions. For example, group meetings of potential adoptive parents help workers to destroy myths about adoption procedures.

The presence of other group members may also encourage people to bargain over the proposed contract terms and to test out the worker's sincerity in stating that many of the terms are negotiable. A group meeting gives people an opportunity to observe the worker in interaction with others besides himself and to form opinions on the worker's competence, interest, and commitment.

The worker can enhance the influence a group will have on its members by selecting people whose descriptive characteristics (mothers with young children, age, sex, or race) or behavioral characteristics (aggressive, withdrawn) will enhance the group interactions. Factors affecting selection of group members will be discussed in Chapter 10.

Not only is the negotiation of contracts a continuing process that involves all systems in a change effort, but the techniques of negotiation are a prototype or model of the influence skills used by the worker throughout the process of change. The worker will continue to adjust to the characteristics of other people and indicate his interest in them as individuals. He will continue to identify purposes, work for clarification, and handle disagreements and resistances. If the worker and the other system have identified clear contract goals, their determination whether they have achieved the goals can be the basis for deciding to renegotiate a new contract or to terminate.

---

[47] Vera Dillon, "Group Intake in a Casework Agency," *Social Casework*: 46 (January 1965), 26–30.

CHAPTER 10

FORMING

ACTION

SYSTEMS

The action system is composed of the social worker and the people he works with to accomplish tasks and achieve method and outcome goals. In any one change effort, the worker may form many different action systems to collect data, assess the problem, make an initial contact, negotiate a contract, or influence the major targets to help achieve the outcome goal.

The action system is the medium through which the worker influences the targets of change. Its effectiveness can be enhanced by careful planning in its formation and operation. The social worker forming action systems must operate within the constraints of three major characteristics of action systems: size, composition, and operating procedures, including the use of time, the place or setting, and norms or procedures governing interaction. These are the topics considered in this chapter.

SIZE

In planning any change effort the social worker must determine what size action systems will be most effective to achieve his purposes and influence the targets. A worker in a community mental health clinic who has been asked for help by a mother of a teen-age boy experimenting with drugs who has been in trouble with the police, courts, and the school must decide if he should (1) try to involve the whole family in an action system, (2) work alone in an action system with the boy, (3) place the boy in an action system with other teen-agers, (4) work individually with school personnel, police, and court workers, or (5) ask the boy and/or his family to accompany him to meetings with school and court personnel. The worker may decide to form several action systems to accomplish these goals.

Further, the worker may realize that the private troubles of this one family in its interactions with one another and with community institutions are similar to many other problems he and other workers in the clinic have encountered. Therefore he could conclude that the clinic should work on the public issue of the social problems of drug use and abuse and the worker and his agency could establish the goals of (1) coordinating existing community services for drug abuse, (2) changing police practices, (3) creating new services, (4) changing existing drug laws, or (5) establishing a drug education program for teen-agers, parents, and staff from community institutions. To achieve these goals the agency could form one-to-one action systems to influence a chief of police, a school superintendent, or a prominent legislator, or it could form group action systems composed of people able to influence the targets of change.[1]

The worker's decision on the most effective and efficient size action system to use is influenced by two major factors: the purpose he hopes to achieve and the characteristics of the target. Although in practice these two factors are related, they can be analyzed separately.

Size and Achievement of Purpose

In order for an action system to be effective in relation to its purposes, the members must possess the necessary bases of influence (knowledge and expertise, material resources and services, legitimate authority,

---

[1] For discussion of social work objectives in working for organization and community change, see Ralph M. Kramer and Harry Specht, *Readings in Community Organization Practice* (Englewood Cliffs, N.J.: Prentice-Hall, Inc., 1969); Robert Morris and Robert Binstock, *Feasible Planning for Social Change* (New York: Columbia University Press, 1966); Murray Ross, *Community Organization: Theory and Principles* (New York: Harper and Row, 1955); and Jack Rothman, "An Analysis of Goals and Roles in Community Organization Practice," *Social Work*, 9 (April 1964): 24–31.

status and reputation, personal attractiveness)[2] and be able to exert influence on the targets of change, which may be within or outside of the action system. The system must also be efficient in accomplishing its purpose with a minimum expenditure of time, effort, and money. Robert Morris and Robert Binstock point out that unnecessary expenditure of resources will do nothing to increase the likelihood of achieving the worker's purpose. Such resources should be conserved for use in reaching other goals.[3]

The most effective size action system to be established for the achievement of a particular purpose could be either a one-to-one or a group action system. Often use also can be made of existing action systems.

ONE-TO-ONE ACTION SYSTEMS. A one-to-one system is frequently the most effective and efficient way to influence the targets of change. The worker himself may possess the necessary influences to achieve his purpose with the target. If the president of the agency's board of directors trusts the worker's knowledge and competence, in one interview he can be convinced to recommend to the board approval of a drug program proposed by the worker.

The worker may also be able to use himself as a role model. His appearance and behavior could have a positive influence on a teen-ager who is dropping out of school and using drugs. If this is not sufficient to influence the youth to accept tutoring to catch up with his classes and end his reliance on drugs, the worker could confront him with the long-range consequences of his behavior. If the worker has established access to a director of a community tutoring program, he can approach him directly and attempt to influence him to accept the boy for tutoring.

If the worker himself does not have the necessary influence to achieve his purpose, he can sometimes form an action system with another individual who will influence the target. Often the only bases of influence available to the worker are professional knowledge and expertness, personal energy, and, occasionally, reputation and personal attractiveness. His influence may be limited to the use of persuasion, which is insufficient if his goal is not perceived by the target as being in its self-interest.[4] For example, the worker may not be able to influence a

[2] Bases of influence and influence processes will be discussed in Chapter 12. Also see Dorwin Cartwright and Alvin Zander, *Group Dynamics* (New York: Harper and Row, 1968), pp. 215–35, and Morris and Binstock, *Feasible Planning for Social Change*, pp. 113–27.

[3] Morris and Binstock, *Feasible Planning for Social Change*, p. 138.

[4] In a study of planning efforts to improve programs and services for older persons, Morris and Binstock, *Feasible Planning for Social Change*, found that rational persuasion was rarely successful in overcoming organizational resistance.

legislator to sponsor a bill to change state drug laws, but he may be able to influence the president of his board of directors, who has business and personal relationships with the legislator, to convince him to sponsor the legislation.

A number of one-to-one action systems may be formed to influence different targets in a change effort. A worker may believe he himself has the necessary knowledge to devise a drug education program for community personnel and that he can individually persuade directors of several agencies to enroll their workers. Or he may put together an action system of influential people who never meet face to face but who agree to attempt to influence targets; he could, for example, individually contact several people who will agree to talk to legislators about changes in drug laws.

GROUP ACTION SYSTEMS. The worker may not be able to mobilize sufficient influence through the use of one-to-one action systems. In order to achieve his purpose he can use a group action system in which people influence one another through their direct interactions. The worker may also choose a group action system because he wants to include many people within the action system in order to save time and money. As in a one-to-one system, the targets of change may be people within or outside the action system.

The worker's purpose may be achieved by bringing people together who can influence each other through their expertness, serve as role models to others in the group, or provide support, encouragement, and friendship to other members. The interaction of people may generate ideas as people build on each other's suggestions, and individuals may develop a commitment to take action on recommendations by the group. If the purpose of the worker can only be achieved through the mobilization of the efforts of a large number of people, a group action system is essential.[5]

Group action systems are effective for people with common problems. The worker's focus could be on helping people with their individual problems, such as helping a teen-ager find a satisfactory life style that does not include drugs. Or the worker could help people work together collectively to make changes in their environment and

---

[5] For discussion of the characteristics of groups, see George Homans, *The Human Group* (New York: Harcourt-Brace, 1950); Helen Northern, *Social Work with Groups* (New York: Columbia University Press, 1969); Michael S. Olmsted, *The Small Group* (New York: Random House, 1959); Robert D. Vinter (ed.), *Readings in Group Work Practice* (Ann Arbor: Campus Publishers, 1967); and Cartwright and Zander, *Group Dynamics.*

their interactions with community institutions, such as assisting parents of mentally retarded children persuade a school board to inaugurate special classes for their children. Group members, with assistance from the worker, can explore together alternative ways of dealing with their problems, discuss consequences of different behavior, decide how to relate to people outside the group, and provide support and encouragement to one another. The worker may believe a group action system for people with common problems is more effective and efficient than a series of one-to-one action systems not only because of the influence members will have on each other, but also because if the people with the problems are powerless as individuals to influence systems in their environment, they may be able to gain power through membership in a large group or organization.

Groups of interested and influential people, who may or may not be directly affected by a problem, can be used to devise and generate support for changes in organizations and the community. A group of prominent citizens, elected and appointed officials, and professional workers could study drug problems and services in a community and recommend a comprehensive community drug-abuse program and changes in existing drug laws. This group may be more effective and efficient than a one-to-one action system because members can learn from one another and can produce information that is not readily available to the worker. If group members who have influence with resistant targets develop a commitment to one another and to the recommendations generated by the group interaction, they may take the major responsibility for influencing the targets.

The worker may also choose a group action system in order to equip people with new skills and knowledge, such as community service personnel who need education about drugs or people who need to develop confidence and skills in handling their children. Although the worker may provide the primary information or bring in experts who will provide it, people in the group also can learn from one another's experience. Of course, the use of groups also saves money and the worker's time.

EXISTING ACTION SYSTEMS. A major factor guiding the social worker's choice of size of action system is whether he can achieve his purpose effectively and efficiently through a one-to-one interaction or through the interactions of people in groups. Rather than forming a new action system, the worker often must decide whether an existing group, such as a family, teen-age gang, living unit in an institution, or members of an organization, should be used. In making this decision, the worker will be guided primarily by his interest in achieving the purpose of the intervention in the most effective and efficient way.

If members of a family need the worker's help with a problem that directly affects all members and may require change in them all, the worker may decide to work with the entire family as an action system. The purpose of the intervention could be to help family members assume different roles within the family, to resolve interpersonal conflicts, or to help the family cope with societal resource systems.

If a worker initially comes into contact with only one member of a family, he will have to decide if he should try to work with the entire family as a unit or with only one member. For example, the worker in the mental health center who has been asked for help by a mother of a teen-age boy may decide he needs to work with both the boy and his family to help them understand how the family's behavior is contributing to the boy's problem and to help them modify that behavior. If the worker's assessment of the problem leads him to decide that the boy should be separated from his family; his purpose would be to achieve the separation. In this case the worker could choose to work in one action system with the boy and another with the family.

In working with an individual family member as a primary target system and actual or potential client system, the worker probably will involve some of the family members in an action system because of their effect on the target, whether the individual is living with his family, is away but will return home, or is away permanently but remains involved in reciprocal interactions with his family. When the worker views the whole family as his action and target systems, he can select and work with certain subgroups. Rather than treating the members of a family as a single unit, Salvador Minuchin and Braulio Montalvo found it effective "to treat various subgroupings by first working with the family's natural subgroupings, then changing the subgroupings as the situation may require and actively manipulating them in relation to the whole family group."[6]

Some workers sequence their activities with families, working at various times with separate subparts and with the complete family. Other workers will only deal with all the members as a unit. Some workers will work only with one family member and will not come into direct contact with other members. Rules cautioning workers always

---

[6] Salvador Minuchin and Braulio Montalvo, "Techniques for Working with Disorganized Low Socio Economic Families," *American Journal of Orthopsychiatry*, 37 (October 1967): 887.

to work with the complete family or always to break the family into subunits are not useful. The purpose of the intervention should be the major consideration in a worker's choice of action system.

The worker's theoretical orientation will influence his purpose and thus his selection of size of action system. If the worker views a family as an interlocking social system which determines roles and behavior for each member, he probably will work with the family as a unit. If he views it as only one part of the environment of an individual family member and believes he should deal directly with the anxieties of that member, he will work primarily with the individual. Irving Spergel notes that in working with individual members of "street groups," the worker can have five overlapping purposes: control of delinquent behavior, rehabilitation or treatment of group members, provision of access to opportunities, value change, and prevention of delinquent activity.[7] He suggests that a worker's purpose can guide him to select a particular group for street work, using the entire group as an action system for some objectives, such as modifying the group's norms and behaviors to achieve control, and singling out individual boys for other purposes, such as connecting some individuals with employment and education opportunities.

When working with individuals who are grouped with other people in a controlled environment such as a classroom or institutional living unit, the achievement of the purpose of the intervention again is a major determinant of the worker's choice of size of action system. If his objective is related to the environment of the individuals, the entire group may be used as the action system, as when meetings of all the children in a particular cottage in a home for delinquent girls are held to establish and maintain house rules. Other groups of children selected from several living units may be formed for other objectives, such as helping children who are ready to leave the institution prepare for the return home. A worker also may work with some children on individual problems.

If the worker's purpose is to strengthen coordination between all members of an organization, such as teachers, child-care workers, recreational specialists, or social workers in a children's institution, he may try to hold regular staff meetings. If he wants to gain support for a service innovation or a new organizational focus from key leverage people with influence over other organization members, he may hold

---

[7] Irving Spergel, "Selecting Groups for Street Work Service," *Social Work*, 10 (April 1965): 49.

a series of individual conversations with these people before approaching the entire membership.[8] Sometimes, of course, a one-to-one action system with a dominant member of an organization will be sufficient to achieve the worker's purpose.

Size and Characteristics of the Target

In making his decision on what size action system to use, the social worker will be influenced by the characteristics of the target that make it willing to become involved in either size system. He may choose a one-to-one system simply because the presence of other people might cause the target to refuse to participate. Noting the similarities and differences between individual and group counseling, Nicholas Hobbs points out that some severely threatened people would find a group situation too frightening and would do better, at least at the beginning of a change effort, in a one-to-one situation.[9] An extremely shy, withdrawn person may need the experience of a satisfying interpersonal relationship with one person—a social worker—before he can trust himself to try out new behavior with others. A person who has trouble forming a good relationship with another but succeeds in achieving a trusting, satisfying relationship with a social worker may resist sharing the worker with other people. Some people may believe their problems are so unique and difficult they can only be helped by a professional expert, and the presence of other people would dilute the change effort.

Other individuals may not wish to talk about problems and personal feelings in front of others and indeed may only discuss them with a worker when they have learned to trust him and are assured the discussion will be confidential. A teacher may be unwilling to discuss in a school staff meeting his feelings of inadequacies in dealing with teenagers who disrupt his classroom, but he will confide in a school social worker and ask for his help. A director of city housing inspection may refuse to meet with the worker and a neighborhood organization to discuss housing violations because he does not want to face the residents' hostility and anger and may insist on a personal interview with the worker.

In some circumstances an individual may agree to a proposal or suggestion made by the worker in a one-to-one system but might refuse if

---

[8] See discussion of the use of leverage people in Chapter 8, Making Intitial Contacts.

[9] Nicholas Hobbs, "Group Centered Psychotherapy," in Carl Rogers (ed.), *Client Centered Therapy* (New York: Houghton Mifflin Co., 1951), pp. 278–319.

other people were present. A chief of police who may be willing to discuss a discretionary arrest policy for drug users with a social worker he has learned to respect and trust might not be open to discussion in a public meeting at which the press is present. A teen-age boy might admit to the worker that he wants to get along better with his parents but would not say this directly to his parents. A community leader who has agreed to accept membership in a task force to recommend a program for problems of drug abuse might be persuaded to accept the chairmanship after the worker has clarified for him the possible tasks for the committee, the amount of time involved, and the help the worker will give. If the worker asked him to be chairman without warning at the first meeting of the task force, he might quickly say no and suggest another member.

While the presence and influence of other people leads some targets and some social workers to choose a one-to-one action system, it causes others to prefer a group action system. People who resist entering into change efforts in meetings alone with the worker may be motivated to begin and remain in a change effort if other people are present. Those who share similar characteristics may be reluctant to discuss their personal problems and feelings alone with a worker but will agree to meet with others like themselves. People may feel that in a group they will not have to talk unless they want to and that they will be able to get ideas, support, and make friends in a group.

People who want to learn how they "come off" to others and who want to practice new behavior in a social situation removed from their daily routines may want to join a group to receive feedback from other group members in addition to the worker. Some people who resist change may believe they can manipulate and control the worker in a group setting. For example, a police chief under attack from some elements in the community demanding police action against teen-age drug users may refuse to see a worker alone and will only meet with him if the head of the narcotics division and the president of the police commission are present.

A target system that refuses to acknowledge that it is part of the problem may insist on a group action system which contains the people it believes are the target. A mother with a child creating problems at school who insists that she is not part of the problem may refuse to meet individually with the worker but will meet with him and a teacher or all members of her family.

It is possible for a person to agree to a specific proposal made by the worker in a group action system who would refuse if he were meeting with the worker alone. If a worker believes the director of his agency would refuse his request to present a proposal for a drug information program to the agency board of directors, he may raise the issue at a staff meeting to obtain support of other workers. A teen-age boy may refuse to admit to the worker that he loses control of his actions when he drinks heavily or takes drugs but can be pressured into admitting it in a group of his peers. An autocratic president of an organization may refuse in individual conversations with a worker to agree to change his practices but may be forced to do so or be removed from office at an organizational meeting.

Thus, the worker's choice of a one-to-one or group action system may be determined by his need to gain the participation of the target in the change effort. His choice is also predetermined if the target will agree to a proposal or suggestion of the worker only in either a one-to-one or group action system.

Use of Several Action Systems of Different Size

In order to achieve his purposes in any change effort, the worker may use several action systems of different size and may work with the same person in both a one-to-one action system and a group action system. For example, when the worker is involved with an existing group or organization, he may meet separately with some individuals or subgroups as well as the group as a whole. He may work with an individual alone for several sessions and then encourage him to join a group. He may also work individually with members of a group to help them participate more effectively in it. He could, for example, plan agendas with the chairman of a group and discuss methods for conducting the meetings or meet individually with members who are not attending meetings or are disrupting them. To help people with personal problems that cannot be handled in the group, the worker can supplement group meetings with individual sessions.

Social workers often consciously combine individual and group action systems. A research project in an urban slum demonstrated that a combination of individual interviews between workers and residents, and membership of residents in a group produced significant change in the residents. The workers were operating on the assumption that individuals who are alienated from society and who have no hope of achieving a more satisfying life may be helped to develop a different self-image by becoming part of a group of people working together to solve common problems.[10] A new self-image may be built by increasing feelings of self-worth and reducing despair and alienation. At the same time these individuals may need individual help from the worker in alleviating their problems and becoming effective participants in the group.

As a change effort unfolds, action systems may expand or contract in size. The effort may begin with a one-to-one contact between the worker and another person; as the effort proceeds, this initial action system can be expanded to include many other members. Then too, a change effort that begins in a group action system may be reduced to several one-to-one systems. A social worker may approach a teenage group, observe a city council meeting, or attend a teachers meeting in order to lay the ground work for later individual contacts with group members.

COMPOSITION

In addition to deciding on the appropriate size action system, the worker must choose, perhaps from a number of candidates, the particular people to include in a specific action system. He will be concerned with putting together the best mix of people who will contribute to and gain from the action system.

The worker must select people who will help the action system itself function smoothly. At the same time he must select those who will help each other learn something from action system membership that can be transferred to other situations and those who will perform tasks outside of the action system to help it achieve its purpose. In considering people who can contribute to both the internal functioning and the external purpose and tasks of the action system, the worker is guided in his selection by two kinds of attributes of potential action system members—descriptive and behavioral. Harvey Bertcher and Frank Maple use concepts from role theory to define these attributes as follows: "A descriptive attribute refers to a position an individual occupies. Position means a category of individuals who are similar in

---

[10] Rudolph Wittenberg, "Personality Adjustment through Social Action," in Frank Riessman, Jerome Cohen, and Arthur Pearl (eds.), *Mental Health of the Poor* (New York: Free Press, 1964), pp. 378–92. Warren C. Haggstrom's article in the same book, entitled "The Power of the Poor" (pp. 205–23), deals extensively with this idea. A similar experience with slum residents is described in Purcell and Specht's case study in Part III.

some respect. A behavioral attribute refers to the way in which a person performs . . . in a position."[11]

Examples of descriptive characteristics or attributes are:
1. Bob is a teen-ager.
2. Jim is a member of a youth gang.
3. Mrs. Jones is a parent of a mentally retarded child.
4. Mrs. Smith is a black resident of Harlem.
5. Mr. Miller is president of the school board.
6. John is a child who has been rejected by his parents.

Examples of behavioral characteristics are:
1. Mr. Smith acts as a compromiser when he is in a group and helps other members find common areas of agreement.
2. Bob plays alone and does not join in any group activity.
3. Mr. Miller usually votes on the school board for appropriations for handicapped children and encourages other members to vote his way.
4. Mrs. Jones is a strict disciplinarian with her children and complains that her husband never helps her with household chores.

The worker can influence both the internal functioning and the accomplishment of external tasks and purposes of an action system by selecting members with appropriate descriptive and behavioral attributes.

Behavioral Attributes Affecting Internal Functioning

The worker forming a group action system will try to determine how each potential member might contribute to the internal functioning of the system. Kenneth Benne and Paul Sheats have identified three types of roles that members play in groups:

1. Group task roles. Participant roles here are related to the task which the group is deciding to undertake or has undertaken. Their purpose is to facilitate and coordinate group effort in the selection and definition of a common problem and in the solution of that problem.
2. Group building and maintenance roles. The roles in this category are oriented toward the functioning of the group as a group. They

---

[11] Harvey Bertcher and Frank Maple, *Group Composition—An Instructional Program* (Ann Arbor, Mich.: Campus Publishers, 1971), p. 4. We have relied on many of the ideas of these authors in our discussion of the impact of descriptive and behavioral attributes on the formation of action systems.

are designed to alter or maintain the group way of working, to strengthen, regulate and perpetuate the group as a group.

3. Individual roles. This category does not classify member roles as such, since the "participations" denoted here are directed toward the satisfaction of the "participant's" individual needs. Their purpose is some individual goal which is not relevant either to the group task or to the functioning of the group as a group.[12]

Group task roles include information seeker, opinion seeker, coordinator, initiator-contributor, energizer, and procedural technician. Group building and maintenance roles are those of the encourager, harmonizer, compromiser, standard setter or ego ideal, and follower. Individual roles include aggressor, blocker, recognition-seeker, self-confessor, dominator, help-seeker, and special interest pleader.[13]

In selecting members of a particular action system, the worker will attempt to select people with heterogeneous behavior attributes who will play different group task and maintenance roles. He also will try to put together a combination of individual roles—imagine a group composed entirely of blockers or self-confessors!

Research studies on group problem solving have found that groups with heterogeneous behavioral attributes produce a higher proportion of high quality, acceptable solutions than do homogeneous groups.[14]

Experience can be given to people in playing different group task and maintenance roles. When the worker's purpose is to alter the roles that people play within an existent group in order to improve its internal functioning, he may form subgroups that will result in altered roles. For example, if a mother ordinarily plays most of the group task roles that the worker wants to help the father develop, he could form a subgroup with the young children and the father which would force the father to gain experience in using task roles within the family.

The responsibility of filling various task and maintenance roles within the system may fall on the worker in a one-to-one action system. By assessing the behavioral attributes of the other person, he can determine what roles he will need to play to keep the system functioning.

---

[12] Kenenth D. Benne and Paul Sheats, "Functional Roles of Group Members," in Leland P. Bradford (ed.), *Group Development* (Washington, D.C.: National Training Laboratories, National Education Association, 1961), p. 52.

[13] Ibid., pp. 53–55.

[14] L. R. Hoffman and P. F. Maier, "Quality and Acceptance of Problem Solutions by Members of Homogeneous and Heterogeneous Groups," *Journal of Abnormal and Social Psychology*, 62 (1961): 401–7; William Shalinsky, "Group Composition as an Element of Social Group Work Practice," *Social Service Review*, 43 (March 1969): 42–49.

Descriptive Attributes Affecting Internal Functioning

Similarity in descriptive attributes of action system members can improve the system's internal functioning. Indeed, people may be hesitant to join an action system unless the members have attributes similar to their own. Similar descriptive attributes can help produce a compatible interactive system, such as a group of parents of mentally retarded children, businessmen, neighborhood residents, or black teen-agers. Common descriptive characteristics can also facilitate communication. The worker himself needs to be aware of his own descriptive attributes (sex, age, race, religion) and assess their impact on his ability to engage people in a one-to-one or group action system. In a summary of research studies on the impact of racial differences on the ability of the worker to form relationships with other people, Alfred Kadushin points out that many nonwhite clients prefer a worker of similar racial background, concluding that "although white workers may be able to understand and empathize with the nonwhite experience, nonwhite workers achieve this sooner, more thoroughly, and at less cost to the relationship."[15]

Other studies indicate that similarities in descriptive characteristics such as sex and age may be important in initial contacts, but their importance in keeping an action system functioning is likely to diminish over time.[16] There are circumstances in which similarity of race, sex, and other characteristics is critical to the purpose of the action system, as with a social worker forming a group of black teen-agers dedicated to developing pride in their black identity or a social worker attempting to influence the quality of service provided by an abortion counseling service operated by the women's liberation movement. However, in most cases there seems to be evidence that the competence of the worker as demonstrated by his behavioral characteristics is more important than his similarities with the other system. For example, Donald Brieland found that although black ghetto residents, all things being equal, preferred black service givers to white, they would prefer a white worker if he were better qualified than a black one.[17] Competence proved to be a more important factor than race.

The importance of competence in the worker has been highlighted

---

[15] Alfred Kadushin, "The Racial Factor in the Interview," *Social Work*, 17 (May 1972): 98.

[16] Alfred Kadushin, "Social Sex Roles and the Initial Interview," *Mental Hygiene*, 42 (July 1958): 354–61.

[17] Donald Brieland, "Black Identity and the Helping Person," *Children*, 16 (September–October 1969): 170–75.

in a number of studies which have examined the impact of the characteristics of the worker on the likelihood that people will continue
in change efforts. These studies indicate that commitment to a change
effort by an individual or a group is enhanced if they perceive that
the worker has special knowledge, expertise, and competence, is interested in them, and is committed to help.[18]

A competent worker can not only overcome but take advantage of
his descriptive differences as compared with other systems. For example, younger workers can learn to establish rapport with the aged.[19]
Mary Stites, a social work graduate student at the University of Wisconsin, Madison, described her experiences at an institution for the aged
as follows:

> Student, youth, and female traits are important influences on my
> relationships with staff, administration, and patients at the institu-
> tion. I am a young person in a student role, and female on top of it
> (in a hospital full of people who view the female as less capable than
> the male). These roles are highlighted by my appearance—I wear short
> skirts, knee-high boots, and have long straight hair. These traits give
> me a lack of credibility with many hospital employees.
>
> Dealing with detrimental aspects of my roles has been a daily process.
> Different stances can be assumed in different situations to achieve a
> working relationship with staff members. . . . I have won the respect of
> our Volunteer Coordinator by careful scheduling, deference to her
> long-standing knowledge of patients, discussions of the worth of vari-
> ous activities, individual patient needs, and the future directions of the
> hospital as a whole. The student role provides opportunities to seek
> advice as well as state opinions, and an advantage can be earned in good
> staff relations by using one approach or another at different times.
>
> Patients run a wide gamut from outright rejection to near hero wor-
> ship. Curiosity about young people motivates some of them to initiate
> a lot of interaction. The men are intrigued by young women working

---

[18] George Levinger, "Continuance in Casework and Other Helping Relationships:
A Review of Current Research," *Social Work*, 5 (July 1960): 47; Norman A.
Polansky and Jacob Kounin, "Clients' Reactions to Initial Interviews," *Human
Relations*, 9, No. 3 (1956): 262; and Cartwright and Zander, *Group Dynamics*, p.
227. Arnold Goldstein studied research programs that indicated attraction between
a potential client and psychotherapist is heightened when the client is led to believe
he will like the therapist and perceives him as "warm" rather than "cold," as having similar attitudes on issues important to the client, and as having high status
within his change agent system. See "Maximizing the Initial Psychotherapeutic
Relationship," *American Journal of Psychotherapy*, 23 (July 1969): 450–51.

[19] Allen Pincus, "Reminiscence in Aging and Its Implications for Social Work
Practice," *Social Work*, 15 (July 1970): 47–53.

in a setting of old to very old, institutionalized people. Some of the older women especially resent the young, female workers.

Patients hung up with the youth thing have been easier [than staff] to reach. Joking and good humor, largely as a means of informing them what young people in general are like, have helped to satisfy their curiosity and relieve their anxiety about new modes of dress and ways of thinking. A tacit assurance that I am not going to force my ways on them is exchanged for an acceptance of me the way I am.

The student/youth role has been to my advantage with many patients, especially those who have some understanding of the meaning of their confinement in a county institution. For them, my chief asset is precisely that I belong more to the changing outside world than to the more stagnant institutional world.

Both the behavioral and descriptive characteristics of the members of an action system will have an impact on its internal functioning. The worker must look for people with heterogeneous behavioral attributes to play different task and maintenance roles within the group, but homogeneous descriptive characteristics can facilitate communication in a group action system. Except when similarity in descriptive characteristics of worker and others is required because of the purpose of the action system, the worker's competence, as demonstrated by his behavioral attributes, is a more important factor in the maintenance of the social worker's relationships with other systems.

In addition to functioning smoothly, the action system must accomplish its purposes. Although workers and theoreticians differ in their emphasis on system maintenance and achievement of purpose, in reality the two are intertwined. A system that is not achieving its purpose cannot maintain itself indefinitely, and a system cannot achieve its purpose unless it is functioning smoothly. The worker forming an action system can assess how different behavioral and descriptive attributes of potential members will affect what each will gain from the action system and be able transfer to other situations, and what each will contribute to the achievement of the purpose of the system.

Behavioral Attributes Affecting Accomplishment of Purpose and External Tasks

Members of both one-to-one and group action systems can serve as behavioral models for other members. Members may not only model the behavior of others within meetings of the action system but also try out the new behavior in their interactions with people in their daily lives.

The worker himself is often a model for members of a one-to-one or group action system. With a street gang, the worker can provide a model of behavior that can be imitated by members; in an action system with an individual who has never had a trusting relationship with another person, he can model open, honest communication. Other members of a group action system also can provide behavioral models for imitation. The group approach provides members with the opportunity to observe other people like themselves who face the same difficulties they do but approach them in different ways.[20] If all the members of a group had similar approaches to handling problems, there would be no opportunity to learn by modeling behavior. Thus the worker may look for heterogeneous behavior attributes of members to provide for alternative models of behavior.

In either a one-to-one or group action system in which the worker's purpose is to change the behavior of targets outside of the system, the worker may find it helpful to include people within the system who have influence over the targets. Unless these people normally exert their influence over the targets, however, this purpose may not be achieved. For example, if the worker wants to influence the operation of a public school system, he might include in his action system an individual who has personal and business relationships with the school board president. However, unless the worker has evidence from past events that the individual will use his relationships to influence the school board president, he cannot anticipate that this will be the case.

Descriptive Attributes Affecting Accomplishment of Purpose and External Tasks

For each action system the social worker forms, he needs to determine what *critical* descriptive attributes of candidates for a system can help it achieve its purpose. This is true whether or not the target and action systems are identical. The experiences of agencies in forming groups made up entirely or partially of children with physical and emotional handicaps who are cut off from or deny themselves satisfying social relationships with their peers were studied by Richard Bond and associates. Workers who considered a handicap as a critical attribute formed groups composed completely of handicapped children, with the advantages that group members could empathize with each other and were protected from social ostracism, and programming and activity could be planned easily. The main disadvantage of this group-

---

[20] Bertcher and Maple, *Group Composition*, p. 17

ing was that it continually isolated the children from their normal peers. A different approach was used by an agency that operated on the theory that many handicapped children have the capacity to work out their problems in a setting where they are not surrounded by youngsters similarly handicapped. Agency workers formed small groups (6 to 10 members) of neighborhood children with a mix of handicapped and "average" youngsters. For *all* the children, the purpose of these groups was to help them "accept and live with children who are different and grow as individuals in the process."[21]

The report on the agency's experience with the second type of groups concluded:

> In some . . . clubs group workers have seen evidences of regression, over-dependency and excessive conformity on the part of handicapped or disturbed children. On the other hand, they have observed in many instances that the handicapped or disturbed child concerned has been able to modify his behavior positively. This has re-inforced their belief that such a child—through the identifications which he develops with the group leader, with other members and with the group as an entity —can derive strengths from association with a group of neighborhood peers and learn to function more adequately in a social situation.[22]

The purpose of these groups led to identification of children who had mixed descriptive attributes—handicapped and nonhandicapped—but had in common the *critical* descriptive attributes of children with a need to learn to get along with peers who are different in some way but similar in age and neighborhood residence.

We suggest, along with others,[23] that the critical descriptive attributes are those that relate to the purpose of the action system. For an action system that will include the targets of change, the critical descriptive characteristics are those that relate to the problems or needs of prospective members that are to be handled in the action system. Social workers often make the mistake of assuming that attributes such as race and socioeconomic status are critical because people are frequently differentiated along these lines, although experience

---

[21] Richard J. Bond *et al.*, "The Neighborhood Peer Group," *The Group* 17 (October 1954): 3 ff.; David R. Preininger, "Reactions of Normal Children to Retardates in Integrated Groups," *Social Work* 13 (April 1968): 75–77, reports on a similar experience with groups of retarded and normal children.

[22] Bond *et al.*, "Neighborhood Peer Group," p. 24.

[23] John H. Wax, "Criteria for Grouping Hospitalized Mental Patients," in *Use of Groups in the Psychiatric Setting* (New York: National Association of Social Workers, 1960) p. 87; and Northern, *Social Work with Groups*, p. 95.

suggests that common problems (being the mother of a child with rheumatic fever) outweigh the importance of such attributes.[24]

A similar point is made by John Wax in discussing the importanc of a common bond of "significant life experience" to hospitalize mental patients:

... The emotional impact of an experience people are living throug together can outweigh the differences among them as to diagnosis socioeconomic status, education, and so on. An orientation group fo newly admitted patients, for example, is effective when focused on con cerns about separation from family and community and anticipatory concerns in relation to the hospital and the illness. Separation and antici patory anxieties do not respect diagnostic, educational, or racial differ ences, and the experience of living with these anxieties and sharing wor on them constitutes a major unifying force for the group.[25]

Thus a descriptive factor such as race is important when it is relate to the purpose of the group. If a worker is forming an action syster to help black teen-agers develop attitudes of black pride and identity race and age obviously are critical attributes. As we noted above, fo other action systems with different purposes, race may not be a critica descriptive attribute.

The social worker also must identify the critical descriptive attri butes of potential members when all or some of the targets are outsid the action system he is forming. Peter Marris and Martin Rein sugges that three crucial tasks are necessary to achieve change in organization or within a community. A reformer "must recruit a coalition of powe sufficient for his purpose; he must respect the democratic traditio which expects every citizen, not merely to be represented, but to pla an autonomous part in the determination of his own affairs; and hi policies must be demonstrably rational."[26]   Marris and Rein's thre crucial tasks indicate that the social worker must include in an actio system for community or organizational change people with power t influence the target system, people who are directly affected by th goals of the worker, and people with expertise about the probler under consideration. However, when they studied community actio programs aimed at problems of poverty in major U.S. cities, they foun it was extremely difficult to integrate the three tasks into one strateg and concluded: "Either you do something primarily because its useful

---

[24] Bertcher and Maple, *Group Composition*, p. 79.
[25] Wax, "Criteria for Grouping," p. 90.
[26] Peter Marris and Martin Rein, *Dilemmas of Social Reform* (New York Atherton Press, 1967), p. 7.

ness is worth testing, or because the community's leaders want it, or because the poor want it. Once there is conflict, you must choose."[27]

To show how the worker could resolve the dilemmas raised by Marris and Rein we will examine what might happen in an action system with representatives of the three kinds of people identified above. For example, consider a social worker in a community mental health center who wants to improve educational services for mentally retarded children. He forms an action system composed of:

1. The people directly affected by the problem—the parents of the children.

2. The targets themselves or people who have influence with the targets, such as the superintendent of public schools, members of the school board, the staff and board members of a private day-care center for mentally retarded children, citizens who are influential with people who vote school tax monies, members of the county board of supervisors, and state legislators.

3. Experts, such as workers from the state departments of education and mental health who have expertise in the education of mentally retarded children as well as knowledge of possible state or federal funding sources. The parents of the children might be considered as experts of another kind, who can testify from personal experience about the inadequacies of present educational facilities and the resultant hardships for their children and themselves.

The underlying assumption of the worker in forming this action system would appear to be that if these people are involved together in studying the problem, they will agree on a plan and methods to implement it and can influence the targets to put the plan in operation. Thus he might anticipate that members will decide that classes at the local public schools are needed for children over five years old and that the private day-care center should provide educational experiences for children under five. For this plan to succeed, the parents must agree to it and perhaps agree to pay fees to the private center. The schools and private day-care center must agree to inaugurate the plans. Members of the action system must agree to influence the funding sources and must have the necessary influence to succeed in gaining appropriations. The state experts must certify the plan as being technically sound and perhaps even help obtain state aid for both educational programs.

In order for this action system to achieve its purpose, the *critical*

---

[27] Ibid., p. 229.

common descriptive attribute of its members is their agreement on policies which will achieve the purpose of the action system—improving educational services for mentally retarded children. If the worker cannot identify this common descriptive attribute in people affected by the problem, the targets or people who have influence over the targets, and experts, he will have to form a different kind of action system to achieve his purpose.

If he decides the critical common descriptive attribute is being directly affected by the problem, he could form an action system of the parents. He could help the parents to identify a major target, such as the school board, and plan a strategy to influence it. He also will have to help them assess the resources and influence they can mobilize to overcome resistances of the school board members. He could also form an action system of experts who can reach agreement and devise a plan to influence the targets through use of this and other action systems. One of these could be an action system of people who share the attributes of being community influentials as well as being interested in mentally retarded children.

Thus the worker can form several action systems, each containing people with common critical attributes, to achieve his purpose. Although he may be influenced in his selection of members of an action system by the interest and influence of people who have access to a target, by his need for expertness in the action system, and by a commitment to democratic values that allows for participation by people affected by the problem, he will need to select people whose common critical descriptive characteristics will enable him to achieve his purpose.

Thus the critical descriptive attribute for members of an action system will depend on the social worker's purpose in forming the group. If his major purpose is to accomplish a specific task, such as improving educational services to the retarded, he may work mainly with influential decision makers who he believes will help him reach that goal. If, on the other hand, his major purpose is to enable people to take action on social problems that directly affect their lives, he may work mainly with the people who are affected by the problem—parents of the mentally retarded. This purpose also can be linked to the purpose of helping people gain a feeling of self-worth and increase their ability to solve other personal problems. If the worker's purpose is to help leaders of major segments of the community work together on common problems, thereby building communications between community groupings, the common critical descriptive attribute may be leadership in a community segment. Often members will be selected because they represent specific interest groups—an active Catholic layman who is on the county board of supervisors, a black college professor who is president of the Urban League, a Mexican-American woman who is an officer of a welfare rights group. The worker may attempt to accomplish more than one purpose, but if conflict arises between the purposes because the members do not share a common critical descriptive attribute, the worker may have to choose one on which he will concentrate.

The worker's theoretical orientation will influence him in his selection of members of an action system. If he believes most community problems arise from a struggle between the powerless and a few elite decision makers who will not change unless forced to, he may choose to organize those without power to confront the status quo. If his orientation leads him to believe decision makers can be influenced through their involvement in a group representing a wide cross section of a community, he will form a different kind of action system.

Combining Attributes for Internal Functioning and Accomplishment of Purpose

Both behavioral and descriptive attributes can be combined to facilitate the internal functioning and the accomplishment of tasks and goals of action systems. While *similar descriptive attributes* of group members set the stage for compatible interaction, *different behavioral attributes* make it likely that each individual will have something useful to contribute to others so that interaction will take the form of mutual responsiveness. Thus we can conclude that effective action systems are homogeneous in regard to members' critical descriptive attributes and heterogeneous in regard to members' behavioral attributes.

Recognizing the effects of the two types of attributes, the social worker forming an action system will attempt to select members:

1. Who will play different task and maintenance roles within the system and thus aid the system's functioning.
2. Who will be compatible and complement the needs of others in the system and be alike enough to be able to communicate and interact.
3. Who will provide behavior models for each other.
4. Who will actively influence the targets outside of the system.
5. Whose critical descriptive attributes are related to the purpose of the action system.

Both Bertcher and Maple and Wax suggest that the worker should seek a balance of attributes in a group, selecting members who represent a range of characteristics on a continuum. In Wax's criteria for grouping hospitalized mental patients, the group is regarded as a section of a spectrum or continuum:

> In composing a group we should avoid mixing patients who represent the extremes of the continuum. . . . For example, we would not mix highly articulate and intelligent patients with patients who are mute and/or extremely limited in intellectual and cultural endowment; nor would we place an extremely shy, fearful, submissive patient with a group of extremely aggressive, exploitative soociopaths . . . our groups will probably do better if they are not confronted with the task of assimilating individuals who are so different that they cannot share the group's common process and aims.[28]

Selecting members on a continuum which avoids two extremes of behavior or descriptive characteristics also helps prevent the formation of subgroups of people with the same characteristics who might subvert the working of the action system.

Any potential member of an action system can be described by a great many descriptive and behavioral attributes. The worker must decide which of these characteristics are the potential members' *critical* attributes, as related to the functioning of the action system and the achievement of its purpose. He assesses the attributes of each member in his attempt to achieve a balance of attributes in a group.

For example, a social worker planning to form a group of patients in a mental hospital to help them prepare for discharge would consider patients as potential members on the basis of a wide range of descriptive attributes related to:

1. Age.
2. Sex.
3. Length of stay in hospital. This may be from six months to several years.
4. Job skills.
5. Educational achievement.
6. Assessments by staff of readiness to leave hospital. The length of the stay could range from one month to a year.
7. Type of living arrangement available to patients when they leave hospital.
8. Race.
9. Religion.

Since the social worker's purpose is to help the patients prepare for discharge, he decides that the critical descriptive attribute for this action

---

[28] Wax, "Criteria for Grouping," pp. 91–92.

system is readiness to leave the hospital. He selects as members those patients who should be ready to leave the hospital within two or three months. Since he wants the group to be compatible and able to share common feelings about leaving the hospital and adjusting to similar experiences in the outside world, he decides to include both sexes and selects members on a continuum of age (e.g., 25–40), level of job skills, educational experience, and type of living arrangement available to them when they leave the hospital. The continuum will make it possible for each member to communicate with some other people who are close to them in age and will encounter similar employment and living problems. Behavioral attributes of prospective members could range on a continuum related to:

1. Expressions by patients of their attitudes about leaving the hospital (fearful of leaving, anxious to leave).
2. Behavior in hospital (cooperative with staff, friendly with other patients, dominates other patients, acts aggressively toward staff).
3. Behavior with visitors and on home visits (shows anger toward family and friends, becomes depressed when home visits are discussed, asks for frequent home visits).

If the worker identifies expressions by patients of their attitudes toward leaving the hospital and behavior with visitors and on home visits as critical behavioral attributes, he will select members with a range of attributes on these factors. Wax suggests that the worker may want to weight groups on the side of relative health, to provide good behavioral models for other group members to imitate. Thus the worker may want to "weight" the group with members who are anxious to leave the hospital. The worker will also use his knowledge about the patients' behavior in the hospital to select members to play different task and maintenance roles in the group.

In assessing the multiple characteristics of each member, the social worker will seek to develop an action system with the proper balance of behavioral and descriptive attributes. A prospective member for a group to study educational services for the mentally retarded could be selected because of several critical attributes:

1. His position in the community (descriptive–influential member of the school board).
2. The way he behaves in that position (often votes for additional school appropriations for handicapped children).
3. His knowledge of or relation to mentally retarded children (member of school board committee on special education).
4. His behavior in interaction with others (acts as a facilitator and

bridge builder in a group and works to reconcile different points of view).

The worker also would assess the prospective member for his possible agreement on goals of the group, his self-interest in relation to its purpose, and his perception of the demands that would be placed on him by belonging to the action system.

Attributes of the Worker

A final factor in determining the best mix of people to put in interaction with one another in a particular action system is the characteristics of the worker himself. The style of the worker, composed of the sum total of his personality and values and predisposition, has far-reaching effects on the relationships he forms.[29] A number of studies have indicated that the style of the worker is one of the most important variables influencing the operation of an action system.[30]

Some workers are more comfortable in conflict situations and others function better in collaborative relationships. Some are more skillful with articulate people and others can work successfully with those who are shy or withdrawn. Some workers can tolerate aggressive, hostile behavior and some cannot. Some are responsive to children, and others are effective with the aging. Often a worker's style and preference for working with people of certain descriptive and behavioral attributes leads him to choose his agency setting, for example, a children's institution, nursing home, or juvenile probation agency. Regardless of his agency setting, however, the action systems a worker utilizes will consist of people with a variety of behavioral and descriptive attributes. He can expect to deal with staff members from his own or other agencies, community influentials, and the families of individual clients. The worker himself needs to be aware of his own descriptive and behavioral attributes and assess their impact on his effectiveness in working with different people in action systems.

---

[29] See Chapter 4, Worker Relationships.
[30] Edward Mullen, "Differences in Worker Style in Casework," *Social Casework*, 50 (June 1969): 347–53; William Reid, "Characteristics of Casework Communication," *Welfare in Review*, 5 (October 1967): 11–19; Hans Strupp and Allen Bergin, "Some Empirical and Conceptual Bases for Coordinated Research in Psychotherapy: A Critical Review of Issues, Trends, and Evidence," *International Journal of Psychiatry*, 7 (February 1969): 18–90.

Availability of Members

Even though the worker has been able to determine the mix of people he needs for an action system, he may not be able to secure it unless he has access to several people who are potential members. Some agencies try to maintain a pool of clients from which workers can select members. Workers who rely on referrals from other agencies or from other staff in their own agencies may specify the descriptive and behavioral attributes they need in prospective members.

It is not always possible to achieve the optimum mix of members. A worker reaching out to an already formed group for an action system may not be able to secure the agreement of all the members to participate. An individual may refuse to join a suggested type of action system. Further, the worker may determine that the preferred intervention plan for an individual is a group action system, but the individual's attributes would not mix with those of other prospective members.

When the worker is unable to achieve the optimum mix of members for an action system, he will have to plan strategies to overcome the deficits. To do this he could alter his program plans, bring guests into the action system, use a co-worker, or form additional action systems to exert influence on targets in a community or organization change effort.

OPERATING PROCEDURES

Social workers can influence the functioning of an action system by the use of time, by planning for the setting or place of interaction, and by establishing norms or rules for interaction and decision making. These factors operate in all systems whether they are one-to-one or group action systems.

Use of Time

The social worker's use of time refers to such factors as (1) length of time for the existence of the action system, (2) length of time between meetings or encounters of the system, (3) length of time devoted to each meeting, and (4) time of day the system meets.

LENGTH OF TIME FOR EXISTENCE OF ACTION SYSTEMS. Some action systems meet only once and accomplish their purpose. This can be the case when a hospital social worker discusses alternatives for aftercare with a patient's family or a group of prospective adoptive parents meets for orientation to the adoption laws of the state. Other action systems meet for a specified length of time. A group of foster parents may be engaged in a 16-session class on child development, or a budget committee of an agency board of directors could agree to meet once a week for a month in order to formulate the agency budget. Other action systems may have no set time limit, as with an individual in treatment at a mental health center or a community committee formed to study problems of drug abuse.

In recent years, agency experiences and research have challenged the assumption that extended individual or group counseling is more effective than short-term counseling. It has been found that "when the worker expects treatment will take about two years for treatment goals to be achieved, it usually takes that long—if he really expects that only three months will be needed, three months often proves sufficient."[31]

In a study of a family service agencies, it was found that families receiving planned short-term treatment (limited to eight interviews) had better outcomes than those receiving extended, open-end treatment. The problems of 85 percent of families receiving short-term help improved, compared to only 64 percent of those given extended casework. Equally important, 17 percent of the extended service families showed some deterioration, compared to only 2 percent of the families receiving brief casework.[32] The report of a program of brief (six-session) group therapy in a child guidance clinic concluded that "the majority of children and parents do not need to continue beyond the brief therapy program."[33]

William Reid believes "durational limits . . . force a concentration of efforts on available goals, leads to better planning in use of time available, and stimulate both practitioner and client to greater effort."[34] Ralph Garcia and Olive Irwin found that the use of time-limited contracts at intake cut down on the dropout rate at a family service agency.[35]

Time can operate as a constraint in the selection of action system

---

[31] Bertcher and Maple, *Group Composition*, p. 60.

[32] William Reid and Ann Shyne, *Brief and Extended Casework* (New York: Columbia University Press, 1969).

[33] Norman Epstein, "Brief Group Therapy in a Child Guidance Clinic," *Social Work*, 15 (July 1970): 38.

[34] William J. Reid, "Target Problems, Time Limits, Task Structure," *Journal of Education for Social Work*, 8 (Spring 1972): 66.

[35] Ralph Garcia and Olive Irwin, "A Family Agency Deals with the Problem of Dropouts," *Social Casework*, 43 (February 1962): 71–75.

members. Workers attempting to form community groups have found that busy citizens often will agree to serve on ad hoc task forces with an established, limited time duration but may be reluctant to serve on a long-term committee.

LENGTH OF TIME BETWEEN MEETINGS OF ACTION SYSTEM. The length of time between meetings or encounters of the action system may be determined by the amount of activity that must be carried on between meetings, the needs of the client, and the urgency of the problem. Lydia Rapoport believes:

... The client should be able to set the frequency and length of time within agreed upon limits, like a self demand schedule. We must have enough faith and be sufficiently free from anxiety ourselves to accept the client's time schedule. There is, after all, no magic in weekly appointments. These may fit our patterns of working, but not the client's immediate needs. The client may need three appointments in a row or one each day for a week. The point is that time is a useful instrument in helping with the management and control of various feelings.[36]

The frequency of meetings may change during the process. For example, in working in a treatment context, some workers taper off the frequency of interviews toward the end to help disengage from the client and evaluate how well the client is making it on his own.

LENGTH OF TIME DEVOTED TO EACH MEETING. The length of time for each meeting of the action system should be related to the purpose of the encounter, the age and attention span of the members, the program or activity planned, and the number of members.[37]

A first interview with a potential client may require over an hour to allow time for all parties to discuss their purposes and for the worker to clarify contract terms, but subsequent encounters may be shorter. Very young children and people who are very ill cannot tolerate long sessions. A meeting with a large number of people will have to last long enough for many of them to have an opportunity to participate.

TIME OF DAY. The time of day for the meeting of the action system can be governed by the availability of the members and the social worker. Whereas a low-income person working in a factory may not be able to meet with a social worker or attend a meeting during the

[36] Lydia Rapoport, "Crisis-Oriented Short-Term Casework," *Social Service Review*, 41 (March 1967): 39.

[37] See Northern, *Social Work with Groups*, p. 103, for a discussion of appropriate length of time for group meetings.

day, mothers with young children in school may prefer daytime meetings.

Thus social workers can use time to ensure the participation of members in the encounters of the action system; to sustain people's interest, participation, and motivation; to meet the requirements of participants; and to provide structure, limits, and impetus for change efforts.

Setting or Place for Interaction

Decisions as to where the action system should meet and how the setting should be arranged will follow from the worker's purpose, the needs of the client, and the residence of the members of the action system. In recent years social workers, especially those working with minority cultural groups and low-income people, have emphasized the importance of meeting people in their own neighborhoods and in familiar settings. People who would be hesitant to seek help or meet in a strange or distant location may be more comfortable on their home ground. Workers who are reaching out to offer services and programs to teen-age gangs or slum residents often must meet them on their own turf if they are to reach them at all. Neighborhood service centers are established in low-income neighborhoods to make services geographically, financially, and psychologically accessible to people who need them.[38]

When working with families in their own homes, the worker can not only demonstrate his interest in helping the family but gain a more complete picture of the family than he could in an office interview.[39] Some families, however, consider it an invasion of privacy to meet with the worker in their own homes; they prefer office visits. The worker must be guided in his choice of setting by his purpose and the client's needs.

Settings also are important to workers who want to influence community organizations. A worker trying to mediate a dispute between

---

[38] See Alfred J. Kahn, *Neighborhood Information Centers* (New York: Columbia University School of Social Work, 1966); Michael March, "The Neighborhood Center Concept," *Public Welfare* April 1968): 97–111; Edward J. O'Donnell and Marilyn M. Sullivan, "Service Delivery and Social Action through the Neighborhood Center—A Review of Research," *Welfare in Review*, 7 (November–December 1969): 1–11; Robert Perlman and David Jones, *Neighborhood Service Centers* (Washington, D.C.: Department of Health, Education, and Welfare, 1967).

[39] Alice Overton and Katherine Tinker, *Casework Notebook* (St. Paul, Minn.: Greater St. Paul United Fund Council, Inc., 1957).

two organizations may want to meet their representatives on neutral territory. A committee to coordinate the services of various agencies in a particular field might hold each meeting at a different agency so all involved can gain a better understanding of programs and services. A worker seeking to influence an organization may decide to attempt to gain the confidence and interest of people within the organization by visiting them on their home ground and learning first hand about their operation.

In addition to the place of meeting, there are other important variables of setting which are related to the purpose of the action system, the planned program and activity, and the nature of the interactions between people. These include the formal or informal arrangement of furniture, privacy, adequate space, lighting, condition of facilities, and indoor or outdoor locations.

Setting often indicates to people with problems what society thinks of them. A dirty, dark, uncomfortable waiting room in a welfare department conveys a clear message to public assistance applicants. It has been found that settings and the atmosphere they create can influence the receptivity of prospective clients. For example, a student social worker who described the intake office of a mental health clinic as "a small, windowless room, with shabby torn chairs, and a large IBM computer clicking constantly," found that "the room becomes rapidly smoked filled, the noise disconcerting, the size of the room confining." Noting that this is the first contact clients have with the center, she judged it to be "hardly a positive one."

Settings also can indicate the kind of behavior that is expected of people. An antiseptic children's home with highly polished floors and rigidly arranged furniture does not need signs to say "No playing allowed here."

It is possible for the worker to combine space and time dimensions in his influence efforts. The life space interview described by David Wineman is an example of a one-to-one action system with maximum flexibility in space and time. In a residential treatment setting for children, the worker intervenes on the spot at the place and time the child's disturbed behavior erupts, perhaps as temper tantrums or fighting.[40] The action system becomes activated in immediate response to the client's needs. The "therapeutic milieu" approach in mental hospitals also is an attempt to intervene in the life space of the patient,

---

[40] David Wineman, "The Life Space Interview," *Social Work*, 4 (January 1959): 3–17.

making the entire ward, not just the worker's office, the treatment setting.

Social workers can use setting to make people comfortable; to gain the confidence of change participants; to secure information about individuals, families, and organizations; to provide neutral ground for parties to a dispute; and to provide a therapeutic climate for change efforts.

Norms for Interaction and Decision Making

Action systems develop governing procedures or norms and rules for interaction and decision making. The democratic norms accepted in American culture often lead to the specification of rules and procedures for group meetings. Left to themselves, groups might establish autocratic procedures reflecting the existing power, economic, and social inequities of the members. Social workers who place a high value on client self-determination recognize the importance of establishing a climate in which all people are free to contribute, and they will try to enhance the ability of action system members to govern themselves. However, members of other systems may expect that since the change agent is the "expert," he should establish the rules and set the pace for interaction.

The amount of permissiveness the worker should maintain with a group has been discussed by Robert Vinter:

The degree of autonomy granted the group should vary with the type of group and its purpose, the treatment goals of the worker, and the member characteristics. With younger, less adequate, or more disturbed clients the worker may greatly limit the autonomy of the group, at least initially. The context and situation within which the group exists may also affect its autonomy: delinquent groups in their own neighborhoods may retain high autonomy, while institutional groups composed of clients with similar problems may have only limited autonomy. High control by the worker tends to induce dependence upon him, reduces the members' assertiveness, and limits the satisfactions which they may achieve within the group. The practitioner may vary the *areas* within which groups have autonomy, as well as the degree of self-determination. Thus, a group may be granted high autonomy with respect to its program of activities, but little choice as to its size and composition.[41]

[41] Robert Vinter, *Readings in Group Work Practice*, p. 43.

The size of the action system will be a factor in determining the nature of the rules for interaction. There have been many studies on the effects of group size on group interaction.[42] In general, they indicate that as groups get larger, the participation and satisfaction of members decrease, requirements for leadership increase, and subgroups begin to form. Large groups and organizations may need to adopt formalized rules, but in order to provide for wide participation they will subdivide into smaller, informal groups. A one-to-one action system of worker and client can operate with flexibility.

The optimum size for any group will vary according to group purpose. For example, if the purpose of the group is to help the participants learn satisfying ways of relating to other people, a small group of from 5 to 10 people will enhance close personal relationships. If the worker is organizing a group of residents of a slum neighborhood to withhold rents or confront their alderman and city officials with the power of numbers, a large number of people will be required.

In institutional settings in which members of the action system are in constant interaction, the size of systems and degree of formality can be varied to provide a variety of experiences. An example is the rehabilitative activities of drug addicts conducted by Synanon, a residential facility:

That the group's purpose is keeping addicts off drugs is given emphasis in formal and informal sessions—called "haircuts" or "pull ups" as well as in spontaneous denunciations, and in denunciations at general meetings. . . . The daily program has been deliberately designed to throw members into continuous mutual activity. In addition to the free, unrestricted interaction in small groups called "synanons," the members meet as a group at least twice each day.[43]

The worker has several options in determining rules for interaction and size of systems. When he is forming his contracts with the clients and members of his action system, the way in which the members of

---

[42] Robert F. Bales and Edgar F. Borgatta, "Size of Group as a Factor in the Interaction Profile," in A. Paul Hare, Edgar F. Borgatta, and Robert F. Bales (eds.), *Small Groups* (New York: Alfred A. Knopf, Inc., 1955), pp. 396–413; Edwin Thomas and Clinton Fink, "Effects of Group Size," *Psychological Bulletin*, 60 (July 1963): 371–84; W. Keith Warner and James S. Hilander, "The Relationship between Size of Organization and Membership Participation," *Rural Sociology*, 29 (March 1964): 30–39.

[43] Rita Volkman and Donald Cressey, "Differential Association and the Rehabilitation of Drug Addicts," in Riessman, Cohen, and Pearl, *Mental Health of the Poor*, pp. 600–619.

the action system may be expected to participate as well as the projected use of time and setting are issues that should be clarified.

In summary, the worker's use of rules for interaction and decision making in an action system will be determined by the purpose of the worker, the characteristics of the members, and the size of the system. These rules will affect the degree of autonomy exercised by members and have an impact on the nature of member interaction.

All of the activity of the worker in forming an action system is aimed at providing the optimum conditions for the ongoing functioning of the system. Through his selection of size of system, members with different or similar characteristics, and operating procedures, the worker is structuring the action system to enable it to achieve its goals. Methods the worker can use to maintain an action system and enhance its functioning throughout its existence are discussed in the following chapter.

CHAPTER 11

MAINTAINING AND

COORDINATING

ACTION SYSTEMS

An action system becomes a social entity after it has been put together by a worker and members begin to interact. In analyzing problems that arise in the internal functioning of the system and threaten the achievement of its purposes, the worker views the action system both from a developmental and a social system perspective.[1]

The developmental perspective is concerned with the history of the interactions of the members of the action system, considering where the relationships among members are now in reference to where they have been and how they might develop in the future. The social system perspective focuses on the internal functioning of the system, including such factors as communication patterns, role distribution, interpersonal relationships, and decision-making procedures.

Problems may arise not only between members of a single action

---

[1] For a discussion of developmental and social system models, see Robert Chin, "The Utility of System Models and Developmental Models for Practitioners," in Warren G. Bennis, Kenneth D. Benne, and Robert Chin (eds.), *The Planning of Change* (New York: Holt, Rinehart & Winston, Inc., 1961), pp. 201–14.

system but between people in different action systems. As has been noted, the worker can form a number of action systems to deal with a particular problem. Unless the efforts of these action systems are coordinated, the systems may be working at cross-purposes, so that they hinder rather than aid the worker and his clients in achieving their goals.

This chapter will discuss (1) problems in the development of effective relationships between members of an action system, (2) problems of internal functioning that may occur at any one point in time, (3) techniques the worker can utilize to resolve problems and maintain the system, and (4) methods he can use to coordinate the work of a number of action systems.

PROBLEMS IN THE DEVELOPMENT OF RELATIONSHIPS

Relationships developed by members of an action system with one another will pass through many different phases or stages. At the same time, members of an action system can pass through many different levels of commitment to the action system and the achievement of its purpose.

An already formed group has a history of developmental stages. When the social worker utilizes such a group, his presence creates a new system which not only will be affected by the past history of the existing group but also will develop new relationships between the worker and the individual members.

The stages of development that systems pass through over time have been identified by a number of writers.[2] At the beginning of a group action system, members may be ambivalent about participating and may not have made a full commitment to working through the system to achieve their individual and group goals. If the members make an initial contract to continue in the action system, they move into a stage of jockeying with other members and the worker for status,

---

[2] Erik Erikson, *Childhood and Society*, 2d ed. (New York: W. W. Norton & Co., Inc., 1963); James Garland, Hubert Jones, and Ralph Kolodny, "A Model for Stages of Development in Social Work Groups," in Saul Bernstein (ed.), *Explorations in Group Work* (Boston, Mass.: University of Boston School of Social Work, 1965), pp. 12–53; Helen Northern, *Social Work with Groups* (New York: Columbia University Press, 1969); Rosemary C. Sarri and Maeda J. Galinsky, "A Conceptual Framework for Group Development," in Robert Vinter (ed.), *Readings in Group Work Practice* (Ann Arbor, Mich.: Campus Publishers, 1967), pp. 72–94. In our discussion of stages of group development, we are relying primarily on concepts developed by our colleagues, Jack Kaufman and Diane Kravetz, and by Garland, Jones, and Kolodny, "Model for Stages of Development."

power, and control in the system. In this process they test out their relationships with one another. If the group members resolve their power and status conflicts and assume appropriate roles within the group, the action system may become cohesive. When it becomes important to its members, they are free to accept individual differences and cooperate. Feelings of mutual acceptance enable members to work together to achieve the tasks and purpose of the action system. After this has been accomplished, the system moves to separation and termination.

Although the stages outlined above refer to group action systems, they can also apply to one-to-one action systems. In these systems the worker and the other person are likely to pass through stages characterized by ambivalence about making an initial contract, maneuvering for position and control, mutual trust and acceptance, and willingness to work together to perform tasks and achieve the purpose of the system.

Three kinds of problems can arise to keep the system from passing smoothly through the different phases or stages of a developmental model. First, some members of a system may be in a different stage than others. In a group action system, some members may be fully committed to the purpose of the system and ready to start working on tasks to achieve it, while others are still ambivalent about belonging to the system and remain uncommitted to the purpose. In a one-to-one action system, the worker may underestimate the readiness of a client to trust him and to discuss his problems freely. If the worker does not allow time for the client to test him and develop confidence in him, the client may refuse to cooperate and drop out.

Second, a change in membership of an action system can impede its development. When a new member is added to a group action system, not only will he be at a different phase than the others, but the other members will have to adjust to him. The changes that occur in the group will depend on the stage of group development it has reached.[3] If the action system has moved beyond the stage of jockeying for status and power into a stage of mutual acceptance, the addition of a new member may cause the system to regress into a status and role struggle until the new member is assimilated. The group will also have to adjust if a member who has been playing an important role in the group leaves the action system. Someone else will have to assume his

---

[3] For a discussion of the addition of new members during different stages of group development, see Robert Paradise, "The Factor of Timing in the Addition of New Members to Established Groups," *Child Welfare*, 48 (November 1968): 524–30.

role, and a role struggle may ensue. When there is a change of workers in either a one-to-one or a group action system, major changes can occur in the system, especially if members are in a stage of trust and dependence upon the worker.

Third, problems can arise if the action system becomes bogged down in a particular stage and thus is not able to move successfully into another stage. It may even regress to a previous stage.[4] If members of the action system do not develop mutual trust, they will not be able to move on to work as a cohesive unit to achieve their purpose. In order to understand why the system is bogged down, the worker must examine the history of the development of the system. He also must apply a social system perspective in investigating current patterns of internal functioning of the action system.

PROBLEMS IN FUNCTIONING

At any one stage in the development of an action system, problems may arise that will prevent the members from accomplishing the tasks at that stage and from moving on through the stages of development to achieve its purpose. Problems in the functioning of action systems can result from (1) role distribution, (2) communications, (3) interpersonal relationships, (4) the distribution of power, (5) conflicting loyalties, (6) conflicting values and attitudes, or (7) the nature of the purpose.[5]

Role Distribution

As noted in the preceding chapter, the worker attempts to select people for the action system who will maintain satisfying working relationshps

---

[4] Some writers suggest that a system can move back and forth between stages—see Chin, "Utility of System Models." Sarri and Galinsky, "Conceptual Framework for Group Development," add a revision phase to their group development model to account for modifications that occur in group structure.

[5] These problem types are based on problem categories developed by Charles Garvin and Paul Glasser in "The Bases of Social Treatment," in *Social Work Practice, 1970* (New York: Columbia University Press, 1970), pp. 149–77, and those devised by Leland P. Bradford, Dorothy Stock, and Murray Horwitz, "How to Diagnose Group Problems," in Leland P. Bradford (ed.), *Group Development* (Washington, D.C.: National Training Laboratories, National Education Association, 1961), pp. 37–50. Garvin and Glasser designate them as problems in various types of structure: communications, sociometric, power, role, and normative. Bradford, Stock, and Horwitz believe problems are derived from conflict or fight, apathy and nonparticipation, or inadequate decision making.

with other members and will be able to play many different roles to help the system accomplish its tasks and purposes. In the functioning of the system, however, people may not always play their expected roles, and some who do assume necessary roles may drop out, leaving the role unplayed. One of the problems the worker may face with an existing group which is a target of change is inadequate performance of task and maintenance roles by group members.

Leland Bradford, Dorothy Stock, and Murray Horwitz point out that group action systems often emphasize task performance. They establish elaborate operating procedures, such as rules of order and subgroup or individual task assignments, that fail to satisfy the socio-emotional needs of the members and thus threaten the maintenance of the system. A group may decide that formal parliamentary procedures make decision making more efficient, but such rules may serve only the needs of the articulate and aggressive members, reduce the amount of creative thinking of all the members, and cause some members to drop out altogether because they are not receiving satisfaction.

On the other hand, Charles Garvin and Paul Glasser indicate that in a one-to-one action system, emphasis often is placed on satisfying the socioemotional needs of the other person and building a relationship between the worker and the other in order to maintain the action system and prevent the other from dropping out. However, if people in the one-to-one system do not also assume task roles to help the system achieve its purpose, the system may either be ineffective or it may disintegrate.

Communications

People who join action systems not only bring to it the potential of playing task and maintenance roles, but also bring established patterns of communicating with others which they will continue to use, especially in the early meetings of the action system. These individual modes of communication may lead to problems of communication within the action system. Some people may attempt to dominate the conversation, while others may be reluctant to speak at all or to participate in the activity, will attempt to change the subject or lead the system off in random discussion, will be inattentive, or will not listen to what is being said.

Some individuals or groups may have been made a part of an action system by a social worker who hopes to change their way of communicating with others. This could be the case with a shy withdrawn individual or a staff group in an organization in which the members do not share information and withhold cooperation in making decisions. The system itself may be too large to allow communication to flow equally among all its members, or the place or setting for the meetings may not be conducive to interactions among the members.

As the members of action systems interact with one another, they may change their manner of communicating with others. In doing so, however, they may choose different methods that create other communication problems for the system.

Interpersonal Relationships

Problems result in a group action system when subgroups and cliques form or some members are made scapegoats or become isolated from the activity. Members may dislike or openly reject one another, and in most groups, it can be expected that individuals will like and respect some members more than others. However, if some subgroups are always in conflict with others and refuse to compromise, and if some people feel rejected by others or reject most of the other members, the action system probably will not be cohesive enough to be able to reach decisions and mobilize itself to achieve its purpose.

Participants also may not like or respect one another in a one-to-one action system. Unless the worker can establish a collaborative or at least a bargaining interpersonal relationship, with the understanding that both parties have something to gain as well as to lose by working together, the other person may reject any relationship with the worker.[6]

In an already formed group that is made a part of an action system, the major problems may be in existing interpersonal relationships. People in the system must be helped to attain a mutually satisfactory level of functioning with one another, and the members must learn to maintain satisfactory interactions with other systems. A child who is rejected or scapegoated at home may be a behavior problem at school, or an organization may be so fraught with cliques and factions that decisions for changes in organizational services cannot be made. When the worker begins his work with these groups, the history of the interpersonal relationships may make it difficult for him to negotiate a contract with them.

---

[6] See Chapter 4, Worker Relationships.

Distribution of Power

The pattern of power and influence relationships within an action system can create additional problems in interpersonal relationships and communications. Some people within the action system may possess more influence than others because of their knowledge and skills, their personal charm, or their existing prestige, position, or reputation.[7]

In a group action system people can use their influence to help the system achieve its purpose. On the other hand, they can use it to control the decisions of the group, coerce some members into deviant behavior, force their ideas on others, or challenge the influence of the worker. The worker himself may be viewed by some members as an authority figure who should not be challenged. If some members of a group action system dominate the group's decisions and activity, others may become apathetic and withdrawn and will not contribute to the group or learn from it. Others may fight back, creating continual dissension in the group, or become subservient followers.

In a one-to-one action system, the other person's influence may be more than, the same as, or less than the worker's. If the other person perceives the worker as lacking both influence and competence, the worker may not be able to achieve his purpose in an action system. On the other hand, if the worker is perceived as having power and influence over the other, as is the case with a social worker in a court or prison, the worker may use his influence inappropriately or the other may not trust the worker.

In an existing group that has become part of an action system, continuing relationships of power and influence can create continual problems for the worker and other members of the system. Examples are an autocratic chairman of a neighborhood group or a dominant parent in a family.

Conflicting Loyalties

For many people who join action systems, their primary allegiances and loyalties are to individuals, groups, and organizations outside of the action system. In both one-to-one and group action systems, the worker can expect the members to be influenced by their outside refer-

---

[7] For discussion of the bases of power and influence, see Chapter 12 below and Dorwin Cartwright and Alvin Zander, *Group Dynamics* (New York: Harper and Row, 1968), pp. 215–35.

ence groups—their families, friends, neighbors. The activities and tasks of the action system can place members in conflict with these reference groups, or action system members may believe they will lose face with people in them. In this case they may resist cooperation with others in the action system, try to change the focus of the action system, or drop out all together.

In many action systems formed to achieve changes in organizations and in the community, people are asked to join the system because of their membership in other organizations. An action system may be composed of leaders of different agencies in the community, a youth council formed of representatives of youth organizations, or an organization task force composed of directors of different organizational units. In this type of action system, members will only be able to agree on policies that will benefit, or at least not harm, the outside organizations. Members may refuse to cooperate and resist any activity they perceive as threatening their outside loyalties.[8]

Conflicting Values and Attitudes

In addition to loyalties to specific groups outside the action system, members also bring to an action system their personal values and attitudes and their standards of what they consider to be acceptable and deviant behaviors. Members of an action system who have similar descriptive characteristics are likely to be compatible, but those who hold sharply divergent values and standards of behavior may not be able to work together. They may not be able to agree on goals or tasks for the action system and may disagree on appropriate operating procedures. If, for example, an individual believes that differences between people should be settled through rational, peaceful discussion, he may have difficulty in accepting the development of norms of operating in a system where people are allowed and encouraged to confront one another with open hostility. Further, this individual would not agree to the use of conflictual strategies with targets outside the action system.

Nature of Purpose

The purpose of the action system can produce problems for the social worker. Members of an action system may resist working together if

---

[8] Martin Rein and Robert Morris, "Goals, Structures and Strategies for Community Change," in *Social Work Practice, 1962* (New York: Columbia University Press, 1962), pp. 127–45.

they believe the purpose of the system is impossible to achieve.[9] If the action system has been given an assignment from another person or organization, it may be unclear about its charge or believe it does not have the knowledge or sufficient manpower to carry out the tasks assigned.

Action system members may believe they lack power to implement their decisions and may lose interest in performing their tasks. For example, if an autocratic principal of a school asks a social worker to form an action system of teachers to recommend ways the school should deal with children who disrupt classrooms, members could believe their work and recommendations will be meaningless because the principal probably will ignore their suggestions. Or members of an action system working for community change may believe they cannot mobilize sufficient influence to affect the targets of change.

The purpose of the action system may seem unimportant to some of its members, or not so important as other problems. Clients may lose interest in working on problems the worker thinks are important instead of those the clients want to work on. Action systems formed to work on problems in organizations or in the community may resent spending time on what may appear to be merely busy work or a diversionary activity to make a show of democratic participation.

RESOLVING PROBLEMS OF FUNCTIONING

In order to resolve the various types of problems that arise in action systems, the social worker must first diagnose the problem and then decide which of several techniques he will employ to deal with it. The worker might (1) assume different roles, (2) change the operating procedures, (3) regulate the use of program and activities, (4) change the membership of the action system, or (5) assist members to diagnose their problems.

Worker's Roles

The worker himself usually must play many different task and maintenance roles to keep the action system functioning. This is especially true in the initial encounters of the system. The worker's diagnosis of the roles played by other members of the action system will help him

---

[9] For reasons why members of a group fight with one another or become apathetic, see Bradford, Stock, and Horwitz, "How to Diagnose Group Problems," pp. 37–44, and the discussion in Chapter 8 above on resistances to change.

determine which specific roles he should play himself. After diagnosing the functioning of a system, the worker may decide he needs to relinquish roles to allow members to play them or to adopt new roles which are missing.

The responsibility of filling various roles rests heavily on the worker in a one-to-one action system because there are not several group members to pick up these roles. Studies of one-to-one action systems indicate that clients identify effective workers as being both warm and accepting (system maintenance) and technically competent (task achievement). Rather than playing all roles himself, however, the worker must assess the potential of the other for assuming roles that will keep the system functioning.

The worker usually will play the "missing member" role when he believes that a function such as clarifying or expediting is not being performed in a group action system.[10] Goldstein et al. describe an experiment in which the worker analyzed groups in psychotherapy to see what roles needed to be played out (missing member roles) and "planted" people in the groups to play out these roles. In the post-meeting reaction forms, the "plant" was viewed by other members as being a helpful person in the group.[11]

Because it is difficult for one worker to carry out all the necessary roles and at the same time keep attuned to all the member interactions, co-workers are often used with families and other groups. Each worker can play out a different role and serve as a role and behavior model. However, workers sometimes tend to form a subgroup of their own. They may be working at cross-purposes with a given person or problem, or they may feel inhibited if they are not completely comfortable with one another. When there is more than one worker with an action system, workers need to plan their roles in relation to group purpose and development, so their differences can be exploited for the benefit of the group rather than serving as a hindrance.

In some circumstances, particularly action systems formed to solve community problems, the worker does not serve as the formal leader or chairman of a group. Rather, he recruits or selects a person from the community as group leader. The leader chosen must be knowledgeable and interested in the task of the group but not strongly identified with any one "side" or "interest" concerned with the problem, so he

---

[10] Ralph M. Kramer and Harry Specht, *Readings in Community Organization Practice*, Englewood Cliffs, N.J.: Prentice-Hall, Inc., 1969), p. 258.

[11] Arnold Goldstein et al., "The Use of Planted Patients in Group Psychotherapy," *American Journal of Psychotherapy*, 21 (October 1967): 767–73.

can play the roles of energizer, harmonizer, orienter, opinion seeker and others that will provide for system maintenance and task performance. The worker may need to help the leader to play appropriate leader roles and himself act out roles that will complement but not compete with those of the formal leader.

By playing different roles himself and assisting others to play appropriate roles, the worker can resolve problems in functioning stemming from problems in role distribution. The worker's behavior in these roles can serve as a model for others in the action system that may help resolve problems in communication (listening to others, encouraging quiet members to participate); in interpersonal relationships (treating other members with respect, indicating points on which subgroups or cliques can come to an agreement); and in distribution of power (lending support to ideas of members who possess little influence).

Operating Procedures

The worker's diagnosis of problems in action system functioning may lead him to suggest changes in operating procedures, such as plans for the use of time, setting, and rules for interaction and decision making. He could, for example, change the place of meetings or shorten or lengthen their time to enhance communications among members.

The worker also may suggest changes in operating procedures and modes of decision making if problems in internal relationships or distribution of power have caused the action system to adopt methods that prevent all members from participating in idea generation and decision making. For example, in order to gain participation from all the members of a group, the worker may use a nominal group procedure, in which the activity is structured so individuals work in the presence of one another using paper and pencil to write ideas, but do not interact verbally. Andre Delbecq and Andrew Van de Ven cite research which indicates that the use of nominal groups can produce a larger number of identified problems, more high-quality suggestions, and more different kinds of solutions than a group in which the members interact verbally. They point out that "the tension created by the nominal group situation where other members at a table are industriously writing maximizes social-facilitation tension which is important for individuals to fully involve themselves in the task at hand."[12]

---

[12] Andre Delbecq and Andrew Van de Ven, "A Group Process Model for Problem Identification and Program Planning," *Journal of Applied Behavioral Science*, 7 (July–August 1971): 474.

Nominal groups also give people who have difficulty in verbal participation an opportunity to express their ideas. Delbecq and Van de Ven
suggest the planned use of both nominal groups and interactional
groups for problem solving.

Use of Program and Activity

The social worker can use program and activities to help resolve problems of functioning at any one time and to facilitate or speed the
development of relationships over time. As Robert Vinter points out,
different activities require different behavior from participants, and
different activities evoke diverse behavior patterns.[13] Thus the worker
can determine what behaviors and attitudes he wants to elicit from
members to resolve problems of internal functioning and to develop
productive relationships, and then design activities to produce the
desired behaviors and attitudes. For example, in a group action system,
if the worker wants to reduce conflicts in interpersonal relationships
and competitiveness between members, he can plan activities that will
require cooperation. If the worker wishes to build confidence and
increase the influence of people with little status or power within the
system, he can plan activities in which these people can excel and which
will give them a sense of mastery. They may even inspire approval and
acceptance by other members.

The worker can also use activities to enhance communication between members with different characteristics in a group action system.
An example is the impact of program activities on mixed groups of
handicapped and average children:

> If the handicapped child is to derive strengths from his relationships
> with other group members, the program activities employed must be
> within the potential ability range of the child and at the same time pro-
> vide a high degree of satisfaction for the other group members. There
> are games . . . which for the insecure child provide the controls and
> limitations which he is seeking and yet allow his more aggressive play-
> mates to act out in a healthy and acceptable manner. Creative crafts
> where premium is not put on perfection or on reproducing a model
> object permit the handicapped child and other group members to pro-
> ceed at their own pace and derive satisfaction from their efforts. In such
> a milieu, where the handicapped child is less likely to be threatened by

---

[13] Robert Vinter, *Readings in Group Work Practice* (Ann Arbor: Campus Publishers, 1967), p. 98.

fear of failure, and the other group members are enjoying themselves, a rapport may develop among members.[14]

Communication can also be enhanced by utilizing activities with an existing group. Rachel Levine has demonstrated this with the use of games in working with low-income families:

The social worker arranged the visits after the family's evening meal, taking along simple play materials. From the first, the children eagerly gathered around the table, but the parents sat apart, watching while the two-year-old was thrust aside. Gradually, both parents began to join in the game and the worker began to include the two-year-old by showing him how to hold and use materials, indirectly demonstrating to the older children and to the parents how he could be taught. In the activity, both parents manipulated, competed, and cheated just as the children did. Gently, the worker introduced rules. In the weeks that followed, as rivalries, cheating, and angry outbursts occurred, the worker would stop the activity, allow each one to have his say, encourage them to bring out their feelings of anger and hurt, and introduce, gradually, acts of fairness and respect for each other. Before many sessions had passed, the visits were awaited with eagerness by all the family.[15]

The worker can also use program and activities to help him communicate with people who have different characteristics than his own. Frank Riessman and Jean Goldfarb, in discussing the value of role playing to low-income people, noted that this technique is amenable to their action-oriented life style. Role playing allows the change agent to reduce the role distance between himself and the disadvantaged person, who might ordinarily be alienated from the social worker and his bureaucratic world.[16]

Program and activities can be planned to help an action system accomplish its tasks at any stage of its development.[17] Thus, when an action system is first formed and members are ambivalent about working together, the worker can plan activities that will provide quick satisfaction to individual members as well as to the whole system and

---

[14] Richard J. Bond et al., "The Neighborhood Peer Group," The Group, 17 (October 1954): 9–10.

[15] Rachel A. Levine, "Treatment in the Home," in Frank Riessman, Jerome Cohen, and Arthur Pearl (eds.), Mental Health of the Poor (Glencoe, Ill.: Free Press, 1964): 329–35.

[16] Frank Riessman and Jean Goldfarb, "Role Playing and the Poor," Group Psychotherapy, 17 (March 1964): 36–48.

[17] See Garland, Jones, and Kolodny, "Model for Stages of Development."

will motivate the members to enter into a contract. When the action system is moving toward termination and members are reluctant to stop working together, ceremonies or rituals are useful to punctuate the ending. A children's group may hold a party; a community committee, a dinner. Further, as members of an action system plan for the ending ritual, they are reminded that termination is about to take place.

Membership of the Action System

The worker's diagnosis of the problems of an action system may lead him to change the membership of the system. Perhaps the worker did not select the proper mix of people for the system or he did not have the opportunity to do so. Perhaps the interactions of people within the system or changes in the outside environment of system members have led to unforeseen problems.

If members of the action system are not able to work together and cannot agree on goals and tasks because their primary loyalties lie outside the system, the worker may need to disband it altogether and form a new system of people whose loyalties and allegiances make it possible to agree on a common purpose and the methods to achieve it. If the values and attitudes of action system members remain sharply divergent, the worker may need to form a new system or encourage dissident members to drop out. Sometimes the worker can reduce problems of conflicting loyalties and values and attitudes by adding new members who are acceptable to all existing members and who possess the requisite skills and influence to find a common purpose and suggest tasks that are acceptable to all. However, when this happens, some of the members of the group may be co-opted, and the purpose of the original action system may be changed.

If problems of functioning stem from the lack of adequate role performance, members can be added who will assume these roles. The action system also can be expanded as additional targets are identified and agree to join the system, or the worker may add new members if he believes the system is not large enough to accomplish its tasks. If the system needs additional expertness or people with influence over targets in order to achieve its original or expanded purpose, the addition of new members can solve these problems.

The worker can prepare a new member for membership in a group action system through individual discussions to acquaint him with the activities of the group. He may need to support new members in their first few meetings by giving them an opportunity to demonstrate their special knowledge or ability and including them in group activities and tasks. The worker also needs to prepare the present members of a group action system for the addition of new members by explaining who they are and why they are joining the group. Workers can use the introduction of new members to provide an opportunity for present members to explain the purpose and activities of the action system. This can intensify members' commitment to the purpose and reinforce the changes they have made through the group experience.

The worker also can change action system membership by encouraging members to drop out of a group system if they are contributing to problems of interpersonal relationships or in the distribution of power. He might suggest leaving to a small clique trying to dominate other members or to an individual who is always being scapegoated by other members and who might be better off in a one-to-one system with the worker or another group action system. If the worker himself is not able to form a satisfying relationship in either a one-to-one system or a group, he may try to find another worker to take his place.

A worker can ease the transition of a change in workers by informing action system members well in advance of his departure. If he feels it is necessary, he should provide an opportunity to discuss feelings about his departure. He could also bring the new worker to several joint co-worker sessions of the action system.

Members' Diagnosis of Problems

It may help the action system if members are involved in a diagnosis of the system's problems of functioning.[18] Chapter 7, Collecting Data, discussed several techniques the worker can use to provide information to all the members on current patterns of communication, distribution of power, and interpersonal relationships. Chapter 9, Negotiating Contracts, discussed feedback mechanisms that can be used in a multiperson system to provide members with information on the other's values, attitudes, and behavior. The worker can use minutes, summary reports, and discussion to help members review their history of work together.

If members themselves are involved in the diagnosis of problems in the way the system is functioning, they may perceive how their own behavior is contributing to the problems of the group. They then may attempt to change their behavior and to gain understanding of other

---

[18] See Bradford, Stock, and Horwitz, "How to Diagnose Group Problems," pp. 45–50, for a discussion of diagnosis and feedback.

members' behavior. In either a one-to-one or group action system, the members themselves may suggest trying out the techniques described above: assume different roles in the system, decline to play a role or help others to play a new role, change the operating procedures of the system, try out a new program or activity, or change the membership of the system.

A diagnosis by all members of an action system can lead to a renegotiation of the contract with the system and a renegotiation of the system's contracts with other systems. Thus if the purpose of the system is not clear, the members can clarify it with one another, or change it and achieve a new sense of purpose. If their purpose and tasks have been assigned to them, they may ask for clarification or point out that the purpose as designed is impossible to achieve and ask for additional help and direction. Diagnosis by the members may even lead to a joint decision to disband.

In encouraging members to diagnose problems of internal functioning, the worker needs to guard against preoccupation with internal processes, which may lead members to neglect the tasks that need to be performed if the system is to achieve its purpose. Because members in such circumstances may become frustrated and lose interest, the worker may have to motivate them by planning activity that will give them a quick feeling of accomplishment.

The process of diagnosis can help the system achieve the very purpose for which it was formed. If the action system is composed of the worker and an existing group such as a family or an organizational group, the worker's major goals may be to improve the internal functioning of the existing group so members can achieve satisfying ways of relating to one another, as well as accomplishing the tasks and goals of the system. If members are helped to diagnose their own functions in the system and to try out new behavior with others, the system functioning may improve. The case study by Foster in Part III illustrates how a social worker forced staff members of a hospital ward to examine how their own attitudes and values had built a ward culture and norms for staff behavior that kept them from meeting the needs of the patients and their families.

When the worker forms an action system with an already existing group, the members are placed in a dual interaction situation. They interact in encounters of the action system and with each other outside of the meetings. The worker's interactions with the action system may increase or reduce problems of functioning of the action system itself as well as the other interactions of the members. It is difficult in this case to distinguish analytically between the problems in functioning of the action system itself and the problems of the members, because the roles of action system members and members of the existing group are so completely interwined. The worker's purpose in working with a formed action system is to help the members improve their functioning so the system can accomplish its purpose. He usually is not interested in building a permanent well-functioning system as an end in itself. However, members may transfer their ability to diagnose problems and their new patterns of interaction to their relations with people in other situations.

COORDINATION OF ACTION SYSTEMS

It has been noted that the worker can form a number of action systems to deal with a problem and that the same person can be involved in several different action systems with different workers. When the worker and his clients are involved in several action systems, it is necessary to coordinate the systems for the benefit of the client.

The Hoffman and Long case study in Part III describes one problem handled by a social worker from a social services department of a neighborhood health center on New York's lower East Side. The major clients were a 52-year-old black man, Mr. Johnson, and his family. The study illustrates how the interplay of a number of systems—social, family, and individual—contributed to the breakdown of a person.

Because of the number of systems connected to the family, a number of action systems came into play. The worker dealt not only with Mr. Johnson, Mrs. Johnson, Mr. and Mrs. Johnson together, and Mr. and Mrs. Johnson and their two children, but with a housing agent, three doctors, Mrs. Johnson's employer, a lawyer from an antipoverty agency, people from Mr. Johnson's union, the Veteran's Administration, Workmen's Compensation, a private loan company, All Saint's Parish, Franklin Settlement, a hospital, Alcoholics Anonymous, and Southern College. In this case the worker had to keep all of these systems functioning for the benefit of his clients.

In his contact with the family members, separately and together in different size action systems, the worker had to keep his focus on the family as an interactive unit and concentrate on his goal of changing the roles and status of different family members. If the worker had not been clear about his goal, one or the other family members, in individual action systems with him, might have subverted it by inducing him into actions that would solve an immediate problem for that member but would undermine his major goal. As Andrew Curry points out, a family member often tries to use the worker in some capacity against other family members.[19]

In his action system with the host of societal systems linked to the Johnson family, the worker found himself "subverting the intrusions of the helping agencies into the family's life whenever these intrusions pushed the husband further into helplessness vis-à-vis the family, or the family further into helplessness vis-à-vis society." Since his major purposes for this action system of representatives of societal systems were clearly to help the family obtain the resources they needed and to maintain themselves as a unit that would provide satisfactions to all its members, he also was able to avoid being induced by any member into action that would subvert his goals. Further, the worker tried not to become too much of an authority himself. Whenever possible, he turned the task of dealing with the agencies over to the family to encourage the family, Mr. Johnson particularly, to increase its feelings of competence.

Thus, with all of the action systems involved in this problem, the worker was consistent in his purpose to increase Mr. Johnson's independence and status and power in the family. Hoffman and Long point out that the problem as it is conceived by a "systems" worker is "how to redress an imbalance of power when dealing with disturbed people in poor families *when the presence of powerful helpers is one of the factors contributing to the imbalance in the first place.*"

The case of the Johnson family illustrates the role of the worker in coordinating and orchestrating several different action systems to ensure that clients do receive the help they need and are not confronted with different or contradictory messages that may aggravate rather than reduce their problems. The case also illustrates the point that no one social worker has all the necessary expertise and resources to help with all the problems he meets. In any action system he deals with people from many resource systems. The social worker, however, often serves as the central person vis-à-vis the client system and coordinates the interactions of members of action systems to ensure that they are consistent with his change purpose. When two or more social workers or other change agents are involved in one problem, often one of them

---

[19] Andrew Curry, "The Family Therapy Situation as a System," *Family Process*, 5 (September 1966): 131–41.

is designated as the central worker, with responsibility for coordination.[20]

Neighborhood service centers attempt to provide coordinated services by locating under one roof several services provided by different change agents. However, studies indicate that proximity in itself can facilitate but cannot ensure coordinated service.[21] Centers have tried different means of coordination, such as case conferences including all workers involved with one problem, central file systems, or assigning an anchor worker with chief responsibility for coordination. A review of research on neighborhood centers indicates that no means of coordination has been wholly effective.[22]

Different workers may work with the same individual in different action systems within a single agency or institution. For example, a patient in a mental hospital might be seen in a one-to-one relationship with a social worker; in occasional family therapy sessions with co-therapists, such as the worker and a psychiatrist; in an activity-centered group led by an occupational therapist; and in regular ward meetings, with many staff present. An institution can be viewed as one large action system composed of several staff members engaged in planned change efforts with the residents. Unless the staff members work as a team with a clear understanding of the role of each and agreement on a treatment plan for the residents, their separate interventions can provide contradictory messages to the residents and frustrate the change goal.

If we view each community agency and societal resource system as an action system, the need becomes apparent for clarity of purpose and internal cooperation on the part of administrative and other staff. Further, as the Johnson case highlights, when many agencies and institutions are interacting with the same people in the community, the need for community coordination between these different action systems becomes obvious. When a social worker is dealing with many action systems on behalf of an individual, family or other group,

[20] Neil Gilbert, "Neighborhood Coordinator: Advocate or Middleman?" *Social Service Review*, 43 (June 1969): 136–44, discusses the role of neighborhood coordinators in an antipoverty agency who functioned as advocates committed to increase the power and influence of neighborhood citizens and as middlemen expediting services delivery between welfare institutions and local citizens.

[21] Robert Perlman and David Jones, *Neighborhood Service Centers* (Washington, D.C.: U.S. Department of Health, Education, and Welfare, 1967) and Edward J. O'Donnell and Marilyn M. Sullivan, "Service Delivery and Social Action through the Neighborhood Center—A Review of Research," *Welfare in Review*, 7 (November–December, 1969): 1–11.

[22] O'Donnell and Sullivan, "Service Delivery and Social Action."

organization, or community, he must try to keep the different action systems from working at cross-purposes in order to make sure their efforts will enhance rather than frustrate his change purpose.

VALUE DILEMMAS

Throughout this and the previous chapter we have emphasized the active role played by the worker in structuring and programming action systems. This active role may appear to include elements of manipulation that deny the other's self-determination, again raising the value dilemmas of flexibility and integrity discussed in Chapter 2.

Several writers and practitioners have wrestled with these dilemmas. Robert Perlman and David Jones, in a study of neighborhood organizers, note that the worker influences the group in innumerable ways.

He will often have brought it into existence, he will be the sustaining force particularly in the early stages of its life, he will be constantly influencing the group's understanding of its situation and the action it takes. Thus the organizer of a social action group stressed, with undoubted sincerity, that the group should make its own decisions, yet it was clear that he and his organization had previously decided the category of people to be recruited into the group, the nature of its activity, the problem it was to be concerned with, and the methods it was to adopt, and to a large extent determined the individual membership of the group, at least in its initial stages. In addition, the worker saw the group within the context of a wider policy of which the group at best was only vaguely aware.[23]

Perlman and Jones note that one safeguard in this situation is that whether he wishes to or not, the worker can rarely control the groups.

As noted in the previous discussion of value dilemmas related to action systems, when the client is part of the worker's action system, the contract between worker and client ordinarily will help ensure that the client's right to self-determination will be enhanced in the action system. However, when targets for change are not clients but are part of an action system, the worker can manipulate the action system to influence the targets to change and thereby to help the client system.

The worker forms, maintains, and coordinates action system to create conditions that will influence the behavior of action system members and help him achieve his outcome goals. The worker's planned use of these factors can enhance his use of other influence processes, the topic of the next chapter.

---

[23] Perlman and Jones, *Neighborhood Service Centers*, p. 58.

CHAPTER 12

EXERCISING

INFLUENCE

The exercise of influence[1] underlies most of the interactional activities of the social worker as he carries out his tasks in a planned change effort. In collecting data in an interview, the worker will try to create a climate conducive to open discussion. In negotiating a contract, he will try to heighten the other person's motivation to participate in the change effort. When forming a task group, he may try to convince a certain person to serve as chairman. The social worker who understands the dynamics of influence processes will be able to harness and use them in conscious ways to facilitate the achievement of outcome and method goals.

Broadly speaking, the term "influence" can be defined as effecting the condition or development of a person or system. In the case of social work, this means having an effect on the achievement of outcome and method goals. Thus a social worker exerts influence in changing an employer's attitude about hiring a client, motivating a

---

[1] As with the term "planned change" discussed in Chapter 2, there is a tendency in the social work literature to use euphemisms with positive or negative connotations such as "leadership," or "manipulation" instead of the term "influence." We prefer the neutral term "influence" because it does not mask the value issues involved in social work practice.

client to leave a mental hospital, or getting a city council member to lend his support to a program.

The exercise of influence is usually a two-way transactional process. Its use depends both on the target's perception of the person attempting to exert influence and on the target's attitude toward being influenced.[2] It is also a two-way process, in the sense that the worker himself will often become a target of other people's influence attempts.

In analyzing influence, this chapter will discuss (1) the bases or sources of influence used by change agents, (2) the processes by which these bases of influence are brought to bear on a situation, and (3) issues related to the use of these processes.

BASES OF INFLUENCE

When the exercise of influence in social work is carefully examined, it is always possible to identify some base of influence the worker brings to bear in order to affect a situation.[3] These bases of influence include (1) knowledge and expertness, (2) material resources and services, (3) legitimate authority, (4) status and reputation, (5) charisma and personal attractiveness, (6) control over the flow of information, and (7) established relationships.

The social worker may directly control or possess any of these resources himself, or he may have access to people who can bring them to bear in a situation. Although these bases of influence will be described separately, they usually are used in combination.

---

[2] While the worker may be exerting influence on a potential or actual member of a client, action, target, or change agent system, in relation to the influence attempt, the other person can be considered a *target* of the worker. We will therefore use the term "target" to refer to the person toward whom the worker is directing his influence efforts. Our use of the term "target" here, as well as throughout the book, however, should not be interpreted as meaning that the person being influenced passively accepts the efforts of the worker.

[3] Our analysis of the bases of worker's influence will utilize concepts that have been developed by many social scientists. See for example Edward C. Banfield, *Political Influence* (New York: Free Press, 1961); Dorwin Cartwright and Alvin Zander, *Group Dynamics* (New York: Harper and Row, 1968); William A. Gamson, *Power and Discontent* (Homewood, Ill.: Dorsey Press, 1968); Robert Morris and Robert Binstock, *Feasible Planning for Social Change* (New York: Columbia University Press, 1966); and Peter H. Rossi, "Theory, Research, and Practice in Community Organization," in Ralph Kramer and Harry Specht (eds.), *Readings in Community Organization Practice* (Englewood Cliffs, N.J.: Prentice-Hall, Inc., 1969), pp. 49–61.

Knowledge and Expertness

The knowledge and expertness of the social worker, acquired through education and experience, is probably the most fundamental basis of influence he possesses. They will vary with each practitioner according to his experience, interests, and capabilities, but common areas of knowledge and expertness can be identified.

The first area of knowledge and expertness is in interpersonal relations. This includes the ability to form and maintain a variety of purposeful relationships based on objectivity, self-awareness, knowledge of interpersonal dynamics and verbal and nonverbal communication. Also included in this area are interpersonal skills, such as conducting interviews, exercising leadership, providing feedback, mediating, and giving support, which are aimed at attitudinal and behavior change. Being able to establish the appropriate social-psychological atmosphere within an action system is another interpersonal skill. In assessing interpersonal relationships and exercising interpersonal skills the worker can be guided by his knowledge of relevant theoretical orientations such as ego psychology, learning theory, and communication theories.

A second area the social worker draws on is his knowledge of planned change processes and the tasks and activities which must be carried out in any planned change effort. The worker's expertise includes the ability to select and use the appropriate analytical and interactional skills and techniques necessary to carry out these tasks and activities. It is this knowledge area that this text is addressed to.

A third area of knowledge relates to the age of the people the change agent works with—children, adolescents, middle-aged, or elderly. Included here is knowledge of developmental stages and tasks, life cycle changes, problems and crises, needs and coping mechanisms, and the effects of physical and other disabilities on behavior at different periods in the life span.

Fourth, most social workers have knowledge of one or more social problem areas, such as delinquency, drug abuse, mental retardation, poverty, child neglect, or inadequate housing. This knowledge includes theories, concepts, and empirical research related to the problem area; approaches to analyzing the problem; methods of intervention; programs and services for dealing with the problem; and related social policy and legislation.

A fifth knowledge area the social worker draws upon is developmental and systems models for understanding the functioning of formal and informal systems such as families, small groups, and communities. This includes knowledge of structures and processes which affect decision making, power, communication, and role allocation.

Finally, social workers possess knowledge about societal resource and service delivery systems such as hospitals, child welfare agencies, schools, governmental departments, and the community in which they are located. This includes knowledge on how the systems operate, special problems in their functioning, the impact they have on the people they serve, how to gain access to them, and social policy and legislation related to the operation of these systems.

Material Resources and Services

Society's contract with change agent systems gives them the right and responsibility to dispense certain material resources.[4] Thus the worker, through his agency sanction and within prescribed limits established by laws, funding sources, and the agency itself, is able to exercise some control over resources such as money, nursing home beds, babies for adoption, and homemaker services. Some change agent systems have the power to grant or to recommend allocation of financial resources to other organizations and groups. Examples are a United Fund which dispenses contributions to member agencies or an agency such as a Model Cities Program or a Community Action Commission that administers the flow of federal or state grants to community organizations and institutions. Although the final decisions on granting money to other organizations may be made by a body of citizens and public officials, social workers employed by these agencies are often in a position to contribute to these decisions.

Material resources also may be available to the worker through people with whom he and the agency have established relationships. The change agent system and the worker may have established access to other community services, perhaps by reaching working agreements with other community institutions to obtain resources for clients. Relationships may also have been established with people who have personal wealth or who exercise control over the expenditure of public, voluntary, or corporate funds. Examples of such influentials are the chairman of a legislative finance committee, the chairman of a United Fund budget committee, an executive of a charitable foundation, or

---

[4] Chapter 1 considers the social work function of dispensing resources.

the president of a corporation that gives money to community enterprises or that loans money to businesses.

Legitimate Authority

Two types of legitimate authority can serve as a base of influence. The first derives from the particular elected or appointed position held in the hierarchy of a group such as an agency, a professional organization, a civic group, or a committee. Within the limits of his position, an individual can invoke his authority over others. A supervisor may tell a worker to rewrite a report, or a chairman may call a meeting to order. This authority is specific to relationships within a given group or organization. It is a characteristic of the position a person occupies rather than of the person himself. It is called "legitimate" because others in the system view the exercise of this authority as a right of the person in that position.[5]

A second type of legitimate authority is directly or indirectly vested in people who are serving certain social control functions. This authority gives them the right to invoke certain sanctions under certain conditions. For example, under agreement with a parole board or judge a social worker can revoke a parole or probation. A social worker who is investigating a child neglect complaint may not have the authority to remove a child from his home, but he can write a report which has an impact on the judge's decision. Social workers may be given the authority to grant or revoke the license of certain facilities, such as foster homes and children's institutions.

Through his own and his agency relationships, the worker also has access to people who have authority. Such people may be able to exercise authority over organized or informal groups, hold positions of formal authority, be part of a dominant faction in another community institution or a legislative body, be elected or appointed officials, or be employed in occupations such as police officer and teacher that grant them control over others.

Status and Reputation

The status and reputation of the social worker serve as another base of influence. The status of the worker may be related to a formal position that he holds in an agency, professional organization, or social or

---

[5] For a discussion of workers' authority positions in agencies, see Yvonne L. Fraley, "A Role Model for Practice," *Social Service Review*, 43 (June 1969): 145–54.

civic group. Unlike legitimate authority, however, status and reputation are attributes of the change agent himself, not the position he holds.

The worker will develop a reputation with former and present members of client, action, target, and change agent systems and with other people. His reputation may lead other people to ascribe to him such qualities as competence, intelligence, objectivity, and trustworthiness.

Within his change agent system the worker may have a position which gives him prestige both within and outside the agency. The worker carries with him the status his change agent system holds within the hierarchy of community agencies and institutions. Some change agent systems have high acceptance and prestige; others are considered to be low-status organizations.

An agency's prestige may be based on the characteristics of its clients. An agency that works with affluent middle-class or upper-class clients may have more prestige than one that works with low-income or minority people. The nature of the problems of the agency clientele (senility in old people, alcoholism, the criminally deviant, emotionally disturbed children) also may influence people's attitudes towards the agency.

Other factors that affect the prestige of an agency are the professional status and other characteristics of its staff, the size of its budget, its reputation for effectiveness and efficiency, and its association with people who have local, state, or national influence. The worker and his change agent system may have relationships with people who have high status in the community because of their reputations and their positions within community groups and institutions. Holders of such status can be in positions in businesses, churches, athletics, the arts, prestigeful social groups, and government, civic, and political organizations.

Charisma and Personal Attractiveness

Some change agents are personally attractive because of their personality, charm, or charisma. These workers have an ability to arouse loyalty and enthusiasm among the people they work with. It is easy for people to find relationships with such workers intrinsically gratifying, and they can identify easily with them. The attraction of the worker for some people may be enhanced by his descriptive characteristics, such as age, sex, or race. Unlike other bases of influence, the worker's personal attractiveness is independent of any formal position he may occupy. His attractiveness can help increase the potency of his other bases of influence.

In some circumstances, charismatic community leaders can be called on to assist the social worker. The worker who has difficulty establishing relationships in a particular community can be helped if a local influential supports his activities.

Control Over Flow of Information

The kinds of decisions people make, the perceptions they hold, and the behavior they engage in are to an extent dependent on the amount and type of information available to them. Thus anyone in a position to control the flow of information which others are dependent upon has a base of influence with respect to them.

The worker derives information from his current and past relationships with people, his knowledge of social problems and resources, his skills in generating information through data collection, and his status and position within his agency and in professional, civic, or social groups. From his position within his change agent and action systems he can use this information selectively in his influence efforts. The worker's communication skills will enhance his use of this base of influence.

An interesting characteristic of control over information as a base of influence is that it is often open to lower status persons in a system. For example, David Mechanic describes how aides in a mental hospital influence the decisions of psychiatrists by manipulating the kinds of information about patients that they pass on to the psychiatrists.[6] Similarly, prospective adoptive parents, who have lower status in the adoption process relationship, will be selective about the kind of personal information they reveal to a worker who is doing an adoption study.

Through his relationships, the worker has access to other people who can control the flow of information to specific individuals, groups, and community organizations and institutions because of their status and positions. Sometimes the worker and his agency have relationships with people who have special access to the mass media, such as staff people or advertisers, and who exercise control over the flow of information to the public.

Established Relationships

In all of the bases of influence discussed above, the change agent may either possess the particular base of influence himself or have access

---

[6] David Mechanic, "Sources of Power of Lower Participants in Complex Organizations," *Administrative Science Quarterly*, 7 (December 1962): 349–64.

to other people who do. These established relationships, the "contacts" that the worker has, can be considered an influence base in themselves.

The worker and his change agent system have established relationships with many people. These may be members of the board of directors of the change agent system; consultants or volunteers of the change agent system; present or past members of client, action, or target systems of the worker or his change agent system; or personal friends of the worker.

The base of influence applied by a social worker in a particular situation may be possessed by the worker himself. This is true of his knowledge and expertness, personal attraction, and status and reputation. Other sources of influence may be possessed or controlled by other people and are available to the social worker because of his own or his agency's relationships with them. Finally, some bases of influence stem from the worker's position in his change agent system. His use of material resources and services, legitimate authority, and control over the flow of information are all enhanced by his role in the system.

Social workers in private practice may possess all of these bases of influence except for those related to the change agent system. Since social workers in private practice have generally first acquired experience in an agency setting, they often establish relationships with other professionals and lay people which they continue to utilize after they move into private practice.

INFLUENCE PROCESSES

In exercising influence a change agent must not only control a base of influence but must be able to bring it to bear on a target system.[7] Four major means of influence (or influence processes) used by social workers to change a target system's behavior, attitudes, and beliefs are: (1) inducement, (2) persuasion, (3) use of relationship, and (4)

---

[7] Many social scientists have identified processes by which one system influences another. Cartwright and Zander, *Group Dynamics*, pp. 219-223, identify four methods of influence: (1) control over gains and costs, (2) persuasion, (3) use of P's (the one influenced) attitude toward being influenced by O (the one viewed as exerting influence), and (4) control over P's environment. Morris and Binstock, *Feasible Planning for Social Change*, p. 117, identify six pathways through which influence is exerted: obligation, friendship, rational persuasion, selling, coercion, and inducement. Gamson, *Power and Discontent*, pp. 72-81, identifies three means of influence: constraints, inducements, and persuasion. Also see Banfield, *Political Influence*, pp. 4-5.

use of environment. The social worker can use some combination of these means of influence to achieve method and outcome goals in performing the various functions of social work practice.

Inducement

The term "inducement" in this context means influencing a target system by providing rewards for complying with an influence effort (positive inducement) or punishing it for not complying (negative inducement). In order to use inducements, the worker must have access to resources or control over sanctions that the target believes can be beneficial or detrimental to its situation.[8] For example, a worker with a community action agency which has access to federal funds and relationships with editors and reporters of the local newspaper may induce a vocational school to offer special English classes and training for Mexican-Americans by offering to obtain federal funds for the programs or threatening to make a public charge that the school is discriminating.

When rewards are used for inducements, the target system may receive the reward only after it makes the desired change. For example, an agency administrator may reward a worker by a promotion only after he has completed special educational courses. A boy in a children's institution may be allowed a home visit after he has completed a week in which he has not fought with other children. In other instances, the worker or a member of his action system may specify in advance what action he expects, receive a commitment from the target system, and reward the system ahead of time, thus obligating the system to perform the desired action. For example, a social worker who is trying to influence his agency colleagues to join him in influencing the agency board of directors to inaugurate a new outreach program for juvenile runaways may agree to support a colleague's proposal for a new program for alcoholics in exchange for the colleague's later help for the juvenile program. Other times a feeling of obligation can be created by rewarding a target system or doing favors for it and not specifying until later what reciprocal action is expected. For example, a worker who has gone out of his way to help a juvenile judge by finding resources for delinquents may later ask the judge for the release of a specific juvenile who has been arrested for the first time on a drug

---

[8] See Gamson, *Power and Discontent,* for discussion of the addition of advantages and disadvantages to influence efforts (pp. 75–79).

possession charge. The president of an agency board who has agreed to serve on a mayor's citizens' task force and has supported the mayor politically may later ask for the mayor's support for an agency's proposal that requires city funds or cooperation. In order for obligations to be used in inducement, the target must recognize or be made to recognize that if it does not repay the obligation, sanctions could be used against it or no future rewards will be provided.

When punishments are used for inducements, the worker or a member of his action system may threaten to evoke the punishment if the target system does not comply, but the actual punishment ordinarily is not used until after the system has failed to do so. For example, a tenant's union may threaten to withhold rents but ordinarily will not do so unless the landlord fails to meet their demands.

Sometimes the offer of rewards and threat of punishments and the request to cash in on obligations are made explicit. The tenants say they will withhold rents, or the worker with the community action program says he will help obtain federal funds for the vocational school. Other times they are implicit. The juvenile judge does not need to be reminded that the social worker has been helpful to him in the past, and the mayor knows he owes the board president favors and that if he does not comply the president may not help him politically in the future.

In order for the worker to use inducements, the other systems must perceive that the worker has control of something the systems want to obtain or do not want to lose, or he can evoke the influence of others who do have control. The systems have to believe that the influencer can and will deliver the reward or punishment. Further, if people are resistant to a change effort because they do not believe it is in their self-interest, the rewards or punishments must be strong enough to make them believe it would be more in their self-interest to comply with the influence effort than not to.[9]

The worker himself may sometimes have sufficient bases of influence to provide rewards and punishments. The worker's control over material resources which is provided by his change agent system can be a powerful base of inducement. If the other system perceives the social worker as having the power to provide resources or services which are essential for his or his family's survival, for example, the social worker

---

[9] See the discussion on coercive power in Cartwright and Zander, *Group Dynamics*, pp. 221–227; and in John R. P. French and Bertram Raven, "The Bases of Social Power," in D. Cartwright (ed.), *Studies In Social Power* (Ann Arbor, Mich.: Institute for Social Research, 1959), pp. 150–67.

probably will be able to induce it to comply with the demands he makes on it.

The social worker with legitimate authority has a powerful resource to use in controlling the behavior of other people. A worker who has authority to grant or take away a license to operate may induce a day-care center or an institution to establish special services. A worker in a prison may induce good behavior in an inmate so he can receive a recommendation for parole or special treatment or can avoid disciplinary treatment. The social worker's position in an agency can provide him with authority over other staff that gives him resources such as salary raises, working assignments, and office space to induce staff members to perform certain behaviors by implying that they will receive future rewards or punishments. The worker who has control over information that another system wants, such as information about procedures to obtain a valued resource like federal funds, may be able to make demands on the system in return for release of the information.

When the worker wants to use inducement with people who have higher status than himself or authority over him, or with people who themselves possess considerable sources of influence, he may need to utilize other people whom he has access to because of his own or his agency's relationships. These people may have access to rewards that the worker's target values and penalties the target wishes to avoid, or the target may be obligated to them. For example, a large financial contributor to an agency may be able to induce an agency board of directors to inaugurate a new program or to change existing policies. A mental hospital superintendent may use his authority to insist that new discharge policies be established. A newspaper editor may threaten to run a series about inadequate treatment of aged people in the county home which would embarrass county officials. The leader of a political party who has control over legislative committee assignments may ask legislators to introduce bills for programs for the unemployed. The membership chairman of a prestigeful social club may ask a new president of a local business who wants to join the club to support a local fund drive. A leader of a tenant's union may threaten slum landlords with legal action or a rent strike.

Reward and punishment can be two sides of the same coin. Complying with the influence efforts will produce a reward (a license to operate a nursing home, additional financial assistance) and noncompliance will produce a punishment (loss of license, reduction in financial resources). Studies of people subjected to inducement have indicated that if punishment is used, the target may develop negative feelings toward the person exerting the influence. They may change only their behavior in response to the threat and not their values, beliefs, or attitudes, and they probably will revert to their former behavior if the punishment is withdrawn. However, if rewards are used, the target may come to be attracted to the person using influence, may adopt his standards and values, and may be motivated to accept future influence attempts from him that do not offer special rewards.[10]

Persuasion

A second major means of influence is persuasion. Rather than relying on the implicit or explicit promise or threat of rewards and punishments, the process of persuasion is directed to the target's voluntary acceptance of the change agent's influence efforts. This willingness to go along with the social worker may be based on the target's conviction that the worker is correct, his appraisal of the worker's standing as an expert, or his acceptance of the legitimacy of the worker's request. As William Gamson points out, the target's conviction that the worker is correct may result from the content of the worker's argument or the target's faith in the expertness of the worker. The target's acceptance of the legitimacy of the worker's request depends on perceiving the worker as being in a position to make the request and perceiving the requested behavior as falling within the norms subscribed to by the target.[11]

The social worker who depends on the content of his argument for persuasion will draw on his resources of knowledge and expertness, skills in communication, and ability to control the flow of information. For example, staff members of a community mental health center may have knowledge of many community problems that the agency could become involved with, but they will select only a few on which they will provide information to the board of directors. By presenting selected information in a logical manner indicating that problems of drug abuse are more serious than other current problems, the workers may persuade the board to establish an action system to assess alternative service approaches to these problems. The social worker working with this action system may provide information only on the service approaches that he believes will be helpful.

---

[10] See summary of research on use of rewards and punishment in Cartwright and Zander, *Group Dynamics*, pp. 221–227; and French and Raven, "Bases of Social Power."

[11] Gamson, *Power and Discontent*, pp. 79–81 and 87–88.

In facilitating communication or reducing conflicts within or between systems, the worker may provide information to members of the systems to give them a better understanding of the point of view of the other people. The social worker who is advocating on behalf of a client with a city housing inspector will provide information on housing violations which he thinks will persuade the inspector to take action on behalf of his client. The social worker who is building new systems will provide information to potential members about its purposes and tasks.

The social worker often is in a special position to control the information used in a persuasion effort. His own change agent system can provide information he can control. For example, the worker can select the information he presents about the nature of the material resources the agency possesses and procedures to be used to obtain them or the information he uses in his recommendations to a court or other legal authority. The worker's position in the agency can provide him with information he may share selectively. For example, a supervisor can control, to some extent, the amount and nature of information about agency policy that he shares with his workers. A worker can withhold or select information about clients in his discusssions with his supervisor or other staff, or with people outside the agency.

The social worker can use his skills in data collection and assessment to generate information to be used in persuasion attempts. When working with members of a multiperson system, he can collect data about members and arrange for feedback of the information to other members. The worker can influence the type of information that is collected, fed back, and assessed by his selection of a data collection technique and feedback mechanisms.

In the examples cited above, the social worker relies on his access to his target system and his ability to provide a logical and effective presentation to persuade others by the content of the information he has gathered. However, the presentation of information alone often will not influence the target's willingness to accept it; the target must be convinced that the persuader is an expert. Cartwright and Zander cite research that indicates the effectiveness of persuasion is dependent on the target's perceptions of the source of the information—i.e., the persuader.[12] It has been suggested that a persuader has "expert power" only if he is perceived by others as having special knowledge or expert-

---

[12] Cartwright and Zander, *Group Dynamics*, pp. 221–227.

ness.[13] Factors that may contribute to the worker's standing as an expert are his established relationships with other people, his authority and sanction to practice social work, his status and reputation, his personal attractiveness, and the perception of the target that the worker has access to special information.[14]

Potential members of client, action, and target systems may accept the worker's statements because his agency affiliation and professional identification certify to them his competence and right to practice social work. The worker may enhance his prestige and credibility by identifying or calling attention to his position in the agency and the agency's position in the community, his professional education and past experiences, and his position in professional and community organizations. Of course if the worker has already established relationships with his target system, the system may automatically consider him an expert. For example, a social worker in a children's institution who has developed cooperative working relationships with all staff members and has been helpful to them in the past may be able to persuade them to form a contract to mediate conflicts that have arisen over boundaries of staff responsibility.

The worker also can use his personal characteristics, such as race, sex, or success in dealing with personal problems like physical handicaps, to enhance his expertness. For example, a black worker may be perceived as having special knowledge about black people, or a physically handicapped worker may be viewed as an expert on the inadequacies of community resources for the physically handicapped. He can also add to his resources by utilizing other people to whom he has access through his own or his agency's relationships. These people may be able to persuade others because of their prestige and reputation for expertness and credibility, their personal characteristics, or because of their access to information. For example, a leader of an organization who has credibility with its members may vouch for the worker's expertness and competence and persuade the group to ask the worker to help them overcome their problems of internal functioning. A director of an agency who is viewed as having special access to knowledge and information about the operation of his agency and the problems of its clients may assist the worker in persuading a school principal to provide job training for agency clients. A prominent doctor viewed as an expert in his area of competence may be asked to

---

[13] French and Raven, "Bases of Social Power."
[14] See discussion on resources of a change agent using persuasion in Cartwright and Zander, *Group Dynamics*, pp. 221–27.

assist the worker in persuading his own agency to utilize existing public health facilities for its clients. A worker may ask people who have experienced the problem of trying to find adequate nursing home care to testify to a county board on the need for more quality nursing homes. A newspaper reporter with a reputation for objectivity may be able to persuade large numbers of people to support a fund-raising drive.

Use of Relationship

A third major category of influence processes is the use of relationship. This means of influence stems from the nature or quality of the interpersonal relationship between the social worker (or the influencer) and the people he is trying to influence. In understanding how this means of influence operates it is useful to distinguish between two of its interrelated factors: who the worker is as a person, and how he manages the interpersonal dynamics in a relationship.

The first factor pertains to the characteristics of the worker as perceived by the target. In contrast to persuasion, the issue here is not the target's rational assessment of the merit of the arguments put forth by the worker or his belief in the worker's expertness. Rather, the concern is with the target's emotional response to the personality of the social worker—how the social worker comes across to him as a person. It is this emotional response which makes people open to the influence of the worker. An individual may find the relationship with the worker to be intrinsically rewarding and want to maintain it, or he might identify with the worker—look up to him, respect him, want to be like him, or see in him a number of characteristics he admires.[15]

This means of influence utilizes the influencer's resource of charisma or personal attractiveness, which is often enhanced by his status and reputation, his legitimate authority, and his descriptive characteristics. For example, a prominent black athlete might be able to get a group of black high school graduates to apply for admission to college. A group of pre-teen-age girls might model their behavior after a respected and liked group leader. A family may agree to continue seeing a social

---

[15] Arnold Goldstein, Kenneth Heller, and Lee Sechrest, *Psychotherapy and the Psychology of Behavior Change* (New York: John Wiley & Sons, Inc., 1966), pp. 73–145, discuss ways of increasing personal attraction. Identification is discussed in Herbert C. Kelman, "The Role of the Group in the Induction of Therapeutic Change," *International Journal of Psychotherapy*, 13 (October 1963): 339–43. Cartwright and Zander, *Group Dynamics*, pp. 221–22, discuss how the change agent can use the target's attitude toward being influenced by the change agent.

worker after the initial interview because they like his personality. As these examples illustrate, the worker can exercise influence himself through the use of relationship or can draw on other people who possess the resources which give them an impact on a given person or group. The exercise of influence through the use of relationship may be deliberate on the part of the influencer or may occur as a by-product of the interaction within a relationship, without conscious use being made of it.

A second facet of the use of relationship in the exercise of influence is the way the worker handles the interpersonal dynamics in a relationship. This means of influence relies heavily on the worker's resource of knowledge and skills in interpersonal relationships.

Various chapters throughout this text have illustrated how the worker makes use of relationship in exercising influence.[16] For example, the worker can enhance a person's motivation to engage in a contract by treating him with respect, demonstrating concern for his needs, and actively involving him in decision making. By pointing out discrepancies between what a person says and does or by providing information which challenges a person's perceptions or self-image, the worker can create discomfort and dissatisfaction which may induce a person to participate in a planned change effort or make him more open to other influence processes, such as persuasion.

Establishing rapport with a client in an interview, calming down an overly excited or angry person, raising some anxiety or enthusiasm in an apathetic person, and feeding ego needs are all examples of the use of influence through relationship. Again, this means of influence may be directly employed by the worker or he may reach a target through another person who has the necessary resources to do so. The use of relationship may be directed at specific behavior or attitudinal change. It can also be utilized to create a psychological atmosphere in a system or to arouse an emotional response in a person which will make the person or system more open to the exercise of other means of influence, such as rational persuasion.

A closer look at the use of relationship would require examining such issues as the nature of verbal and nonverbal communications, what the worker responds to and when and how he does so, and theories of interpersonal relationships. To do the subject justice would require an in-depth analysis of interpersonal relationships which is beyond the scope of this book. However, the importance of this skill

---

[16] See especially Chapters 4, 8, and 9.

area for social work should be emphasized and its pursuit in other sources encouraged.[17]

Use of Environment

A fourth means by which change agents exercise influence is through manipulation of the immediate physical and social environment. The term "physical environment" here means the physical attributes of the setting in which people are interacting. "Social environment" refers to the composition of the one-to-one or group action system utilized, the activities engaged in, and the norms or regulations that govern people's interactions.

In comparison to other influence processes, the use of environment might be thought of as an indirect means of influence. It is based on the concept that people's behavior and attitudes are affected by the nature of their immediate social and physical environment.[18]

In order to use environmental manipulation the worker must possess the necessary knowledge resource, that is, knowledge of the impact that the immediate environment has on people, and the ability to structure or make changes in the environment.[19] In some situations both conditions are easily met. For example, a worker arranges chairs in a circle to promote greater interaction, or a worker offers a client a cup of coffee to help him relax. At the other extreme, a drastic change in milieu, such as placement of a child in a foster home, requires a great deal of knowledge about the impact of such a change on the child and his family and the kinds of foster homes which might be suitable. Effecting such a change requires access to the resource (foster home), legal authority to make the change, and skill in preparing the natural parents, the child, and the foster parents for the change. As with the other means

---

[17] See, for example, Robert R. Carkhuff, *Helping and Human Relations*, Vols. I and II (New York: Holt, Rinehart & Winston, Inc., 1969), and Paul Watzlawick, Janet Beavin, and Don D. Jackson, *Pragmatics of Human Communication* (New York: W. W. Norton & Co., 1967).

[18] For further discussion on the use of environment as a means of influence, see Cartwright and Zander, *Group Dynamics*, pp. 222–23, and Ronald Lippitt, Jeanne Watson, and Bruce Westley, *The Dynamics of Planned Change* (New York: Harcourt, Brace & World, Inc., 1958), pp. 110–12.

[19] The impact of environment is discussed in Roger G. Barker, *Ecological Psychology* (Stanford, Cal.: Stanford University Press, 1968); John and Elaine Cumming, *Ego and Milieu* (New York: Atherton Press, 1962); Harold M. Proshansky, William H. Ittleson, and Leanne G. Rivlin, *Environmental Psychology* (New York: Holt, Rinehart & Winston, Inc., 1970); and Robert Sommer, *Personal Space: The Behavioral Basis of Design* (Englewood Cliffs, N.J.: Prentice-Hall, Inc., 1969).

of influence discussed in this chapter, the worker may exert the influence himself or rely on another person who possesses the appropriate resources to reach the target system. For example, a social worker serving as an advisor to the chairman of a neighborhood council may suggest ways of structuring the council meetings which will promote greater member participation in the decision-making processes of the council. The chairman, however, is the person who is in the position to implement the suggestions.

The exercise of influence as the basis of many of the planned change skills and activities of the social worker is particularly evident in the use of environment. For example, in data collection the system from which the data are being gathered can be structured in ways that involve both the social and physical environments. In collecting data on a family, the worker might set up a rule that each person has a certain time to tell how he perceives the family's problems, during which other members of the family must listen without interrupting. Or the worker may ask the family to engage in some task together, such as planning for a vacation, so he can observe the family interaction. He might also vary the composition of the group, having parents interact with and without the children present. As another example, the worker can use a variety of different program activities and different settings in a children's group to place different demands on the children and provide data on how they cope with these various situations.

Manipulation of the physical and social environment is particularly important in the formation and structuring of action systems. Chapters 10 and 11 discussed in some detail the effects on the functioning of the action system of such factors as composition (size and membership), time and location of meetings, operating rules and procedures, and the activities engaged in by members.

One way of examining the impact of the physical environment is in terms of the direct constraints it places on physical activity as well as the opportunities for activity and interaction it provides.[20] If the chairs in a day room of a mental hospital ward are placed around the perimeter of the room, people will tend to sit where the chairs are; chairs placed in small conversational groupings allow more opportunity for casual interaction among the patients. A home for the aged located on the outskirts of the city, with no nearby public transportation, makes it difficult for residents to get into town, and visitors may curtail their

---

[20] For an extensive discussion on environmental therapy, see Cumming and Cumming, *Ego and Milieu.*

visits because it is inconvenient. A social worker in a children's institution who has his office located in the cottage where the children live, instead of in a central administration building, will have more opportunity to become a part of the cottage life and to interact informally with the children.

A second way the physical environment influences people is through the information about values and attitudes it conveys. A drab and dreary waiting room in a public welfare office or a medical clinic tells the clients the value that society places on them and the services they are receiving. A social worker in an institution who always keeps his office door closed may be saying "don't bother me" to a client who might want to see him. An open door, on the other hand, can often be considered an invitation to drop in.

A third perspective on the environment is the help it provides in restoring and maintaining psychological orientation and general feelings of comfort.[21] For example, many homes for the aged allow residents to bring with them favorite small furnishings such as a chair or end table, in order to ease the transition into the institution. Geriatric mental patients can be helped to maintain their psychological orientation to time and place by putting up large clocks and calendars and decorations which give cues as to the seasons and the passage of time. Another example is the case of an elderly male patient in a mental hospital—a retired farmer—who often wandered into other patients' rooms. This was not surprising since all the room entries looked alike and the room numbers were small and difficult to read. When some pictures depicting farm scenes were placed on his door, the wandering into other rooms ceased.

ISSUES IN THE EXERCISE OF INFLUENCE

Several issues can arise in the social worker's use of the different means of influence described above. These can involve combination of the means of influence, the limitations of influence resources, the communication of influence, the cost of exercising influence, and value implications of the use of influence.

---

[21] Cumming and Cumming, *Ego and Milieu*, p. 95, point out that many pictures, chairs, and other furnishings which intellectuals find attractive seem austere and "unhomelike" to working-class people. They point out that the goal of the worker is to help the client, not to improve the client's taste.

Combining Means of Influence

The social worker will often use more than one means of influence, simultaneously or in succession. For example, a teen-ager on probation may initially maintain contact with his social worker because of fear of having his probation revoked (negative inducement). Eventually, however, he may grow to like and respect the worker and continue seeing him because he finds the relationship itself rewarding (use of relationship) and may value the practical help the worker is able to provide him (positive inducement). A worker may follow a suggestion of his supervisor because he accepts the legitimate authority of the supervisor. As he recognizes that the supervisor's suggestions are usually helpful, he may begin to view him as an expert and follow his advice because he is convinced of its merits (persuasion). A social worker might hang his diplomas on his office wall (use of environment) to enhance his resources of status or expertness, which in turn might make him more able to use persuasion. Or a worker might use persuasion to get someone to join an action system and then structure the action system to help that person feel comfortable with the other members.

When a social worker lacks the appropriate resources to influence a target system, there are generally two options open. First, he may utilize the resources he does have to get a third party with the appropriate resources to influence the target system for him. A social worker from a county social services department may want to influence the behavior of some of his clients who are patients in a nursing home by making certain changes in the physical or social environment of the home. Though he may lack the legitimate authority to make such changes, he can use his persuasion resources to get the administrator of the institution to make the desired changes.

The second option open to the social worker is to use his available means of influence to obtain the needed resources from a third system. For example, a social worker might use persuasion or an inducement such as the promise of favorable publicity to get a sporting goods firm to donate athletic equipment to his community center. He can then use this equipment as an inducement to get neighborhood children to attend the center.

The above examples illustrate the varied ways in which the social worker can utilize his influence resources and employ means of influence, in succession and in combination, to reach a target system. It is useful, then, to view the worker's exercise of influence in relation to an overall strategy of influence activity.

Limitations of Influence Resources

Another major consideration in the exercise of influence relates to the nature of the influence resource or base of influence being used. Resources are situation specific—that is, something which may serve as a resource in one situation may not be a resource in another. For example, the threat of withdrawal of funds may be a powerful inducement for an agency which is highly dependent on that money. But to another agency which has multiple sources of funding and a larger overall budget, the threat of withdrawal of the same amount of funds might not be as powerful an inducement resource. A person with status and reputation with white middle-class members of a community may not command the respect of blue-collar workers or blacks in that community. A union leader who holds the threat of a strike may have a powerful bargaining tool, but he will not be able to call a strike on any issue at any time. The issue must be made to appear of vital concern to the union members.

Generally, the less tangible the influence resource, the more its applicability is limited by the target's perceptions and evaluations of the resource. If a change agent is not perceived as an expert or as being knowledgeable, he will not be able to use persuasion to influence a target. If a teen-age boy does not identify with the worker, the worker will not be able to serve as a role model in changing the boy's behavior.

Though all resources are situation specific, some are more generalized than others. Money is a generalized tangible resource because it can be converted into many different kinds of inducement resources. Within a given system, status and reputation may be a more generalized resource than legitimate authority because they are attributes of the influencer himself rather than of the position he holds in the system.

In each new situation the worker will have to reassess the applicability and availability of the different bases of influence that can be brought to bear on that situation.

Communication of Influence

In any use of influence, the effort has to be communicated to the target. While verbal communications are most often used, written and other nonverbal communications also can be effective. Nonverbal communications such as gestures and tone of voice are especially important when use of relationship is the means of influence.

The worker can use nonverbal communication to bring other peoples' resources, as well as his own, to bear on a situation. A typical example is the stationery of many social agencies, which lists the members of the board of directors, who are often influential people in the community, on their letterheads. A news story about the beginning of a new program illustrated with a picture of some prominent personality is another such example.

Written communications include letters, memorandums, reports, agendas, case summaries, minutes of meetings, news releases, and advertisements. A social worker who is trying to persuade a vocational training program to accept a client might write a letter of referral which presents the information on the client in such a way that he is seen as meeting the eligibility criteria for the program (control over the flow of information). An agenda which a committee chairman sends out in advance to committee members can influence how the meeting is run (use of social environment).

The media through which the influence effort is communicated may have an impact on the effectiveness of the effort. For example, when using rational persuasion to solicit financial or other support for a program, a personal letter might receive more serious consideration than a form letter. As another example, people may be more reluctant to turn down a request to attend a meeting if the request is made in person or over the phone than if the request is communicated via a letter or memorandum.

Cost of Exercising Influence

The cost of exercising influence is another factor that the worker will have to evaluate. Cost may be measured in several different terms.

First, there is the cost involved in using up or depleting one's influence resources. Both material and nonmaterial resources may be spent in exercising influence. When money is used as an inducement, it is gone after it has been spent. If the worker cashes in on an obligation incurred by a worker in another agency, this inducement resource may also be depleted. Repeated use of an influence resource will sometimes diminish its value. The presentation of information about the plight of residents in the inner city may be an effective persuasion resource when people hear these facts for the first time, but after repeated use they become used to it, and it loses some of its potency. The same is true of sit-ins and other such demonstrations used in inducement. What made them initially effective was their novelty and shock value. People are now more blasé about such things.

There are some resources which do not get used up when employed in an influence effort, for example, the worker's resource of expertness. In fact, such a resource may be enhanced through use. If the worker gives useful advice, his status may increase in the eyes of other people. An organizer who has staged a successful rent strike may establish his credibility at being able to command an inducement resource, and he may be able to rely on the threat of the use of this resource in the future instead of actually having to carry off the strike.

A related point is that a worker might be tempted to employ a bluff. He may threaten to invoke a sanction which he really has no control over, or he may incur an obligation he does not intend to honor. While there may be no initial cost in such a situation because no actual resource is being used up, the use of bluff can increase the cost of future influence efforts if the bluff is called or if he is called upon to honor his obligations. The loss of credibility and the relationships he may damage in such situations mean that a greater amount of resources will have to be spent in future influence efforts to reestablish credibility and relationships.

A second way of analyzing costs is in terms of restrictions that the exercise of influence places on future alternatives for action. If a depletable resource is being used in the influence effort, the worker must consider what alternate uses could have been made of that resource. For example, the money a community center director spends on remodeling a gymnasium might have been used to raise the salaries of his staff.

The exercise of influence can also restrict future options of the worker because of the effects it may have on ongoing and future relationships. The use of negative inducement often arouses resistance and hostility and affects the target's perception of the influencer. Once the worker operates in the context of a conflictual relationship, it is difficult for him to assume roles such as a mediator and to use other means of influence, such as persuasion.[22] The exercise of influence, especially negative inducement, also may polarize positions in a family or community at a time when they should remain fluid because negotiation is still possible. Or it may have the effect of mobilizing a previously dormant group to oppose the goals of the worker (sometimes referred to as "backlash"). Dealing with the backlash or trying to restore relationships in a polarized system can put a further drain on the worker's influence resources.

The worker can incur obligations in the exercise of influence, espe-

---

[22] It may be helpful to review the discussion on this point in Chapter 4.

cially when he lacks the appropriate resources in a given situation. In order to mount a public information campaign, a neighborhood group might need office facilities and equipment to reproduce materials such as posters or leaflets. A community center might be willing to make its facilities available to the group if it promises to lend its assistance to the center's next fund-raising drive. If the neighborhood group had its own facilities, they would not need to incur such an obligation. The cost of fulfilling these obligations in the future must then also be considered an allocation of resources which might limit future alternatives.

A third aspect of the cost of exercising influence is the cost involved in monitoring change. Especially in the case of a resistant target, where negative inducement is being used, the target's behavior must be continually monitored in order to apply any negative sanctions. The behavior of a person on parole must be monitored to see if he is complying with the conditions of his release from prison. The threat of having his parole revoked might be the only reason he is maintaining certain behaviors. In contrast, when persuasion is used, the person changes his behavior or attitudes because he sees it as in his own self-interest. There is no need to monitor and control the administration of rewards or sanctions. Aside from any ethical considerations, this is why persuasion is often preferable to negative inducement.

A final cost to be considered in any influence process is the cost involved in communicating the effort. In many cases this cost may be negligible. For example, a promise for support of a program can be elicited verbally through a phone call. In other cases however, such as when trying to influence a large group of people by persuasion, there may be a high cost involved in collecting information and getting it to the people, perhaps through leaflets and advertisements.

Value Implications

To some extent the imposition of values is inherent in any change effort. It is not to be expected, therefore, that any of the various means of influence discussed in this chapter would be devoid of manipulative aspects. They do vary in their ethical implications, however. Because inducement places the greatest amount of restraints on a person, it might be considered the most problematic influence process from an ethical point of view. In some respects the use of environment and relationships is even less ethically desirable, because it can influence people's behavior without their conscious realization.[23]

Within a democratic framework, persuasion is the most ethical form of influence. As Dorwin Cartwright and Alvin Zander note, when persuasion is being used the influencer does not apply any extraneous rewards or punishment to get the target to accept his message. The target is constrained only by his own evaluation of the merits of the influencer's message, though this evaluation may be colored by his feeling toward the influencer. Thus the target remains in control of his own behavior.[24] Given equal alternatives, the social worker would opt for the use of persuasion. The alternatives, however, are rarely equal.

---

[23] For further discussion on some of these issues see Goldstein, Heller, and Sechrest, *Psychotherapy and Behavior Change*, pp. 8–9, and Robert Perlman and David Jones, *Neighborhood Service Centers* (Washington, D.C.: U.S. Department of Health, Education, and Welfare, 1967), p. 58.

[24] Cartwright and Zander, *Group Dynamics*, p. 221.

CHAPTER 1

Termination is not just some point reached at the end of the planne
change effort, but an integral part of the whole process which th
worker carefully prepares for and helps bring about. Skills in terminat
ing a planned change effort and disengaging from relationships are a
necessary as skills in initiating the effort and engaging people in it
The way the process is brought to an end can affect the success of th
whole change effort and future relationships between the worker an
members of the client, action, and target systems.

The groundwork for termination is laid throughout the planne
change process. Time limits established in the beginning provide
target date to work toward and against which progress can be meas
ured. The formulation of clear and specific outcome goals makes i
easier to assess the extent to which they have been realized.

In addition to this groundwork, there are specific things the worke
must do near the end of the planned change effort to help bring it t
a successful conclusion. This chapter will consider three aspects of thi
skill area: (1) evaluation of the change effort, (2) disengaging from
relationships, and (3) stabilization of the change effort. The worke
may be terminating with different persons at different times in th

planned change effort, but the focus here will be on termination with the client and action systems at the end of the process.

EVALUATION

Evaluation should be a continuing activity throughout the planned change process. After each task has been completed, the worker must determine if it has accomplished its purpose and decide if the methods or goals of the change effort should be readjusted or redefined. From time to time the worker and client or action systems may engage in a broader review and assessment of the progress being made, particularly if no time limits have been established. Reaching some impasse or getting "bogged down" should signal the need to take stock and reassess what is being done. While the evaluation at the end of the process is more comprehensive, it should be a continuation of the evaluative activity throughout the planned change process. Many of the points in regard to the content of an evaluation are applicable to the periodic evaluations performed by the worker and other systems during the process.

There are two major reasons why the social worker reviews and evaluates the change effort. The first has to do with his professional obligation to the client and action system members to indicate to what extent the outcome goals agreed upon in his contract with them have been realized. The credibility of the profession of social work rests on its ability to demonstrate that it can bring about the changes it claims to be able to make. Though this is usually considered to be a research problem, it is not just that. Generalizations about social work intervention must be based on a large number of cases, but it is still necessary to measure change in individual planned change efforts. The better the practitioner does in demonstrating and documenting the results of his work in each case, the easier it will be to conduct needed research. Thus the first reason for evaluation and review stems from the fact that the worker is accountable for the results of his planned change effort to the specific client as well as to the general public which supports the profession.

A second reason for the evaluation is that an explicit review and assessment of failures and accomplishments can be a valuable learning experience for those involved in the planned change effort, including the worker. It can help consolidate the lessons learned as a result of going through the planned change effort and can enhance the ability of the client or action system to cope with similar situations in the future. Thus even if mistakes were made and not all the outcome goals were realized, if those involved learned why the goals were not accomplished and how to avoid similar mistakes in the future, the planned change effort will have some payoff. This is especially important for an action system that continues to function as an ongoing system after the worker terminates with it.

Content of the Evaluation

There are two general areas to be considered in making an evaluation of the planned change effort—outcome and process. The major consideration is the outcome, or what has been accomplished. In what way is the problem or situation different now than at the beginning of the planned change effort? How do the changes compare with the outcome goals?

A legitimate evaluation is only possible if outcome goals are clearly and specifically defined in terms which are capable of measurement (see Chapter 6). The absence of initial outcome goals may tempt the practitioner to justify the outcomes as evaluation targets, whether or not he caused these outcomes or was aiming to bring them about.[1] Without clarity in outcome goals, there is the danger that the practitioner will state his purpose post hoc in terms of what was accomplished, rather than measuring accomplishments against initial purposes. Such a practice can become a means for circumventing accountability to the client and others.

Besides clarity in goals, in order to measure change there needs to be a clear picture of where things started from, i.e., a baseline. In this regard it is useful to think of two levels of baseline measurement. The first is for outcome goals which involve producing some kind of "end product," such as a report on day-care needs in the community, or obtaining or providing some kind of resource or service for a client. In such cases the baseline is simply the absence of the product or the service, although the quality of the product or the adequacy of the service obtained will have to be considered in the evaluation. When the outcome goal involves some change in the state of the functioning of a system or a change in behavior, the task of describing the initial conditions, i.e., measuring the baseline, becomes more complex.

---

[1] Robert Chin, "Evaluating Group Movement and Individual Change," in *Use of Groups in the Psychiatric Setting* (New York: National Association of Social Workers, 1960), p. 38.

For example, suppose the outcome goal in a planned change effort is to improve the coordination of services to the mentally retarded in a given community. As a result of the social worker's efforts a permanent coordinating committee is established in the community. But the mere existence of this new committee doesn't necessarily mean that the outcome goal (improvement in the coordination of services) has been achieved. The committee is a vehicle for such coordination, not the proof of its accomplishment. To demonstrate that there has actually been an improvement in the coordination of services there first must be an operational measure of coordination, such as number of agencies with overlapping functions or number of referrals made between agencies. Then a change in the amount of coordination from the baseline to termination must be demonstrated.

Depending on goals and baselines, lack of change is not always a sign of failure. In working with an elderly person who has just become widowed, the social worker may offer supportive services with a goal of helping the widow to maintain her current level of independent living in the community. Without such supportive services she might be expected to have difficulties living alone. Her health might begin to deteriorate, so that she eventually would require institutional care. In such cases maintenance of a level of functioning, rather than change, represents a legitimate and successful outcome. Thus, both baselines and outcome goals are needed in evaluating outcomes.[2]

The evaluation must account for negative as well as positive outcomes. There is always the possibility of a situation (or aspects of a situation) worsening or deteriorating by the time the point of termination is reached. In fact, lack of progress or deterioration may cause the client or worker to decide to terminate the effort earlier than expected. There are often unintended consequences or negative side effects in a planned change effort. The solution to one problem may bring other problems to the surface. In his initial planning the worker must try to anticipate such possibilities, and his evaluation should make mention of his success or lack of sucess in doing so.

The evaluation of outcome goals is really a kind of accounting procedure. The positive outcomes (intended as well as unintended) must be weighed against the negative outcomes (anticipated as well as

---

[2] We recognize the possibility of unanticipated positive changes in areas where no baseline data were collected or explicit goals established. While these changes will be discussed in the evaluation, baselines with regard to them can only be viewed in retrospect.

unanticipated). By comparing the gains with the losses, a balanced picture of the situation at the point of termination can become evident. For example, a tenant organization might win a concession from the housing authority by staging a large demonstration, but a negative outcome of their effort could be the loss of support of certain groups in the community. If this support is important for the future growth of the organization, then the gains must be weighed against the loss.

A second aspect of the evaluation of the planned change effort focuses on the process by which the outcome goals have been achieved. This includes an evaluation of the techniques, methods, and strategies used, as well as an examination of the roles played by the change agent himself and by the change agent system.

In evaluating the methods used it is helpful to differentiate between effectiveness and efficiency. Effectiveness pertains to the extent to which the methods used were effective in accomplishing the goal or objective. Efficiency pertains to the effort or cost expended to attain the goal or objective. While it may be effective to drive a thumbtack into a wall using a sledgehammer, it is not very efficient because the application of a smaller force could do the job just as well. Thus a method is efficient if the outcome can be achieved at the least possible cost.

Cost can be measured in terms of money, time, psychological stress, reduced status, and lost alternative courses of action. Could a worker have accomplished the same goals by working with a family for three months instead of six? Were the additional gains in the final three months worth the expenditure of additional time? What else could the worker or the family have done with that time? Or could the same policy changes have been achieved through continued meetings with the welfare board rather than the holding of large-scale demonstratons? Instead of using up their resources on these demonstrations, would an alternative project have had a greater overall payoff for the organization? While such questions are, of course, considered in the worker's initial planning, they must be looked at again at the end of the planned change effort in light of his actual experience. It may be playing the Monday morning quarterback to speculate on how things might have been done differently, but such critical exploration provides the climate for professional growth.

Another question that should be asked in evaluating the methods used in the planned change effort is *why* change occurred. How did the methods work? What helped and what hindered the process? Did changes (positive or negative) occur because of or in spite of the worker's intervention? Can the changes be attributed to factors identified by the worker? These are questions which can only be answered definitively by well-designed research studies.[3] This kind of inquiry on the part of the practitioner, however, can help sensitize him to factors to be explored and hypotheses to be tested in research. It can also give him ideas on ways of experimenting with and modifying his own procedures and techniques in future cases.

Another aspect of the evaluation of the methods of the planned change effort is an evaluation of the worker himself in his performance of the change agent role and an evaluation of the change agent system of which he is a part. The worker should be prepared to evaluate his own performance and how it contributed to and hindered the attainment of the goals of the planned change effort. While self-evaluation is useful, feedback from clients and others involved in the effort can serve as an important check on the worker's self-perception. When one's image as a competent professional is at stake, self-perception may not be very objective. It is tempting to take credit for success while blaming failure on others.

In cases where the worker is likely to have continuing relationships with members of the client and action systems, as in working with committees and community groups, their evaluation of him and the image he establishes during the current change effort will affect their acceptance of him in future efforts. The feedback the worker receives from others will to an extent depend on the quality of the relationships he has established. How free do the clients or others feel to voice criticism of the worker or the change agent system? How anxious is the worker when receiving feedback, and how does he communicate this anxiety to others?

The client's evaluation of the agency and its services may take place informally through discussions with the worker, or the agency may find a way to structure such evaluations more formally through the use of evaluation forms or interviews.[4] If social workers see clients as consumers of their services, as people who have valid opinions and

---

[3] In evaluative research a well-known, documented phenomenon is that improvement often results from the mere fact of participating in a treatment program, regardless of the specific nature of the treatment. It may be that expectations of improvement or belief in the methods are sufficient to bring about some change. The "sugar pill" (placebo) is a common example.

[4] For a good example of using clients to evaluate services, see Rachel A. Levine, "Consumer Participation in Planning and Evaluation of Mental Health Services," *Social Work*, 15 (April 1970): 41–46.

points of view, they will seek out their opinions and suggestions on ways of improving the agency and its services.

Data Collection for Evaluation

At the time of termination the worker's evaluation must be supported by relevant data. In cases where several people are involved in or affected by the outcome of the planned change effort, the worker will use his skills in data collection to assess different perceptions of the outcome. Some members of a client or action system may feel that a given outcome is good, while others may disagree. The two groups may be using similar or different standards or values in making their judgments. In a problem assessment it is important to assess why people are evaluating a given social condition or behavior as a problem. Likewise, it is important to determine how people view and evaluate the outcomes of a change effort. People can agree on a course of action or on an outcome for different reasons. If the worker will again work with some of these people in the future it is good for him to understand their value systems.

The kind of data the worker uses to support his evaluation will, of course, affect its credibility. Use of the worker's or client's subjective judgments of change is usually not enough, because they leave too much room for distortion.[5] The worker's data should be as objective as possible and should be based on a variety of sources. If data are collected throughout the planned change process, it will be easier to assess changes. Comparisons between baseline data and data collected at the end of the planned change process provide the best evidence for outcomes.

The worker does have some opportunities to assess the client system by structuring situations or taking advantage of those that present themselves. When the client system is also the target system, the worker can use his periods of absence, such as vacations, as a means of assessing how the client system gets along without his help. If outcome goals involve the acquisition of social skills, the worker can structure tasks for the client that require use of these skills in their natural setting, under realistic conditions. Evaluation based on the client's behavior in the worker's office has many limitations. When the client is involved in the evaluation process, the way he goes about the evalua-

---

[5] See for example Ann Shyne, "Evaluation of Results in Social Work," *Social Work*, 8 (October 1963): 26–33.

tion and how much responsibility he takes for it can provide an additional source of data for the worker.

The issue of timing is important in collecting data to support an evaluation. Since the possibility exists that the outcomes achieved by the end of the planned change effort might not last, some sort of follow-up evaluation at some time after termination is desirable. But there are problems associated with such follow-up studies. There are value questions such as the extent to which such a follow-up after termination represents a transgression of the client's right to privacy. There are also practical problems. The longer the worker waits to do the follow-up, the more confidence he can have that the desirable behaviors or conditions have remained, but the more difficult it becomes to disentangle effects attributable to the planned change effort from those related to the current life situation of the client system.

DISENGAGING FROM RELATIONSHIPS

The evaluation process discussed above takes place in the psychological context of "endings." The importance of understanding the psychological context of "beginnings" and of assessing the individual's motivations and resistances to engage in a planned change process were pointed out in Chapter 8. Similarly, the worker must understand the dynamics of "endings" and be prepared to cope with a variety of reactions to it. The prospects of termination may be accompanied by ambivalent feelings, particularly if participation in the action system has been a rewarding experience.

James Garland, Hubert Jones, and Ralph Kolodny have noted a number of reactions which typically take place in groups in the process of termination. They are seen as devices employed by members to avoid and forestall termination on the one hand and to face up to and accomplish it on the other. These reactions, which may occur in any size action system, include:

1. Denial. Members simply "forget" that the worker has told them about termination. They may act surprised and ask when the group will begin again.

2. Regression. There is a backsliding in ability to cope with interpersonal and organizational tasks. The group returns to previous levels of functioning. Disagreements that were previously settled may erupt again. Demands for dependence on the leader may increase, and there may be outbursts of anger toward one another, toward the leader, and toward the idea of termination.

3. Expression of need. Members feel that the worker will continue with the group if they show that they still need his services. There may be an increase in problematic behavior, verbal pleas for continuing help with problems may be expressed, or new problems may be brought up. The members may have become very aware of the kinds of problems that intrigue the worker and use this knowledge to manipulate him.

4. Recapitulation. Earlier modes of interaction and group activities may be revived and may at times be regressive. Members may request that activities they engaged in early in the history of the group be repeated. Reminiscing and recapitulation of group experiences often take place, and discussion may center on the minute details of earlier events.

5. Evaluation. This is closely related to recapitulation. Garland, Jones, and Kolodny note that "the process of repeating earlier events or relational stages, in addition to serving the need to recapture an experience that is slipping away, also may become part of the process of evaluating the meaning and worth of the experience."

6. Flight. There are two kinds of flight. One represents a destructive reaction to separation in which there is denial of any positive meaning of the group experience. Members may exhibit a variety of rejecting and rejection-provoking behaviors to prove that the agency or worker either didn't care for them or is terminating the group in retaliation for their bad behavior. In the second kind of flight, which is positive, constructive moves are made toward disengaging from the group. Members find new groups, activities, or friends outside the group, while continuing as members. Garland, Jones, and Kolodny note that "new contacts, which may be started well in advance of termination, serve to substitute for interests and gratifications which will no longer be fulfilled after the group's end. They also represent a broadening and maturing of interests and skills."[6]

While Garland, Jones, and Kolodny considered these reactions in the context of groups, many of the same dynamics can be observed in one-to-one relationships as well. They also note that a variety of these behaviors may occur in a single action system around the period of ter-

---

[6] James Garland, Hubert Jones, and Ralph Kolodny, "A Model for Stages of Development in Social Work Groups," in Saul Bernstein (ed.), *Explorations in Group Work* (Boston, Mass.: University of Boston School of Social Work, 1965), pp. 41–44.

mination. Further, there may be several different reactions within a single meeting. These reactions may not occur in any particular sequence, but in flashes or clusters. Milder forms of these reactions can sometimes be noted at the end of single interviews or group meetings, as well as at the end of a series of meetings.

In understanding the psychological context of endings, the worker's reactions, as well as those of the client and action systems, must be taken into consideration. The worker may have his own problems disengaging from his relationships. As Helen Northern states:

> The social worker is not immune from feelings about terminating with members of the group. Facing termination stirs up feelings about both the members and his role in the group. It is natural that a worker will feel pleased about the progress of the group and his part in it. It is natural, too, that he will feel a sense of loss, for it is not easy to separate from persons with whom one has developed a meaningful relationship. Termination also stirs up feelings about the quality of the worker's performance, for example, certain guilt feelings for not having had the time or the skill to have been more helpful to more members. The worker may have doubts about the nature and the permanence of the gains made by the members, leading to a desire to hang onto the group.[7]

If the worker is not clear about his own feelings regarding termination, he can easily get caught up in the client system's reactions, especially if that system is attempting to prolong the change effort. The feeling that time is running out, whether from a single session or from a series of sessions, sometimes creates pressure in the action system to bring out new problems. This is one reason why it is important to set time limits at the beginning of the planned change effort.

To prepare clients for termination, it is useful for the worker to be clear in the beginning about the planned termination date and to get the client system used to periodic reviews of progress and evaluation. Several weeks before the actual termination, the client system should be reminded of it, and references to it should be made more frequently from then on. William Reid and Ann Shyne found that in planned short-term casework, where termination dates were set in advance, the clients were apt to see termination in neutral terms, as part of the structure of the service. In contrast, those who were given open-ended casework services were more likely to see the end of serv-

---

[7] Helen Northern, *Social Work with Groups* (New York: Columbia University Press, 1969), p. 233.

ice in negative terms, as having come about because of insufficient progress.[8]

Sometimes it is useful to decrease the frequency or duration of contacts with the client or action system toward the end of the planned change process. This tapering off provides a gradual way for the client or action system to withdraw from the relationship and to assume greater responsibilities for the tasks performed by the worker. But this is not always possible, especially with a community task group which is likely to increase the frequency of its meetings near the end in order to meet a deadline. Since such final meetings can create strains in the interpersonal relationships in the action system, it is useful to have some sort of final ceremony, like a dinner or party, to release pressures. This is especially important if the worker has a stake in maintaining good relationships among the members of the action system so they can be called upon to work together at some future time. In other kinds of groups, the planning for some kind of an ending ritual or ceremony can serve as a reality reminder that termination is taking place.

If the worker is leaving before the end of a planned change effort and is being replaced by a new worker, it may be useful for both workers to hold a joint session or two with the client or action system. This is especially important if the old worker enjoys a good relationship with the client or action system, because he then can help legitimate the new worker. A social work student wrote about such an experience this way:

At the first contact I introduced the new worker to the client, a foster home child. We'd talk a little, maybe go have a coke, and then I'd take the youngster home myself. The next time I'd pick up the youngster and we'd pick up the new worker and go do something together. Then we'd all go to the foster home, the youngster would introduce the new worker to his foster parents and we'd talk a while. The next time the new worker would pick up the youngster and bring him to the office and leave us alone to say goodbye. He'd then take the youngster home. The kid continued to write to me for about six months and of course I wrote back. He needs to experience that someone could leave but continue caring about him. The relationship changed to a purely friendship one as the new worker gradually assumed responsibility for the working part of the relationship.

---

[8] William Reid and Ann Shyne, *Brief and Extended Casework* (New York: Columbia University Press, 1969), p. 124.

Finally, as in the above example, the worker may need to redefine his relation with the client or action system. If there will be no continuing contact, this is not necessary. The worker may make himself available to the client system on an emergency basis or leave the door open for the client system to return should the services of the worker be needed again. The worker should clarify with the client system the nature and extent of his continuing relationship with them past the point of termination. In a sense, a new contract or understanding is being negotiated.

When involved in community projects, the worker may be dealing with members of the action system again in the future. Therefore there may not be any termination of relationships, though there is a termination of the specific planned change effort. Sometimes there may be what Roland Warren refers to as a transformation of the action system.[9] For example, a task force established to see if a day-care center is needed may become the board of directors of the center when it is established. When the action system is thus transformed, the worker will have to reclarify his role with the group.

With ongoing community and organizational systems, one change effort unfolds from another. For example, the action systems in a health planning council or community action agency might change, but the worker and his agency will have an ongoing relationship to institutions, agencies, and groups and individuals in the community in an ongoing change effort consisting of many ad hoc efforts that terminate.

STABILIZATION OF THE CHANGE EFFORT

A third major task the worker must be concerned with at the time of termination is the stabilization and generalization of the change effort. He needs to assess the steps which must be taken to make sure that the positive changes and gains will be maintained after he is no longer involved. For example, in the Foster case study in Part III, the residents on the hospital ward were helping to maintain an undesirable role expectation for patients. After helping to initiate some changes, the worker had to build into the ward system an ongoing seminar for new residents, since they represented a potential force to return the system to its previous definition of the "good" patient. Thus the worker must assess what factors may counteract the change effort and

---

[9] Roland Warren, *The Community in America* (Chicago: Rand McNally & Co., 1963).

take steps to prevent such an occurence. To help stabilize the change, the worker looks for the kind of continuing support the client system might need and arranges for it.

In assessing needs with regard to the stabilization of change, the worker will explore the increased ability of the client system to cope with its own problems. He will try to evaluate how, as a result of the planned change effort, the client or action system has increased its capacity to cope with similar situations in the future. Roland Lippitt, Jeanne Watson, and Bruce Westley point to some questions which the worker should explore with the client:

Has the helping relationship been specific only to certain types of problems, or has it provided the basis for attacking a variety of new and unpredictable problems? Has there been any provision for incorporating the kind of function performed by the change agent into the permanent structure of the system, and can such a provision be made? Is there a need for periodic examinations of the system's ongoing operations to identify new sources of difficulty and dispose of them before they become serious? Has the client system been helped to learn how to identify problems which are beyond its resources and how to obtain help if such problems arise?[10]

On the community level, Warren raises the issue of "systematic residue" of the change effort. What kind of informal or formal community relationships remain as a result of the planned change effort? Will the community be better able to take action in the future because of its experience and these relationships? What kind of leadership has developed?[11]

By making himself available should the need arise, the worker can sometimes provide all the continuing support or help that is needed. He might also arrange with another change agent or community resident to provide whatever continuing services the client system might need. In cases where the client needs some ongoing service such as a homemaker or visiting nurse, the worker may help arrange for these services and check to make sure that they are being provided.

When the worker is not likely to come into contact with the client again, he may arrange for someone else to monitor the client's progress. For example, he might ask the visiting nurse to inform him if the client is experiencing any difficulties. In such cases the worker is in

---

[10] Ronald Lippitt, Jeanne Watson, and Bruce Westley, *The Dynamics of Planned Change* (New York: Harcourt, Brace and World, Inc., 1958), pp. 234–35.
[11] Warren, *Community in America*, pp. 319–320.

fact getting people who will be in contact with the client to serve as referral agents. In other cases the worker might himself check up on the progress of a client. If a client has been referred to a vocational training program, for example, the worker might call either the client or the school to find out how he is doing.

Because the community worker is likely to have continuing contacts with client and action system members, it is easier for him to monitor changes. Newspaper reports, minutes of meetings, and other such sources allow him to keep tabs on community groups.

In comparison to the great deal of attention which has been paid to the area of beginnings in the social work literature, termination has been a relatively neglected topic. There has been a tendency to view termination as the point which is reached when progress is no longer being made. We believe termination should be viewed as an integral part of the whole planned change effort. The social worker carefully prepares for termination and helps bring it about. The way the change effort process is brought to an end affects both the success of his effort and his future relationships with those involved.

PART III

CASE
STUDIES

_____

FRANCIS P. PURCELL

AND

HARRY SPECHT

THE HOUSE ON

SIXTH STREET

The extent to which social work can affect the course of social problems has not received the full consideration it deserves. For some time the social work profession has taken account of social problems only as they have become manifest in behavioral pathology. Yet it is becoming increasingly apparent that, even allowing for this limitation, it is often necessary for the same agency or worker to intervene by various methods at various points.

In this paper, the case history of a tenement house in New York City is used to illustrate some of the factors that should be considered in selecting intervention methods. Like all first attempts, the approach described can be found wanting in conceptual clarity and systematization. Yet the vital quality of the effort and its implications for social work practice seem clear.

Reprinted with permission of the National Association of Social Workers, from *Social Work*, Vol. 10, No. 4, (October 1965), pp. 69–76.

The case of "The House on Sixth Street" is taken from the files of Mobilization For Youth (MFY), an action-research project that has been in operation since 1962 on New York's Lower East Side. MFY's programs are financed by grants from several public and private sources. The central theoretical contention of MFY is that a major proportion of juvenile delinquency occurs when adolescents from low-income families do not have access to legitimate opportunities by which they can fulfill the aspirations for success they share with all American youth. The action programs of MFY are designed to offer these youths concrete opportunities to offset the debilitating effects of poverty. For example, the employment program helps youngsters obtain jobs; other programs attempt to increase opportunities in public schools. In addition, there are group work and recreation programs. A wide variety of services to individuals and families is offered through Neighborhood Service Centers: a homemaking program, a program for released offenders, and a narcotics information center. Legal services, a housing services unit, a special referral unit, and a community development program are among other services that have been developed or made available. Thus, MFY has an unusually wide range of resources for dealing with social problems.

THE PROBLEM

"The House on Sixth Street" became a case when Mrs. Smith came to an MFY Neighborhood Service Center to complain that there had been no gas, electricity, heat, or hot water in her apartment house for more than four weeks. She asked the agency for help. Mrs. Smith was 23 years old, Negro, and the mother of four children, three of whom had been born out of wedlock. At the time she was unmarried and receiving Aid to Families with Dependent Children. She came to the center in desperation because she was unable to run her household without utilities. Her financial resources were exhausted—but not her courage. The Neighborhood Service Center worker decided that in this case the building—the tenants, the landlord, and circumstances affecting their relationships—was of central concern.

A social worker then visited the Sixth Street building with Mrs. Smith and a community worker. Community workers are members of the community organization staff in a program that attempts to encourage residents to take independent social action. Like many members in other MFY programs, community workers are residents of the particular neighborhood. Most of them have little formal education, their special contribution being their ability to relate to and communicate with other residents. Because some of the tenants were Puerto Rican, a Spanish-speaking community worker was chosen to accompany the social worker. His easy manner and knowledge of the neighborhood enabled him and the worker to become involved quickly with the tenants.

Their first visits confirmed Mrs. Smith's charge that the house had been without utilities for more than four weeks. Several months before, the city Rent and Rehabilitation Administration had reduced the rent for each apartment to one dollar a month because the landlord was not providing services. However, this agency was slow to take further action. Eleven families were still living in the building, which had twenty-eight apartments. The landlord owed the electric company several thousand dollars. Therefore, the meters had been removed from the house. Because most of the tenants were welfare clients, the Department of Welfare had "reimbursed" the landlord directly for much of the unpaid electric bill and refused to pay any more money to the electric company. The Department of Welfare was slow in meeting the emergency needs of the tenants. Most of the children (forty-eight from the eleven families in the building) had not been to school for a month because they were ill or lacked proper clothing.

The mothers were tired and demoralized. Dirt and disorganization were increasing daily. The tenants were afraid to sleep at night because the building was infested with rats. There was danger of fire because the tenants had to use candles for light. The seventeen abandoned apartments had been invaded by homeless men and drug addicts. Petty thievery is common in such situations. However, the mothers did not want to seek protection from the police for fear that they would chase away all men who were not part of the families in the building (some of the unmarried mothers had men living with them—one of the few means of protection from physical danger available to these women—even though mothers on public assistance are threatened with loss of income if they are not legally married). The anxiety created by these conditions was intense and disabling.

The workers noted that the mothers were not only anxious but "fighting mad"; not only did they seek immediate relief from their physical dangers and discomforts but they were eager to express their fury at the landlord and the public agencies, which they felt had let them down.

The circumstances described are by no means uncommon, at least not in New York City. Twenty percent of all housing in the city is still unfit, despite all the public and private residential building completed since World War II. At least 277,500 dwellings in New York City need major repairs if they are to become safe and adequate shelters. This means that approximately 500,000 people in the city live in inferior dwelling units and as many as 825,000 people in buildings that are considered unsafe. In 1962 the New York City Bureau of Sanitary Inspections reported that 530 children were bitten by rats in their homes and 198 children were poisoned (nine of them fatally) by nibbling at peeling lead paint, even though the use of lead paint has been illegal in the city for more than ten years. Given the difficulties involved in lodging formal complaints with city agencies, it is safe to assume that unreported incidents of rat bites and lead poisoning far exceed these figures.

The effect of such hardships on children is obvious. Of even greater significance is the sense of powerlessness generated when families go into these struggles barehanded. It is this sense of helplessness in the face of adversity that induces pathological anxiety, intergenerational alienation, and social retreatism. Actual physical impoverishment alone is not nearly so debilitating as poverty attended by a sense of unrelieved impotence that becomes generalized and internalized. The poor then regard much social learning as irrelevant, since they do not believe it can effect any environmental change.

INTERVENTION AND THE SOCIAL SYSTEMS

Selecting a point of intervention in dealing with this problem would have been simpler if the target of change were Mrs. Smith alone, or Mrs. Smith and her co-tenants, the clients in whose behalf intervention was planned. Too often, the client system presenting the problem becomes the major target for intervention, and the intervention method is limited to the one most suitable for that client system. However, Mrs. Smith and the other tenants had a multitude of problems emanating from many sources, any one of which would have warranted the attention of a social agency. The circumstantial fact that an individual contacts an agency that offers services to individuals and families should not be a major factor in determining the method of intervention. Identification of the client merely helps the agency to define goals; other variables are involved in the selection of method. As Burns and Glasser have suggested:

It may be helpful to consider the primary target of change as distinct from the persons who may be the primary clients. . . . The primary target of change then becomes the human or physical environment toward which professional efforts via direct intervention are aimed in order to facilitate change.[1]

The three major factors that determine MFY's approach to the problem were (1) knowledge of the various social systems within which the social problem was located (i.e., social systems assessment), (2) knowledge of the various methods (including non-social work methods) appropriate for intervention in these different social systems, and (3) the resources available to the agency.

The difficulties of the families in the building were intricately connected with other elements of the social system related to the housing problem. For example, seven different public agencies were involved in maintenance of building services. Later other agencies were involved in relocating the tenants. There is no one agency in New York City that handles all housing problems. Therefore, tenants have little hope of getting help on their own. In order to redress a grievance relating to water supply (which was only one of the building's many problems) it is necessary to know precisely which city department to contact. The following is only a partial listing:

No water—Health Department
Not enough water—Department of Water Supply
No hot water—Buildings Department
Water leaks—Buildings Department
Large water leaks—Department of Water Supply
Water overflowing from apartment above—Police Department
Water sewage in the cellar—Sanitation Department

The task of determining which agencies are responsible for code enforcement in various areas is not simple, and in addition one must know that the benefits and services available for tenants and for the community vary with the course of action chosen. For example, if the building were taken over by the Rent and Rehabilitation Administration under the receivership law, it would be several weeks before services would be re-established, and the tenants would have to remain in the building during its rehabilitation. There would be, however, some compensations: tenants could remain in the neighborhood—indeed, in the same building—and their children would not have to change schools. If, on the other hand, the house were condemned by the Build-

---

[1] Mary E. Burns and Paul H. Glasser, "Similarities and Differences in Casework and Group Work Practice," *Social Service Review*, Vol. 37, No. 4 (December 1963), p. 423.

ings Department, the tenants would have to move, but they would be moved quickly and would receive top relocation priorities and maximum relocation benefits. But once the tenants had been relocated—at city expense—the building could be renovated by the landlord as middle-income housing. In the Sixth Street house, it was suspected that this was the motivation behind the landlord's actions. If the building were condemned and renovated, there would be twenty-eight fewer low-income housing units in the neighborhood.

This is the fate of scores of tenements on the Lower East Side because much new middle-income housing is being built there. Basic services are withheld and tenants are forced to move so that buildings may be renovated for middle-income tenants. Still other buildings are allowed to deteriorate with the expectation that they will be bought by urban renewal agencies.

It is obvious, even limiting analysis to the social systems of one tenement, that the problem is enormous. Although the tenants were the clients in this case, Mrs. Smith, the tenant group, and other community groups were all served at one point or another. It is even conceivable that the landlord might have been selected as the most appropriate recipient of service. Rehabilitation of many slum tenements is at present nearly impossible. Many landlords regard such property purely as an investment. With profit the prime motive, needs of low-income tenants are often overlooked. Under present conditions it is financially impossible for many landlords to correct all the violations in their buildings even if they wanted to. If the social worker chose to intervene at this level of the problem, he might apply to the Municipal Loan Fund, make arrangements with unions for the use of non-union labor in limited rehabilitation projects, or provide expert consultants on reconstruction. These tasks would require social workers to have knowledge similar to that of city planners. If the problems of landlords were not selected as a major point of intervention, they would still have to be considered at some time since they are an integral part of the social context within which this problem exists.

A correct definition of interacting social systems or of the social worker's choice of methods and points of intervention is not the prime concern here. What is to be emphasized is what this case so clearly demonstrates: that although the needs of the client system enable the agency to define its goals, the points and methods of intervention cannot be selected properly without an awareness and substantial knowledge of the social systems within which the problem is rooted.

DEALING WITH THE PROBLEM

The social worker remained with the building throughout a four-month period. In order to deal effectively with the problem, he had to make use of all the social work methods as well as the special talents of a community worker, lawyer, city planner, and various civil rights organizations. The social worker and the community worker functioned as generalists with both individuals and families calling on caseworkers as needed for specialized services or at especially trying times, such as during the first week and when the families were relocated. Because of the division of labor in the agency, much of the social work with individuals was done with the help of a caseworker. Group work, administration, and community organization were handled by the social worker, who had been trained in community organization. In many instances he also dealt with the mothers as individuals, as they encountered one stressful situation after another. Agency caseworkers also provided immediate and concrete assistance to individual families, such as small financial grants, medical care, homemaking services, baby-sitting services, and transportation. This reduced the intensity of pressures on these families. Caseworkers were especially helpful in dealing with some of the knotty and highly technical problems connected with public agencies.

With a caseworker and a lawyer experienced in handling tenement cases, the social worker began to help the families organize their demands for the services and utilities to which they were legally entitled but which the public agencies had consistently failed to provide for them.

The ability of the mothers to take concerted group action was evident from the beginning, and Mrs. Smith proved to be a natural and competent leader. With support, encouragement, and assistance from the staff, the mothers became articulate and effective in negotiating with the various agencies involved. In turn, the interest and concern of the agencies increased markedly when the mothers began to visit them, make frequent telephone calls, and send letters and telegrams to them and to politicians demanding action.

With the lawyer and a city planner (an agency consultant), the mothers and staff members explored various possible solutions to the housing problem. For example, the Department of Welfare had offered to move the families to shelters or hotels. Neither alternative was acceptable to the mothers. Shelters were ruled out because they would not consider splitting up their families, and they rejected hotels because they had discovered from previous experience that many of the "hotels" selected were flop-houses or were inhabited by prostitutes.

The following is taken from the social worker's record during the first week:

> Met with the remaining tenants, several Negro men from the block, and [the city planner]. . . . Three of the mothers said that they would sooner sleep out on the street than go to the Welfare shelter. If nothing else, they felt that this would be a way of protesting their plight. . . . One of the mothers said that they couldn't very well do this with most of the children having colds. Mrs. Brown thought that they might do better to ask Reverend Jones if they could move into the cellar of his church temporarily. . . . The other mothers got quite excited about this idea because they thought that the church basement would make excellent living quarters.

After a discussion as to whether the mothers would benefit from embarrassing the public agencies by dramatically exposing their inadequacies, the mothers decided to move into the nearby church. They asked the worker to attempt to have their building condemned. At another meeting, attended by tenants from neighboring buildings and representatives of other local groups, it was concluded that what had happened to the Sixth Street building was a result of discrimination against the tenants as Puerto Ricans and Negroes. The group—which had now become an organization—sent the following telegram to city, state, and federal officials:

> We are voters and Puerto Rican and Negro mothers asking for equal rights, for decent housing and enough room. Building has broken windows, no gas or electricity for four weeks, no heat or hot water, holes in floors, loose wiring. Twelve of forty-eight children in building sick. Welfare doctors refuse to walk up dark stairs. Are we human or what? Should innocent children suffer for landlords' brutality and city and state neglect? We are tired of being told to wait with children ill and unable to attend school. Negro and Puerto Rican tenants are forced out while buildings next door are renovated at high rents. We are not being treated as human beings.

For the most part, the lawyer and city planner stayed in the background, acting only as consultants. But as the tenants and worker became more involved with the courts and as other organizations entered the fight, the lawyer and city planner played a more active and direct role.

RESULTANT SIDE-EFFECTS

During this process, tenants in other buildings on the block became more alert to similar problems in their buildings. With the help of the community development staff and the housing consultant, local groups and organizations such as tenants' councils and the local chapter of the Congress of Racial Equality were enlisted to support and work with the mothers.

Some of the city agencies behaved as though MFY had engineered the entire scheme to embarrass them—steadfastly disregarding the fact that the building had been unlivable for many months. Needless to say, the public agencies are overloaded and have inadequate resources. As has been documented, many such bureaucracies develop an amazing insensitivity to the needs of their clients. In this case, the MFY social worker believed that the tenants—and other people in their plight—should make their needs known to the agencies and to the public at large. He knew that when these expressions of need are backed by power—either in numbers or in political knowledge—they are far more likely to have some effect.

Other movements in the city at this time gave encouragement and direction to the people in the community. The March on Washington and the Harlem rent strike are two such actions.

By the time the families had been relocated, several things had been accomplished. Some of the public agencies had been sufficiently moved by the actions of the families and the local organizations to provide better services for them. When the families refused to relocate in a shelter and moved into a neighborhood church instead, one of the television networks picked up their story. Officials in the housing agencies came to investigate and several local politicians lent the tenants their support. Most important, several weeks after the tenants moved into the church, a bill was passed by the city council designed to prevent some of the abuses that the landlord had practiced with impunity. The councilman who sponsored the new law referred to the house on Sixth Street to support his argument.

Nevertheless, the problems that remain far outweigh the accomplishments. A disappointing epilogue to the story is that in court, two months later, the tenants' case against the landlord was dismissed by the judge on a legal technicality. The judge ruled that because the electric company had removed the meters from the building it was impossible for the landlord to provide services.

Some of the tenants were relocated out of the neighborhood and some in housing almost as poor as that they had left. The organization that began to develop in the neighborhood has continued to grow, but it is a painstaking job. The fact that the poor have the strength to continue to struggle for better living conditions is something to wonder at and admire.

IMPLICATIONS FOR PRACTICE

Social work helping methods as currently classified are so inextricably interwoven in practice that it no longer seems valid to think of a generic practice as consisting of the application of casework, group work, or community organization skills as the nature of the problem demands. Nor does it seem feasible to adapt group methods for traditional casework problems or to use group work skills in community organization or community organization method in casework. Such suggestions—when they appear in the literature—either reflect confusion or, what is worse, suggest that no clearcut method exists apart from the auspices that support it.

In this case it is a manifestation of a social problem—housing—that was the major point around which social services were organized. The social worker's major intellectual task was to select the points at which the agency could intervene in the problem and the appropriate methods to use. It seems abundantly clear that in order to select appropriate points of intervention the social worker need not only understand individual patterns of response, but the nature of the social conditions that are the context in which behavior occurs. As this case makes evident, the social system that might be called the "poverty system" is enduring and persistent. Its parts intermesh with precision and disturbing complementarity. Intentionally or not, a function is thereby maintained that produces severe social and economic deprivation. Certain groups profit enormously from the maintenance of this system, but larger groups suffer. Social welfare—and, in particular, its central profession, social work—must examine the part it plays in either maintaining or undermining this socially pernicious poverty system. It is important that the social work profession no longer regard social conditions as immutable and a social reality to be accommodated as service is provided to deprived persons with an ever increasing refinement of technique. Means should be developed whereby agencies can affect social problems more directly, especially through institutional (organizational) change.

The idea advanced by MFY is that the social worker should fulfill his professional function and agency responsibility by seeking a solution to social problems through institutional change rather than by focusing on individual problems in social functioning. This is not to say that individual expressions of a given social problem should be left unattended. On the contrary, this approach is predicated on the belief that individual problems in social functioning are to varying degrees both cause and effect. It rejects the notion that individuals are afflicted with social pathologies, holding, rather, that the same social environment that generates conformity makes payment by the deviance that emerges. As Nisbet points out ". . . socially prized arrangements and values in society can produce socially condemned results."[2] This should direct social work's attention to institutional arrangements and their consequences. This approach does not lose sight of the individual or group, since the social system is composed of various statuses, roles, and classes. It takes cognizance of the systemic relationship of the various parts of the social system, including the client. It recognizes that efforts to deal with one social problem frequently generate others with debilitating results.

Thus it is that such institutional arrangements as public assistance, state prisons, and state mental hospitals, or slum schools are regarded by many as social problems in their own right. The social problems of poverty, criminality, mental illness, and failure to learn that were to be solved or relieved remain, and the proposed solutions pose almost equally egregious problems.

This paper has presented a new approach to social work practice. The knowledge, values, attitudes, and skills were derived from a generalist approach to social work. Agencies that direct their energies to social problems by affecting institutional change will need professional workers whose skills cut across the broad spectrum of social work knowledge.

---

[2] Robert K. Merton and Robert A. Nisbet (eds.), *Contemporary Social Problems* (New York: Harcourt, Brace, & World, 1961), p. 7.

ZELDA P. FOSTER

HOW SOCIAL WORK
CAN INFLUENCE
HOSPITAL
MANAGEMENT OF
FATAL ILLNESS

In recent years caseworkers in hospital settings have been urged to broaden the base of their practice and to assume greater responsibility for effecting needed social changes. However, little has been written about how the caseworker can influence the organization in which he works to provide benign and therapeutic influences for all its clients or how he can deliberately effect such changes. This paper will describe the steps and processes of a clinical social worker who intervened actively and purposefully to modify the ward culture for a group of hospital patients.

The setting is the hematology service of a veterans' hospital. The

Reprinted with permission of the National Association of Social Workers, from *Social Work*, Vol. 10, No. 4, (October 1965), pp. 30–45.

majority of the forty men in this service are married, fathers, and breadwinners and range in age from 25 to 40. They have been admitted for treatment for serious blood diseases: Hodgkin's disease, leukemia, or lymphoma. While periods and degrees of chronicity vary, life expectancy is drastically reduced for all patients. They are followed by the hospital, as inpatients and outpatients, throughout the course of their illness.

THE WARD THAT WAS

To understand why and how the social worker became engaged in a four-year process of wardwide environmental intervention, it is important to understand the ward culture he encountered, joined, and ultimately challenged. By ward culture is meant the patterned ways staff, patients, and families regarded, responded to, and communicated with one another. Of early significance to the social worker was the fact that this culture perpetuated a clearly defined patient role. The troublesome aspect was that this role seemed to prohibit free choices and decisions. Staff and patient culture interlocked to promote and maintain defined patient and doctor roles.

Staff Culture

The structure derived from the staff's commitment to protecting these patients from learning the names and nature of their diseases. Staff had long ago concluded that patients could not bear such knowledge without devastating fear and anguish. Substantiating this assumption was the traditional medical viewpoint that it is correct and humanitarian to protect the patient from unnecessary emotional pain. The psychological justification was that denial is an essential defense against unacceptable pain. This theory reinforced a role model for the doctor that attributed to him the responsibility for knowing what is best for the patient. In turn, the role of other staff members was to carry out the doctor's prescription, free of the burden of decision-making. The coping patterns that developed out of the role ascribed to the doctor by his professional training and by society were not unusual. They were no doubt intensified because the staff was dealing with a patient group whose illnesses would be fatal despite their efforts. Staff's reaction to the fatally ill patient, medical failure, and their own feelings of helplessness included the use of individual defense mechanisms. The composite of individual and corporate defenses was formalized into a group pattern that took definite shape and became ritualized.

The doctors developed and acted out a stereotyped view of their behavior. They suppressed questions, offered evasive answers, and provided direct reassurance to offset any patient doubts. For his own good, the patient was not encouraged to express feelings, reactions, or doubts. Thus, staff culture defined how the patient should respond to his illness.

Patients' Responses

The patients readily learned what was expected of them. Those who deviated—who did not respond to their cues—were viewed by staff as problem patients and an effort was made to help them conform. The patients should not be viewed as helpless victims of this philosophy. They were also participants in the system and, in complying with staff expectations, promoted the philosophy. Most patients did not ask questions, did not insist on receiving accurate knowledge of their disease, and did not share feelings and fears with staff.

Families

The responsibility of sharing the secret diagnosis with the doctor and of protecting the patient from gaining knowledge about his disease was left to the patient's family. If the family had insisted on sharing the information with the patient, it would have been permitted, but they were never encouraged to do so. This arrangement initiated two important processes. (1) The family was left alone with their ambivalent feelings about this new role because the staff was so committed to protecting the patient that relatives could not be helped to weigh alternatives. Only when the family was determined that the patient should know would any information be revealed. Most families, while ambivalent, feared the patient's reaction and decided to spare him from what they felt would be painful to him. (2) Staff were relieved when relatives were apprised of the situation. Now by not informing the patient they were also carrying out the family's wishes.

A result of this system was that the family and doctor bypassed the patient and excluded him from decision-making. Thus, the family became part of the ward culture, and found the role of relative clearly prescribed. They saw patients as helpless, dependent, and incapable of self-assertion. Therefore, they must take action on the patient's behalf. Financial matters, future planning, and concerns of children were not referred to the patient. Since these patients were generally married men who until recently fully supported their families, role reversal occurred suddenly—husband and father roles were canceled out by the patient role.

The patients seemed to quietly accept that their families had taken over. This reaction was viewed as justification for staff philosophy. Staff did not recognize that they had created a self-fulfilling prophecy by requiring behavior that conformed to their own preconceived attitudes. Actually, the doctor, patient, and family roles had been staged and on the surface the performance seemed flawless. The players knew their parts and each part interlocked with and supported the others.

SEARCH FOR ALTERNATIVES

The social worker's function was similar to that in most medical settings—helping patients and families with the medical and social problems resulting from illness. Since the social worker shared the views of the staff culture, he hoped to help prevent patients from feeling the sorrow and pain of fatal illness. However, it is the nature of casework to study how social and external forces relate to inner feelings and how they impinge on each other. This approach forced the social worker to examine his role. If the patient role is viewed as the way the individual responds to and attempts to meet social expectations, it is clear that here role expectations solidified the kind of defense mechanisms that most people under great stress try to adopt. What was not clear was the extent of the strain on those patients who found only partial psychological relief and were only partially able to adopt the rigidly defined role offered them. At what cost was the patient excluded from sharing his needs, dilemmas, or wishes with his family? Would another type of ward culture offer patients a wider choice or better alternatives? The social worker's prime concern with each individual patient was his feelings, thoughts, and attitudes. As he began to explore the inner world of these patients, he opened to public view what had previously been unshared and even taboo. The strains that patients and families experienced as they attempted to play their parts became visible.

Many patients described feelings of rejection, isolation, and abandonment. They felt cut off from other people and sensed the stigma attached to discussing their feelings and diseases. They were aware of questions brushed aside, brusque answers, and deliberate evasions and half-truths. These reinforced their disturbing fantasies and feelings of despair and hopelessness. Direct reassurance had failed to dispel the underlying anxiety. Instead, it was interpreted as evidence of staff disinterest and aroused the patients' suspicion and distrust.

Estrangement from family was another common problem. Patients complained that they were not made aware of family problems and conflicts and were left out of family planning and decision-making. Relatives appeared upset; their reactions seemed artificial. Patients pondered the meaning of these reactions, alone and afraid.

Patients were ambivalent about what they wanted to find out. On the one hand, there was a need to be more connected with reality, and on the other, a wish to be defended against it. What type of help would permit the patient to resolve this dilemma? Pivotal to this question was the recognition that while it was the patient's dilemma, the existing ward culture attempted to solve it for him. The social worker utilized individual approaches to try to help the patient resolve the conflict, but this alone was not sufficient. It was also necessary to intervene in the ward culture, specifically in the communication system between doctors and patients.

CHANGING THE CULTURE

As a first step, the worker shared the patients' feelings with the staff. The staff's initial reaction was to deny that the patients had such thoughts. Then they modified their viewpoint and attributed the emergence of these thoughts to the act of casework exploration. They still held that the best way to handle these feelings was with reassurance and repression. Now the doctors reassured more and the patients accepted it less because a new element had been introduced into the ward culture. With better communication between the patients and staff, it became increasingly difficult not to hear or feel.

How the social worker was able to demonstrate the need for social change in the ward culture is illustrated in the following cases.

1.

Mr. M, a 25-year-old patient with chronic leukemia, learned that his wife had melanoma. He requested help in planning for their infant child in the event that both died or one was left chronically ill. The social worker presented the family situation to the doctors. They readily saw that this man's problems would not be alleviated by evasive reassurance. After an initial reaction of helplessness (they had "nothing to offer this dying man," they said) they were able, with the social worker's guidance, to help him do what he wanted to do—plan for his family. They saw and accepted their responsibility for giving him the facts about his illness. After frankly sharing with him the nature and prognosis of his disease, they waited. Everyone wondered what would happen to a patient who had been given the burden of knowing he would die.

Mr. M spoke frankly and calmly to the social worker of his poor prognosis. He sorrowfully imagined his child growing up and never knowing him. He feared for his wife—a dependent girl who strongly relied on him. Questions of why this had happened to them revealed his inner sense of outrage. At the same time he established a goal, or perhaps a defense—to be strong and remain intact so that he could emotionally support and plan for his family in this crisis.

The social worker encouraged the doctors to share their empathy and concern with Mr. M. A new phenomenon developed—a relationship between patient and staff, characterized by mutual trust, openness, and equality. The staff regarded Mr. M as a person to admire and proudly pointed to his independence, responsibility, and strength. Without recognizing it, the staff had modified the role image of a patient, and Mr. M was referred to as an "ideal" patient. For the first time ward culture offered rewards and approval for a different coping pattern. With this change in social expectations, Mr. M found a source of personal prestige and privilege. He lived his remaining one and one-half years constructively involved in making important decisions, developing relationships, and fulfilling his need to be integrated with himself and external reality.

For staff, this was a unique patient, and would have remained so, had not two others quickly come to their attention.

2.

Mr. P, a 30-year-old engineer, was found shortly after admission to have leukemia. He had planned to be married in two months and the doctors advised his parents to tell the fiancee the truth so she could make her decision. The parents refused. Several weekly sessions of medical-social work ward rounds were spent discussing the moral dilemma of this case. The social worker explained that the dilemma existed because the patient was excluded from decision-making. Unable to persuade the social worker to intervene with the parents, the doctors considered telling the fiancee themselves, but knew that this was not legal. The staff struggled, and the social worker encouraged the expression of their resistance and doubt. Emotions were intense. The doctors felt frustrated. This was an area in which they rarely had to make a decision because the ward culture had previously promoted a clear course of action. Moreover, the social worker challenged them by not insisting that the parents tell the fiancee. The doctors' feelings of helplessness and anger were not resolved. The patient was reluctantly told his diagnosis, simply because the staff had no other choice.

Mr. P immediately told his fiancee, who wanted to marry him in spite of his disease. After a series of interviews with the social worker, Mr. P decided that he could not freely marry under these circumstances. The staff reacted to his decision with sadness because the fiancee wished desperately and pathetically to marry him. However, they also felt a sense of relief, as if a burden had been lifted. The patient had, in effect, told them that he could accept and wrestle with his own problem.

3.

Mr. K, 29, discovered that he had leukemia when he opened and read a slip of paper he was carrying to the laboratory. Prior to this, he had often questioned the social worker as to whether he had anemia or something worse. After reading the diagnosis, he immediately went to the doctor and demanded an explanation. The doctor told him it was a terrible mistake made by the secretary. Mr. K remained unconvinced and said that he had opened the lab slip in order to confirm his suspicions. He assured the doctor that it would be a relief "to know the score." Once the doctor admitted the diagnosis and answered Mr. K's questions about the probable course of his disease, Mr. K came to the social worker and freely shared his mixed feelings of shock, relief, and sadness. Like Mr. M and Mr. P, he felt he must be involved with reality. In the course of work with him, he agreed to tape several interviews for teaching purposes with ward physicians. In these he explained how he felt about the period of life left to him and how important it was for him to know his prognosis. He saw this activity as an important contribution to helping others and derived considerable ego satisfaction from it. A highly social and sensitive person, he referred other patients who had shared their troubled thoughts with him to the social worker. Having developed a stake in the way his illness was being handled, he created a subtle impact on patient culture. Mr. M and Mr.

P related primarily to and influenced staff culture; Mr. K related more to the patient group.

These three cases, which occurred in a relatively short period of time, had been handled differently but this did not result in disaster. The patients appeared to be functioning well, talking more freely with their doctors, and obviously liked and trusted them and showed new self-reliance. These patients were successful in bringing about significant social change in the ward milieu. For the first time it became a matter of ward policy to consider the willingness and capacity of each patient to know his diagnosis. Furthermore, the majority of patients were considered capable of understanding the nature of their diseases. The ward culture was influenced strongly by this expressive, questioning, assertive, and independent majority. The good patient was no longer one who silently submitted to his fate, but one who courageously faced his disease and continued in his role as husband, father, and breadwinner. The improved communication system between doctor and patient fostered a mutual respect that had not existed previously. Patients were able to view the doctor more realistically and had less of a need to invest him with magical, omnipotent powers.

MAINTAINING THE CHANGED CULTURE

Some of the foregoing changes have become self-perpetuating. Natural carriers of the culture are long-term or readmitted patients, a relatively stable nursing staff, and a social worker who remained on the service for four years. The rotation of medical residents on a three-month cycle is potentially disruptive. The social worker assumed that each new group of residents would require exposure to some of the processes other doctors had experienced in the early stages of ward change. Their willingness to be involved in a process involving examination of their own intense feelings and their acceptance of the right of another discipline to challenge their philosophy have naturally varied. It is possible that the social worker would not have been able to handle this process consistently if he had not himself been a solidly integrated part of the ward culture. Certainly this facilitated the development of skills that sped up the process of acculturating resident physicians, as well as providing him with an important knowledge of the ward power structure and significant leverage points.

Specialized skills are required to maintain a ward culture of this type, i.e., one that provides the patient with a range of choice in coping with his disease. Such a culture is highly dependent on the staff's willingness and ability to offer the patients consistent and stable support. It requires a continued openness of communication, respect for individual differences, belief that a person with a fatal disease can have a self-determining life, and a capacity for meaningful interpersonal relationships with patients. In such a culture, the patients tend to develop strong positive feelings for the service and the staff. They feel and respond to the genuine and long-term investment and involvement with them, derive a sense of security from the knowledge that a relationship will be offered them throughout the course of their illness—one that is related to their individualized needs and feelings—and develop a stake in continuing or perpetuating such an ambience.

Another factor in maintaining the ward culture is related to the selection of casework methods to be utilized with this patient group. One aspect of this is especially relevant. It involves the management of ego defense mechanisms. The patients tend to share readily feelings of depression, anxiety, and discomfort if the caseworker is willing to hear them. However, these realistic feelings frequently mask more permeating and pervasive fears that immobilize and overwhelm them. Therefore, it is important to reach these underlying feelings and free the patient to share his more primitive and nightmarish thoughts. Fantasies of punishment and death frequently break through the ego defenses and leave the patient at the mercy of his unresolved conflicts and their concomitant anxiety. It has been shown that only as the patient is able to put his worst thoughts and fears outside himself is he able to relinquish the tormenting and fruitless struggle against a harsh and unrelenting reality and become engaged in a process directed at helping him plan and make decisions for his remaining life and his family's future. Most patients experience a feeling of relief and freedom in sharing deeper feelings. Recognition of the capacity to control their behavior, if not their fears, does much to reduce the feelings of helplessness and frustration.

It is recognized that modifications in ward culture inevitably raise new problems. Patients have varying capacities to recognize and integrate their poor prognoses, internalize their anxiety, and meet a complex of social roles. Although the new ward culture offers a broader range of coping patterns, it may not provide adequate protection for those patients in need of external supports to maintain essential defenses of denial. Experience has shown that many patients can make successful adjustments to fatal illness based on a well-developed connection with reality. Some cannot. Better techniques are needed to provide a ward social system that can meet the needs of all.

LYNN HOFFMAN

LORENCE LONG

A SYSTEMS

DILEMMA

INTRODUCTION:
EDGAR H. AUERSWALD, M.D.

The current shift of interest, reflected in public policy, from the production of goods to the provision of services, has caused a major re-examination of the nature of the services the individual can expect from his society. This re-examination is producing a number of insights, some of them shocking. In particular, we are learning that many of the systems we have created to deliver services are, in the name of "progress" and "civilization," contributing to the conditions of human distress they were designed to alleviate.

Much has been written lately about how service systems of one kind or another subvert their announced goals—how a welfare system perpetuates poverty, or how the medical profession creates iatrogenic illness. There has not been very much written, however, about how several systems inadvertently combine *in their day to day operations*

Reprinted with permission of *Family Process*, 8 (September 1969): 211–34.

in such a way as to frustrate each others' activities, and how, in so doing, they destroy in varying degrees the lives of people, or render it difficult for them to improve their lives. We have all been much too tightly locked in our own niches by training, experience, and various types of private interest to see this kind of interlock. It comes into sharp perspective only when one studies the problems of a single person in terms of his total life space, his "ecology."

This paper represents an effort to describe one such situation in a family as viewed from a community health services program designed to approach human crises as ecological phenomena, and to explore and respond to them within this framework. We have found that the best way to organize our view of the environmental field people move in is according to the diverse systems which make it up, so we have labeled our theoretical base "ecological systems theory."[1] What is of particular interest to the behavioral scientist in the situation described is that neither individual nor family diagnosis, nor the contributions of the larger systems (in this case a housing system and a system of medical care) will, if viewed separately, explain the state of the man in question. Only when the contributions of all of these systems are made clear, and their interrelationships explored, do the origins of the phenomena described begin to emerge.

This study investigates the context of a man's breakdown. In the first part of the story, evidence about the social systems in which he moved will be presented, in order to trace out factors that may have contributed to his collapse. The second part describes an attempt to intervene in some of these systems in order to get him back on his feet. A single person is the focus of the study, but the entire ecological field—individual within family within wider social network—is the area under consideration.

A special interest of this paper has been to document the peculiar nature of communications in this area. These communications were characterized by dissonances, self-contradictions and confusions, and may be seen as part of the scapegoating process which pushes individuals and their families, especially if they are poor, into positions of increasing powerlessness.

Finally, the question will be asked: does this "systems" way of looking at individual dysfunction bring with it a different way of dealing with it, or is what we shall be describing merely traditional social work?

---

[1] E. H. Auerswald, "Interdisciplinary vs. Ecological Approach," *Family Process*, 7, 202–215, 1968.

The central character of our story, Charles Johnson, is a fifty-two year old black man who worked for eleven years as a chef in a proprietary nursing home. His wife, Bernice, works in a home for brain-damaged children, and before he quit his job, they made enough to keep their 15 year old daughter, Lorna, in private school, and their 19 year old daughter, Gail, in college. Mr. Johnson was brought to the attention of the social services department of a neighborhood health center on New York's lower East Side because of the following dilemma:

Mr. and Mrs. Johnson's combined income was above the limit for the low-income housing apartment which they had occupied for 17 years, and the New York City Housing Authority was trying to evict them. The neighborhood was in the throes of a severe housing shortage, so that there was little prospect of finding decent housing at a rent they could afford. Mr. Johnson had for some years been subject to dizzy spells, in addition to drinking a sizable amount of liquor each day, and twice he had fallen while at work. The second time, three years before, he was taken to Bellevue, and his wife was told he was an epileptic. He had been having dizzy spells more frequently in the past months, and this prompted the Housing Authority agent, who wished to help the Johnsons, to suggest that he get a statement from a doctor saying that the spells were serious enough to put his working future in doubt. This would allow him to quit work and collect disability payments, and at the same time, the family's income would be sufficiently reduced to enable them to stay on in their apartment.

Mr. Johnson agreed with the Housing agent that this might be the best thing to do, and his wife supported this opinion. Unfortunately, the drop in income would mean that the family could no longer continue to keep the two girls in school without extra financing. Quitting work would also seriously undermine Mr. Johnson's status both outside of and within his family, particularly in regard to his wife.

Mr. Johnson was thus in a peculiar situation. It is the type of situation in which a person is punished by the social system on one set of grounds for functioning and on another set of grounds for not functioning. Mr. Johnson is being a good husband and father and is obeying society's rules for upward mobility by providing for his family and by giving his children an education which will guarantee them more opportunities than he had. However, to continue to provide these opportunities, he must depend to some extent on governmental subsidies, such as low income housing. To keep this housing, he must now fulfill the requirements of being a poor person by reducing his income and lowering his ambitions. Thus he is caught. If he persists in being the model American father who works, he throws his family into the streets. If he gives up his job and accepts disability payments, he continues to provide for his family but at a cost of personal dignity and a diminution of hopes for his children. One is reminded of Gregory Bateson's classic image for paradoxical systems (applied here to the Russellian logical paradox):

A mechanical model of such an oscillating or paradoxical system may be of use to the reader. Such a model is the ordinary electric buzzer or house bell. This machine consists of an electro-magnet acting upon an armature (a light metal spring) through which the current which activates the magnet must pass. The armature is so placed that the circuit is broken whenever the magnet is active and causes the spring to bend. But the current is re-established by the relaxation of the spring when the magnet ceases to act. We may translate this system into logical propositions by labeling that position of the spring which closes the circuit as "yes"; and labeling the contrasting position which breaks the circuit as "no." The following pair of propostions can then be stated:

1. If the spring is in "yes," the circuit is closed and the electro-magnet operates; therefore the circuit must go to "no."

2. But if the spring is in "no," the magnet is not operating, and the spring must therefore go to "yes."

Thus the implications of "yes" involve "no"; and the implications of "no" involve "yes." The model illustrates precisely the Russellian paradox, inasmuch as the "yes" and "no" are each of them being applied at two levels of abstraction. In Proposition I, "yes" refers to position, while "no" refers to direction of change. The "no" to which "yes" is an answer is therefore not the same as the "no" which is an answer to "yes."

This matter of the paradoxes is here discussed at some length because it is impossible to go far in thinking about communication and codification without running into tangles of this type, and because similar tangles of levels of abstraction are common in the premises of human culture . . . and in psychiatric patients.[2]

In studying paradoxical systems in human affairs, the usual emphasis has been on the conflicts between levels of messages exchanged by persons in on-going relationships, mainly families (witness the large

---

[2] J. Ruesch and G. Bateson, *Communication: The Social Matrix of Psychiatry* (New York: Norton, 1951), pp. 194–95.

"double-bind" literature).[3] This is too narrow a view when one starts to look at lower class city families which, being poor, uneducated, isolated, and often from an alien culture, cannot go through the smallest life crisis without becoming encrusted with parent-like figures who represent the acculturation and controlling systems of the wider society. These systems seldom act collaboratively, and are more often than not in conflict with one another. As a result, a person may be caught in a paradoxical situation in a family which is in turn caught in paradoxical situations within the systems designed to help the family or person.

It could also be observed that at this point in the history of American benevolence, helping institutions have begun to carry out a coercive function beneath a genuinely charitable intent.[4] Our national welfare system has become notorious for legislation whose covert policy seems designed to break up or weaken poor families and place their members into self-perpetuating cycles of helplessness. Thus an attitude of benevolence is itself beginning to be a self-contradiction in many of our helping settings. If the proponents of the double-bind theory are right, in a situation where one party is extremely dependent on another, an action which is supposed to help the weaker party but has a punishing result can be particularly devastating.

With these thoughts in mind, it might be useful to frame our narrative in terms of the many contradictory messages (if not truly paradoxical in Bateson's double-level sense) received by Mr. Johnson from persons in various systems during the period after the Housing Agent suggested he stop work. Of course, one must not forget that the receiver of a message is also collaborating with, or even eliciting the message. In addition, our arbitrary picking out of particular messages is a reduction of what in real life is a much more complicated, many-messaged affair.

It was in mid-October, 1967, that the Housing Agent contacted the social services department of the Health Service for advice in locating a doctor who would certify Mr. Johnson too ill to work. A social worker was assigned to the case and talked to the Housing Agent about it. He then called the Johnson's home. Only Mrs. Johnson was in, but she was glad to speak to the worker. His case report states:

Mrs. J. spoke anxiously of her husband's condition. She equated him with the brain-damaged children with whom she works. His drinking

---

[3] G. Bateson, D. Jackson, J. Haley and J. Weakland, "A Note on the Double Bind—1962," *Family Process*, 2, 154–161, 1963.

[4] K. Keniston, "How Community Mental Health Stamped Out the Riots (1968–1978)," *Transaction*, July/August, 21–29, 1968.

complicated the seizure problem, and it seemed to be getting worse. He had been missing work more lately. Worker arranged for Mr. and Mrs. J. to meet with him.

The Housing Agent and the wife were both contributing to the original dilemma, but for different reasons. Mrs. Johnson saw her husband heading for collapse, where the Housing Agent seemingly saw him as capable of working, but in a position where the best strategy would be for him to opt out, claiming the "seizures" as an excuse.

The social worker now met with the couple together for the first time. His impression was of the well-known team: "dominating" wife and "passive" husband. During the interview, the wife took over as spokesman for the husband. The matter of what to do in relation to the eviction threat was discussed, with Mr. Johnson saying that he had thought of quitting his job so as to bring the income level down. Mrs. Johnson then suggested that she could quit instead. The worker asked them how they would decide who should quit work, and remarked later in his notes: "There seemed to be no answer." Mr. Johnson next turned the subject to his dizzy spells and how they affected his working. The worker asked him to tell the full story of his illness to the doctor the Housing Agent had arranged for him to see at the Health Service, because the medical opinion could help to stave off the impending eviction. He stressed that Mr. Johnson should tell his own story, not let his wife tell it for him.

At this point, Mr. Johnson took his leave, explaining that he had to baby-sit for their pre-school youngest daughter, Maureen. After her husband had gone, Mrs. Johnson again expressed anxiety about his "seizures" and his increased drinking, and said that he slept most of the time when he was at home. She preferred his sleeping, because when he was awake, he would often explode over nothing, and his "grouchiness," as she termed his behavior, was hard to take. Sometimes he would even try to hit her, but she claimed she was the stronger and got the better of him in any physical fight. Thus the message from Mrs. Johnson seemed to be: stay at home and sleep and we'll have less trouble. On the other hand, it was Mrs. Johnson who was most committed to seeing that her daughters got a good education, and if this commitment were to be fulfilled, she could not afford to let her husband stay at home and sleep. There were contradictory aspects to her attitude too.

Up to now, Mr. Johnson had not talked very much for himself. However, during an interview with Mr. Johnson alone, just before the appointment with the doctor, the worker was able to uncover points of pride in Mr. Johnson's opinion of himself. He was proud of his skills as a cook and proud of his position of responsibility as supervisor of a large and busy kitchen where complicated diets for sick people had to be adhered to. He had held the same position for many years. He was naturally disheartened by the increased frequency of the dizzy spells and unnerved by the fear that one more "seizure" at work might cause him to be fired. Caught in the grip of a self-fulfilling prophecy, in that his fear of having the seizures was part of what provoked them, Mr. Johnson would clearly be vulnerable to messages from others confirming these fears. As an example of Mr. Johnson's easily crumbled sense of personal rights and gloomy expectations, here is an excerpt from the worker's account of the interview:

Worker said, Your wife said the other day that you had had two seizures on the job, and that one more would mean the end of the job. Is that so?

Mr. J. said, Yes. Worker said, who made that ruling? The insurance company? (Wife had previously mentioned the insurance company in that connection.) Mr. J. said, No, well, you see when I had the last seizure at work—when I had my head injury—as the Hospitals Department inspector was coming in the door, I was going out on a stretcher. My boss told me that the inspector said that one more seizure and he'd have to let me go.

Worker asked, Is that just the inspector's idea, or is that a ruling by the Department of Hospitals? Mr. J. said, I don't know. Worker asked, Exactly how did your boss tell it to you? Mr. J. said, He said the inspector said, if a man falls out like that, you can't keep him, can you?

Worker said, Would you like me to try to find out if there really is such a regulation, or if this was just an off-hand remark by the inspector? Mr. J. responded, I'd be delighted.

The next chapter of the story concerns Mr. Johnson's visit to the doctor. A new set of opinions now fell out, containing a new proliferation of contradictory meanings. Mr. Johnson had been coming to the Health Service since 1964 for physical complaints, and in the course of his first work-up, the doctor learned and noted down that he customarily drank up to a quart of liquor a day. A look at the medical chart reveals that the statement "chronic alcoholic" is written at the bottom of every subsequent entry in the chart, no matter which department in the clinic Mr. Johnson came to, or for what reason. In discussing his "drinking problem" with the social worker, Mr. Johnson said that he usually kept whiskey by him on the job, "because if I feel shaky, I take a drink, and then I'm usually all right." However, Mr. Johnson's doctor had told him that "anyone who takes a drink before six o'clock in the evening is an alcoholic." The medical record converts this opinion into a disease syndrome by analogy with other biological diagnoses found in medical charts. Yet no doctor proposed a treatment plan. There is a confusion here between explicit moral disapproval of drinking on the one hand, and exoneration of alcoholism as a medical condition on the other. The opinion of it as a medical condition is kept in the chart and not made explicit.

This confusion reappears, with a new twist, in the encounter with the different doctor who examined Mr. Johnson at the time of the referral to the social service department. The worker had sent this doctor a long memo explaining the importance the medical opinion would have in regard to the family's housing. Initially, the worker had accepted the request from the Housing Agent: "Certify this man as unable to work." But the conversation with Mr. Johnson raised doubts in the worker's mind about the advisability of removing the support that work represented to him, and the memo reflected the worker's ambivalence. The following statement was issued by the doctor:

Apparently patient is a lazy, indifferent, passive immature, dependent, inadequate personality who cannot maintain a responsible position for any appreciable length of time. He prefers alcohol to anticonvulsive medications and indeed, at times, his convulsions may be merely "rum fits" or delirium tremens. Apparently the best that can be expected with this individual is that he can be productive on occasions as long as he is "mothered" by his wife and society. I would suggest that he not be moved from his present apartment since his present income is likely to vanish at any moment of stress.

The worker feared that his memo had sounded too protective to the doctor, and had called forth this anti-mothering response. He phoned Mr. Johnson, expecting him to be upset. On the contrary, Mr. Johnson said that his interview with the doctor had gone very well. The doctor had behaved in a kind and benevolent manner to him and had told him that he wouldn't have to worry about being moved after the Housing Authority read what he was going to write in his statement.

The worker then called the doctor, who said that he was only willing to sign a statement that Mr. Johnson was a chronic alcoholic. The worker called a lawyer at an anti-poverty agency, who told him that to show this diagnosis to the Housing Authority would not stop the family's eviction; on the contrary, it would ensure it. The worker then appealed to a doctor further up the clinic hierarchy, who issued a diagnosis of "chronic seizure disorders and labile hypertension," and stated that Mr. Johnson should be permitted to remain in his present apartment as the stress of moving at this time might prove harmful. The wording here was important, as it did not tie the Johnson's continuing occupancy of their apartment to Mr. Johnson's decision about work.

The worker was just about to mail this statement to the Housing Authority when he learned that Mr. Johnson had just had a bad dizzy spell at work and had decided to quit for good. In view of his situation as we have described it, this event was not surprising. There were many conflicting pressures for and against his continuing to work, both within the circle of Mr. Johnson's immediate and daily relationships, and within the circle of helpers around the family. The explanation that a human being cannot continue to function under the strain of this kind of bell-buzzer fibrillation may be as reasonable a way to see his collapse as to trace it to a single aspect, whether this be a "dependent personality," a "dominating wife," the "over-mothering of society," or some mysterious physical condition such as "chronic seizure disorder."

Whatever its cause, Mr. Johnson's decision to quit his job, which occurred a little more than two weeks after the Housing Agent first called the Health Service, created a new configuration. Now, not loss of housing but a far more difficult loss to repair came into question: a man's loss of executive function and social place. In particular, a shift in the relationship between husband and wife had taken place, leaving the wife on top and the husband on the bottom. This shift had been hanging in the air for a long time, but it was only now, when the outer social systems finally got into the act, that it became sanctioned and fixed. Three doctors, a Housing Agent, Mrs. Johnson, Mr. Johnson, possibly his boss, and to some extent the case worker, all became implicated in a process which caused Mr. Johnson to accept, and/or provoke, a label of helplessness.

Now a two-fold job presented itself: first, to get Mr. Johnson out of the sick man's seat and back on his feet; second, while this was being attempted, to work out the changed economics of family life now that Mr. Johnson no longer contributed an income. This second task alone meant endless casework time that had to be devoted to dealing with a multitude of institutions and agencies. A list of these institutions will give an idea of the forest of helpers that had sprung up around the Johnson family: the Health Service, with its various departments;

O.E.O. Legal Services; the Housing Authority; Mr. Johnson's union; the Veteran's Administration; Workmen's Compensation; a private loan company; All Saints Parish; Franklin Settlement; and Southern College.

Rather than describe in detail how the worker helped the Johnsons to deal with all these agencies, one single example will be presented: the raising of funds so that the oldest girl could finish the year at Southern College, where she was now a junior. Neither Gail nor Lorna were doing too well at school, and Mrs. Johnson said she had never tried to look for scholarship aid to Gail, "because my daughter is not the brightest person in the world." It seemed that Gail had been in a subdued struggle with her mother for some time. The main issue had become the low-status black college in the South that Gail had chosen to go to, which affronted the mother's school and social expectations for her. Two years before, the girl had begun to get migraine headaches, and the psychiatrist she saw commented to Mrs. Johnson that they might stem from the mother's feelings about Gail's college. The mother denied this, but the headaches stopped after this suggestion was made, and Gail was allowed to attend the college. The worker, sensing the importance of keeping Gail in school, offered to help Mrs. Johnson find a source of scholarship funds. What was done in the work around getting the scholarship was to build on the upwardbound motivation of Mrs. Johnson, which required her to keep her daughter in college at any price. The alternate current in Mrs. Johnson—let daughter fail and come back home to reconstitute an unhealthy family triangle—was strong, and all the more so because it was not recognized. Insight therapy was not particularly suited to this family and it seemed more logical to strengthen the conscious drive toward achievement by offspring.

In order to give an idea of the number of fund-raising operations that took place over a two and a half month period between four persons and seven systems, a list is appended (see Appendix) telling what each of these transactions consisted of in chronological order. Multiply this sequence many times, and you begin to see how much time and energy of persons and agencies has to be poured into the vacuum left when even an unassuming cook like Mr. Johnson relinquishes his share of the social burden.

The last part of this story will describe what was done to reverse the machinery which had created an invalid out of Mr. Johnson. The worker had already been consulting with a psychiatrist at the Health Service about the case and now asked him to meet with Mr. and Mrs.

Johnson. This psychiatrist looked at the situation through two sets of glasses: the medical one, which would support the assumption that Mr. Johnson suffered from some physical condition, epilepsy or alcoholism or some combination of both, and the "ecological" one, which would widen the focus of the investigation to include non-biological factors. What he found tended to support the hypothesis that social and environmental factors rather than purely physical ones were at work.

First of all, he discovered that ever since the "seizure" three years before, Mr. Johnson had been taking large dosages of Dilantin and Librium (tranquilizers) and Phenobarbital. It was only *after* this time that the dizzy spells began to manifest themselves. On seeking further medical advice, Mr. Johnson was told that they were preludes to seizures: "aura." Because of the dizzy spells, his dosages were increased. He was now constantly feeling dizzy and constantly terrified that another seizure was coming on. He found that a drink of whiskey would dispel the dizziness for a while, and gradually upped his liquor consumption to about a quart a day. The dizzy spells continued, now augmented by the large amounts of medication and the large amounts of drink. Further visits to doctors brought increased dosages of drugs which brought on more dizziness which prompted him to drink more. There was also some doubt as to the nature of Mr. Johnson's seizures. The psychiatrist summed up his opinion on the medical aspects of Mr. Johnson's condition thus:

In a review of the chart, and on careful questioning, I can find no evidence that Mr. Johnson has ever had a seizure since the first one that brought him to Bellevue. There is a notation that he had a couple of blackout spells which turn out, on questioning both Mr. Johnson and his wife, to be fainting spells, not seizures. These can be reasonably explained as resulting at least in part from the combination of sedative and anesthetic (alcoholic) drugs he was taking, as can his dizzy spells. His EEG is normal (slow, but this is compatible with sedation).

The psychiatrist pointed out to Mr. Johnson the possibility that far from helping him, the drugs were in part responsible for the dizzy spells. A few days later, an incident occurred which helped Mr. Johnson to see that he could do without medication. Mrs. Johnson interpreted a vague remark on the part of her husband, mistakenly as it turned out, as a suicide threat. She took away the store of medication he had amassed, fearing that he would overdose himself with pills. Mr. Johnson reported to the worker that while he was deprived of his usual medication, he had no serious dizzy spells.

At the same time, the psychiatrist looked at the family factors which might be contributing to Mr. Johnson's difficulties. He learned that the onset of Mr. Johnson's heavy drinking coincided with the birth of his youngest daughter, six years before, at which time his wife stopped having sex relations with him. His drinking was opposed by Mrs. Johnson until he had his second "seizure." After that, he was able to defend his drinking on the ground that it kept him from having his spells. At the same time, Mr. Johnson was accepting more and more the position of sick and disabled one. This at least brought him concern from his wife. She also seemed to be more comfortable in a situation in which she held the reins.

The psychiatrist presented his over-all impression of the case as follows:

In my opinion, Mr. Johnson is a passive dependent man who has gradually accepted the role of an epileptic individual provided for him by those about him. There is no evidence that he is epileptic. He is an alcoholic. But even his alcoholism seems to be secondary to his sense of exclusion from his family resulting from his wife's sexual withdrawal and what seems to be a coalition of females (wife and three daughters) who find it easier for him to be powerless than to deal with him as the head of the household. Secondary gain is provided for him as the result of the actions of the Department of Public Housing and his wife's provision of mothering for her "sick" husband (child).

The psychiatrist recommended to Mr. Johnson's doctor that he withdraw all sedative drugs and suggested that the worker confront the family with the dynamics which were placing Mr. Johnson in the invalid role and work to re-establish Mr. Johnson's status as man of the house. He stressed particularly the need to get Mr. and Mrs. Johnson back together as a married pair.

At this point, a disagreement arose between the psychiatrist and the social worker. Acting on a cue from Mr. Johnson, who had said he wanted to get "dried out," the worker suggested that he be hospitalized for this purpose. This would also allow Mr. Johnson's physical condition to be assessed in a setting where his intake of both drugs and alcohol would be controlled. The psychiatrist argued that hospitalization might reinforce the label of invalid which was already hanging over Mr. Johnson's head. He also feared that a new set of medical authorities might pick up and re-affirm the old label of epileptic from Mr. Johnson's previous hospital record. For these reasons, he felt it would be best to hold off on hospitalization. Until, as will be seen, Mr. Johnson himself broke the stalemate, the worker continued to see the family every week, and the question of hospitalization remained open.

For the next two and a half months, an uneasy stasis prevailed in the family, perhaps related to the uneasy stasis between the psychiatrist and the worker, who still differed on the subject of hospitalization. Mr. Johnson lay around the house and continued to drink, and Mrs. Johnson complained to the worker about his drinking but continued to supply him with his daily allotment. Even though she also complained about the fact that Mr. Johnson's drinking cost her forty dollars a week, it was clear that she had a stake in keeping alive the idea that her husband needed to drink. Once, for instance, in the period just after Mr. Johnson had quit work, the worker called and was told by Mrs. Johnson that they had had a terrible weekend. Mr. Johnson had accidentally spilled the bottle of liquor she had bought him to last the weekend, and she had no money to replace it. She said he had been in great pain, which was hard on her too, as she couldn't bear to see him suffer. Also, he was difficult to handle when he couldn't get his liquor. During his next meeting with the couple, the worker asked Mr. Johnson about what had happened. Mr. Johnson said that he had knocked the bottle onto the kitchen floor. "I washed the kitchen floor with gin," he said. "I felt real bad about that." The worker asked, "How did you feel without your liquor?" Mr. Johnson said, "Lonely." Otherwise, he had apparently got through the weekend quite well.

Mrs. Johnson also preferred to have her husband stay at home, drinking or doped up, because she had less trouble keeping the upper hand. In a later interview with the worker, she said (the interview record is being quoted):

One thing that has been better since he's been home is that we've had fewer arguments. We used to argue all the time. My whole married life has been nothing but arguments. . . .

Worker asked, These arguments, who wins them—half and half, or do you win most, or does he? Mr. J. said quickly, She wins them all. Mrs. J. said, Well, there's never any agreement, so nobody wins. Worker said, But usually you do what you feel must be done, whatever happens about the argument. Mrs. J. said, Yes.

During this time, the worker kept pushing on a number of fronts, all designed to move the see-saw that had locked with Mrs. Johnson in the up position and Mr. Johnson in the down one. During an interview in mid-February, the see-saw started to loosen. Among other things, the worker was trying to get Mr. Johnson to think about going back to work. If he had part-time work, it would not affect his housing eligibility. Mr. Johnson countered by describing all the panicky feelings and dizziness he was getting whenever he ventured out. Mrs. Johnson moved in too, saying that work was out of the question until Mr. Johnson stopped drinking. Her fear was that Mr. Johnson would get a job, they would lose their housing, he would collapse, and they would then be left without sufficient income to pay for more expensive quarters. She brought up hospitalization again and said with some feeling that she would like to see progress. The worker said that in his opinion progress for Mr. Johnson was tied to two things: working and having sexual relations with his wife. The couple started talking about the difficulties they had in being intimate together, a subject which they were not accustomed to airing and which put the wife on the spot for a change. The worker put her on the spot again by bringing up her failure to register their youngest child for a Headstart program, an intention she had expressed in the first interview, months before. Of course, her not having done this meant that her husband, who was now at home all the time, was perpetually baby-sitting. Mrs. Johnson promised to try to register the child, but ended the meeting by complaining about her husband's growing resentment at having to baby-sit.

The meeting seemed to have broken some kind of dam. The next day, Mr. Johnson had another "seizure" as he went out to buy some liquor. He was taken to the Health Service, where a doctor gave him a prescription for sedative drugs and sent him home. The worker came to see him as soon as possible; he felt now that not talk but action was required, and pushed for hospitalization. Mr. Johnson seemed genuinely eager to go ahead. He said that he seemed to be going down the drain and he wanted to prevent that. Mrs. Johnson for the first time began to show signs of doubt about hospitalizing her husband, but the worker said that he would go ahead and make plans, because Mr. Johnson had said he was ready. The wife called the worker several days later and said that if Mr. Johnson did not stop drinking, she herself was going to have to quit work; she had come home that evening and found him asleep when he should have been taking care of the little girl. It was an interesting message: "I want my husband to stop drinking so that he can baby-sit for me better," but it seemed her way of supporting the decision to go ahead with hospitalization.

The worker now turned his efforts to finding a hospital which would allow the clinic some measure of control over Mr. Johnson's case. The hospital he found was satisfactory in this respect to the psychiatrist, who now supported the plan. However, the psychiatrist still wished to guard against the danger that the wife might interpret the move as a further proof that her husband was sick and thus offset any good it might do. Before Mr. Johnson went into the hospital, the psychiatrist had one more meeting with the couple. In it he pointed out that Mrs. Johnson, by supplying her husband with liquor, helped to incapacitate him, both as a breadwinner and a bed-partner. He was particularly concerned to expose the wife's share in the problems of the husband, which both preferred to define as belonging to the husband alone. He did this, not by telling the wife all the ways in which she was dominating or babying her husband, but by putting her on the other end of a fulcrum. If Mr. Johnson was willing to give up drinking, as well as the benefits of the invalid position, Mrs. Johnson must make some concessions which would prevent him from lapsing back and would help to restore his sense of worth as a husband and head of the house. This particularly meant sex, as the psychiatrist emphasized strongly.

In a subsequent interview with the worker, Mrs. Johnson said that she could understand why the psychiatrist had criticized her, but that she didn't give Mr. Johnson liquor to hurt him, only because it was easier for her when she did so. She thought he ought to be strong enough to resist it. She also brought up the question of sex, which the psychiatrist had pushed her on; she said she didn't want to seem uncooperative, but she could not promise to begin sleeping with Mr. Johnson because she didn't want to promise anything that was not going to happen. The worker said that it was not so much a matter of sleeping or not sleeping, but if she was going to work at keeping him a nonparticipant in family life, then this whole effort would be for nothing. If, on the other hand, Mr. Johnson was going to be helped to regain his place in the family, then they could work with his being hard to get along with. Mrs. Johnson seemingly got the point and agreed, but the worker did not feel her heart was in it.

The evening of Mr. Johnson's departure for the hospital did not go very smoothly. Mrs. Johnson kept postponing their leaving, even though Mr. Johnson and the worker, who was accompanying them, were anxious to get going. After an elaborate dinner, which the worker shared, Mr. Johnson got up just as coffee was being served and said that he was nervous and wanted to go. The worker got up with him and they began to put on their coats. Mrs. Johnson stopped them, saying to Mr. Johnson that it was not polite to drag people off before they had a chance to finish their coffee. Everybody sat down again until coffee was finished. Several other distractions were engineered by Mrs. Johnson, including the temporary loss of her house keys. The worker said later that he had expected some resistance on the wife's part but that he had not been prepared for such a dazzling display.

In the first days after Mr. Johnson came home from getting "dried out," he felt poorly, and his wife seemed especially remote and downcast. Efforts to plug him into Alcoholics Anonymous were not successful, and within a month he was back drinking again with his old cronies, who during his period of abstinence had begun to call him "The Preacher." However, he was much picked up in heart, was eating well for the first time in years, and had begun actively to look for work. The worker had to terminate the case at this point, after arranging for it to be taken over by another case worker. Subsequent developments were both hopeful and unhopeful.

On the unhopeful side, as Mr. Johnson began to act more self-assured, his wife was becoming more and more unhappy. At one point, she threatened to desert the family if Mr. Johnson did not stop drinking totally. There was a possibility that she might replace Mr. Johnson as the invalid; five years before she had been seeing a psychiatrist intensively, and had nearly been hospitalized at that time. However, she began to see the new social worker regularly, and this seemed to help her keep going.

Another unfortunate event was that the Housing Agent had expressed opposition to Mr. Johnson's working full-time again, telling him that if he did, the family would still have to leave their apartment. The original worker phoned the agent to check on this, and the agent, after trying to get him to agree that Mrs. Johnson was a terrible housekeeper (also grounds for ineligibility), said that it might be "more humane" to tell Mr. Johnson that it was the end of the line as far as his ever working again was concerned, rather than let him get his hopes up. This was particularly discouraging from the worker's point of view. Even if some changes could be brought about in the family system, it was difficult to believe that much permanent good could be done when the systems outside the family remained so fixed.

However, Mr. Johnson turned the tables on those who had consigned him to the dust-bin. He found a summer job cooking for a camp. When he returned, the owner of the camp offered him another job in the city at a very good wage. His old employer was also asking him to come back, arranging for him to work in such a way that his income level would no longer be a problem. Mr. Johnson decided to accept the second alternative, but was faced with the task of turning down the first. The new social worker was prepared to do the task for Mr. Johnson, on the premise that it was so difficult that it might immobilize him and the downward spiral would begin all over again. But the next time Mr. Johnson came in, he told the worker that he had settled the matter himself and was already back at work.

The starring—and unexpected—development was that Gail, who had been doing marginally at college, was getting A's and B's at midterm. It would be encouraging to believe, and consistent with family theory, that the opening up of difficulties between husband and wife had the advantage of setting Gail free from the family triangle she seemed to have been caught in, thus allowing her to succeed on her own. It would also be encouraging to believe that the thirty operations described in the Appendix were not in vain.

This story has been told in some detail in order to show how an elaborate interplay of systems—social, familial, individual—contributed to the breakdown of a person, a breakdown which might otherwise seem to be the result of some disorganizing process within the person himself. We started with the paradoxical social situation, centering on housing, which Mr. Johnson was caught in. Peeling off this outer layer, we saw how the social dilemma was reflecting and reinforcing a long-standing marital dilemma which also contained contradictory elements, such as Mrs. Johnson objecting to her husband's drinking while supplying him with liquor. Getting down to the layer of biological health, we saw how the medical system was putting Mr. Johnson in another impossible position, mainly by giving him drugs which caused him to have dizzy spells for which it prescribed more drugs.

We also attempted to trace, through an analysis of recorded or observed communications between Mr. Johnson and the persons in the systems around him, the subtle ways in which a scapegoat is created. We saw that the communications were characterized by a confusion of benevolent/derogatory attitudes, intricately masked. There is no direct evidence that white persons in the helping agencies were influenced by the fact that Mr. Johnson was black, but some of their expressed attitudes resembled stereotyped white opinions about the "passive" or "shiftless" black male who is nevertheless treated in a kindly manner because he is not accountable. This study has not gone into the effect of national social issues, but the week that Mr. Johnson started drinking again was also the week that Dr. Martin Luther King was killed. How much the tensions sparked by this event were reflected in the life of any particular black family is open to conjecture, but this is another factor which cannot be pushed aside.

The Johnsons will probably continue to experience difficulties in their lives together. There is at least a hope that the oldest girl may continue to hold her own at college and get out of the vicious dependency cycles that have trapped her parents. The worker may also have prevented Mr. Johnson from getting fixed in the invalid position he was clearly headed for. It is equally possible that he will still fall back into that position, or that his wife or a daughter may have to fill a similar one.

Whatever its outcome, this case illustrates the breadth and complexity of the context the worker in a low-income area has to struggle with in his efforts to help an individual or a family. We began by saying that helping systems may inadvertently combine to cause harm to their mutual clients. If we have demonstrated that in at least one case this was so, then the question may properly be raised: How does one work in such a situation? And is this way of working, which we have here put into a "systems" framework, radically different from traditional or even newer models of social work? Our answer is yes, for reasons which we shall try to suggest below.

In working with the Johnsons, it was found necessary to add to individual or family "treatment" sessions, which are a standard part of social work procedure, a set of strategies directed toward the various systems which impinged on the family. The expectation for this approach was developed in the first home visit:

Worker said, You know, I haven't been sure that my role in this situation has been clear to you. People in our society have to deal with big organizations like the Housing Authority or the hospital. It's my job to see that they get what they need, and that they don't get stepped on or forgotten. . . . People can get pretty mad sometimes when they have to deal with the Housing Authority. Mrs. J. responded, Yes, you sure can. As a matter of fact, I understood that was what your role was.

The worker's role, as presented above, resembles in many ways the models of social case work involving systems intervention which Scott Briar calls "social broker" and "advocate" models.[5] In these models, the worker becomes a super-authority who mediates between the family and the agencies, guiding his clients through the maze of services they are entitled to and fighting for their rights. In our story, the

---

[5] S. Briar, "The Current Crisis in Social Casework," *Social Work Practice*, 19–33, 1967.

worker was attempting a very different kind of operation. Throughout his involvement, he found himself subverting the intrusions of the helping agencies into the family's life whenever these intrusions pushed the husband further into helplessness *vis à vis* the family, or the family further into helplessness *vis à vis* society. While attempting to equalize the skew in these concentric sets of relationships, the worker also tried not to become too much of an authority himself. Whenever he could, he turned the task of dealing with the agencies back to the family, using this tactic to resist becoming too omnipotent a figure in family affairs.

Why it is so important to attain an equity in the total balance of relationships—individual within family and family within society—is perhaps explained by Montague Ullman in his essay, "A Unifying Concept Linking Therapeutic and Community Process." Ullman has made an interesting bridge between a condition perceived as social: poverty, and a condition perceived as individual: mental illness, using the concept of power:

We are suggesting that poverty and mental illness are expressions of an inequity in power relationships. Poverty emerges as the material precipitate of an underlying insistent imbalance in economic opportunity, while neurosis may be defined as the internalized reflection of existing inequities in the day to day lives of people.[6]

The writers would qualify Ullman's use of the term "power" by putting it in an ecological context. As an ecologist knows, if one species in an interdependent grouping becomes too successful—too powerful—it only invites its own demise. Power, in looking at such groupings, is a matter of total equilibration, not of strength of individual parts, because only when all parts are in balance, does each operate at an optimum level.

How to redress an imbalance of power when dealing with disturbed people in poor families *when the presence of powerful helpers is one of the factors contributing to the imbalance in the first place* is the problem as it is conceived by a "systems" worker. Specific tactics seem to fall naturally out of this way of putting the matter. Each intervention, the whole process in fact, serves a double purpose: a piece of help, a suggestion, or a task, is pursued not only for itself but because it also helps to equalize the balance of power in whatever arena is in

---

[6] M. Ullman, "A Unifying Concept Linking Therapeutic and Community Process," speech presented at the American Psychiatric Association meeting in Detroit, May, 1967.

question, or in several at once. For instance, if one looks at the Appendix, it will be clear that the worker initiated few of the contacts needed to raise the scholarship. Most of this work was done by Mrs. Johnson. Assigning this task to Mrs. Johnson was done not only to give her a chance to materially help her daughter, but to demonstrate her competence at a time when the family sessions, with their emphasis on re-establishing the husband's strength in relation to his wife, tended to plunge her into despair, and possibly into the same helpless state she was herself in five years before. It also, as explained above, prevented the worker from taking too much initiative.

This tack, applied to Mr. Johnson, was not quite so successful. He was given the task of applying to all the agencies which he thought might provide him with funds while he sank into dependency. In the visit described above, the worker tried to encourage him:

Mr. J. said that he intended to go over to the Veterans' office and the union today, but he had this dizzy spell. He didn't know if the Veterans Aid applied. Worker said, It would be good to find that out. Mr. J. said, Would you want to find out about it? Worker said, Well, I really think it is better if people do for themselves where they can. Why don't you call tomorrow . . . and then Monday I'll check with you to see how far you have gone.

However, as Mr. Johnson went through the process of tackling these agencies—public welfare, the Veteran's Adminstration, and the like—it became clear that they took as much as they gave, especially the last symbol of a black man's financial independence (until recently): his insurance policy. The worker began to feel that this task was fatally untherapeutic for a man whose sense of worth he was trying to rebuild, even though he wanted to be sure that there would be some cushion in the event the worst happened. He took it upon himself to see that the demands of Workmen's Compensation were met, so that the family had funds to function with. But this taking over was done in the context of supporting Mr. Johnson in the family sessions, where a major goal was to reinforce his status as a husband and father.

Except for the contact with workmen's compensation and a few critical interventions to support Mrs. Johnson's scholarship efforts, the worker's own actions in regard to outer systems turned out to be mainly resistive. What he did was to block the confusing and double-binding communications from social and medical authorities who insisted on placing Mr. Johnson in the invalid position. When the Housing Agent turned out to be extremely rigid in this regard, the worker blocked the agent's access to the medical system. The agent could not certify Mr. Johnson's helplessness without the medical system's cooperation. The worker would not return calls; he would deliver quite unsatisfactory written documents well beyond deadlines set by the agent. When it became necessary for the Johnsons to deal with the Housing Authority themselves, the worker referred them to a lawyer who specialized in housing matters.

The worker also had to frustrate his own system, the medical one, in its customary functioning. The psychiatrist had intervened directly with the physician to reverse the pattern of increasing Mr. Johnson's medication. This step had one consequence not reported in the body of this paper: when the doctor who had been prescribing the drugs saw Mr. Johnson again, he took the small reserve of pills Mr. Johnson had stored up against a panic and hurled them into a wastebasket. Fortunately, the worker was present and was able to support Mr. Johnson through this crisis. Nevertheless, such incidents underscore the need for training in greater skill in systems intervention. On this evidence, it seems that hell hath no fury like a helping system scorned.

The above discussion has highlighted some of the strategies that emerge when attempting to apply a "systems" approach to social work in poor communities. Perhaps the most obvious difference between traditional social work and the type of activity described herein is this: the more traditional model does not see the persons who are helpers of a given individual or family (and this includes the social worker himself) as part of the problem to be attacked. If reducing inequities of power within all the interlocking systems inhabited by a distressed person is the therapeutic task, the role of the helper is going to have to be re-cast. It will be increasingly harder to separate the specialist in "emotional" problems from the specialist in "community" problems. In fact, if these practitioners do not combine to produce a new type of helper, they may find themselves atrophied stubs on a form which has developed very different limbs.

For the time being, however, this form is still evolving. The worker in this study found himself doing combination-work for which there is as yet no training and only the beginnings of a theoretical base. Lacking this, it would seem best to present case stories such as this one in an interim attempt to document some of the perplexities the worker meets and has to deal with on this new frontier.

APPENDIX

Number of Operations Needed to Secure College Assistance Funds for
Miss J., Nov. 28, 1967 to Feb. 12, 1968

a1. 11-28-67. Mrs. J. speaks to worker about problem of college
assistance for daughter. Illness of Mr. J. has made it impossible
for family to provide this money.

a2. 12-7-67. Worker calls Urban League for information. He is
referred to College Assistance Program.

a3. Same date. Worker gives information to Mrs. J., who makes
appointment with College Assistance Program for December
19. Persons in that office give her conflicting information about
who to go to, but someone finally comes in and makes an
appointment with the right person.

a4. 12-11-67. Mrs. J. calls Sam Arcaro, who used to work for Franklin
Settlement House and who is in touch with a donor interested
in Miss J.

a5. 12-12-67. Mr. J. and worker go to see Father Arcy at All Saints
Parish. The family are members of that parish and Mr. J is a
well-known figure there.

a6. Same date. Fr. Arcy writes to President of Southern College,
where Miss J. is a student. Fr. Arcy tells Mr. J. to get in touch
with Mrs. Xavier, who is head of the Parish Scholarship Fund.
Since Mr. J. and Mrs. Xavier have a feud going, the worker
and the family decide that Mrs. J. might be the best one to
approach her.

a7. The President of Southern College refers the matter to college
loan officer, and writes Fr. Arcy to that effect.

a8. 12-18-67. Miss J. comes home from college. Worker talks with
her; she is not particularly happy at school, but she wants to
continue.

a9. 12-19-67. Miss J. and her mother go to College Assistance Program where she is given an application for a National Defense
Loan.

a10. Same week. Miss J. goes to see Mr. Watson at Franklin Settlement.

a11. Same week. Miss J. goes to see Sam Arcaro.

a12. Miss J. goes to see Fr. Arcy too. She is sick with the flu during
the last part of her vacation, and does not follow up on any of
these appointments.

a13. Miss J. returns to college in South Carolina.

a14. 1-4-68. Mrs. J. calls Mr. Watson, finds that he is waiting for
Miss J. to return.

a15. 1-5-68. Mrs. J. goes to see Mr. Watson, who says that Franklin
Settlement will help with some money, but cannot give the
whole amount.

a16. Same date. Mrs. J. contacts Sam Arcaro, who says that Miss J. gave him the impression that she wanted to transfer when she talked with him. He will not act until this is clarified.

a17. Same date. Mrs. J. writes to Miss J. at college, asking her to contact Mr. Arcaro.

a18. 1-14-68. Mrs. J. has been trying to reach Mrs. Xavier for weeks. Finally she succeeds, only to learn that Mrs. Xavier only raises money, she does not dispense it. Mrs. J. is referred to the Diocesan Scholarship Fund, represented by Father Chipworth and Mrs. York.

a19. Week of 1-14-68. Worker calls Mrs. York and finds that Miss J. must apply herself. They only have limited funds and cannot give the whole amount.

a20. 1-22-68. Worker calls Miss J. in South Carolina, asking her to respond to Mr. Arcaro and the Diocesan Scholarship Committee. Miss J. is not in; worker does not reach her.

a21. Same date. A letter arrives from Miss J. She very much wants to live off-campus, and has made arrangements to do so; her mother approves. Miss J. thinks this will solve the problem of her unhappiness at school.

a22. 1-23-68. Worker calls Father Chipworth, a friend, who also knows the family. He agrees to give $300.

a23. 1-23-68 to 1-26-68. Mrs. J. makes a number of attempts to reach the college business manager to get a postponement of the date when fees are due. He is never in when she calls.

a24. 1-24-68. Miss J. calls worker two days after his call. Worker tells her that the log-jam has been broken.

a25. 1-28-68. Diocesan Scholarship Committee votes the $300 that Fr. Chipworth had promised.

a26. 1-30-68. Fr. Borden, pastor of All Saints Parish, writes the $300 check and sends it to Miss J. at college. He sends it to the dormitory, which instead of forwarding it to her new address, returns it to her home address in New York.

a27. Same date. Mrs. J. contacts Franklin Settlement, which immediately comes through with the remaining funds.

a28. Same date. Worker writes to college business manager for delay in fee due date.

a29. 2-2-68. Returned scholarship check sent by Mrs. J. to Miss J. Fees are now paid.

a30. 2-12-68. Worker receives letter from college business manager, dated February 9, granting delay in due date for fees. See step 29.)

(During this period the worker had twelve family interviews with the parents, parts of which were spent working out the next step in the above process. However, the worker's main business during this time was related to the health of Mr. J., and other issues arising from that. Our society expects low income, sometimes disorganized families, under stress from illness and other factors, to negotiate a complex assortment of systems in order to survive. It is a remarkable achievement that the members of the Johnson family were able to play such a significant part in this particular issue of raising scholarship funds.)

Bibliography

AGUILAR, IGNACIO. "Initial Contacts with Mexican-American Families." *Social Work*, 17 (May 1972): 66–70.

ALINSKY, SAUL D. *Reveille for Radicals*. Chicago: University of Chicago Press, 1946.

ARGYRIS, CHRIS. "Explorations in Consulting-Client Relationships." In Warren Bennis, Kenneth Benne, and Robert Chin (eds.), *The Planning of Change*, pp. 434–57. 2nd ed. New York: Holt, Rinehart & Winston, 1969.

ARTHUR, A. Z. "A Decision-Making Approach to Psychological Assessment in the Clinic." *Journal of Consulting Psychology*, 30 (October 1966): 435–38.

BALES, ROBERT F.; and BORGATTA, EDGAR F. "Size of Group as a Factor in the Interaction Profile." In A. Paul Hare, Edgar F. Borgatta, and Robert F. Bales (eds.), *Small Groups*, pp. 396–413. New York: Alfred A. Knopf, 1955.

BANFIELD, EDWARD C. *Political Influence*. New York: Free Press, 1961.

BARKER, ROGER G. *Ecological Psychology*. Stanford, Cal.: Stanford University Press, 1968.

BARTLETT, HARRIET M. *The Common Base of Social Work Practice*. New York: National Association of Social Workers, 1970.

BEIER, ERNEST. *The Silent Language of Psychotherapy*. Chicago: Aldine Publishing Co., 1966.

BENNE, KENNETH D. "Some Ethical Problems in Group and Organizational Consultation." In Warren Bennis, Kenneth Benne, and Robert Chin (eds.), *The Planning of Change*, pp. 595–604. 2nd ed. New York: Holt, Rinehart & Winston, 1969.

BENNE, KENNETH D., and SHEATS, PAUL. "Functional Roles of Group Members." In Leland P. Bradford (ed.), *Group Development*, pp. 51–59. Washington, D.C.: National Training Laboratories, National Education Association, 1961.

BENNIS, WARREN. "Personal Change through Interpersonal Relations." In Warren Bennis (ed.), *Interpersonal Dynamics: Essays and Readings on Human Interaction*, pp. 357–94. Rev. ed. Homewood, Ill.: Dorsey Press, 1968.

BENNIS, WARREN G.; BENNE, KENNETH D., and CHIN, ROBERT. *The Planning of Change*. New York: Holt, Rinehart & Winston, 1961.

BENNIS, WARREN G.; BENNE, KENNETH D., and CHIN, ROBERT. *The Planning of Change*. 2nd ed. New York: Holt, Rinehart & Winston, 1969.

BERLIN, IRVING N. "Resistance to Change in Mental Health Professionals." *American Journal of Orthopsychiatry*, 39 (January 1969): 109–15.

BERNSTEIN, SAUL. "Self-Determination: King or Citizen in the Realm of Values." *Social Work*, 5 (January 1960): 3–8.

BERTCHER, HARVEY, and MAPLE, FRANK. *Group Composition—An Instructional Program*. Ann Arbor, Mich.: Campus Publishers, 1971.

BIESTECK, FELIX B. *The Casework Relationship*. Chicago: Loyola University Press, 1957.

BILLINGSLEY, ANDREW. "Bureaucratic and Professional Orientation Patterns in Social Casework." *Social Service Review*, 38 (December 1964): 400–407.

BISNO, HERBERT. "A Theoretical Framework for Teaching Social Work Methods and Skills, with Particular Reference to Undergraduate Social Welfare Education." *Journal of Education for Social Work*, 5 (Fall 1969): 5–17.

BOND, RICHARD J.; BURNS, VIRGINIA; KOLODNY, RALPH; and WARREN, MARJORY C. "The Neighborhood Peer Group." *The Group*, 17 (October 1954): 3 ff.

BORGATTA, EDGAR, and CROWTHER, BETTY. *A Workbook for the Study of Social Interaction Processes*. Chicago: Rand McNally & Co., 1965.

BRADFORD, LELAND P.; STOCK, DOROTHY; and HORWITZ, MURRAY. "How to Diagnose Group Problems." In Leland P. Bradford (ed.), *Group Development*, pp. 37–50. Washington, D.C.: National Training Laboratories, National Education Association, 1961.

BRAGER, GEORGE A. "Advocacy and Political Behavior." *Social Work*, 13 (April 1968): 5–15.

BRAGER, GEORGE A. "The Indigenous Non Professional Worker: A New Approach to the Social Work Technician." *Social Work*, 10 (April 1965): 33–35.

BRAGER, GEORGE A. "Institutional Change: Perimeters of the Possible." *Social Work*, 12 (January 1967): 59–69.

BRAGER, GEORGE A., and BARR, SHERMAN. "Perceptions and Reality— The Poor Man's View of Social Services." In G. Brager and F. Purcell (eds.), *Community Action against Poverty*, pp. 72–80. New Haven, Conn.: College and University Press, 1967.

BRAGER, GEORGE A., and JORRIN, VALERIE. "Bargaining: A Method in Community Change." *Social Work*, 14 (October 1969): 73–83.

BREDEMEIER, HARRY C. "The Socially Handicapped and the Agencies." In Frank Riessman, Jerome Cohen, and Arthur Pearl (eds.), *Mental Health of the Poor*, pp. 88–109. New York: The Free Press, 1964.

BRIAR, SCOTT. "Clinical Judgment in Foster Care Placement." *Child Welfare*, 42 (April 1963): 161–169.

BRIELAND, DONALD. "Black Identity and the Helping Person." *Children*, 16 (September–October, 1969): 170–75.

BURKE, EDMUND. "Citizen Participation Strategies." *Journal of the American Institute of Planners*, 34 (September 1968): 287–94.

BURNS, MARY E., and GLASSER, PAUL H. "Similarities and Differences in Casework and Group Work Practice." *Social Service Review*, 34 (December 1963): 416–28.

CARKHUFF, ROBERT R. *Helping and Human Relations*. Vols. I and II. New York: Holt, Rinehart & Winston, 1969.

CARTWRIGHT, DORWIN. "Achieving Change in People." In Warren Bennis, Kenneth Benne and Robert Chin (eds.), *The Planning of Change*, pp. 698–705. New York: Holt, Rinehart & Winston, 1961.

CARTWRIGHT, DORWIN, and ZANDER, ALVIN. *Group Dynamics*. New York: Harper and Row, 1968.

CHIN, ROBERT. "Evaluating Group Movement and Individual Change." In *Use of Groups in the Psychiatric Setting*, pp. 34–35. New York: National Association of Social Workers, 1960.

CHIN, ROBERT. "The Utility of System Models and Developmental Models for Practitioners." In Warren G. Bennis, Kennth D. Benne and Robert Chin (eds.), *The Planning of Change*, pp. 201–14. New York: Holt, Rinehart & Winston, 1961.

CHURCHILL, SALLIE. "Social Group Work: A Diagnostic Tool in Child Guidance." *American Journal of Orthopsychiatry*, 35 (April 1965): 581–88.

CLOWARD, RICHARD A., and EPSTEIN, IRWIN. "Private Social Welfare's Disengagement from the Poor: The Case of Family Adjustment Agencies." In Mayer Zald (ed.), *Social Welfare Institutions*, pp. 623–644. New York: John Wiley & Sons, 1965.

COCH, LESTER, and FRENCH, JOHN R. P. "Overcoming Resistance to Change." *Human Relations*, 11 (1948): 512–32.

CUMMING, JOHN, and CUMMING, ELAINE. *Ego and Milieu.* New York: Atherton Press, 1962.

CURRY, ANDREW. "The Family Therapy Situation as a System." *Family Process*, 5 (September 1966): 131–41.

DELBECQ, ANDRE, and VAN DEVEN, ANDREW. "A Group Process Model for Problem Identification and Program Planning." *Journal of Applied Behavioral Science*, 7 (July–August 1971): 466–92.

DILLON, VERA, "Group Intake in a Casework Agency," *Social Casework*, 46 (January 1965): 26–30.

EATON, JOSEPH. "Science, 'Art', and Uncertainty in Social Work." *Social Work*, 3 (July 1958): 3–10.

EPSTEIN, IRWIN. "Professional Role Orientations and Conflict Strategies." *Social Work*, 15 (October 1970): 87–92.

EPSTEIN, IRWIN. "Social Workers and Social Action: Attitudes Toward Social Action Strategies." *Social Work*, 13 (April 1968): 101–8.

EPSTEIN, NORMAN. "Brief Group Therapy in a Child Guidance Clinic." *Social Work*, 15 (July 1970): 33–38.

ERIKSON, ERIK. *Childhood and Society.* 2nd ed. New York: W. W. Norton & Co., 1963.

FELLNER, IRVING A. "Recruiting Adoptive Applicants." *Social Work*, 13 (January 1968): 92–100.

FRALEY, YVONNE L. "A Role Model for Practice." *Social Service Review*, 43 (June 1969): 145–54.

FRENCH, JOHN R. P., and RAVEN, BERTRAM. "The Bases of Social Power." In D. Cartwright (ed.) *Studies in Social Power*, pp. 150–67. Ann Arbor, Mich.: Institute for Social Research, 1959.

GAMSON, WILLIAM A. *Power and Discontent.* Homewood, Ill.: Dorsey Press, 1968.

GARCIA, RALPH, and IRWIN, OLIVE. "A Family Agency Deals with the Problem of Dropouts." *Social Casework*, 43 (February 1962): 71–75.

GARLAND, JAMES; JONES, HUBERT; and KOLODNY, RALPH. "A Model for Stages of Development in Social Work Groups." In Saul Bernstein (ed.), *Explorations in Group Work*, pp. 12–53. Boston, Mass.: University of Boston School of Social Work, 1965.

GARVIN, CHARLES, and GLASSER, PAUL. "The Bases of Social Treatment." In *Social Work Practice, 1970*, pp. 149–177. New York: Columbia University Press, 1970.

GILBERT, NEIL. "Neighborhood Coordinator: Advocate or Middleman?" *Social Service Review*, 43 (June 1969): 136–44.

GOLDSTEIN, ARNOLD P. "Maximizing the Initial Psychotherapeutic Relationship." *American Journal of Psychotherapy*, 23 (July 1969): 430–51.

GOLDSTEIN, ARNOLD P.; GASSNER, SUZANNE; GREENBERG, ROGER; GUSTIN, ANN; LAND, JAY; LIBERMAN, BERNARD, and STREINER, DAVID. "The Use of Planted Patients in Group Psychotherapy." *American Journal of Psychotherapy*, 21 (October 1967): 767–73.

GOLDSTEIN, ARNOLD; HELLER, KENNETH; and SECHREST, LEE. *Psychotherapy and the Psychology of Behavior Change*. New York: John Wiley & Sons, 1966.

GORDON, RAYMOND. *Interviewing: Strategy, Techniques and Tactics*. Homewood, Ill.: Dorsey Press, 1969.

GORDON, WILLIAM E. "A Critique of the Working Definition." *Social Work*, 7 (October 1962): 3–13.

GORDON, WILLIAM E. "Knowledge and Value: Their Distinction and Relationship in Clarifying Social Work Practice." *Social Work*, 10 (July 1965): 32–39.

GOULDNER, ALVIN W. "Anti-Minotaur: The Myth of a Value-Free Sociology." In Warren Bennis, Kenneth Benne, and Robert Chin (eds.), *The Planning of Change*, pp. 604–18. 2nd ed. New York: Holt, Rinehart & Winston, 1969.

GREENSPOON, J. "Verbal Conditioning and Clinical Psychology." In A. J. Bachrach (ed), *Experimental Foundations of Clinical Psychology*, pp. 510–53. New York: Basic Books, 1962.

GREENWOOD, ERNEST. "The Practice of Science and the Science of Practice." In Warren Bennis, Kenneth Benne, and Robert Chin (eds.), *The Planning of Change*, pp. 73–82. New York: Holt, Rinehart & Winston, 1961.

GURSSLIN, ORVILLE R.; HUNT, RAYMOND G.; and ROACH, JACK L. "Social Class and the Mental Health Movement." In Frank Riessman, Jerome Cohen, and Arthur Pearl (eds.), *Mental Health of the Poor*, pp. 57–67. New York: Free Press, 1964.

HAAS, WALTER. "Reaching Out—A Dynamic Concept in Casework." *Social Work*, 4 (July 1959): 41–45.

HAGGSTROM, WARREN C. "Can the Poor Transform the World?" In Ralph Kramer and Harry Specht (eds.), *Readings in Community Organization Practice*, pp. 301–14. Englewood Cliffs, N.J.: Prentice-Hall, Inc., 1969.

HAGGSTROM, WARREN C. "The Power of the Poor." In Frank Reissman, Jerome Cohen, and Arthur Pearl (eds.), *Mental Health of the Poor*, pp. 205–23. New York: Free Press, 1964.

HALL, JULIAN C.; SMITH, KATHLEEN; and BRADLEY, ANNA K. "Delivering Mental Health Services to the Urban Poor." *Social Work*, 15 (April 1970): 35–39.

HALLECK, SEYMOUR L. "The Impact of Professional Dishonesty on Behavior of Disturbed Adolescents." *Social Work*, 8 (April 1963): 48–55.

HARDCASTLE, DAVID A. "The Indigenous Non Professional in the Social

Service Bureaucracy: A Critical Examination." *Social Work*, 16 (April 1971): 56–63.

HOBBS, NICHOLAS. "Group Centered Psychotherapy." In Carl Rogers (ed.), *Client Centered Therapy*, pp. 278–319. New York: Houghton Mifflin Co., 1951.

HOFFMAN, L. R., and MAIER, P. F. "Quality and Acceptance of Problem Solutions by Members of Homogeneous and Heterogeneous Groups." *Journal of Abnormal and Social Psychology*, 62 (1961): 401–7.

HOLLIS, FLORENCE. *Casework—A Psychosocial Therapy*. New York: Random House, 1972.

HOMANS, GEORGE. *The Human Group*. New York: Harcourt-Brace, 1950.

HOSHINO, GEORGE, and WEBER, SHIRLEY. "Outposting in the Public Welfare Services." *Public Welfare*, 31 (Winter 1963): 8–14.

JOLESCH, MIRIAM. "Strengthening Intake Practice through Group Discussion." *Social Casework*, 40 (November 1959): 504–10.

KADUSHIN, ALFRED. "Diagnosis and Evaluation for (Almost) all Occasions." *Social Work*, 8 (January 1963): 12–19.

KADUSHIN, ALFRED. "The Racial Factor in the Interview." *Social Work*, 17 (May 1972): 88–98.

KADUSHIN, ALFRED. "Social Sex Roles and the Initial Interview." *Mental Hygiene*, 42 (July 1958): 354–61.

KADUSHIN, ALFRED. *The Social Work Interview*. New York: Columbia University Press, 1972.

KAHN, ALFRED J. *Neighborhood Information Centers*. New York: Columbia University School of Social Work, 1966.

KAHN, ROBERT, and CANNELL, CHARLES. *The Dynamics of Interviewing*. New York: John Wiley & Sons, 1957.

KAPLAN, ABRAHAM. *The Conduct of Inquiry: Methodology for Behavioral Science*. San Francisco: Chandler Publishing Co., 1964.

KEITH-LUCAS, ALAN. "A Critique of the Principle of Client Self-Determination." *Social Work*, 8 (July 1963): 66–71.

KELMAN, HERBERT C. "Manipulation of Human Behavior: An Ethical Dilemma for the Social Scientist." In *Journal of Social Issues*, 21 (1965): 31-46.

KELMAN, HERBERT C. "The Role of the Group in the Induction of Therapeutic Change." *International Journal of Psychotherapy*, 13 (October 1963): 399–430.

KRAMER, RALPH M., and SPECHT, HARRY. *Readings in Community Organization Practice*. Englewood Cliffs, N.J.: Prentice-Hall, Inc., 1969.

KRAVETZ, DIANE F., and ROSE, SHELDON D. *Contracts in Groups: A Workbook*. Dubuque, Iowa: Kendall-Hunt Publishing Co., 1973.

LANDY, DAVID. "Problems of the Person Seeking Help in Our Culture." In *Social Welfare Forum, 1960*, pp.127–44. New York: Columbia University Press, 1960.

LESSOR, RICHARD, and LUTKAS, ANITA. "Two Techniques for the Social Work Practitioner." *Social Work*, 16 (January 1971): 67 ff.

LEVINE, RACHEL A. "Consumer Participation in Planning and Evaluation of Mental Health Services." *Social Work*, 15 (April 1970): 41–46.

LEVINE, RACHEL A. "Treatment in the Home." In Frank Riessman, Jerome Cohen, and Arthur Pearl (eds.), *Mental Health of the Poor*, pp. 329–335. Glencoe, Ill.: Free Press, 1964.

LEVINGER, GEORGE. "Continuance in Casework and Other Helping Relationships: A Review of Current Research." *Social Work*, 5 (July 1960): 40–51.

LEWIS, OSCAR. *La Vida*. New York: Random House, 1965.

LINDBLOM, CHARLES E. "The Science of 'Muddling Through.' " In Fred M. Cox *et al.*, *Strategies of Community Organization: A Book of Readings*, pp.291–301. Itasca, Ill.: F. E. Peacock Publishers, 1970.

LIPPITT, RONALD; WATSON, JEANNE; and WESTLEY, BRUCE. *The Dynamics of Planned Change*. New York: Harcourt, Brace & World, 1958.

LIPSKY, MICHAEL. "Protest as a Political Resource." *American Political Science Review*, 42 (December 1968): 1144–58.

LITWAK, EUGENE. "An Approach to Linkage in 'Grass Roots' Community Organization." In Fred M. Cox *et al.*, *Strategies of Community Organization: A Book of Readings*, pp. 126–38. Itasca, Ill.: F. E. Peacock Publishers, 1970.

LITWAK, EUGENE, and MEYER, HENRY. "A Balance Theory of Coordination between Bureaucratic Organizations and Community Primary Groups." *Administrative Science Quarterly*, 11 (June 1966): 31–58.

LONDON, PERRY. *The Modes and Morals of Psychotherapy*. New York: Holt, Rinehart & Winston, 1964.

MABLEY, ALBERTINA. "Group Application Interviews in a Family Agency." *Social Casework*, 47 (March 1966): 158–64.

MARCH, MICHAEL. "The Neighborhood Center Concept." *Public Welfare*, 26 (April 1968), pp. 97–111.

MARRIS, PETER, and REIN, MARTIN. *Dilemmas of Social Reform*. New York: Atherton Press, 1967.

MAYER, JOHN E., and TIMMS, NOEL. *The Client Speaks: Working Class Impressions of Casework*. New York: Atherton Press, 1970.

MECHANIC, DAVID. "Sources of Power of Lower Participants in Complex Organizations." *Administrative Science Quarterly*, 7 (December 1962): 349–64.

MEYER, CAROL. *Social Work Practice: A Response to the Urban Crisis*. New York: Free Press, 1970.

MILLER, HENRY. "Value Dilemmas in Social Casework." *Social Work*, 13 (January 1968): 27–33.

MILLER, HENRY, and TRIPODI, TONY. "Information Accrual and Clinical Judgment." *Social Work*, 12 (July 1967): 63–69.

MILLS, C. WRIGHT. *The Power Elite.* New York: Oxford University Press, 1957.

MILLS, C. WRIGHT. *The Sociological Imagination.* New York: Oxford University Press, 1959.

MINUCHIN, SALVADOR, and MONTALVO, BRAULIO. *An Approach for Diagnosis of the Low Socio-Economic Family.* Psychiatric Research Report 20, American Psychiatric Association, February 1966, pp. 163–174.

MINUCHIN, SALVADOR, and MONTALVO, BRAULIO. "Techniques for Working with Disorganized Low SocioEconomic Families." *American Journal of Orthopsychiatry*, 37 (October 1967): 880–87.

MORRIS, ROBERT, and BINSTOCK, ROBERT. *Feasible Planning for Social Change.* New York: Columbia University Press, 1966.

MULLEN, EDWARD. "Differences in Worker Style in Casework." *Social Casework*, 50 (June 1969): 347–53.

NATIONAL ASSOCIATION OF SOCIAL WORKERS. "Working Definition of Social Work Practice." *Social Work*, 3 (April 1958): 5–9.

NORTHEN, HELEN. *Social Work with Groups.* New York: Columbia University Press, 1969.

O'DONNELL, EDWARD J., and SULLIVAN, MARILYN M. "Service Delivery and Social Action through the Neighborhood Center—A Review of Research." *Welfare in Review*, 7 (November–December 1969): 1–11.

OLMSTED, MICHAEL S. *The Small Group.* New York: Random House, 1959.

OVERALL, BETTY, and ARONSON, H. "Expectations of Psychotherapy in Patients of Lower Socio Economic Class." *American Journal of Orthopsychiatry*, 33 (April 1963): 421–30.

OVERTON, ALICE. "The Issue of Integration of Casework and Group Work." *Social Work Education Reporter*, 16 (June 1968): 25–27 and 47.

OVERTON, ALICE, and TINKER, KATHERINE. *Casework Notebook.* St. Paul, Minn.: Greater St. Paul United Fund and Council, Inc., 1957.

PARADISE, ROBERT. "The Factor of Timing in the Addition of New Members to Established Groups." *Child Welfare*, 47 (November 1968): 524–30.

PEARL, ARTHUR, and RIESSMAN, FRANK. *New Careers for the Poor.* New York: Free Press, 1965.

PERLMAN, HELEN HARRIS. "Intake and Some Role Considerations." *Social Casework*, 41 (April 1960): 171–77.

PERLMAN, HELEN HARRIS. *Social Casework—A Problem Solving Process.* Chicago: University of Chicago Press, 1957.

PERLMAN, ROBERT, and JONES, DAVID. *Neighborhood Service Centers.* Washington, D.C.: U.S. Department of Health, Education and Welfare, 1967.

PILIAVIN, IRVING. "Restructuring the Provision of Social Services." *Social Work*, 13 (January 1968): 34–41.

PINCUS, ALLEN. "Reminiscence in Aging and Its Implications for Social Work Practice." *Social Work*, 15 (July 1970): 47–53.

POLANSKY, NORMAN A., and KOUNIN, JACOB. "Clients' Reactions to Initial Interviews." *Human Relations*, 9, No. 3 (1956): 237–64.

PREININGER, DAVID R. "Reactions of Normal Children to Retardates in Integrated Groups." *Social Work*, 13 (April 1968): 75–77.

PROSHANSKY, HAROLD M.; ITTELSON, WILLIAM H.; and RIVLIN, LEANNE, G. *Environmental Psychology.* New York: Holt, Rinehart & Winston, 1970.

RAPOPORT, LYDIA. "Crisis-Oriented Short-Term Casework." *Social Service Review*, 41 (March 1967): 31–43.

REID, WILLIAM. "Characteristics of Casework Communication." *Welfare in Review*, 5 (October 1967): 11–19.

REID, WILLIAM J. "Target Problems, Time Limits, Task Structure." *Journal of Education for Social Work*, 8 (Spring 1972): 58–68.

REID, WILLIAM, and SHYNE, ANN. *Brief and Extended Casework.* New York: Columbia University Press, 1969.

REIN, MARTIN, and MORRIS, ROBERT. "Goals, Structures and Strategies for Community Change." In *Social Work Practice, 1962*, pp. 127–45. New York: Columbia University Press, 1962.

RIESSMAN, FRANK. "The Helper Therapy Principle." *Social Work*, 10 (April 1965): 27–32.

RIESSMAN, FRANK, and GOLDFARB, JEAN. "Role Playing and the Poor." *Group Psychotherapy*, 17 (March 1964): 36–48.

RILEY, PATRICK V. "Family Advocacy: Case to Cause and Back to Case." *Child Welfare*, 50 (July 1971): 374–83.

ROGERS, CARL R. *Freedom to Learn.* Columbus, Ohio: Charles E. Merrill Publishing Co., 1969.

ROGERS, CARL R. *On Becoming a Person.* Boston, Mass.; Houghton Mifflin Co., 1961.

ROSENBLATT, AARON. "The Application of Role Concepts to the Intake Process." *Social Casework*, 43 (January 1962): 8–14.

ROSENFELD, JONA M. "Strangeness between Helper and Client: A Possible Explanation of Non-Use of Available Professional Help." *Social Service Review*, 38 (March 1964): 17–25.

ROSENTHAL, DAVID. "Changes in Some Moral Values Following Psychotherapy." *Journal of Consulting Psychology*, 19 (November 1955): 431–36.

Ross, Murray. *Community Organization: Theory and Principles.* New York: Harper and Row, 1955.

Rossi, Peter H. "Theory, Research, and Practice in Community Organization." In Ralph Kramer and Harry Specht (eds.), *Readings in Community Organization Practice*, pp. 49–61. Englewood Cliffs, N.J.: Prentice-Hall, Inc., 1969.

Rothman, Jack. "An Analysis of Goals and Roles in Community Organization Practice." *Social Work*, 9 (April 1964): 24–31.

Sarri, Rosemary C., and Galinsky, Maeda J., "A Conceptual Framework for Group Development." In Robert Vinter (ed.), *Readings in Group Work Practice*, pp. 72–94. Ann Arbor, Mich.: Campus Publishers, 1967.

Sarri, Rosemary; Galinsky, Maeda; Glasser, Paul; Siegel, Sheldon; and Vinter, Robert. "Diagnosis in Group Work." In Robert Vinter (ed.), *Readings in Group Work Practice*, pp. 39–71. Ann Arbor, Mich.: Campus Publishers, 1967.

Schmidt, Julianna. "The Use of Purpose in Casework Practice." *Social Work*, 14 (January 1969): 77–84 .

Schwartz, William. "Private Troubles and Public Issues: One Social Work Job or Two?" In *The Social Welfare Forum, 1969*, pp. 22–43. New York: Columbia University Press, 1969.

Schwartz, William. "The Social Worker in the Group." In *Social Welfare Forum 1961*, pp. 146–71. New York: Columbia University Press, 1961.

Selltiz, Claire; Jahoda, Marie; Deutsch, Morton; and Cook, Stanley. *Research Methods in Social Relations.* New York: Holt, Rinehart & Winston, 1959.

Shalinsky, William. "Group Composition as an Element of Social Group Work Practice." *Social Service Review*, 43 (March 1969): 42–49.

Shapiro, Joan. "Group Work with Urban Rejects in a Slum Hotel." In *Social Work Practice, 1967*, pp. 148–64. New York: Columbia University Press, 1967.

Shyne, Ann. "Evaluation of Results in Social Work." *Social Work*, 8 (October 1963): 26–33.

Simon, Herbert A. *Administrative Behavior.* New York: Free Press, 1957.

Siporin, Max. "Situational Assessment and Intervention." *Social Casework*, 53 (February 1972): 91–109.

Smalley, Ruth. *Theory for Social Work Practice.* New York: Columbia University Press, 1967.

Sommer, Robert. *Personal Space: The Behavioral Basis of Design.* Englewood Cliffs, N.J.: Prentice-Hall, 1969.

Soyer, David. "The Right to Fail." *Social Work*, 8 (July 1963): 72–78.

SPECHT, HARRY. "Casework Practice and Social Policy Formulation." *Social Work*, 13 (January 1968): 42–52.

SPECHT, HARRY. "The Deprofessionalization of Social Work." *Social Work*, 17 (March 1972): 3–15.

SPECHT, HARRY. "Disruptive Tactics." In Ralph Kramer and Harry Specht (eds.), *Readings in Community Organization Practice*, pp. 372–86. Englewood Cliffs, N.J.: Prentice-Hall, 1969.

SPERGEL, IRVING. "Selecting Groups for Street Work Service." *Social Work*, 10 (April 1965): 47–55.

STREAN, HERBERT S. "Role Theory, Role Models, and Casework: Review of the Literature and Practice Applications." *Social Work*, 12 (April 1967), 77–87.

STRUPP, HANS, and BERGIN, ALLEN. "Some Empirical and Conceptual Bases for Coordinated Research in Psychotherapy: A Critical Review of Issues, Trends, and Evidence." *International Journal of Psychiatry*, 7 (February 1969): 18–90.

STUDT, ELLIOTT. "Social Work Theory and Implications for the Practice of Methods." *Social Work Education Reporter*, 16 (June 1968): 22–27.

SUNLEY, ROBERT. "Family Advocacy: From Case to Cause." *Social Casework*, 51 (June 1970): 347–57.

SUNLEY, ROBERT. "New Dimensions in Reaching-Out Casework." *Social Work* 13 (April 1968): 64–74.

THELEN, HERBERT A. *Dynamics of Groups at Work*. Chicago: University of Chicago Press, 1954.

THOMAS, EDWIN. "Selecting Knowledge from Behavioral Science." In Edwin Thomas (ed.), *Behavioral Science for Social Workers*, pp. 417–24. New York: Free Press, 1967.

THOMAS, EDWIN, and FINK, CLINTON. "Effects of Group Size." *Psychological Bulletin*: 60 (July 1963): 371–84.

THOMAS, EDWIN J.; POLANSKY, NORMAN A.; and KOUNIN, JACOB. "The Expected Behavior of a Potentially Helpful Person." *Human Relations*, 8 (1955): 165–175.

THOMPSON, ANDREW, and ZIMMERMAN, ROBERT. "Goals of Counseling: Whose? When?," *Journal of Counseling Psychology*, 16 (March 1969): 121–25.

TRIPODI, TONY, and MILLER, HENRY. "The Clinical Judgment Process: A Review of the Literature." *Social Work*, 11 (July 1966): 63–69.

VINTER, ROBERT D. (ed.). *Readings in Group Work Practice*. Ann Arbor: Campus Publishers, 1967.

VINTER, ROBERT D. "The Social Structure of Service." In Edwin J. Thomas (ed.), *Behavioral Science for Social Workers*, pp. 193–206. New York: Free Press, 1967.

VINTER, ROBERT D., and SARRI, ROSEMARY. "Malperformance in the

Public School: A Group Work Approach." *Social Work*, 10 (January 1965): 3–13.

VOLKMAN, RITA, and CRESSEY, DONALD. "Differential Association and the Rehabilitation of Drug Addicts." In Frank Riessman, Jerome Cohen, and Arthur Pearl (eds.), *Mental Health of the Poor*, pp. 600–619. New York: Free Press, 1964.

WADE, ALAN D. "The Social Worker in the Political Process." In *The Social Welfare Forum, 1966*, pp. 52–67. New York: Columbia University Press, 1966.

WALTON, RICHARD E. "Two Strategies for Social Change and Their Dilemmas." In Fred M. Cox *et al.*, *Strategies of Community Organization: A Book of Readings*, pp. 343–349. Itasca, Ill.: F. E. Peacock Publishers, 1970.

WARNER, W. KEITH, and HILANDER, JAMES S. "The Relationship between Size of Organization and Membership Participation." *Rural Sociology*, 29 (March 1964): 30–39.

WARREN, ROLAND. *The Community in America*. Chicago: Rand McNally and Co., 1963.

WARREN, ROLAND. *Studying Your Community*. New York: Free Press, 1965.

WARREN, ROLAND L. *Truth, Love and Social Change and Other Essays on Community Change*. Chicago: Rand McNally & Co., 1971.

WARREN, ROLAND L. *Types of Purposive Social Change at the Community Level*. Brandeis University Papers in Social Welfare, No. 11. Waltham, Mass., 1965.

WATSON, GOODWIN. "Resistance to Change." In Warren G. Bennis, Kenneth D. Benne, and Robert Chin (eds.), *The Planning of Change*, pp. 488–97. 2nd ed. New York: Holt, Rinehart & Winston, 1969.

WATZLAWICK, PAUL. "A Structured Family Interview." *Family Process*, 5 (September 1966): 256–71.

WATZLAWICK, PAUL; BEAVIN, JANET; and JACKSON, DON D. *Pragmatics of Human Communication*. New York: W. W. Norton & Co., 1967.

WAX, JOHN H. "Criteria for Grouping Hospitalized Mental Patients." In *Use of Groups in the Psychiatric Setting*, pp. 87–92. New York: National Association of Social Workers, 1960.

WEBB, EUGENE; CAMPBELL, DONALD; SCHWARTZ, RICHARD; and SECHREST, LEE. *Unobtrusive Measures: Nonreactive Research in the Social Sciences*. Chicago: Rand McNally & Co., 1966.

WHITMAN, PEARL S., and OPPENHEIMER, SONYA. "Locating and Treating the Mentally Retarded." *Social Work*, 11 (April 1966): 44–51.

WILENSKY, HAROLD L., and LEBEAUX, CHARLES N. *Industrial Society and Social Welfare*. New York: Russell Sage Foundation, 1958.

WILKIE, CHARLOTTE. "A Study of Distortion In Recorded Interviews."
    Social Work, 8 (July 1963): 31–36.
WINEMAN, DAVID. "The Life Space Interview." *Social Work*, 4 (January 1959): 3–17.
WITTENBERG, RUDOLPH. "Personality Adjustment through Social Action." In Frank Riessman, Jerome Cohen, and Arthur Pearl (eds.),
    Mental Health of the Poor, pp. 378–92. New York: Free Press,
    1964.
WOLINS, MARTIN. "Group Care: Friend or Foe?" *Social Work*, 14
    (January 1969): 35–53.
YOUNG, PAULINE. *Scientific Social Surveys and Research*. 4th ed. Englewood Cliffs, N.J.: Prentice-Hall, 1966.
ZALD, MAYER N. "Organizations as Polities: An Analysis of Community
    Organization Agencies." In Fred M. Cox *et al.*, *Strategies of Community Organization: A Book of Readings*, pp. 91–100. Itasca, Ill.:
    F. E. Peacock Publishers, Inc., 1970.

Name Index

Aguilar, Ignacio, 169, 333
Alinsky, Saul D., 190, 333
Argyris, Chris, 44, 74, 333
Aronson, H., 174n, 340
Arthur, A. Z., 115n, 333
Auerswald, Edgar H., 309, 310n

Bachrach, A. J., 337
Bales, Robert F., 225n, 333
Banfield, Edward C., 248n, 254n, 333
Barker, Roger G., 263n, 333
Barr, Sherman, 335
Bartlett, Harriet M., 4, 65n, 108n, 333
Bateson, Gregory, 312, 313
Beavin, Janet, 263n, 344
Beier, Ernest, 71, 333
Benne, Kenneth D., 35n, 43n, 44n, 49, 56n, 74, 77, 82, 103, 136, 140n, 147, 205, 206n, 227n, 333–334, 335, 338, 344
Bennis, Warren, 35n, 43n, 44n, 49, 56n, 74, 77, 82, 103, 136, 140n,

147n, 187n, 227n, 334, 335, 337, 338
Bergin, Allen, 218n, 343
Berlin, Irving N., 147, 148, 334
Bernstein, Saul, 45n, 46, 228n, 280n, 334, 336
Bertcher, Harvey, 204, 205, 210n, 212n, 215, 220n, 334
Biesteck, Felix B., 74, 334
Billingsley, Andrew, 55n, 149n, 334
Binstock, Robert, 147n, 154, 195n, 196n, 248n, 254n, 340
Bisno, Herbert, 65, 334
Bond, Richard J., 210, 211n, 239n, 334
Borgatta, Edgar F., 126n, 225n, 334
Bradford, Leland P., 206n, 230n, 235n, 241n, 334
Bradley, Anna K., 145n, 337
Brager, George A., 51, 55n, 56n, 59n, 67n, 68n, 76, 77, 79, 81n, 82, 149n, 158n, 334, 335
Bredemeier, Harry C., 143, 148n
Briar, Scott, 115, 326n, 335

347

Subject Index

THE BOOK MANUFACTURE

Social Work Practice: Model and Method was composed at NAPCO Graphic Arts, Inc., New Berlin, Wisconsin; printing and binding were by R. R. Donnelley & Sons Company, Crawfordsville, Indiana. Internal design was by the F. E. Peacock Publishers art department. Cover design was by Charles Kling and Associates. The type is Janson with various sizes of Spartan display.